Introduction to
Crochet

Golden Hands Books

Marshall Cavendish
London and New York

Credits
Photographs in Part 1 by
Alan Duns, except p.3 The Victoria & Albert Museum/John Freeman Ltd.,
p.5–9, 12, 23, 29 Bruce Scott; p.12 (bottom) Peter Watkins
Drawings by Barbara Firth

Edited by Nicky Hayden

Published by Marshall Cavendish Publications Limited
58 Old Compton Street,
London W1V 5PA

© Marshall Cavendish Publications Limited 1974, 1975

This material was first published by Marshall Cavendish
Publications Limited in *How to Improve your Crochet
Techniques* and *The Crochet Collection*

This volume first published 1975

Printed in Great Britain by The Artisan Press

ISBN 0 85685 116 7

Introduction

This book is a complete introduction to the traditional craft of crochet, from the simple starting chain to the complicated openwork of filet crochet—and beyond! With a simple hook and a ball of yarn you can create beautiful stitches which can be used in thousands of different ways. If you're a beginner, in part one you'll find all the basic steps you need to start, and if you are an experienced crochet worker there are over a hundred stitches and techniques which you will be able to use, including Irish crochet; Tunisian crochet; chevrons; Aran; patterns, stripes and checks; surface crochet; blocks; borders and edgings and much, much more. In addition, there are two beginners' garments—a useful 'his and hers' cardigan and a patchwork slip-on, plus five simple accessories for you to make. As an added bonus there is the Crochet Collection, which contains 50 attractive and varied patterns for men and women, babies and children and of course for the home: in fact a wide selection with which to practise all the skills and techniques in the first half of the book.

Contents

Crochet know-how

Crochet is a rewarding and practical craft, both simple and quick to work once the basic steps have been mastered. Just as with knitting, however, there is a correct way to produce the best results and tricks-of-the-trade to give a professional finish.

If you are interested in learning how to crochet or would like to add to your knowledge about some of the more unusual crochet techniques, the following pages will prove invaluable. The beginner will find that she can soon master the basic steps which are set out clearly and simply and produce her first garment—the crochet cardigan has been designed specifically with the beginner in mind.

The more experienced crochet worker will find many ways to improve her skills and dozens of beautiful stitches, which she may be tempted to adapt to her own designs.

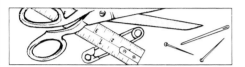

The tools required
A rigid metal centimetre/inch rule
Scissors
Blunt-ended sewing needles
Rustless steel pins
Polythene bag in which to keep work clean
Iron and ironing pad or blanket
Cotton cloths suitable for use when pressing

Know your hooks
Crochet hooks are now available in metric sizes and since the hook does not hold any stitches but merely the working loop, they are all produced to the same, easily manageable length. The larger the metric number, the larger the size of the hook.

Tunisian crochet hooks are also available in metric sizes but because the working method for Tunisian crochet requires a number of stitches to be held on the hook, they are produced in varying lengths to accommodate the correct number of stitches required. Again, the larger the metric number the larger the hook.

ISR hooks	old Wool sizes	ISR hooks	old Cotton sizes
7.00	2	2.00	1½
6.00	4	1.75	2½
5.50	5	1.50	3½
5.00	6	1.25	4½
4.50	7	1.00	5½
4.00	8	0.75	6½
3.50	9	0.60	7
3.00	10		
2.50	12		
2.00	14		

Crochet Abbreviations

alt	alternate(ly)	**dtr**	double treble	**rep**	repeat
approx	approximate(ly)	**foll**	follow(ing)	**RS**	right side of work
beg	begin(ning)	**gr**	group(s)	**ss**	slip stitch in crochet
ch	chain(s)	**grm**	gramme(s)	**sl st**	slip stitch in seaming
cl	cluster(s)	**htr**	half treble	**st(s)**	stitch(es)
cm	centimetre(s)	**in**	inch(es)	**tog**	together
cont	continu(e) (ing)	**inc**	increase	**tr**	treble
dec	decrease	**ISR**	International size range of hooks	**tr tr**	triple treble
dc	double crochet	**No.**	number	**WS**	wrong side of work
		patt	pattern	**yrh**	yarn round hook
		rem	remain(ing)		

SYMBOLS
An asterisk, (*), given in a pattern row denotes that the stitches shown after this sign must be repeated from that point.

Square brackets, [ ], denotes instructions for larger sizes in the pattern.
Round brackets, ( ), denote that this section of the pattern is to be worked for all sizes.

Tension—this is the most important factor in successful crochet. Unless you obtain the tension given for each design, you will not obtain satisfactory results.

Know your yarns
'Yarn' is the word used to describe any spun thread, fine or thick, in natural fibres such as wool, cotton, linen, silk, or in man-made fibres such as Acrilan, Orlon, Nylon or Courtelle.
The word 'ply' indicates the number of spun single threads which have been twisted together to produce a specific yarn. Each single thread may be spun to any thickness so that reference to the ply does not necessarily determine the thickness of the finished yarn, although the terms 2 ply, 3 ply and 4 ply are often used to mean yarns of a recognized thickness.
The following ply classification is broadly applicable to the majority of hand-knitting yarns, whether made from natural fibres, man-made fibres or a blend of both.
Baby yarns are usually made from the highest quality yarns and are available in 2, 3 and 4 ply, also double knitting weights. Baby Quicker-knit yarns are equivalent to a 4 ply but because they are very softly twisted, they are light in weight.
2, 3 and 4 ply yarns are available in natural fibres, man-made fibres, or a blend of both, usually made by twisting two spun single threads together—but there are exceptions to this.
Double knitting yarns are usually made from four spun single threads—although there are exceptions to this—twisted together to produce hard-wearing yarns, virtually double the thickness of 4 ply yarns.
Chunky and double double knitting yarns are extra thick yarns which are ideal for heavier, outdoor garments such as children's anoraks.

Some of these yarns are oiled to give greater warmth and protection.
Crepe yarns are usually available in 4 ply qualities—sometimes called 'single crepe'—and double knitting qualities—called 'double crepe'. They are more tightly twisted than normal yarns and produce a smooth, firm fabric which is particularly hard-wearing.

Very important

Since there is no official standardization, yarns marketed by various Spinners often vary in thickness and yardage. As most yarns are marketed by weight, rather than yardage, even the density of dye used to produce certain colours in each range can result in more or less yarn in each ball, although the structure of the yarn is exactly the same.

If it is impossible to obtain the correct yarn quoted in the instructions, another comparable yarn may be used, provided the same tension as given in the pattern is achieved. The Great Yarn Chart shows equivalent yarns which will work up to the appropriate tension, but it is still essential to work a tension sample before beginning any design.

Always buy sufficient yarn at one time to ensure that all the yarn used is from the same dye lot. Yarn from a different dye lot may vary slightly in colour.

Yarns and metrication

When purchasing yarns, it is advisable to check on the weight of each ball, as they now vary considerably due to the introduction of the metric system. Although this system has already been adopted by most of the Spinners, large stocks of yarn in standard ounces will take some time to run out, so this confused situation will be with us for some time.

Here is a conversion table, giving comparable weights in ounces and grams.

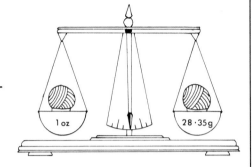

Measurements and metrication

Conversion from Imperial measurements in inches and yards to centimetres and metres is already taking place. To assist the reader, all measurements in these chapters will be given first in metric sizes, followed by comparable Imperial sizes. A conversion chart, showing sizes in centimetres and inches is given on page 64.

Success depends on tension

To make any design successfully it is essential to obtain the correct tension stated in the pattern. This means that the same number of stitches and rows to the centimetre/inch—as originally obtained by the designer—must be achieved. As a beginner, it is vital to keep on practising and trying to obtain the correct tension. If it is impossible to hold both the yarn and hook comfortably and at the same time obtain the correct tension, then change the hook size. If there are too many stitches to the centimetre/inch, try using one size larger hook; if there are too few stitches to the centimetre/inch, try using one size smaller hook. Too many stitches to the centimetre/inch means that the tension is too tight and too few stitches means that the tension is too loose.

This advice applies not only to the beginner but to all crochet workers beginning a new design. It is so often overlooked on the assumption that the reader's tension is average and therefore accurate. The point to stress is that although all patterns are carefully checked, the original designer of the garment may have produced a slightly tighter, or looser tension than average and all the measurements of the garment will have been based on calculations obtained from this original tension.

Always test that the correct tension is being achieved by working at least a 10.0cm (4in) square. A few minutes spent on this preparation lays the successful foundation for any garment. If it is overlooked, a great deal of work may be undertaken before the error in size is realized. Even half a stitch too many or too few can result in the completed garment being 5.0cm (2in) too large or too small.

Once a tension sample has ben worked, lay it on a flat surface and pin it down. Place a firm rule on the sample and mark out 5.0cm (2in) with pins. Count the number of stitches between the pins very carefully, then check the number of rows to 5.0cm (2in) in the same way.

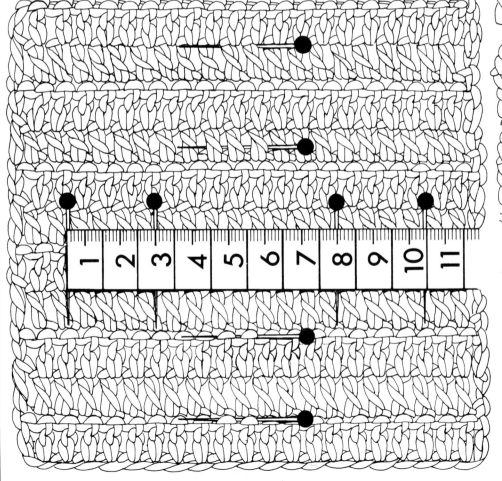

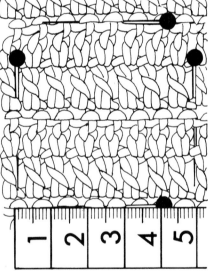

Opposite: This charming crochet purse is of late nineteenth century Irish origin. The delicate Irish lace crochet is backed with pure white silk and the tasseled cord is worked in tubular crochet.

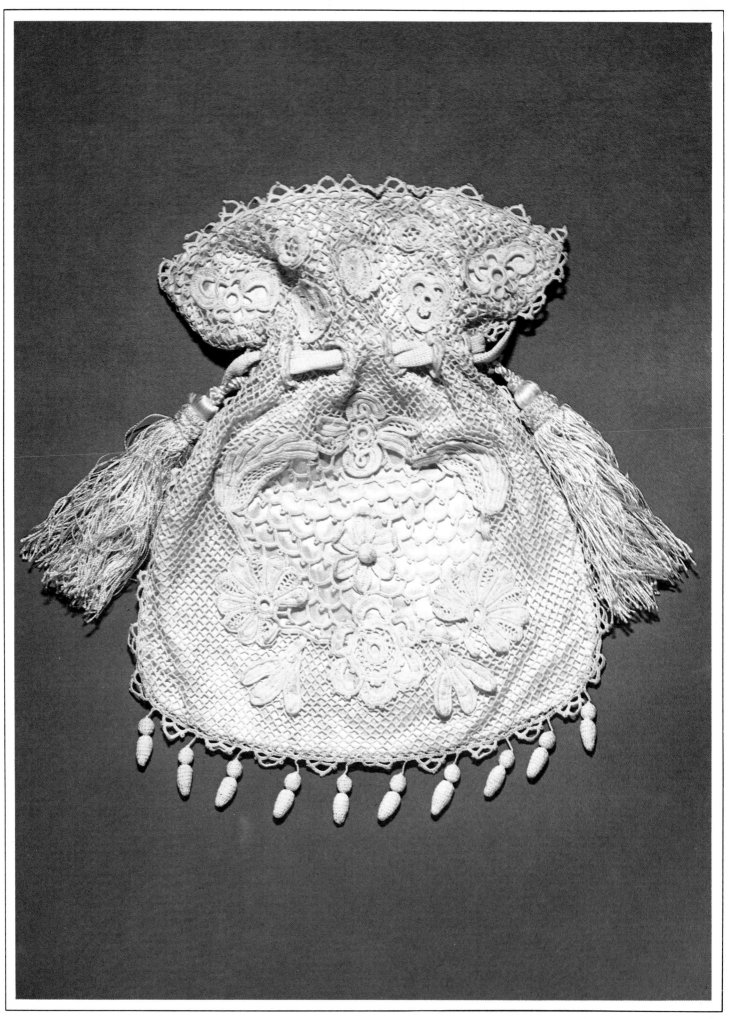

The basic steps

All crochet begins with a slip loop, just as in knitting. The stitches are worked by simply pulling one loop through another and however complicated a stitch may appear, it is merely a variation of this method, always finishing with one loop left on the hook once the stitch has been completed. This loop is a working loop only and is not counted as a stitch. It is the last loop to be fastened off at the end of the crochet, by breaking off the yarn, drawing it through the last loop then pulling this end up tightly.

Holding yarn and hook
Loop the end of a ball of yarn over the index and second finger of the left hand, then under the third finger and round the little finger. Hold the hook in your right hand in the same way as a pen or pencil, gripping the shank firmly between the thumb and forefinger and resting the hooked end against the tip of the second finger.

To make a slip loop
Hold the end of a ball of yarn between the thumb and forefinger of the left hand, using the right hand form a loop and hold this in position with the left hand, allowing the long end of the yarn to stay at the back of the loop. Hold the crochet hook in your right hand, insert the hook

through the loop from the front, catch the long end of the yarn in the hook and pull this loop through, allowing it to stay on the hook. Pull the long end of yarn downwards to tighten the loop.

How to begin
Before you can begin to crochet you must first make a length of loops, or chain stitches, which form a foundation row just as casting on does in knitting.

To make chain stitches.
Hold the hook with the slip loop just made in the right hand and the yarn in the left hand. Pass the hook under, then over the top of the yarn in your left hand, abbreviated as 'yrh', catching the yarn in the curve of the hook. Hold the knot of the slip loop firmly down between the thumb and forefinger of the left hand, then draw the yarn through the loop on the hook from the back to the front. One chain has been made, abbreviated as 'ch', and one working loop is left on the hook. Repeat this action into the chain just made until you have the required length, taking care to move your thumb and forefinger up the chain to hold the stitch you have just made very firmly and allowing the yarn to flow freely over the fingers of the left hand.

Turning chains
Before beginning to work any crochet stitches, it is important to realize the significance of turning chains and the part they play in forming the fabric. Because of the depth of most crochet stitches, it is necessary to add extra chains at the beginning of each row to bring the hook up level with the stitch being used for this row. These are called turning chains, abbreviated as 'turning ch', and the number varies depending on the stitch being worked. They form the first stitch of every row and to compensate for this, the first stitch of every row must be missed and the actual pattern stitch must be worked into the second stitch of the previous row. At the end of each row, the last stitch is then worked into the turning chain of the previous row. Turning chains give a neat, firm edge to the work and unless otherwise stated in a pattern, they form the first stitch, whether working in rows or rounds. Throughout these chapters, the turning chain will be given at the beginning of the row, although some patterns give instructions for working them at the end of the row before turning the work—the important point to remember is that they count as the first stitch of the row. The following table is a guide to the number of turning chains required to give the

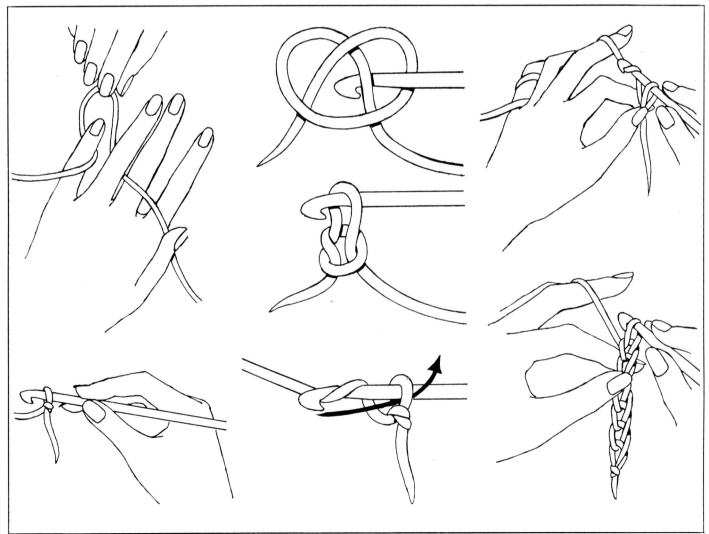

right depth for the stitch being worked:

Double crochet   —1 or 2 turning chains
Half treble   —2 turning chains
Treble   —3 turning chains
Double treble   —4 turning chains
Triple treble   —5 turning chains

Basic stitches

To work a slip stitch, abbreviated as 'ss'.
Make the required number of ch. *Insert the hook from front to back into the second ch from the hook, yrh and draw loop through both the ch and loop on hook, (one ss has been made), repeat from * into each ch to end.

To work a double crochet, abbreviated as 'dc'.
Make the required number of ch plus one extra ch, i.e., 11ch for 10dc.
1st row Insert the hook from front to back into the 3rd ch from hook, *yrh and draw a loop, through (2 loops on hook), yrh and draw through both loops on hook. (1dc has been made with the 2 missed ch counting as the turning ch), insert the hook from front to back into the next ch and repeat from * into each ch to end. Turn the work so that the last stitch of the row becomes the first stitch of the next row.
2nd row 1ch to count as first dc, miss first dc, *insert the hook from front to back under both loops at the top of the next dc, yrh and draw a loop through. (2 loops on hook), yrh and draw through both loops on hook. repeat from * into every dc, working last dc into turning ch at end of row. Turn.
Repeat the 2nd row for the required length. Fasten off.

To work a half treble, abbreviated as 'htr'.
Make the required number of ch plus one extra ch, i.e., 11ch for 10htr.
1st row Yrh, insert the hook from front to back into the 3rd ch from hook, *yrh and draw a loop through, (3 loops on hook), yrh and draw through all 3 loops on hook, (1htr has been made with the 2 missed ch counting as the turning ch), yrh, insert hook from front to back into the next ch and repeat from * into each ch to end. Turn the work so that the last stitch of the row becomes the first stitch of the next row.
2nd row 2ch to count as first htr, miss first htr, *yrh, insert the hook from front to back under both loops at the top of the next htr, yrh and draw a loop through, (3 loops on hook), yrh and draw through all 3 loops on hook, repeat from * into every htr, working last htr into turning ch at end of row. Turn.
Repeat the 2nd row for the required length. Fasten off.

To work a treble, abbreviated as 'tr'.
Make the required number of ch plus 2 extra ch, i.e., 12ch for 10tr.
1st row Yrh, insert the hook from front to back into the 4th ch from hook, *yrh and draw a loop through, (3 loops on hook), yrh and draw through 2 loops on hook, (2 loops on hook), yrh and draw through 2 loops on hook. (1tr has been made with the 3 missed ch counting as the turning ch), yrh, insert the hook from front to back into the next ch and repeat from * into each ch to end. Turn the work so that the last stitch of the row becomes the first stitch of the next row.
2nd row 3ch to count as first tr, miss first tr, *yrh, insert the hook from front to back under both loops at the top of the next tr, yrh and draw a loop through, (3 loops on hook), yrh and draw through 2 loops on hook, (2 loops on hook), yrh and draw through 2 loops on hook, repeat from * into every tr, working last tr into turning ch at end of row. Turn.
Repeat the 2nd row for the required length. Fasten off.

Slip stitch

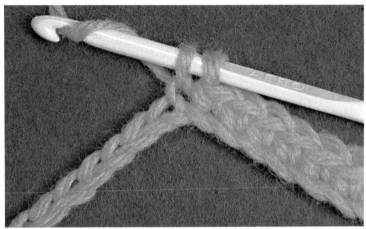

Double crochet

Half treble

Treble

Shaping up to crochet

Shaping in crochet is achieved by means of increasing the number of stitches in a row to make the fabric wider, or decreasing the number of stitches in a row to make the fabric narrower. Various methods are used, either by working one more or less stitch at each end of a row, or in the course of a row, by means of additional chains to increase the width, or slipped stitches to decrease the width. Because of the depth of most crochet stitches, unless the shaping is worked very neatly an unsightly gap will be left in the fabric, spoiling the appearance of the completed garment.

How to increase

To increase one stitch at each end of a row
Work the required turning chain, then instead of missing the first stitch, work into this stitch to increase one stitch at the beginning of the row. At the end of the row, work 2 stitches into the turning chain instead of one.

To increase one stitch in the middle of a row
Work in pattern until the position for the increase is reached, work 2 stitches instead of one in to the next stitch, then continue in pattern to the end of the row.

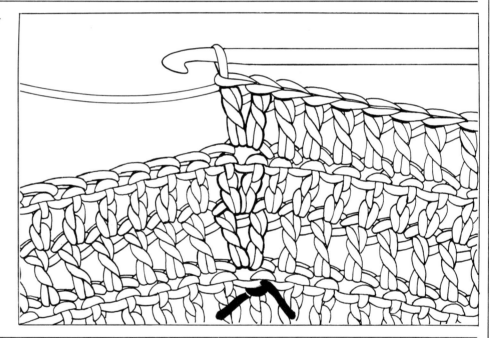

To increase several stitches at the beginning of a row
Before beginning to work in pattern, make a chain equivalent to one less than the extra number of stitches required plus the correct number of turning chains for the stitch being worked. As an example. if 6 stitches are to be increased when working in treble, make 5 extra chain plus 3 turning chain, making a total of 8 in all. Work the next treble for the new row into the 4th chain from the hook, then work 1 treble into each of next 4 chain. Continue working in treble across the row, noting that the position of the turning chain is now at the beginning of the increased stitches.

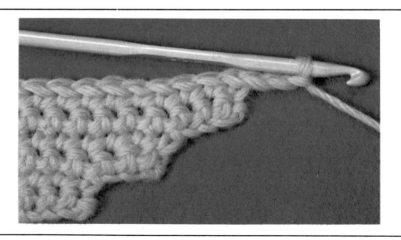

To increase several stitches at the end of a row
This can be worked in two ways. The first method is to make a separate length of chain in the correct yarn for the exact number of stitches required and join with a slip stitch to the top of the first stitch of the last row, break off the yarn and fasten off and leave for the time being. Work in pattern to the end of the row where the increased stitches are required, then work one stitch into each of the separate length of chain.

The second method is to make provision for these extra stitches at the beginning of the previous row. As an example, if 6 stitches are to be increased at the end of the next row when working in treble, make 10 chain at the beginning of the previous row, miss first chain, work one slip stitch into each of the next 6 chain and leave the other 3 for the first treble of the row, then work in treble to the end of the row. Turn and work back in treble to the 6 slipped stitches, then work one treble into each slip stitch.

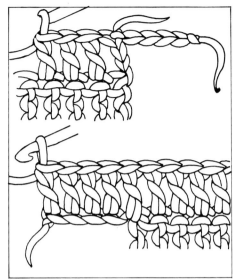
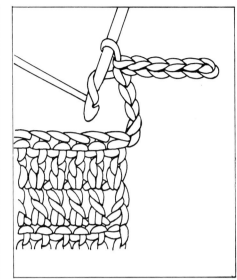

How to decrease

To decrease one double crochet at each end of a row
Make 1 turning ch and miss the first double crochet, insert hook into next stitch and draw loop through, insert hook into next stitch and draw loop through, (3 loops on hook), yrh and draw through all loops on hook—called dec 1—, work one double crochet into each double crochet until 2 double crochet and the turning chain of the previous row remain, dec 1 as at the beginning of the row, work the last double crochet into the turning chain.

To decrease one half treble at each end of a row
Make 2 turning chain and miss the first half treble, yrh, insert hook into next stitch and draw loop through, insert hook into next stitch and draw loop through, (4 loops on hook), yrh and draw through all loops on hook—called dec 1—, work one half treble into each half treble until 2 half treble and the turning chain of the previous row remain, dec 1 as at the beginning of the row, work the last half treble into the turning chain.

To decrease one treble at each end of a row
Make 3 turning chain and miss the first treble, yrh, insert hook into the next stitch and draw loop through, yrh and draw through 2 loops on hook, yrh, insert hook into next stitch and draw loop through, yrh and draw through 2 loops on hook, (3 loops on hook), yrh and draw through all loops on hook—called dec 1—, work one treble into each treble until 2 treble and the turning chain of the previous row remain, dec 1 as at the beginning of the row, work the last treble into the turning chain.

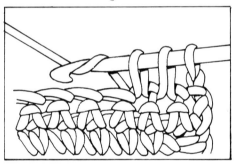
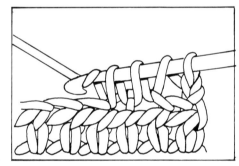
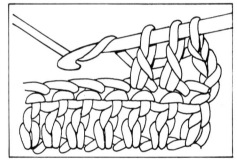

To decrease one stitch in the middle of a row
Work in pattern until the position for the decrease is reached, then dec 1 over the next 2 stitches as given for decreasing at each end of a row, and continue in pattern to the end of a row.

To decrease several stitches at the beginning of a row
Slip stitch over the required number of stitches to be decreased and into the next stitch, work the required number of turning chains to form the first stitch, then continue in pattern to the end.

To decrease several stitches at the end of a row
Work in pattern along the row until the required number of stitches to be decreased remain, noting that the turning chain of the previous row must be counted as one of the stitches, then turn the work and leave these stitches unworked.

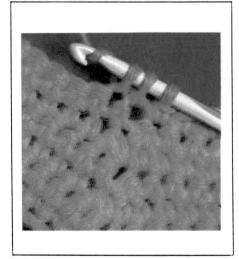
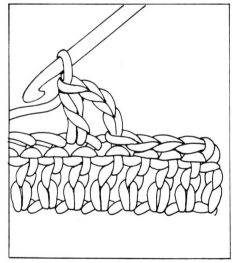

Helpful hints!
When increasing or decreasing in the middle of a row, mark the position where the shaping is to be worked with a length of coloured thread.

To work a double increase, follow the same instructions but work 3 stitches instead of 2 into the foundation stitch.
To work a double decrease, follow the same instructions but work across 3 stitches instead of 2 before completing the decreasing.

Crochet in rounds

The word 'round' refers to the working method, where the work is not turned at the end as when working in rows but is continued round and round to form a flat, or tubular fabric, joining the last stitch of each round to the first.

When this method is used to produce a flat fabric, an infinite variety of shapes may be formed which may be used as large, separate motifs, or a number of smaller motifs which may then be joined together to form cushions, afghans or blankets and even garments. Each motif may be worked in one single colour, or each round in a different colour to produce a multi-coloured, patchwork effect. Providing the same thickness of yarn is used throughout, it is an ideal way of using up oddments of yarn to make colourful and economical pram and cot blankets.

Where the method of working in rounds is used to produce a tubular fabric, it has the same effect as knitting in rounds to make a fabric without seams.

To work a flat fabric in rounds
To keep the fabric flat, it must begin with a small number of stitches, which are then increased on every round until the required diameter is achieved. This shaping can be achieved either by means of additional stitches or chain spaces.

To make a circular motif
Begin by making 4 chain to form the centre of the motif. Loop the chain round to form a circle and join the last chain to the first chain by means of a slip stitch. Into this circle work twice the number of stitches of the original chain, using the required number of chain to form the first stitch and joining the last stitch to the top of the turning chain with a slip stitch. 8 stitches. On the next round, work the turning chain to count as the first stitch, then work one stitch into the same place as the base of the turning chain and continue working 2 stitches into each stitch to the end, joining as before. 16 stitches. On each subsequent round, increase a total of 8 stitches by increasing in the first and every alternate stitch in the next round; in the first and every following 3rd stitch in the next round; in the first and every following 4th stitch in the next round, then continue in this way depending on the size of motif required.

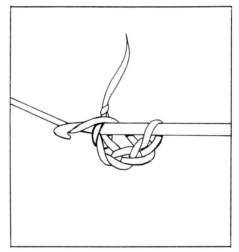
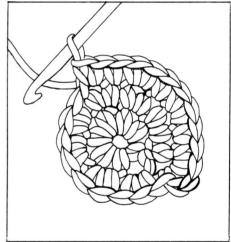

To make a square motif
Make the centre circle as given for the circular motif, having about 6 chain. If only one colour is being used, each round can be worked without having to break off the yarn.

1st round 3ch to count as first tr, 2tr into circle, 2ch, (3tr into circle, 2ch) 3 times. Join with a ss to 3rd of first 3ch.

2nd round 2ch, (3tr, 2ch, 3tr) into first 2ch space to form corner, *1ch, (3tr, 2ch, 3tr) into next 2ch sp, rep from * twice more. Join with a ss to first of first 2ch.

3rd round 3ch to count as first tr, 2tr into first ch space beyond ss join of previous round, 1ch, *(3tr, 2ch, 3tr) into corner 2ch space, 1ch, 3tr into next 1ch space, 1ch, rep from * twice more, (3tr, 2ch, 3tr) into last 2ch space, 1ch. Join with a ss to 3rd of first 3ch.

4th round 2ch, 3tr into next 1ch space, 1ch, *(3tr, 2ch, 3tr) into corner 2ch space, 1ch, (3tr into next 1ch space, 1ch) twice, rep from * twice more, (3tr, 2ch, 3tr) into last 2ch space, 1ch, 3tr into last 1ch space. Join with a ss to first of first 2ch. Fasten off.

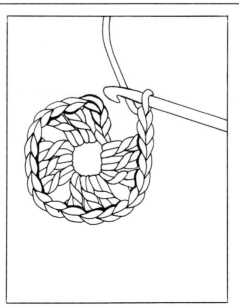
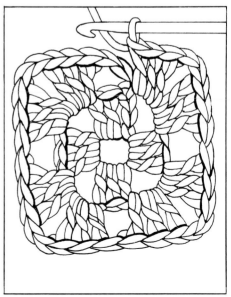

If a separate colour is being used for each round, each colour must be broken off at the end of the round. Each colour for this motif is coded as A, B, C and D.

Using A, make the centre circle and work the 1st round as given for the square motif. Break off A.

2nd round Join in B to any 2ch space with a ss, 3ch to count as first tr, 2tr into same ch space, *1ch, 3tr, 2ch and 3tr into next 2ch space to form corner, rep from * twice more, 1ch, 3tr into same ch space as beg of round, 2ch. Join with a ss to 3rd of first 3ch. Break off B.

3rd round Join in C to any 2ch space with a ss, 3ch to count as first tr, 2tr into same ch space, *1ch, 3tr into next 1ch space, 1ch, 3tr, 2ch and 3tr into corner 2ch space, rep from * twice more, 1ch, 3tr into next 1ch space, 1ch, 3tr into same ch space as beg of round, 2ch. Join with a ss to 3rd of first 3ch. Break off C.

4th round Join in D to any 2ch space with a ss, 3ch to count as first tr, 2tr into same ch space, *1ch, (3tr into next 1ch space, 1ch) twice, 3tr, 2ch and 3tr into corner 2ch space, rep from * twice more, 1ch, 3tr into next 1ch space, 1ch, 3tr into next 1ch space, 1ch, 3tr into same ch space as beg of round, 2ch. Join with a ss to 3rd of first 3ch. Fasten off.

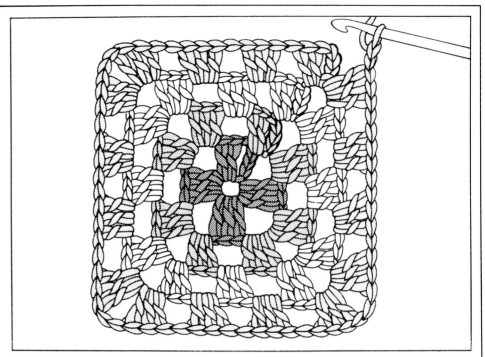

To work a tubular fabric in rounds
The fabric must begin with the required number of chains to give the total circumference of the item being made. Because the right side of the work is always facing you, even basic stitches, such as trebles, will have a different appearance. If the work is to be divided at any point and continued in rows, this difference in appearance must be taken into account at the onset. In this case, each round will be joined to the first stitch but the work will then be turned, just as when working in rows, and continued along the reversed side of the fabric.

To work tubular fabric without turning
Make the required number of chains and join the last chain to the first by means of a slip stitch, taking care to see that the length of chain does not become twisted. Work the required number of turning chains to form the first stitch and miss the first chain, then work one stitch into each chain to end. Join the last stitch to the top of the turning chain with a slip stitch. Continue in this way for the required length, then fasten off.

To work tubular fabric turning each round
Make the required number of chains and work the first round as given for tubular fabric without turning. After joining the round with a slip stitch, turn the work so that the other side of the fabric is facing you, make the required number of turning chains and miss the first stitch, then continue in pattern to the end of the round, joining with a slip stitch as before. Continue in this way for the required length, or until the point where the work is to be divided is reached, then continue working in rows, without joining.

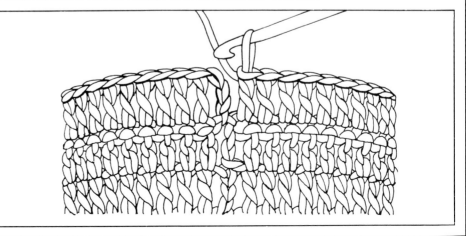

Finishing touches

The making up of a garment and any additional finishing touches can make or mar the final results. It is essential to pay attention to the correct handling of the yarn which has been used, to the best methods of seaming the finished sections and to the way of making, or applying any individual trimmings.

Handling yarns
Each yarn, whether it is made from natural or man-made fibres, requires a different method of handling in making up and after care. The Home Laundering Consultative Council has compiled a washing, ironing and dry-cleaning code in respect of hand knitting yarns and the

relative symbols are shown on most ball bands. Read these instructions very carefully before attempting to press any of the sections. If you have not used the correct yarn given in the instructions, check and make absolutely sure that the substitute you have chosen needs pressing, regardless of what instructions are given in the making up section of the pattern.

	HOT	WARM	COOL	DO NOT IRON
IRONING				
DRYCLEAN	(A)	(P)	(F)	(X)
	Usual dry cleaning	Normally drycleanable in most solvents. If drycleaned inform cleaner of composition of yarn.	Drycleanable in some solvents It is important that the cleaner is informed of the composition of the yarn if dry-cleaning is to be undertaken.	DO NOT DRYCLEAN

Blocking and pressing
As so many of the yarns now available do not require pressing, it is not always necessary to block out each section to the correct size and shape. However, any crochet stitch which is very open in texture will benefit if it is blocked out, then covered with a damp cloth and left until the cloth is absolutely dry.

If pressing is advised, place each section right side down on an ironing pad and pin it evenly round the edges to the pad. Once the piece is pinned out, making sure that it is not stretched and that the stitches and rows run in straight lines, check with a rule that the width and length are the same as those given in the instructions. Using a clean damp, or dry cloth and a warm or cool iron, as given in the instructions, press the piece evenly, putting the iron down and lifting it up again without moving it across the surface of the cloth. Allow the piece to cool before removing the pins.

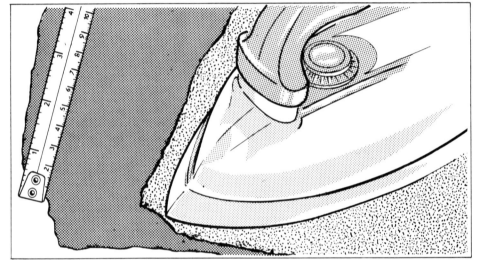

Seaming
Crochet sections may be joined together either by means of a blunt ended sewing needle threaded with the same yarn, or by means of a crochet hook and double crochet. The choice of seaming will depend on the finished article but the double crochet method gives a very firm edge, which can look most effective when it is worked on the right side of the item, giving added interest to the fabric.

Back stitch seam
Using a blunt ended needle threaded with yarn, begin by working two or more small stitches, one on top of the other, to secure the yarn, *with the needle at the back of the work, move approximately 0.5cm (¼in) along the seam to the left, insert the needle through to the front of the work then take it back along to the right and insert it into the end of the previous stitch, repeat from * to the end of the seam. Fasten off securely.

Oversewn seam
Using a blunt ended needle threaded with yarn, secure the yarn as given for back stitch seam, *pass the needle over the top of the two edges, through from the back to the front and pull the yarn through, repeat from * to the end of the seam. Fasten off securely.

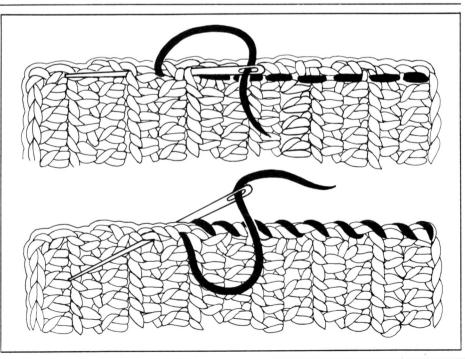

Double crochet seam
Insert the crochet hook from front to back through the edge stitch of both pieces to be joined, put the yarn round the hook and pull loop through, then complete one double crochet in the usual way, insert the hook approximately 0.5cm (¼in) along to the left from the last double crochet and work another double crochet. Continue in this way until the seam is completed, then fasten off.

Finishing touches
Casing or herringbone stitch
This method is used to finish the waist of a skirt or trousers. Cut the elastic to the size required and join into a circle. Mark off the waistband and elastic into quarters, then pin the elastic into position on the wrong side of the work. Taking care to distribute the crochet evenly, hold the waistband over the fingers of the left hand. Thread a blunt ended needle and secure the yarn to the fabric. Take the yarn over the elastic and insert the sewing needle lightly through the fabric from right to left, draw the yarn through, take the yarn back over the elastic to the top edge about two stitches along, insert the sewing needle lightly through the fabric from right to left again and draw the yarn through. Continue in this way all round the waistband. Fasten off securely.

Picking up stitches
This method is widely used for finishing neckbands and borders. Have the right side of the work facing and join in the yarn with a slip stitch. Keeping the yarn at the back of the work, insert the crochet hook through the edge from front to back, pull the yarn through and complete the stitch as given in the instructions. To ensure that stitches are picked up evenly and are well spaced, mark each section with pins at regular intervals and pick up the same number of stitches between the pins.

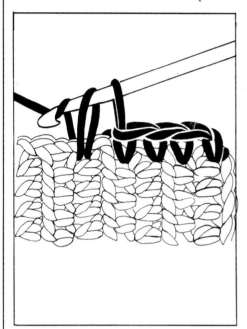
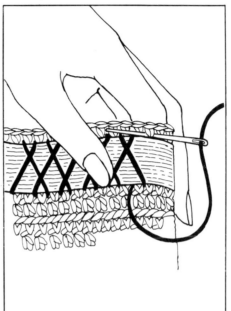
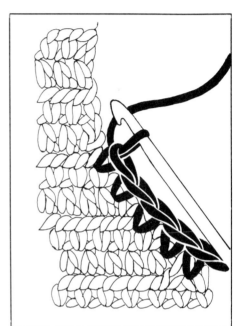

Twisted cords
The number of strands of yarn required will vary according to the thickness of the cord and the yarn being used. Take the required number of stands and cut them into lengths 3 times the length of the finished cord. Enlist the aid of another person, each one taking one end of the strands and knotting them together, then insert a pencil into each knot. Each person should twist the strands to the right until they are tightly twisted. Holding the strands taut, fold them in half at the centre and knot the 2 ends together. Holding the knot, give the cord a sharp shake, then smooth it from the knot to the folded end to even out the twists. Make another knot at the folded end, cut through the folded loops and tease out the ends.

needle threaded with yarn, insert the needle at one edge of the card and under the strands, taking them all together, then fasten off securely. Cut through the strands of yarn at the other untied edge of the card. Finish the tassel by winding an end of yarn several times round the top folded ends and fasten off securely, leaving an end long enough to sew the tassel to the garment.

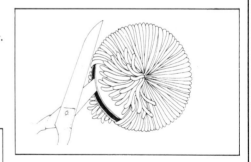

Threading beads or sequins on to yarn
To thread beads or sequins on to a ball of yarn before beginning to work with it, fold a length of sewing cotton in half and thread a fine sewing needle with both cut ends, leaving a loop of cotton. Pass the end of the ball of yarn to be used through the loop of cotton and slide beads or sequins on to the needle, down the cotton and on to the yarn.

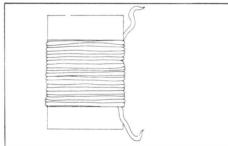

Pompons
Cut 2 circles of cardboard to the size required for the finished pompon, then cut a circle from the centre of each. Place the 2 pieces of card together and wind the yarn evenly round until the centre hole is nearly filled, then thread the yarn into a blunt ended sewing needle to completely fill the centre. Cut through the yarn round the outer edge, working between the 2 pieces of card. Take a piece of yarn and tie very securely round the centre of the pompon and between the 2 pieces of card, leaving an end long enough to sew the pompon to the garment. Cut away the card and trim pompon to shape.

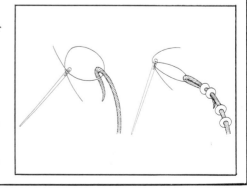

Tassels
Cut a piece of cardboard the width of the required length of the tassel. Wind the yarn round and round the card until the desired thickness is obtained. Using a blunt ended

Buttonholes & buttons

Neat buttonholes, either horizontal or vertical, can easily be worked in one with the main fabric or incorporated into a separate band. Chain button loops are simple to work and are ideal for use on baby garments and frog fastenings add an original touch to any basic garment.

Horizontal buttonholes
Work until the position for the buttonhole is reached. Where this is required as part of the main fabric, finish at the centre front edge before working the buttonhole row. On the next row, work a few stitches to where the button-hole is required, work two or more chains to take the size of the button being used, miss the same number of stitches in the row below, then pattern to the end of the row. On the next row, work in pattern over the chains in the previous row to complete the buttonhole.

Vertical buttonholes
When using short stitches, such as double crochet or half treble, work until the position for the buttonhole is reached. On the next row work a few stitches to where the buttonhole is required, turn, then work the required number of rows over these stitches to take the size of button being used, ending at the inner edge. Work in slip stitch down the inner edge of the rows just worked to the last complete row worked and pattern to the end of this row. Work across these remaining stitches for the same number of rows as the first side, then continue across all the stitches to complete the buttonhole. When a longer stitch, such as treble, is being used, work as given for vertical buttonhole ending at front edge. Do not break off yarn. Using a separate length of yarn, begin at inner edge of buttonhole and complete second side to match first side. Break off yarn. Return to the original yarn and continue across all the stitches to complete the buttonhole.

Button loops
These should be worked on the last row of any edge where buttonholes are required. Work the edging as given in the instructions until the last row is reached. Mark the position of the buttons on the edging, then continue in pattern for the last row, making button loops as the markers are reached by working two or more chains to take the size of button being used, miss the same number of stitches in the row below, then continue in pattern to the next marker. Make the required number of loops in the same way.

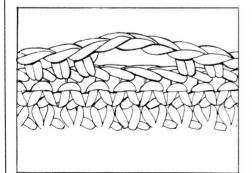

Frog fastening
The size and thickness of the fastening will depend on the type of garment being trimmed. As an example, use a No.5.00 (ISR) crochet hook and 3 strands of double knitting yarn to make approximately 80ch. Fasten off and darn in the ends. Twist into shape and sew together, as shown.

Buttons

It is often very difficult to find buttons which exactly match the yarn used for a garment, or the correct size of button required. Crochet covered buttons are simple to work and provide an inexpensive way of adding individual touches to any garment.

Lilac button

Use No.2.50 (ISR) hook and 4 ply yarn. Make 3ch. Join with a ss to first ch to form circle.
1st round 2ch to count as first htr, 7htr into circle. Join with a ss to 2nd of first 3ch. 8 sts.
2nd round 2ch to count as first htr, working in to back loop only of each st, work 1htr into base of first 2ch, 2htr into each htr to end. Join with a ss to 2nd of first 2ch. 16 sts.
3rd round 2ch, 1htr into back loop only of each htr to end. Join with a ss to 2nd of first 2ch.
4th round As 3rd.
5th round 1ch to count as first dc, *miss 1htr, 1dc into each of next 2htr, rep from * to end. Join with a ss to first ch. 11 sts.
6th round 1ch, *1dc into next dc, miss 1dc, rep from * to end. Join with a ss to first ch. 6sts.
Complete as given for small blue button.

Gold button

Use No.3.00 (ISR) hook and glitter yarn. Make 2ch. Into first of these 2ch work 8dc, do not join. Into each dc work 2htr. Join with a ss to first htr.
Break off yarn, thread through each st round edge, draw up and fasten off securely.

Pink button worked spirally

Use No.3.00 (ISR) hook and double knitting yarn. Make 2ch. Into first of these 2ch work 8dc, do not join. Cont working in rounds without joining, work (2dc into next dc, 1dc into next dc) 12 times, (there will now be 20 sts in round), or until work is required size.
Next round Work 1dc into each dc all round, do not join.
Next round (dec round) (Miss 1dc, 1dc into next dc) 10 times, do not join.
Insert cotton wool or button mould into cover and cont to dec in this way until hole is filled. Fasten off.

Yellow button with petals

This requires a button mould 2.5cm (*1in*) diameter with 2 or 4 holes in it. Use No.2.50 (ISR) hook and 4 ply yarn. Make 3ch. Join with a ss to first ch to form circle.
1st round 1ch, 8dc into circle. Join with a ss to first ch. 9 sts.
2nd round 1ch, 1dc into same place, 2dc into each dc to end. Join with a ss to first ch. 18 sts.
3rd round 1ch, 1dc into each dc to end. Join with a ss to first ch.
4th round As 3rd.
5th and 6th rounds As given for small blue button.
Complete as given for small blue button.
Petals
Make 3ch. Join with a ss to first ch to form circle. Into circle work (1dc, 2tr, 1dc) 5 times. Join with a ss to first dc. Fasten off.
Centre
Leaving a long end make 2ch. Into the first of these 2ch work (yrh, insert hook into ch and draw a loop through, drawing it up to 1.5cm (½*in*)) 3 times, yrh and draw through all 7 loops on hook, 1ch. Fasten off leaving a long end of yarn.
Sew petals to top of button. Thread 2 ends of centre through the holes of button, pull up tightly and fasten off at back.

Ring button

This requires a ring 2.5cm (*1in*) diameter. Use No.3.00 (ISR) hook and double knitting yarn. Using first colour, make 3ch. Join with a ss to first ch to form circle.
1st round 1ch, 11dc into circle. Join with a ss to first ch. 12 sts. Break off yarn.
2nd round Join in 2nd colour, 1ch, hold the ring behind the work, then working over the ring make 1dc into base of 1ch, 2dc into each dc to end. Join with a ss to first ch.
Fasten off.

Small blue button

Use No.2.50 (ISR) hook and 4 ply yarn. Make 3ch. Join with a ss to first ch to form circle.
1st round 1ch, 5dc into circle. Join with a ss to first ch. 6 sts.
2nd round 1ch, 1dc into same place, 2dc into each dc to end. Join with a ss to first ch. 12 sts.
3rd round 1ch, 2dc into next dc, *1dc into next dc, 2dc into next dc, rep from * to end. Join with a ss to first ch. 18 sts.
4th round 1ch, 1dc into each dc to end. Join with a ss to first ch.
5th round 1ch, 1dc into next dc, *miss 1dc, 1dc into each of next 2dc, rep from * to last dc, miss last dc. Join with a ss to first ch. 12 sts.
6th round 1ch, *miss 1dc, 1dc into next dc, rep from * to last dc, miss last dc. Join with a ss to first ch. 6 sts.
Break off yarn leaving an end long enough to sew on button. Insert button mould into cover, thread yarn through rem sts, draw up and fasten off securely.

Light green button

Work as given for small blue button but turn cover inside out before inserting button mould.

Two-colour blue button

Work as given for small blue button, working first 3 rounds in one colour and remaining rounds in 2nd colour.

Dark green button

Use No.2.50 (ISR) hook and 4 ply yarn. Make 3ch. Join with a ss to first ch to form circle.
1st round 1ch, 7dc into circle. Join with a ss to first ch. 8 sts.
2nd round 3ch to count as first tr, 1tr back into 8th dc of last round, 1tr into next dc beyond the 3ch, 1tr into base of 3ch, *1tr into next dc of last round, 1tr back into previous dc, rep from * to end. Join with ss to 3rd of first 3ch.
3rd round Ss into sp between 2tr, 1ch to count as first dc, 1dc into same place, 1dc between next 2tr, *2dc between next 2tr (i.e. into the sp between the 2 crossed tr), 1dc between next 2tr (i.e., between the pairs of crossed tr), rep from * to end. Join with a ss to first ch.
4th round 1ch to count as first dc, miss 1dc, *1dc into next dc, miss 1dc, rep from * to end. Join with a ss to first ch.
5th round As 4th.
Complete as given for small blue button.

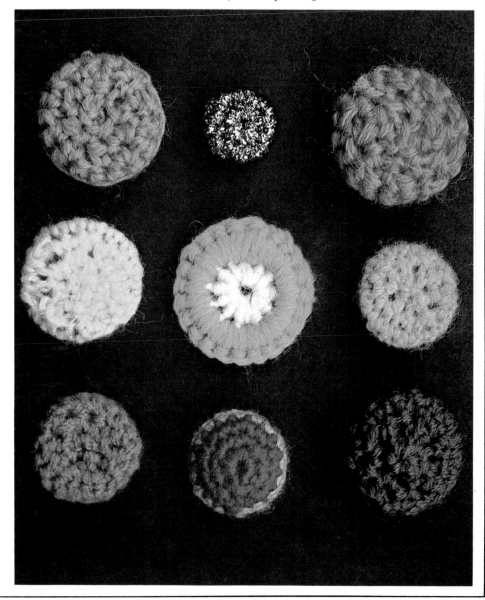

Edgings & braids

Crochet edgings and braids can either be applied directly to the main fabric, or worked as a separate strip and then sewn to the fabric. They can be thick of fine, depending on the type of yarn being used—bold and wide multi-coloured bands or narrow and delicate strips of lace. Their uses are almost too numerous to list—edgings for household linens, baby garments and fashion garments, or separate braids worked as hatbands, cushion and curtain trimmings or neat belts.

Edgings

An edging is usually applied directly to the main fabric as a means of neatening openings, such as neckbands, or as an additional decorative trimming.

Crab stitch edging

This is one of the simplest edgings, being worked in double crochet either in rows or rounds. Work along the edge in double crochet and if this is a circular opening, join with a slip stitch to the first stitch. Do not turn the work but work another row or round of double crochet back along the edge already worked, making one double crochet into each double crochet and working from left to right instead of from right to left. Fasten off.

Picot edging

There are many variations of picot edging but this method is simple to work in rows or rounds. Work along the edge in double crochet and if this is a circular opening, join with a slip stitch to the first stitch and turn, making sure that you have a nunber of stitches divisible by 2 plus one. On the next row or round, work 1ch to count as the first dc and miss the first dc ,*1dc into next dc, 3ch, ss into first of these 3ch to form picot, 1dc into next dc, rep from * to end. Fasten off.

Cluster edging

Work along the edge in double crochet, making sure that you have a number of stitches divisible by 2 plus one. Turn.
Next row 2ch to count as first dc and 1ch sp, * miss next dc, (yrh, insert hook into next dc and draw through a loose loop) 4 times into same dc, (9 loops on hook), yrh and draw through all loops on hook, 1ch, rep from * to last 2dc, miss 1dc, 1dc into last dc. Fasten off.

Shell edging.

Work along the edge in double crochet, making sure that you have a number of stitches divisible by 4 plus one. Turn.
Next row 1ch to count as first ss, *miss 1dc, 4tr into next dc, miss 1dc, 1ss into next dc, rep from * to end. Fasten off.

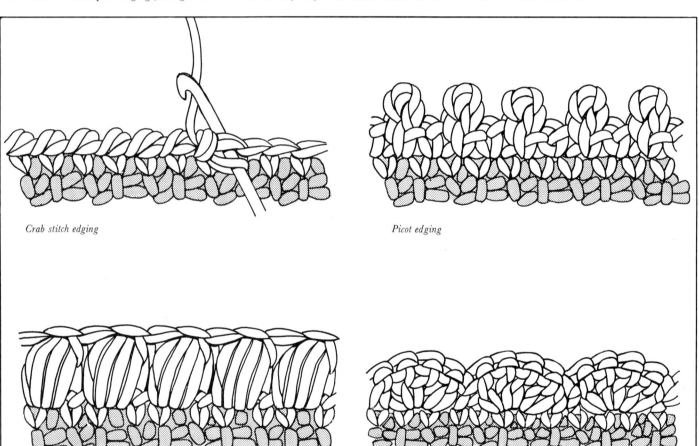

Crab stitch edging

Picot edging

Cluster edging

Shell edging

Separate edgings

These edgings are worked for the required length and then sewn in place to the main fabric.
Picot edging
*Make 3ch, into the first of these 3ch work 2dc, do not turn but repeat from * until the edging is the required length. Fasten off.
Ring picot edging
*Make 5ch, into the first of these 5ch work 1tr, do not turn but repeat from * until the edging is the required length. Fasten off.
Lace ring edging
Each ring is formed and one side worked into before making the next ring then, when the required length has been made, the second side of each ring is completed.
1st row *Make 10ch, remove hook from last ch and insert into first ch, draw loop of last ch through first ch to form ring, work 6dc along one side of ring, rep from * until edging is required length. Do not fasten off.
2nd row *Work 6 more dc into this ring along other side of ch, ss into side of last dc of previous ring, rep from * until each ring has been completed. Join with a ss to first dc. Fasten off.

Braids

These braids may be used as trimmings, or the wider examples can be used to make attractive belts.

Ric rac braid
Make 5ch.
1st row Into 5th ch from hook work 1dc. Turn.
2nd row 4ch, work 1dc into dc of previous row.
Turn.
Repeat the 2nd row for the required length.
Fasten off.

Birds eye braid
Worked in 2 colours, coded as A and B. Using
A, make a number of chain divisible by 3 plus
one, joining in B on last chain. Do not break
off A.
1st row Using B, 1ch to count as first dc, *4ch,
miss 2ch in A, 1dc into next ch, rep from * to
end, work 2 more dc into end ch then rep from
* along the other side of commencing ch, work
1 more dc into the last ch. Break off B.
2nd row With RS of work facing insert hook
from front to back into the last of the commencing ch in A, keeping the hook behind the
row in B draw a loop of A through, 2ch to count
as first htr, working only into the missed sts of
the commencing ch and holding the 4ch loops
in B forward and working behind them, work
1htr into each of next 2ch, *2htr into next ch,
1htr into next ch, rep from * to end, 2ch, ss into
last ch noting that this is the same ch as the last
st in B, 2ch, then cont along other side of work in
same way. Break off A.
3rd row With RS of work facing, rejoin B to
2nd of 2ch at beg of 2nd row, 1ch to count as
first dc, *insert hook under the 4ch loop and
work 1dc into next htr catching the 4ch loop at
the same time, 1dc into each of next 2htr, rep
from * to end, do not turn but work a row of
crab st back along this edge. Fasten off.
Rep 3rd row and crab st along other edge to
complete braid.

Chevron braid
Worked in 2 colours, coded as A and B. Using
A, make a chain the required length, making
sure that you have a number of stitches
divisible by 4 plus 3 and one extra turning
chain.
1st row Using A, into 3rd ch from hook work
1htr, 1htr into each ch to end. Do not break off
A but work 2ch, 1ss into same ch as last htr,
2ch, then continue along other side of commencing ch, working 1htr into each ch to end,
2ch, 1ss into same ch as last htr, 2ch. Join with a
ss to 2nd off first 2ch. Fasten off.
2nd row With RS of work facing join B with a
ss to 2nd of first 2ch, 1ch to count as first dc,
1dc into each of next 2htr, *miss 1htr, insert
hook into space between the 2 rows along
commencing ch and immediately below the next
htr (the htr after the missed htr), yrh and draw
a loop through long enough to reach to the top
of the row being worked, insert hook into the
missed htr, yrh and draw through 2 loops on
hook, yrh and draw through rem 2 loops,
1htr into each of next 3htr, rep from * to end,
2ch, 1ss into end of commencing ch, 2ch, 1ss
into first htr along other side, 1ch to count as
first dc, **1dc into each of next 3htr, insert hook
into same space as first long st on other side,
yrh and draw a long loop through, insert hook
into next htr, yrh and draw through 2 loops on
hook, yrh and draw through rem 2 loops, rep
from ** to last 3htr, 1dc into each of next 3htr,
2ch, 1ss into end of commencing ch, 2ch, 1ss
into 2nd of first 2ch along other side, then
continue along this side.
3rd row *3ch, (yrh, insert hook into same st as
last ss, yrh and draw a loop through, yrh and
draw through 2 loops on hook) twice, yrh and
draw through all 3 loops on hook, miss 3dc, 1ss
in to next dc, rep from * to end, 2ch, 1ss into
end of commencing ch, 2ch, 1ss into first dc
along other side, then rep from * along this side.
Fasten off.

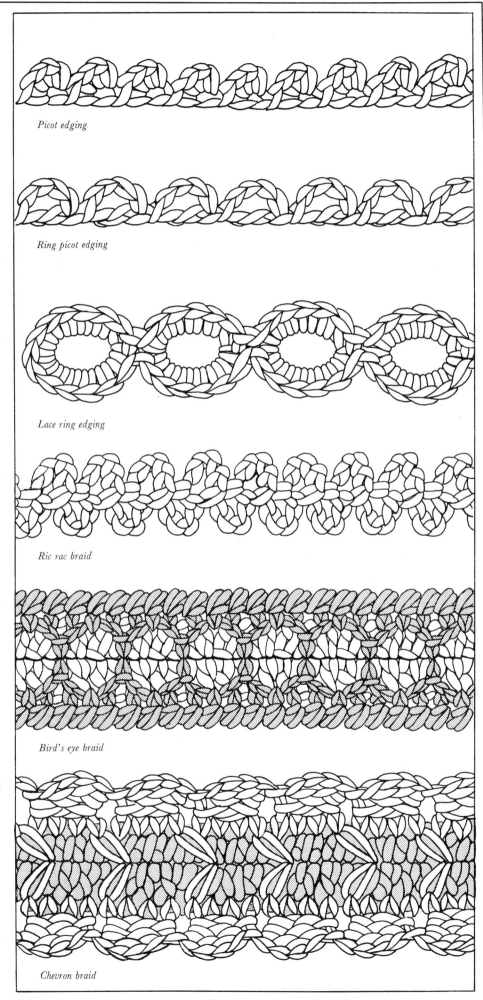

Picot edging

Ring picot edging

Lace ring edging

Ric rac braid

Bird's eye braid

Chevron braid

New ways of shaping

The usual way of shaping, by increasing or decreasing stitches at a given point has already been explained but a far more interesting effect can be achieved by working a section from side edge to side edge and using stitches of different depths, or turning at a given point in a row, to form the shaping. These methods are an ideal way of working a full skirt, a beret, matinee jacket or something as simple as a man's tie. Before beginning to work a section using different stitches, it is essential to ensure that the fabric formed will complement any other sections which may be worked in the normal way. Because they are worked from side edge to side edge, the stitches which form the fabric will lie vertically in rows instead of horizontally. The narrowest part of the section should be worked in double crochet which will form a dense fabric, with half trebles used for the next shaped section and the widest part may then be worked in trebles or a patterned stitch.

Shaping by turning

This method is also worked from side edge to side edge and the shaping is achieved by turning at a given point in a row and leaving the remaining stitches unworked for the time being. Begin by making this simple tie, to see how easily this method of shaping may be worked. You will need 1 x 50 grm ball of a 4 ply yarn, an oddment of contrast colour for the edging and a No.3.00 (ISR) crochet hook. Make 261ch in the usual way.

1st row Into 3rd ch from hook work 1dc, 1dc into each ch to end. Turn.
Work 2 more rows dc.
4th row (shaping row) 1ch, miss first dc, 1dc in to each of next 99sts, 1ss into each of next 10sts, turn.
5th row Ss into each of next 10ss, 1dc into each dc to end. Turn.
6th row 1ch, miss first dc, 1dc into each of next 89dc, 1ss into each of next 10dc, turn.
7th row As 5th.
Rep 4th and 5th rows once more. Work 3 more rows dc across all sts. Fasten off.
Edging Using B and with RS of work facing, work round all edges in dc. Join with a ss to first dc. Fasten off.

Shaping by using different stitches

This method is most effective when it is used to shape a skirt. Before beginning, you must first determine the length of skirt required and the tension which will be achieved using the hook size and yarn selected, over both double crochet and trebles or a patterned stitch. The correct position for the shaping must also be worked out to give a good swing to the skirt. As an example, say the required skirt length is 53.5cm (*21in*) from waist to lower edge, the first position for shaping should occur approximately 7.5cm (*3in*) below the waist and the second position approximately 15.0cm (*6in*) below the waist. For each 7.5cm (*3in*) less in overall length, allow approximately 0.5cm ($\frac{1}{4}$*in*) less to each shaping position, i.e., on a skirt with an overall length of 30.5cm (*12in*), allow 5.5cm (*2¼in*) to the first shaping position and 11.5cm (*4½in*) to the second position.

The pattern given here uses a 4 ply yarn and a No.3.50 (ISR) crochet hook to give a skirt length of 53.5cm (*21in*). Allow 8 x 50 grm balls for a 91.5cm (*36in*) hip size and 1 additional ball for each subsequent size. The correct tension is 20tr and 22dc to 10.0cm (*4in*).
Make 111ch and beg at waist, working from top to lower edge.
1st row (RS) Into 3rd ch from hook work 1dc, 1dc into each of next 14ch, 1htr into each of next 16ch, 1tr into each of next 78ch. Turn. 110 sts.
2nd row 3ch to count as first tr, 1tr into each of next 77tr, 1htr into each of next 16htr, 1dc into each of next 16dc. Turn.
3rd row 1ch to count as first dc, 1dc into each of next 15dc, 1htr into each of next 16htr, 1tr into each tr to end. Turn.
The 2nd and 3rd rows form the pattern and are repeated throughout. Continue in pattern until work measures 68.5cm (*27in*) from beginning, or required length measured across waist edge. Fasten off. Join cast on edge to cast off edge, leaving an opening for a zip fastener. Sew in zip, Sew elastic inside waist edge using casing stitch. Use one of the edgings given earlier to neaten lower edge.

Shaping using turning and different stitches

Both of these methods may be combined to produce a beret, or an interesting fluted sleeve which will give an original touch to an otherwise plain jersey or dress. Here again, the finished depth and the position for the shaping must first be determined. A vertical striped effect can quite easily be obtained by working an even number of rows in two or more colours.

Beret
Make the required number of chain to fit the depth of crown. Work 1 row treble.
2nd row 3ch to count as first tr, miss first tr, 1tr into each tr to last 12 sts, 1dc into each of next 6 sts, turn, leaving rem 6 sts unworked.
3rd row Ss into each of first 6dc, 1tr into each tr to last 6 sts, 1dc into each of next 2 sts, turn.
4th row Ss into each of first 2dc, 1tr into each tr to last 6ss, turn.
5th row Ss into each of first 6sts, 1tr into each st to end. Turn.
Work 2 rows tr across all sts. Repeat from the 2nd row until lower edge fits round head. Fasten off. Join cast on edge to cast off edge. Gather up top of crown. Work 2 rounds dc round lower edge. Fasten off. Trim with pompon.

Fluted sleeve.

The pattern given here uses the same yarn, hook size and tension as given for the skirt, to give a sleeve seam of 12.5cm (*5in*), to fit an armhole on an 86.5cm (*34in*) bust size. Make 22ch and work from side edge to side edge.
1st row (RS) Into 4th ch from hook work 1tr, 1tr into each ch to end. Turn. 20 sts.
2nd row 3ch to count as first tr, 1tr into each tr to end. Turn.
Shape top
Next row 3ch, work 1htr into 3rd of these 3ch from hook to increase 2 sts, 1tr into each tr to end. 22 sts.
Next row 3ch, 1tr into each of next 19tr, 1htr into next htr. Turn.
Next row 3ch, work 1htr into 3rd of these 3ch to increase 2 sts, 1htr into each of next 2htr, 1tr into each tr to end. Turn. 24 sts.
Next row 3ch, 1tr into each of next 19tr, 1htr into each of next 3htr, 1tr into each tr to end. Turn.
Cont inc in this way, rep last 2 rows 4 times more. 32 sts.
Next row 5ch, work 1dc into 3rd of these 5ch, 1dc into each of next 2ch to inc 4 sts, 1htr into each of next 12htr, 1tr into each tr to end. Turn.
Next row 3ch, 1tr into each of next 19tr, 1htr into each of next 12htr, 1dc into each of next 3dc, 1dc into turning ch. Turn.
Cont inc in this way, rep last 2 rows twice more. 44 sts. Work 12 rows patt as now set without shaping, ending at top edge.
Next row Ss across first 4dc and into next dc, 1ch to count as first dc, patt to end. Turn. 40 sts.
Next row Patt to end. Turn.
Rep last 2 rows twice more. 32 sts.
Next row Ss across first 2htr and into next htr, 2ch to count as first htr, patt to end. Turn. 30 sts.
Next row Patt to end. Turn.
Rep last 2 rows until 20tr rem. Work 1 more row tr. Fasten off. Join cast on edge to cast off edge to form underarm seam. Set sleeve into armhole, easing in fullness at shoulder.

Opposite, (l. to r.): Sections of skirt and beret, the completed tie, and a section of the sleeve showing the shaping using different stitches and turning rows. Top: the finished skirt, beret and sleeve.

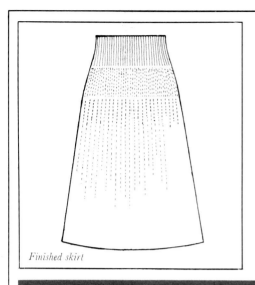

Finished skirt

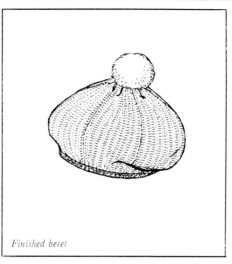

Finished beret

Finished sleeve

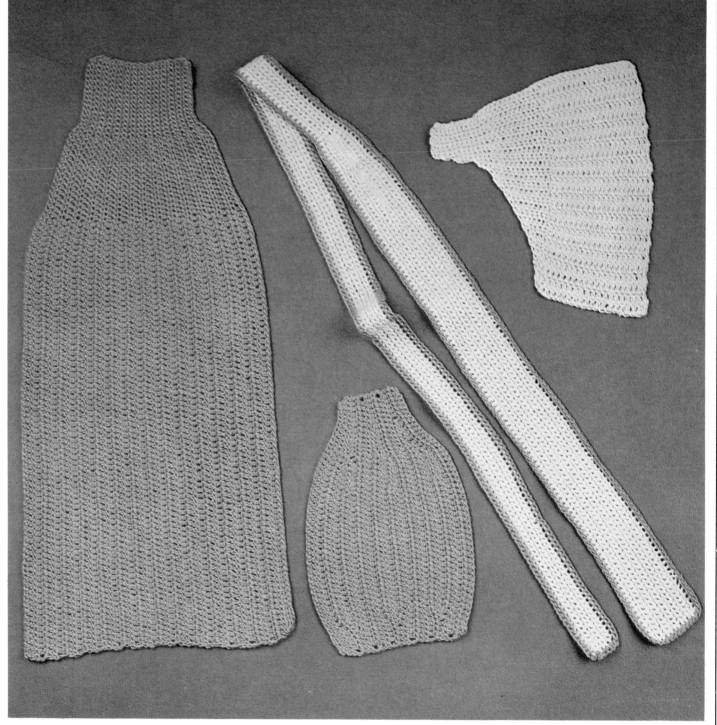

Stripes are so simple

Striped effects are the quickest and simplest way of giving even the most basic stitches a completely different look, or a perfectly plain garment the couture touch. They can be incorporated into an all-over pattern, or used as bands of contrast colours round the welt or cuffs of a jersey. Providing yarns of the same thickness are used, they can be an interesting and economical way of using up oddments.

Horizontal stripes

These may be formed by working 2, 4, 6 or more even number of rows in each colour in turn, carrying the yarn not in use up the side of the work until it is required again. If an odd number of rows is worked for each stripe, care must be taken to ensure that the number of colours used will allow for the yarn to be at the correct end of the work when it is required again, otherwise each colour must be broken off and rejoined again. To bring a new colour into use at the beginning of a row, work the last stitch of the previous row until 2 loops remain on the hook, then draw the new colour through these 2 loops to complete the stitch. Turn the work and continue with the new colour, bringing in each subsequent colour in the same way.

Checked effects can be achieved on a striped background by working vertical rows of chains directly on to the right side of the fabric at regular intervals.

Vertical stripes

These are a little more difficult to work, as the colours must be changed at several points during the course of the same row. When the stripes are narrow, using only 2 or 3 stitches for each colour, it is quite simple to bring in each new colour as it is required, carrying the yarn not in use across the back of the work until it is required again.

For wider stripes, however, it is not advisable to use this method as, apart from the waste of yarn, there is a tendency to carry the yarn across too tightly causing the fabric to pull out of shape. It is much better to divide each colour into small, separate balls before beginning to work and use a separate ball of yarn for each stripe.

One important point to remember is that vertical, or diagonal stripes worked by carrying the yarn across the back of the stitches produce a fabric of double thickness, whilst stripes worked by using separate balls of yarn give a fabric of normal thickness.

Bringing in a new colour for vertical or horizontal stripes

Unless each new colour is brought into use correctly the edge of each stripe will be blurred and out of line. To work these samples, use 2 colours coded as A and B.

Carrying yarn across back of work

On a right side row where the yarn is carried across the back of the work, *work one stitch less than the required number of stitches in A, work the next stitch with A leaving the last 2 loops of the stitch on the hook, pick up B and take it over A then conplete the stitch with B, work one stitch less than the required number of stitches in B, work the next stitch with B leaving the last 2 loops of the stitch on the hook, pick up A and take it over B than complete the stitch with A, repeat from * to the end of the row bringing in colours as required.

On a wrong side row where the yarn is carried across the front of the work, *work one stitch less than the required number of stitches in A, work the next stitch with A leaving the last 2 loops on the hook, bring A forward to front of work, pick up B and take to back of work then complete stitch with B, work one stitch less than the required number of stitches in B, work the next stitch with B leaving the last 2 loops on hook bring B forward to front of work, pick up A and take to back of work then complete stitch with A, repeat from * to the end of the row bringing in colours as required.

Using separate balls of yarn

On a right side row where the yarn is changed at the back of the work, *work one stitch less than the required number of stitches in A, work the next stitch with A leaving last 2 loops on hook, keeping yarn at back of work twist B to the right under and over A and complete stitch with B, work one stitch less than the required number of stitches in B, work the next stitch with B leaving the last 2 loops on hook, keeping yarn at back of work twist A under and over B and complete stitch with A, repeat from * to the end of the row, bringing in colours as required.

On a wrong side row where the yarn is changed at the front of the work, *work one stitch less than the required number of stitches in A, work the next stitch with A leaving the last 2 loops on hook, keeping A at front of work twist B to the right under and over A and across to the back of the work and complete the stitch with B, work one stitch less than the required number of stitches in B, work the next stitch with B leaving the last 2 loops on hook, keeping B at front of work twist A to the right under and over B and across to the back of the work and complete the stitch with A, repeat from * to the end of the row, bringing in colours as required.

Diagonal stripes

Narrow or wide diagonal stripes are worked in the same way as vertical stripes, either by carrying the yarn across the back of the work or by using separate balls of yarn for each stripe. The diagonal effect is achieved by moving one stitch in each colour to the left or right, as desired. The sample given here shows how to work a narrow stripe slanting to the right, using 2 colours coded as A and B.
Using A, make 29ch.
1st row Into 3rd ch from hook work 1dc, 1dc into each ch to end. Turn. 28dc.
Commence striped patt.
1st row (RS) Using A, 1ch to count as first dc, miss first dc, 1dc into next dc joining in B on last loop, *using B, work 1dc into each of next 2dc joining in A on last loop, using A, work 1dc into each of next 2dc joining in B on last loop, rep from * to last 2 sts, using B, work 1dc into each of last 2dc. Turn.
2nd row Using B, 1ch to count as first dc, miss first dc, 1dc into next dc joining in A on last loop, *using A, work 1dc into each of next 2dc joining in B on last loop, using B, work 1dc into each of next 2dc joining in A on last loop, rep from * to last 2 sts, using A, work 1dc into each of last 2dc. Turn.
3rd row Using A, 1ch to count as first dc, miss first dc, *using B, work 1dc into each of next 2dc joining in A on last loop, using A, work

1dc into each of next 2dc joining in B on last loop, rep from * to last 3 sts, using B, work 1dc into each of next 2dc joining in A on last loop, using A, work 1dc into last dc. Turn.
4th row Using A, 1ch to count as first dc, miss first dc, *using B, work 1dc into each of next 2dc joining in A on last loop, using A, work 1dc into each of next 2dc joining in B on last loop, rep from * to last 3 sts, using B, work 1dc into each of next 2dc joining in A on last loop, using A, work 1dc into last dc. Turn.
5th row Using B, 1ch to count as first dc, miss first dc, 1dc into next dc joining in A on last loop, *using A, work 1dc into each of next 2dc joining in B on last loop, using B, work 1dc into each of next 2dc joining in A on last loop, rep from * to last 2 sts, using A, work 1dc into each of last 2dc. Turn.
6th row Using A, 1ch to count as first dc, miss first dc, 1dc into next dc joining in B on last loop, *using B, work 1dc into each of next 2dc joining in A on last loop, using A, work 1dc into each of next 2dc joining in B on last loop, rep from * to last 2 sts, using B, work 1dc into each of last 2dc. Turn.
7th row Using B, 1ch to count as first dc, miss first dc, *using A, work 1dc into each of next 2dc joining in B on last loop, using B, work 1dc into each of next 2dc joining in A on last loop, rep from * to last 3 sts, using A, work 1dc into each of next 2dc joining in B on last loop, using B, work 1dc into last dc. Turn.
8th row Using B, 1ch to count as first dc, miss first dc, *using A, work 1dc into each of next 2dc joining in B on last loop, using B, work 1dc into each of next 2dc joining in A on last loop, rep from * to last 3 sts, using A, work 1dc into each of next 2dc joining in B on last loop, using B, work 1dc into last dc. Turn.
These 8 rows form the pattern.

Chevron stripes

These are worked in the same way as horizontal stripes, using an even number of rows and as many colours as required. If more than 3 colours are used, however, it is advisable to break off the yarn at the end of each stripe, rather than carry it up the side of the work until it is required again. This sample is worked in 3 colours, coded as A, B and C.
Using A, make 38ch.
1st row (RS) Into 3rd ch from hook work 1dc, 1dc into each of next 6ch, 3dc into next ch, 1dc into each of next 8ch, insert hook into next ch and draw loop through, miss 1ch, insert hook into next ch and draw loop through, yrh and draw through 3 all loops on hook, 1dc into each of next 8ch, 3dc into next ch, 1dc into each of last 8ch. Turn.
2nd row 1ch to count as first dc, (insert hook into next dc and draw loop through) into each of next 2dc, yrh and draw through all 3 loops on hook, 1dc into each of next 6dc, 3dc into next dc, 1dc into each of next 8dc, insert hook into next dc and draw loop through, miss 1dc, insert hook into next dc and draw loop through, yrh and draw through all 3 loops on hook, 1dc into each of next 8dc, 3dc into next dc, 1dc into each of next 6dc, (insert hook into next dc and draw loop through) into each of next 2dc, yrh and draw through all 3 loops on hook, 1dc into last dc. Turn.
The 2nd row forms the pattern. Work in stripes of 2 rows B, 2 rows C and 2 rows A throughout.

Horizontal stripe

Check pattern

Yarn across back

Using separate balls

Diagonal stripes

Chevron stripes

19

Jacquard & patchwork

Small jacquard designs, such as squares and diamonds, may be used to produce an all-over pattern or a large, single motif can be used most effectively to highlight a plain background. Random patchwork effects can also be used to produce a most interesting and original fabric.

An all-over jacquard pattern may be worked by carrying the yarn not in use across the back of the fabric but for single motifs and patchwork patterns, separate balls of yarn should be used for each colour. In both methods, each new colour must be bought into use correctly, as

shown in the previous Chapter.
Basic stitches, such as double crochet, half trebles or trebles should be used for these patterns, otherwise the definition of the motif, or patches, will be lost.

Jacquard patterns
Just as in knitting, these motifs may be worked from a chart where each colour in the pattern is shown as a separate symbol, or from row-by-row instructions where each colour is coded with

a letter, such as A and B. The method used is largely a matter of personal choice. The first sample shown here gives row instructions only and in the 2 following samples, the first few rows are given out in full and the motif is then

completed from the appropriate chart—in this way you will soon become familiar with both methods.

Square jacquard pattern
This pattern requires multiples of 7 plus 3 and 2 extra turning chain, using 2 colours coded as A and B. Using A, make 26ch.

1st row (RS) Into 4th ch from hook work 1tr, 1tr into each ch to end. Turn. 24tr.

2nd row 3ch to count as first tr, miss first tr, 1tr into each tr to end. Turn.

3rd row Using A, 3ch to count as first tr, miss first tr, work 1tr into each of next 2tr joining in B on last loop, *using B, work 1tr into each of next 4tr joining in A on last loop, using A, work

1tr into each of next 3tr joining in B on last loop, rep from * to end but do not join in B at end of last rep. Turn.

4th row As 3rd.
These 4 rows form the pattern.

Diamond jacquard pattern
This pattern requires multiples of 6 plus 1 and 2 extra turning chain, using 2 colours coded as A and B. Using A, make 33ch.

1st row (RS) Using A, into 4th ch from hook work 1tr, 1tr into next ch joining in B on last loop, *using B, work 1tr into next ch joining in A on last loop, using A, work 1tr into each of

next 5ch joining in B on last loop, rep from * to last 4ch, using B, work 1tr into next ch joining in A on last loop, using A, work 1tr into each of last 3ch. Turn. 31tr.

2nd row Using A, 3ch to count as first tr, miss first tr, 1tr into next tr joining in B on last loop, *using B, work 1tr into each of next 3tr joining in A on last loop, using A, work 1tr into each

of next 3tr joining in B on last loop, rep from * to last 5 sts, using B, work 1tr into each of next 3tr joining in A on last loop, using A, work 1tr into next tr, 1tr into 3rd of first 3ch. Turn.
Continue in pattern as given in chart below, repeating 10 rows for required length.

Butterfly motif
Work out the position for the motif against a double crochet background, allowing 26 sts and 28 rows to complete the butterfly.

1st row (RS) Using A, 1ch to count as first dc, miss first dc, 1dc into each of next 13dc joining

in B on last loop, using B, work 1dc into each of next 3dc joining in A on last loop, using A, work 1dc into each of next 9dc. Turn.

2nd row Using A, 1ch to count as first dc, miss first dc, 1dc into each of next 7dc joining in B on last loop, using B, work 1dc into each of

next 6dc joining in A on last loop, using A, work 1dc into each of next 4dc joining in C on last loop, using C, work 1dc into each of next 2dc joining in A on last loop, using A, work 1dc into each of next 6dc. Turn.
Continue working in pattern as given in chart.

Patchwork patterns
Although patchwork fabrics may appear complicated, they are quite simple to work. Each patch is worked over the same number of stitches and rows but the order in which the different patches and colours are used gives each section a completely different appearance.
The patches can be worked in a continuous strip to the required length and the required number of strips may then be joined together to form pram and cot covers, cushion covers or afghans and blankets. A really colourful effect can be achieved by using oddments of yarn.
The sample shown here has been worked in 6 colours, coded as A, B, C, D, E and F, using a Double Knitting yarn and a No.4.00 (ISR) crochet hook, to give each patch a width of 10cm (*4in*) and a depth of 10cm (*4in*).

1st patch
Using A, make 18ch.
1st row (RS) Into 4th ch from hook work 1tr, 1tr into each ch to end. Turn. 16tr.
2nd row 3ch to count as first tr, miss first tr, 1tr into each tr to end. Turn.
Rep 2nd row 6 times more. Fasten off.

2nd patch
1st row Join in B and work 2nd row as given for 1st patch.
2nd row Using B, as 1st row.
Rep these 2 rows 3 times more, using C, D and E. Fasten off.

3rd patch
1st row Join in F, 3ch to count as first tr, miss

first tr, work 1tr into each of next 17tr joining in A on last loop, using A, work 1tr into each of next 8tr. Turn.
2nd row Using A, 3ch to count as first tr, miss first tr, work 1tr into each of next 7tr joining in F on last loop, using F, work 1tr into each of next 8tr. Turn.
Rep last 2 rows once more. Break off F and A.
5th row Join in B, 3ch to count as first tr, miss first tr, work 1tr into each of next 7tr joining in C on last loop, using C, work 1tr into each of next 8tr. Turn.
6th row Using C, 3ch to count as first tr, miss first tr, work 1tr into each of next 7tr joining in B on last loop, using B, work 1tr into each of next 8tr. Turn.
Rep last 2 rows once more. Fasten off.

4th patch
1st row Join in D and work 2nd row as given for 1st patch. Turn.
Rep last row 3 times more. Break off D.
5th row Join in E and F and work 1st row as given for 3rd patch.
6th row Using F and E work 2nd row as given for 3rd patch.
Rep last 2 rows once more. Fasten off.
These 4 patches form the pattern and are repeated throughout for the required length, varying the order in which they are worked and the colours used on each subsequent patch. Make as many more strips as are needed in the same way, again varying the sequence in which the patches are worked and the colours used for each patch.

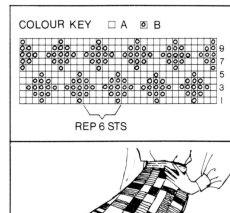

COLOUR KEY □ A ⊡ B

REP 6 STS

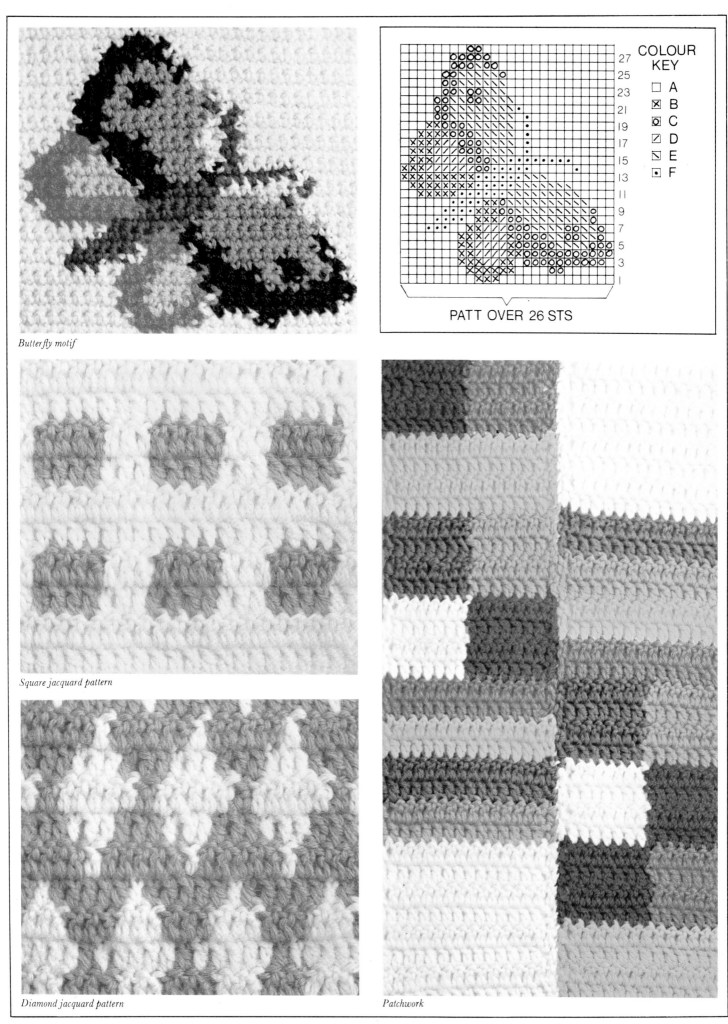

Butterfly motif

COLOUR KEY

☐ A
☒ B
⊘ C
◱ D
◲ E
⊡ F

PATT OVER 26 STS

Square jacquard pattern

Diamond jacquard pattern

Patchwork

21

Filet crochet

The word 'filet' means 'net' and this form of crochet is one of the simplest to work to produce a lacy fabric with numerous uses. It is made up of two basic stitches—the chain and the treble. The trebles are worked in groups to produce a solid block and the spaces between each block are formed by chains, to correspond with the number of trebles over which each space is worked.

Many beautiful and intricate designs can be incorporated into this method, working from a chart as given for the motifs in Chapter 26, or a simple all-over net fabric may be produced.

Basic filet net
This is formed by a single treble with a 2 chain space between each treble. Make a chain having multiples of 3 plus one and an extra 4 chain, e.g., 32ch.

1st row (RS) Into 8th ch from hook work 1tr, noting that the 7 missed ch form a 2ch space on the lower edge, 3ch to count as the first tr and another 2ch space along the top edge, *2ch, miss 3ch, 1tr into next ch, rep from * to end. Turn.

2nd row 5ch to count as first tr and 2ch space, miss first tr and 2ch space, 1tr into next tr, * 2ch, miss 2ch space, 1tr into next tr, rep from * working last tr into 5th of first 7ch. Turn. The 2nd row forms the pattern, ending each subsequent row with 1tr into 3rd of first 5ch.

Blocks and spaces
On to this basic net background, simple or more complicated patterns of blocks and spaces may now be built up.

Blocks worked over spaces.
These are formed by working 1tr into the corresponding tr of the previous row, 2tr into the next 2ch space and 1tr in to the next tr, forming a block of 4tr, the last of which belongs to the next space.

Spaces worked over blocks.
These are formed by working 1tr into the first tr of the block, 2ch, miss the next 2tr and work 1tr into the last tr of the block.

To begin a first row with a block.
Make 3 extra ch to count as the first tr and work the next tr into the 4th ch from hook, then complete the first block of 4tr by working 1tr into each of the next 2ch.

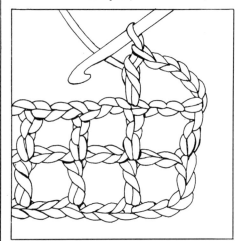

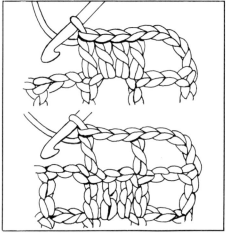

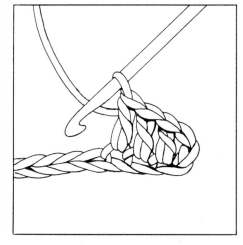

To begin a first row with a space.
Make 7 extra ch to count as the 2ch space along the lower edge, the first tr and 2ch space along top edge, then work the next tr into the 8th ch from hook.

tr, rep from * working last tr into 5th of first 7ch. Turn.

3rd row 5ch to count as first tr and 2ch space, miss first 3tr, *1tr into next tr, 2ch, miss 2ch space, 1tr into next tr, 2ch, miss 2tr, rep from * to end, 1tr into 3rd of first 3ch. Turn.

4th row 5ch to count as given for 3rd row, *1tr into next tr, 2tr into 2ch space, 1tr into next tr, 2ch, miss 2ch space, rep from * to end, 1tr into 3rd of first 5ch. Turn.

5th row 5ch to count as 3rd row, miss 2ch space, *1tr into next tr, 2ch, miss 2tr, 1tr into next tr, 2ch, miss 2ch space, rep from * to end.

working last tr into 3rd of first 5ch.
The 2nd to 5th rows form the pattern.

Filet pattern using double blocks
Make a chain having multiples of 12 plus 7 and 2 extra chain, e.g., 33ch.

1st row Into 4th ch from hook work 1tr, 1tr into each of next 5ch, *2ch, miss 2ch, 1tr into next ch, 2ch, miss 2ch, 1tr into each of next 7ch, rep from * to end. Turn.

2nd row 3ch to count as first tr, miss first tr, 1tr into each of next 6tr, *2ch, miss 2ch, 1tr into next tr, 2ch, miss 2ch, 1tr into each of next

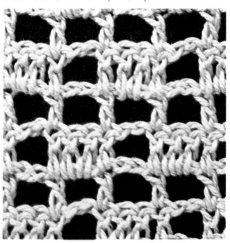

Simple pattern of alternating blocks and spaces
Make a chain having multiples of 6 plus 4 and an extra 4 chain, e.g. 32ch.

1st row (RS) As 1st row of basic filet net.

2nd row 3ch to count as first tr, 2tr into 2ch space, 1tr into next tr, *2ch, miss 2ch space, 1tr into next tr, 2tr into 2ch space, 1tr into next

7tr, rep from * to end working last tr into 3rd of first 3ch. Turn.

3rd row 5ch to count as first tr and 2ch, miss first 3tr, 1tr into next tr, 2ch, miss 2tr, 1tr into next tr, **(2tr into next 2ch space, 1tr into next tr) twice, (2ch, miss 2tr, 1tr into next tr)

twice, rep from * to end, working last tr into 3rd of first 3ch. Turn.

4th row 5ch to count as first tr and 2ch, miss first tr and 2ch, 1tr into next tr, 2ch, miss 2ch, *1tr into each of next 7tr, 2ch, miss 2ch, 1tr into next tr, 2ch, miss 2ch, rep from * to end, 1tr into 3rd of first 5ch. Turn.

5th row 3ch to count as first tr, miss first tr, 2tr into first space, 1tr into next tr, 2tr into next space, 1tr into next tr *(2ch, miss 2tr, 1tr into next tr) twice, (2tr into next space, 1tr into next tr) twice, rep from * to end, working last tr into 3rd of first 5ch. Turn.
The 2nd to 5th rows form the pattern.

Shaping in filet crochet

Attractive borders for household linens may be worked which have an interesting serrated edge. This is achieved by decreasing or increasing blocks or spaces at a given point.

To increase a block at the beginning of a row

Make 5ch, into the 4th ch from hook work 1tr, 1tr into next ch then work 1tr into the last st of the previous row. One block has been increased.

To increase two blocks

Make 8ch, into 4th ch from hook work 1tr, 1tr into each of next 4ch then work 1tr into the last st of the previous row.

To increase a space at the beginning of a row

Make 7ch to count as (2ch space at the end of the previous row, 3 to count as the first tr of the new row and another 2 for the top of the space between the first tr and the next st of the previous row), 1tr into first tr of the row (edge st).

To increase a block at the end of a row

Make provision for the increase at the beginning of the previous row by working 7ch, miss first ch and ss into each of next 3ch, noting that the remaining 3ch will count as the first tr of the row being worked, then continue in pattern to the end of the row. At the end of the following row, where the increase is required, work 1tr into each of the 3ss. One block has been increased.

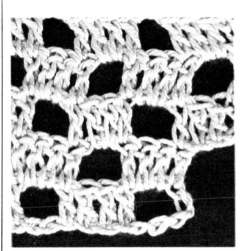

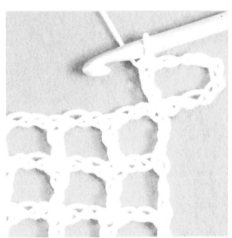

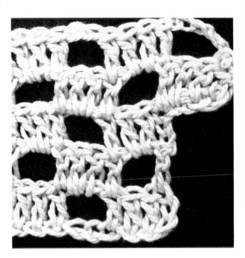

To increase a space at the end of a row

Work as given for increasing a block at the end of a row but when the position for the increase is reached, miss next 2ss, 2ch, work 1tr into last ss. One space has been increased.

To decrease a block or a space at the beginning of a row

Ss across each of the first 3 sts and into the 4th st, make 3ch to count as the first tr or 5ch to count as the first tr and 2ch space, then continue in pattern. One block or space has been decreased.

To decrease a block or space at the end of a row

Work in pattern to within the last block or space, then turn and miss these stitches and continue in pattern for the next row.

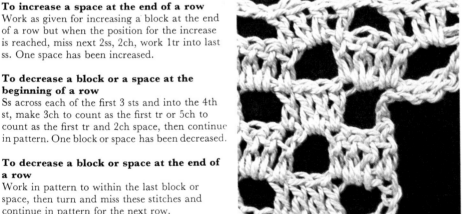

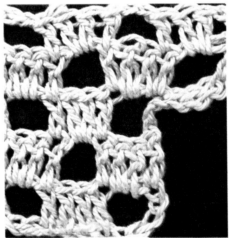

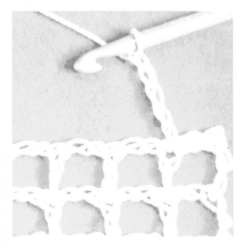

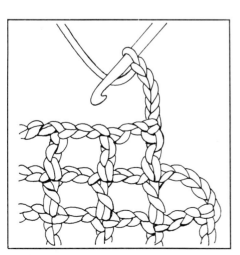

Simple filet edging

This edging is worked by using the exact number of stitches to give the width and continuing until it is the required length. Make 17ch.

1st row (RS) Into 8th ch from hook work 1tr, 1tr into each of next 3ch, (2ch, miss 2ch, 1tr into next ch) twice. Turn.

2nd row 5ch to count as first tr and 2ch space, miss first tr and 2ch space, 1tr into next tr, 2tr into 2ch space, 1tr into next tr, 2ch, miss next 2tr, 1tr into next tr, turn, noting that one space has been decreased.

3rd row 7ch to increase one space, 1tr into first tr, 2tr into 2ch space, 1tr into next tr, 2ch, miss next 2tr, 1tr into next tr, 2ch, 1tr into 3rd of first 5ch. Turn.
The 2nd and 3rd rows form the pattern.

Looped & woven fabrics

Fun-fur fabrics can be produced either by means of loop stitches, chain stitches or by applying cut ends of yarn to a mesh background. Any of these methods can be used for an all-over fabric or separate bands can be worked as collars and cuffs. They are fun to work and they all provide a thick, warm fabric, particularly suitable for pram or cot covers. Worked in a thick, soft cotton they also make ideal bath or nursery rugs.

A simple filet background may be used to achieve interesting woven fabrics, either by threading yarn in contrast colours through each chain space of the background, or by applying vertical chains directly on to the background.

Loop fur stitch

Each loop is formed round the 1st and 2nd fingers of the left hand on the back of the fabric as it is worked. The position of each loop can be placed one above the other into every stitch on every alternate row, to give a dense fabric, or they can be worked into every alternate stitch and into the stitches between the loops on the following alternate row, to form a thinner fabric.

To work this sample make 31ch.
1st row (RS) Into 3rd ch from hook work 1dc, 1dc into each ch to end. Turn. 30dc.
2nd row 1ch to count as first dc, miss first dc, *insert hook into next dc, hold yarn across 1st and 2nd fingers of left hand and extend yarn to required height by lifting 2nd finger, keeping hook to the right of the yarn over the finger place hook over yarn lying between 2nd and 3rd fingers and draw loop through dc, keeping hook to the left of the loop over the finger yrh from main ball of yarn and draw through both loops on hook, remove 2nd finger from loop—called loop 1—, rep from * to last dc, 1dc into last dc. Turn.
3rd row 1ch to count as first dc, miss first dc, 1dc into each st to end. Turn.
The 2nd and 3rd rows form the pattern.

Chain fur stitch

Here the fur effect is formed by chains which are worked across the back of the fabric, to give a close, curly texture.
To work this sample make 32ch.
1st row (RS) Into 4th ch from hook work 1tr, 1tr into each ch to end. Turn. 30tr.
2nd row 1ch to count as first dc, miss first tr, *1dc into back loop only of next tr, 10ch, rep from * to end working last dc into 3rd of first 3ch. Turn.
3rd row 3ch to count as first tr, miss first dc, *1tr into the missed loop of the next tr of the previous alternate row, rep from * to end working last tr into first ch of last row. Turn.
The 2nd and 3rd rows form the pattern.

Cut fur stitch

This method requires a mesh background, into which separate, cut ends of yarn are looped. As with loop fur stitch, the thickness of the fabric may be altered by the positioning of the loops and the number of strands of yarn which are used. To work this sample make 32ch for the mesh background.
1st row (RS) Into 4th ch from hook work 1dc, *1ch, miss 1ch, 1dc into next ch, rep from * to end. Turn.
2nd row 1ch to count as first dc, 1ch, *1dc into next 1ch space, 1ch, rep from * to end, 1dc into 2nd of first 3ch. Turn.
The 2nd row forms the pattern, noting that on subsequent rows the last dc is worked into first ch.
To add the loops. First cut yarn into 12.5cm (5in) lengths. Take 2 strands of yarn and fold in half. With RS of mesh background facing, insert hook horizontally under the first dc of the 1st row, put the folded loop of yarn over the hook and draw through the work, place the 4 ends of yarn over the hook and draw through loops on hook, then pull up tightly to secure. Repeat into every dc, or every alternate dc, as required.

Woven fabrics

The methods shown here can be used to produce colourful plaid effects, which are ideal for travelling rugs and afghans. Oddments of the same thickness of yarn may be used for the applied vertical stripes and the background fabric shown here is a simple filet net. Instructions for this can be found in the previous section, on page 22.

Using woven strands of yarn

Make a simple filet net background to the required width and length, as given in Chapter 11 but having a single treble with 1 chain space between each treble instead of 2 chain spaces. Cut lengths of yarn to the same length as the background, allowing approximately 15.0cm (6in) extra at each end for fringing. Take 2 or 3 strands together at a time and with RS of background facing, begin at lower right hand corner. Thread yarn under first chain in 1st row, over first chain in 2nd row, then continue in this way to top right hand corner. Begin again at lower edge, take yarn over 2nd chain in 1st row, under 2nd chain in 2nd row, then continue in this way to top edge. Repeat into each space across fabric, varying colours as required.

Using crochet chains of yarn

Make a simple filet net background as given when using woven strands of yarn, to the required width and length. Using 2 balls of yarn together in colours as required, make a slip loop and place on hook. With RS of filet background facing, begin at lower right hand corner and hold yarn at back of work, insert hook into first chain space in 1st row to back of work, yarn round hook then draw loop through to front of work and through loop on hook. Continue in this way, working into each chain space to top edge. Fasten off securely. Begin again at lower edge and work in same way into each of the 2nd chain spaces to the top edge. Repeat into each chain space across fabric.

Woven plaid fabric

This requires a filet background to the required width and length, using groups of two blocks of 2 trebles and two 1 chain spaces worked above each other throughout. Make a number of chain divisible by 8 plus 5 and 2 extra turning chain, e.g., 31ch.
1st row Into 4th ch from hook work 1tr, 1tr into each of next 3ch, *(1ch, miss 1ch, 1tr into next ch) twice, 1tr into each of next 4ch, rep from * to end. Turn.
2nd row 3ch to count as first tr, miss first tr, 1tr into each of next 4tr, *(1ch, miss 1ch space, 1tr into next tr) twice, 1tr into each of next 4tr, rep from * to end working last tr into 3rd of first 3ch. Turn.
Rep the 2nd row for the required length, working in stripes of 4 rows of one colour and 2 rows of contrast colour throughout.
Using two or three strands of yarn together, beg in at lower right hand corner and weave yarn over and under each chain as given for first woven sample, using first colour for first pair of chain spaces and second colour for second pair throughout.
This fabric can be adapted in many different ways by varying the number of blocks and chain spaces and also the number of colours used.

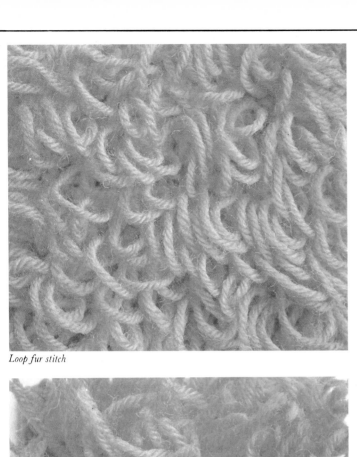

Loop fur stitch

Chain fur stitch

Cut fur stitch

Woven fabric using strands of yarn

Woven fabric using crochet chains of yarn

Woven plaid fabric

Irish crochet

Irish crochet

There are two distinct types of Irish crochet, which both have different working methods. The traditional form is the heavier of the two and each motif, or 'sprig', is worked separately over a length of yarn to give it an almost three dimensional effect and then joined together into an all-over pattern by means of a net background, called 'filling'.

The finer version, sometimes called 'baby Irish crochet' because it was so often used to trim elaborate layettes, is worked continuously into square or circular sections, beginning with a central motif around which a filling is then worked. Each section is then joined together with a series of picot bars or smaller motifs.

Traditional Irish crochet

To work the authentic method, it is first necessary to plan the shape and size of fabric required by tracing out the design on a piece of strong paper or linen. As each separate motif is completed, it should be tacked into position on the plan. The motifs are then joined together by a filling of chains, or picot bars, to form an all-over fabric. A much simpler method, however, is to work the background first to the required size and then apply the separate motifs directly on to the net.

Here we give samples of 2 net fillings and a selection of sprigs.

Honeycomb filling

This simple net background requires multiples of 4 chain plus 1 and 5 extra turning chain. When working to a plan, as each sprig is reached, join it by means of a slip stitch where it touches the filling.

1st row Into 10th ch from hook work 1dc, *6ch, miss 3ch, 1dc into next ch, rep from * to end. Turn.

2nd row 9ch, 1dc into first 6ch space of previous row, *6ch, 1dc into next 6ch space, rep from * to end working last dc into 9ch loop. Turn.

The 2nd row forms the pattern.

Diamond picot filling

This net background is joined as given for honeycomb filling and requires multiples of 4 chain plus 1 and 6 extra turning chain.

1st row Into 3rd ch from hook work 1dc to form picot, 1ch, miss 7ch, 1dc into next ch, *(4ch, 1dc into 3rd ch from hook to form picot) twice, 1ch, miss 3ch of foundation row, 1dc into next ch, rep from * to end. Turn.

2nd row 7ch, 1dc into 3rd ch from hook, 1ch, 1dc into 1ch space between picots in next loop, *(4ch, 1dc into 3rd ch from hook to form picot) twice, 1ch, 1dc into 1ch space between picots of next loop, rep from * to end working last dc into last ch space after picot on end loop. Turn.

The 2nd row forms the pattern.

Irish crochet rings

First estimate the length of separate thread required to complete a ring. Coil the separate thread into a ring by winding it 2 or 3 times round a finger. Working from front to back through the ring, join in the correct yarn with a slip stitch, then work 1 round of double crochet into the ring. Join with a slip stitch to first double crochet to complete the ring.

Where a series of rings are required, complete half of the first ring only, continue working in double crochet over the separate thread until the next position is reached, then coil the yarn and complete half of the 2nd ring only. Continue in this way until the required number of rings have been formed, then complete each ring by working the 2nd half, slip stitching along the length of thread between each ring.

Irish crochet rose motif

Using the correct yarn, coil the end 3 or 4 times round a finger, remove the ring and secure with a slip stitch.

1st round 2ch to count as first dc, work 17dc into ring. Join with a ss to 2nd of first 2ch. 18dc.

2nd round 6ch, miss 2dc, 1htr into next dc, *4ch, miss 2dc, 1htr into next dc, rep from * 3 times more, 4ch, miss last 2dc, Join with a ss to 2nd of first 6ch. 6 loops.

3rd round Into each 4ch space work (1dc, 1htr, 3tr, 1htr, 1dc). Join with a ss to first dc. 6 petals.

4th round Ss into back of nearest htr of 2nd round, *5ch, pass ch behind petal of previous round and ss into back of next htr of 2nd round rep from * 5 times more working last ss into same htr as first ss.

5th round Into each 5ch space work (1dc, 1htr, 5tr, 1htr, 1dc). Join with a ss to first dc.

6th round Ss into back of ss of 4th round, *6ch, pass ch behind petal of previous round and ss into back of next ss of 4th round, rep from * 5 times more working last ss into same place as first ss.

7th round Into each 6ch space work (1dc, 1htr, 7tr, 1htr, 1dc). Join with a ss to first dc. Fasten off.

Irish crochet shamrock motif

Estimate the length of separate yarn required, allowing enough to form the stem. Using correct yarn make 16ch.

1st round Into 16th ch from hook work 1dc, (15ch, 1dc into same ch as last dc) twice.

2nd round Working over separate length of yarn work 22dc into each 15ch loop. Join with a ss to first dc. 3 petals.

3rd round Working over separate length of yarn, *miss first dc of petal, 1dc into each of next 20dc, miss last dc of petal, rep from * twice more. Join with a ss to first dc.

4th round Make 25ch to form stem, working over separate length of yarn into 2nd ch from hook work 1dc, 1dc into each ch to end. Join with a ss to first dc on first petal. Fasten off.

Fine Irish crochet

The samples shown here give 2 methods of joining. The first incorporates a net background to form a square motif. The second forms a round motif and these are then joined together with a smaller motif. Both examples may be used to produce exquisite place mats, tray cloths or tablecloths.

Shamrock and crown medallion

Make 16ch.

1st round Into 16ch from hook work 1dc, (15ch, 1dc into same ch as first dc) twice.

2nd round Work 24dc into each ch loop. Join with a ss to first dc.

3rd round Work 1dc into each dc. Join with a ss to first dc.

4th round Ss into each of next 3dc counting join as 4th ss, **1dc into next dc, *4ch, 1dc into 3rd ch from hook to form picot, 5ch, 1dc into 3rd ch from hook to form picot, 1ch—called 1 picot loop—, miss 4dc, 1dc into next dc, rep from * twice more. 1 picot loop, miss 4dc of first leaf and 4dc of next leaf of shamrock, rep from ** ending with 1 picot loop. Join with a ss to first dc. 12 picot loops.

5th round Ss into centre of first picot loop between picots, 1dc into same loop, *8ch, 1dc between picots of next picot loop, turn, 1ss into loop just made, 3ch, 9tr into same loop, 1tr into next dc, 4ch, turn, miss first 2tr, 1tr into next tr, **1ch, miss 1tr, 1tr into next tr, rep from ** twice more, 1ch, miss 1tr, 1tr into top of 3ch, 4ch, 1dc into 3rd ch from hook, 2ch, 1dc into same loop, (4ch, 1dc into 3rd ch from hook, 5ch, 1dc into 3rd ch from hook, 2ch, 1dc between picots of next picot loop) twice, rep from * omitting 1dc at end of last rep. Join with a ss to first dc.

6th round Ss up side of tr and into each of next 3ch, 1dc into same space, *4ch, 1dc into 3rd ch from hook, 5ch, 1dc into 3rd ch from hook, 2ch, miss 1 space, 1dc into next space, 4ch, 1dc into 3rd ch from hook, 5ch, 1dc into 3rd ch from hook, 2ch, miss 2 spaces, 1dc into next loop, (4ch, 1dc into 3rd ch from hook, 5ch, 1dc into 3rd ch from hook, 2ch, 1dc between picots of next loop) twice, 4ch, 1dc into 3rd ch from hook, 5ch, 1dc into 3rd ch from hook, 2ch, 1dc into first space of next block, rep from * omitting 1dc at end of last rep. Join with a ss to first dc.

7th round Ss into centre of first picot loop, 1dc into same loop, *8ch, 1dc between picots of next loop, turn, 1ss into loop just made, 3ch, 9tr into same loop, 1tr into next dc, 4ch, turn, miss 2tr, 1tr into next tr, **1ch, miss 1tr, 1tr into next tr, rep from ** twice more, 1ch, miss 1tr, 1tr into top of 3ch, 4ch, 1dc into 3rd ch from hook, 2ch, 1dc into 3rd ch from hook, 5ch, 1dc into 3rd ch from hook, 2ch, 1dc between picots of next loop) 4 times, rep from * omitting 1dc at end of last rep. Join with a ss to first dc.

8th round Ss up side of tr and into each of next 3ch, 1dc into first space, *4ch, 1dc into 3rd ch from hook, 5ch, 1dc into 3rd ch from hook, 2ch, miss 1 space, 1dc into next space, 4ch, 1dc into 3rd ch from hook, 5ch, 1dc into 3rd ch from hook, 2ch, miss 2 spaces, 1dc into next loop, (4ch, 1dc into 3rd ch from hook, 5ch, 1dc into 3rd ch from hook, 2ch, 1dc between picots of next loop) 4 times, 4ch, 1dc into 3rd ch from hook, 5ch, 1dc into 3rd ch from hook, 2ch, 1dc into first space of next block, rep from * omitting 1dc at end of last rep. Join with a ss to first dc. Fasten off.

Wheel motif

Make 8ch. Join with a ss to first ch to form circle.

1st round Work 18dc into circle. Do not join.

2nd round *1dc into each of next 2dc, 2dc into next dc, rep from * 5 times more. Do not join. 24 dc.

3rd round *1dc into each of next 3dc, 2dc into next dc, rep from * 5 times more. 30dc.

Cont inc in this way on next 3 rounds. Join with a ss to first dc. 48dc.

7th round 1dc into same place as ss, *5ch, miss 1dc, 1dc into next dc, rep from * ending with 2ch, 1tr into first dc. 24 loops.

8th and 9th rounds *5ch, 1dc into next loop, rep from * ending with 2ch, 1tr into tr of previous round.

10th round *10ch, miss 1 loop, 1dc into next loop, rep from * to end, 10ch. Join with a ss to tr of previous round.

11th round Work 15dc into each 10ch loop. Join with a ss to first dc.

12th round 1dc into same place as ss, 1dc into each of next 6dc, *into next dc work (1dc, 3ch, 1dc, 5ch, 1dc, 3ch, 1dc), 1dc into each of next 14dc, rep from * ending last rep with 1dc into each of last 7dc. Join with a ss to first dc. Fasten off.

Work 2nd motif in same way for first 11 rounds.

12th round (joining round) 1dc into same place as ss, 1dc into each of next 6dc, *into next ds work 1dc, 3ch, 1dc, 2ch, ss into corresponding 5ch loop on 1st motif, 2ch, 1dc, 3ch and 1dc into same dc of 2nd motif, *, 1dc into each of next 14dc, rep from * to *, then complete as given for 1st motif.

Joining motifs

Make 6ch. Join with a ss to first ch to form circle.

1st round Work 8dc into circle. Join with a ss to first dc.

2nd round 1dc into same place as ss, *4ch, 1dc into next dc, rep from * ending with 1ch, 1tr into first dc. 8 loops.

3rd round *5ch, 1dc into next loop, 10ch, 1dc into next loop, rep from * ending with ss into tr of previous round.

4th round *5dc into next 5ch loop, 6dc into next 10ch loop, ss into 5th ch on free picot between motifs, 6dc into same 10ch loop, rep from * to end. Join with a ss to first dc. Fasten off.

Top to bottom: Wheel motif; Diamond picot filling; Irish crochet rings; Rose motif; Shamrock motif; Shamrock and crown medallion; Honeycomb filling

27

Tunisian crochet

This interesting technique is a combination of both knitting and crochet, worked on a single, long hook instead of a pair of needles. Although the overall term applies to this method of working, it is very often referred to as 'Afghan stitch'. This is rather misleading, as it implies that only one stitch is used, instead of the numerous and varied stitches which form most attractive fabrics.

This technique begins in the same way as crochet, with the required length of chains and a working loop on the hook. When making the initial length of chains, you will not require any extra chains for turning—a chain length of 20 will give you exactly 20 working stitches. The first row is worked from right to left into each chain, keeping the last loop of each stitch on the hook, then the 2nd row, which is, in fact, the completion of the 1st row, is worked back again from left to right without turning the work, reducing the loops along the row until only the working loop remains. With this method, the right side of the work is always facing you. The fabric produced is very strong and hard-wearing and, depending on the stitch used, the finished appearance can resemble crochet or look deceptively like knitting. Because of the working method, Tunisian crochet sometimes produces as bias effect but this tendency can be overcome by working the stitches fairly loosely. Always pull the yarn round the hook adequately through the stitch and, when working back along a row from left to right, never pull the first stitch through so tightly that you flatten the height of the row.

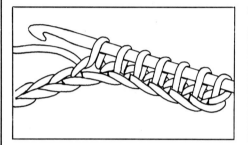 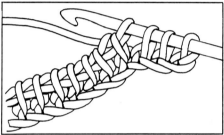 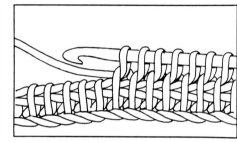

Plain or basic Tunisian stitch
Make any number of chain.
1st row Insert hook into 2nd ch from hook, yrh and draw loop through ch, *insert hook into next ch, yrh and draw loop through ch, rep from * to end. Do not turn work. The number of loops on the hook should be the same as the commencing ch.
2nd row Working from left to right, yrh and draw through first loop on hook, *yrh and draw through 2 loops on hook, rep from * to end. Do not turn work. Working loop only remains on hook.
3rd row *Insert hook from right to left behind the vertical thread of the next st, yrh and draw loop through, rep from * into each vertical thread to end. Do not turn.
4th row As 2nd.
The 3rd and 4th rows form the pattern, always ending with a 4th row.

Tunisian treble stitch
Make any number of chain.
1st row Yrh, insert hook into 3rd ch from hook, yrh and draw loop through ch, yrh and draw through 2 loops on hook, *yrh, insert hook into next ch, yrh and draw loop through ch, yrh and draw through 2 loops on hook, rep from * to end. Do not turn.
2nd row As 2nd row of basic Tunisian stitch.
3rd row 1ch to count as first st, *yrh, insert hook from right to left behind vertical thread of the next st, yrh and draw loop through, yrh and draw through 2 loops on hook, rep from * to end. Do not turn.
4th row As 2nd.
The 3rd and 4th rows form the pattern, always ending with a 4th row.

Tunisian stocking stitch
Make any number of chain. Work 1st and 2nd rows as given for basic Tunisian stitch.
3rd row *Insert hook from front to back between vertical threads and below top edge of next st of previous row, yrh and draw loop through fairly loosely, rep from * to end. Do not turn.
4th row As 2nd.
The 3rd and 4th rows form the pattern, always ending with a 4th row.

Tunisian cluster stitch
Make a number of chain divisible by 8 plus 5. Work 1st, 2nd and 3rd rows as given for basic Tunisian stitch.
4th row Yrh and draw through 3 loops, *3ch, yrh and draw through 5 loops, (i.e. the loop on the hook and the next 4 loops), rep from * to last 2 loops, 3ch, yrh and draw through rem 3 loops, (i.e. the loop on the hook and rem 2 loops). Do not turn.
5th row *Insert hook into each of next 3ch and draw a loop through each, insert hook into top of cluster and draw a loop through, rep from * to end drawing the last loop through the edge st. Do not turn.
6th row As 2nd.
The 3rd to 6th rows form the pattern, always ending with a 4th or 6th row.

Shaping in Tunisian crochet
These fabrics can be shaped to make garments, just as with knitting and crochet. The usual methods are given here, together with instructions for making buttonholes.
Increasing a stitch at the right hand edge
To increase one stitch at the right hand edge, make one chain then insert the hook behind the vertical thread of the first stitch, (edge stitch), yrh and draw loop through, continue in pattern to the end of the row.
Increasing a stitch at the left hand edge
To increase one stitch at the left hand edge, this must be worked on a even numbered row. Yrh and draw through one loop, 1ch, *yrh and draw through 2 loops, rep from * to the end of the row. On the next row patt to the last stitch, insert hook into the 1ch and draw a loop through, insert hook into the last stitch and draw a loop through.
Increasing 2 or more stitches at the right hand edge
Make the required number of chain then work basic stitch into each chain and the first vertical thread (edge stitch) and continue in pattern to end.
Increasing 2 or more stitches at the left hand edge
Using a separate length of yarn make the required number of chain and leave for time being. Work in pattern to the end of the row then work in basic stitch into each of the separate chain.

Decreasing one stitch at the right hand edge
Insert the hook behind 2 vertical threads, yrh and draw through one loop only, continue in pattern to the end of the row.
Decreasing one stitch at the left hand edge
Work as given for decreasing at the right hand edge by inserting the hook behind the last 2 vertical threads together, yrh and draw through one loop only.
Working a buttonhole
Work in pattern from right to left to the position where the buttonhole is required, wind the yarn round the hook for the required number of stitches for the buttonhole, miss this number of stitches in the previous row and continue in pattern to end. On the following row, work off each loop of yarn as if it were a stitch.

Basic Tunisian stitch

Increasing 2 or more stitches at right hand edge

Tunisian treble stitch

Increasing 2 or more sts at left hand edge

Tunisian stocking stitch

Tunisian cluster stitch

Decreasing 1 stitch at right hand edge

Increasing 1 stitch at right hand edge

First step of working a buttonhole

Increasing 1 stitch at left hand edge

Working a buttonhole

Aran crochet

Crochet stitches can be combined to form fabrics which have the appearance of Aran patterns. The patterns can be built up against a plain background, either in the row-by-row working instructions or by applying surface stitches to the background when it has been completed.

The fabric formed has a raised, three-dimensional effect very similar to Aran knitting but is much less complicated to work. A traditional Aran yarn should be used to work these stitches, which have a wide range of uses, including fashion and household designs.

Crochet rib stitch

This stitch is worked from side edge to side edge and requires sufficient chains to give the depth of ribbing. Make any number of chain.

1st row (RS) Into 3rd ch from hook work 1dc, 1dc into each ch to end. Turn.

2nd row 1ch to count as first dc, miss first dc, *work 1dc into horizontal loop below top loop of next dc, rep from * ending with 1dc into turning ch. Turn.

The 2nd row forms the pattern.

Crochet moss stitch

Make a number of chain divisible by 2 plus one extra chain.

1st row (RS) Into 3rd ch from hook work 1ss, *1htr into next ch, 1ss into next ch, rep from* to end. Turn.

2nd row 2ch to count as first htr, miss first ss, *1ss into next htr, 1htr into next ss, rep from * to end, 1ss into 2nd of first 2ch. Turn.

The 2nd row forms the pattern.

Crochet cluster stitch in panels

Make a number of chain divisible by 6 plus 4 and 1 extra chain, e.g. 29ch.

Base row (RS) Into 3rd ch from hook work 1dc, 1dc into each ch to end. Turn. 28 sts.

1st row 3ch to count as first tr, miss first dc, 1tr into each of next 3dc, *(yrh, insert hook into next dc and draw loop through very loosely) 4 times into same dc, yrh and draw through all 9 loops on hook—called 1Cl or cluster—, 1Cl into next dc, 1tr into each of next 4dc, rep from * to end. Turn.

2nd row 1ch to count as first dc, miss first tr, 1dc into each of next 3tr, *(work 1dc into next st inserting hook under st horizontally from front to back and round stem—called 1Fdc—) twice, 1dc into each of next 4tr, rep from * working last dc into 3rd of first 3ch. Turn.

3rd row 3ch to count as first tr, miss first dc, 1tr into each of next 3dc, *1Cl into each of next 2 sts, 1tr into each of next 4dc, rep from * working last tr into first ch. Turn.

The 2nd and 3rd rows form the pattern.

Crochet zig-zag stitch

Make a number of chain divisible by 8 plus 6 and 2 extra turning chain, e.g. 32ch.

Base row (RS) Into 4th ch from hook work 1tr, 1tr into each ch to end. Turn. 30 sts.

1st row 2ch, miss first tr, work 1tr round stem of next tr inserting hook from back to front—called RtB—, 1Rtb round each of next 3tr, *work 1tr round stem of next tr inserting hook from front to back—called RtF—, 1RtF round each of next 3tr, 1RtB round each of next 4tr, rep from * to end, 1tr into turning ch loop. Turn.

2nd row 2ch, miss first st, work 1RtF round each of next 4 sts, *work 1RtB round each of next 4 sts, 1RtF round each of next 4 sts, rep from * to end, 1tr into turning ch loop. Turn.

3rd row 2ch, miss first st, work 1RtF round next st, *work 1RtB round each of next 4 sts, 1RtF round each of next 4 sts, rep from * to last 4 sts, 1RtB round each of next 3 sts, 1tr into turning ch loop. Turn.

4th row 2ch, miss first st, work 1RtF round each of next 3 sts, *work 1RtB round each of next 4 sts, 1RtF round each of next 4 sts, rep from * to last 2 sts, 1RtB round last st, 1tr into turning ch loop. Turn.

5th row 2ch, miss first st, work 1RtF round each of next 2 sts, *work 1RtB round each of next 4 sts, 1RtF round each of next 4 sts, rep from * to last 3 sts, 1RtB round each of next 2 sts, 1tr into turning ch loop. Turn.

6th row As 5th.
7th row As 4th.
8th row As 3rd.
9th row As 2nd.
10th row As 1st.
11th row As 4th.
12th row As 3rd.
13th row As 5th.
14th row As 5th.
15th row As 3rd.
16th row As 4th.

These 16 rows form the pattern.

Crochet Trinity stitch

Make a number of chain divisible by 2 plus 1 and 1 extra turning chain, e.g. 30ch.

Base row (RS) Into 3rd ch from hook work 1dc, 1dc into each ch to end. Turn. 29 sts.

1st row 1ch to count as edge st, *2ch, yrh, insert hook into next dc and draw a loop through loosely, yrh and draw through one loop on hook, (3 loops on hook), yrh, insert hook into same dc and draw a loop through loosely, (5 loops on hook), yrh and draw through 4 loops, yrh and draw through rem 2 loops—called Bl—, 1ss into next dc, rep from * to last 2 sts, Bl into next dc, 1ss into 2nd of first 2ch. Turn.

2nd row 1ch to count as edge st, *1ss into next Bl, 1dc into next ss, rep from * to last 2 sts, 1ss into Bl, 1dc into first ch. Turn.

3rd row 1ch to count as edge st, *1ss into next ss, Bl into next dc, rep from * to last 2 sts, 1ss into next ss, 1dc into first ch. Turn.

4th row 1ch to count as edge st, *1dc into next ss, 1ss into next Bl, rep from * to last 2 sts, 1dc into next ss, 1dc into first ch. Turn.

5th row 1ch to count as edge st, *Bl into next dc, 1ss into next ss, rep from * to last 2 sts, Bl into next dc, 1dc into first ch. Turn.

The 2nd to 5th rows form the pattern.

Surface crochet

Ridges of double crochet are worked on to the background fabric to form mock cables, or to enclose areas of patterned stitches, as shown in the diagrams.

To work surface crochet

Have the right side of the work facing you and join in the yarn with a slip stitch to the lower edge of the fabric. It is important to note that the yarn must be kept at the front of the work and if you hold it to the right of the stitch to be worked, the stitch leans slightly to the left and when the yarn is held to the left, the stitch leans slightly to the right. To work straight, vertical lines, either singly or in pairs, alternate the position of the yarn, first to the left and then to the right. To work diagonal lines, keep the yarn in the same direction as the slant stitch.

To work a straight surface line

Join the yarn and hold it on the RS of the work to the left of the hook, insert the hook under the first row to be worked and out to the front again, yrh and draw a loop through, yrh and draw through 2 loops on hook (one surface dc has been completed), hold the yarn at the right of the hook, insert the hook into the same hole at the top of the last surface dc, under the next row and out to the front again, yrh and draw a loop through, yrh and draw through 2 loops on hook. Continue in this way until the line is completed.

Rib pattern (worked across)

Moss stitch

Clusters in panels

Zig-zag pattern

Trinity stitch

Surface crochet

31

To work a diagonal surface line slanting to the left.
Join in the yarn and hold it on the RS of the work to the left of the hook, insert the hook under the first row to be worked and out to the front again, yrh and draw a loop through, yrh and draw through 2 loops on hook, (one surface dc has been completed), keep the yarn to the left of the hook, insert the hook one stitch to the left level with the top of the surface dc just completed and out to the front again, yrh and draw a loop through, yrh and draw through 2 loops on hook. Continue in this way until the line is completed.

To work a diagonal surface line slanting to the right
Work as given for diagonal line slanting to the left, keeping the yarn at the right of the hook and working each surface dc to the right.

In the diagrams given here, each square represents one stitch and one row of double crochet background. The single arrows indicate one line of surface crochet and the double arrows, 2 lines of surface crochet. Where the pattern lines converge, work both the lines into the same space. Where the lines intersect, cross the lines as indicated. The horizontal dotted lines indicate one pattern repeat.

Basic stitches

Reversible ridged double crochet
Make the required number of chain and one extra turning chain.
1st row (RS) Into 3rd ch from hook work 1dc, work 1dc into each ch to end.
2nd row 1ch to count as first dc, miss first dc, work 1dc into each dc to end working into back loop only of each dc of previous row, ending with 1dc into 2nd of first 2ch.
The 2nd row forms the pattern, ending with 1dc into first ch.

Reversible ridged half treble
Make the required number of chain and one extra turning chain.
1st row (RS) Into 3rd ch from hook work 1htr, work 1htr into each ch to end.
2nd row 2ch to count as first htr, miss first htr, work 1htr into each htr to end working into back loop only of each htr of previous row, ending with 1htr into 2nd of first 2ch.
The 2nd row forms the pattern.

Reversible ridged treble
Make the required number of chain and 2 extra turning chain.
1st row (RS) Into 4ch ch from hook work 1tr, work 1tr into each ch to end.
2nd row 3ch to count as first tr, miss first tr, work 1tr into each tr to end working into back loop only of each tr of previous row, ending with 1tr into 3rd of first 3ch.
The 2nd row forms the pattern.

Double treble
Make the required number of chain and 3 extra turning chain.
1st row (RS) Yrh twice, insert hook from front to back into 5th ch from hook, *yrh and draw loop through, (4 loops on hook), yrh and draw through 2 loops on hook, (3 loops on hook), yrh and draw through 2 loops on hook, (2 loops on hook), yrh and draw through rem 2 loops on hook, (1dtr has been made with the 4 missed ch counting as the turning ch), yrh twice, insert hook from front to back into next ch and rep from * working into each ch to end.
2nd row 4ch to count as first dtr, miss first dtr, work 1dtr into each dtr to end, ending with 1dtr into 4th of first 4ch.
The 2nd row forms the pattern.

Triple treble
Make the required number of chain and 4 extra turning chain.
1st row (RS) Yrh 3 times, insert hook from front to back into 6th ch from hook, *yrh and draw loop through, (5 loops on hook), yrh and draw through 2 loops, (4 loops on hook), yrh and draw through 2 loops on hook, (3 loops on hook), yrh and draw through 2 loops on hook, (2 loops on hook), yrh and draw through rem 2 loops on hook, (1tr tr has been made with the 5 missed ch counting as the turning ch), yrh 3 times, insert hook from front to back into next ch and rep from * working into each ch to end.
2nd row 5ch to count as first tr tr, miss first tr tr, work 1tr tr into each tr tr to end, ending with 1tr tr into 5th of first 5ch.
The 2nd row forms the pattern.

Eyelet treble
Make a number of chain divisible by 2 plus 1 and 2 extra turning chain.
1st row (RS) Into 4th ch from hook work 1tr, work 1tr into each ch to end.
2nd row 3ch to count as first tr, miss first tr, *1ch, miss 1tr, 1tr into next tr, rep from * to end, working last tr into 3rd of first 3ch.
3rd row 3ch to count as first tr, miss first tr, *1tr into 1ch, 1tr into next tr, rep from * to end, ending with 1tr into 1ch, 1tr into 3rd of first 3ch.
The 2nd and 3rd rows form the pattern.

Leaf stitch
Make a number of chain divisible by 2 and one extra turning chain.
1st row (RS) Into 3rd ch from hook work 2dc, *miss 1ch, work 2dc into next ch, rep from * to last 2ch, miss 1ch, 1dc into last ch.
2nd row 2ch to count as first st, miss first dc, *miss 1dc, work 2dc into next dc, rep from * to end, 1dc into turning ch.
The 2nd row forms the pattern.

Open treble
Make a number of chain divisible by 2 plus 1 and 2 extra turning chain.
1st row (RS) Into 5th ch from hook work 1tr, *1ch, miss 1ch, 1tr into next ch, rep from * to end.
2nd row 3ch to count as first tr, miss first tr, *1ch, 1tr into 1ch sp, rep from * to end.
The 2nd row forms the pattern.

Treble variation
Make the required number of chain and 2 extra turning chain.
1st row (RS) Into 4th ch from hook work 1tr, work 1tr into each ch to end.
2nd row 3ch to count as first tr, yrh, insert hook between first and 2nd tr and work 1tr, *yrh, insert hook between next 2tr and work 1tr, rep from * to end, ending with 1tr between last tr and first 3ch.
The 2nd row forms the pattern.

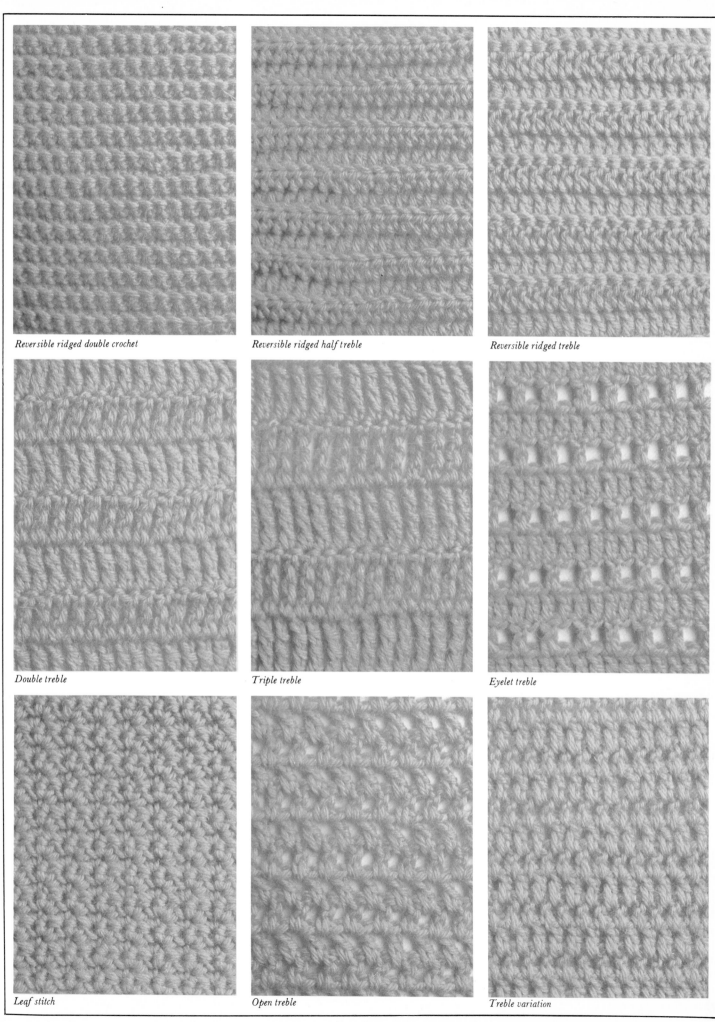

Reversible ridged double crochet

Reversible ridged half treble

Reversible ridged treble

Double treble

Triple treble

Eyelet treble

Leaf stitch

Open treble

Treble variation

33

Arch stitches

Mesh stitch

Make a number of chain divisible by 4 plus 1 and 5 extra turning chain.

1st row (RS) Into 10th ch from hook work 1dc, *5ch, miss 3ch, 1dc into next ch, rep from * to end.

2nd row 5ch, 1dc into 3rd ch of first 5ch loop, *5ch, 1dc into 3rd ch of next 5ch loop, rep from * to last loop, 5ch, 1dc into 6th of first 9ch, 2ch, miss 2ch, 1tr into next ch.

3rd row 6ch, *1dc into 3rd ch of next 5ch loop, 5ch, rep from * to end, 1dc into 3rd of first 5ch.

4th row 5ch, 1dc into 3rd ch of first 5ch loop, * 5ch, 1dc into 3rd ch of next loop, rep from * to last loop, 5ch, 1dc into 3rd ch of last loop, 2ch, 1tr into 1st of first 6ch.

The 3rd and 4th rows form the pattern.

Arch mesh stitch

Make a number of chain divisible by 4 plus 1 and 4 extra turning chain.

1st row (RS) Into 7th ch from hook work 1dc, 2ch, miss 1ch, 1tr into next ch, *2ch, miss 1ch, 1dc into next ch, 2ch, miss 1ch, 1tr into next ch, rep from * to end.

2nd row 1ch to count as first dc, miss first tr, *2ch, 1tr into next dc, 2ch, 1dc into next tr, rep from * to end, working the last dc into 4th of first 6ch.

3rd row 3ch to count as first tr, miss first dc, *2ch, 1dc into next tr, 2ch, 1tr into next dc, rep from * to end, working last tr into first 1ch.

4th row As 2nd row but working last dc into 3rd of first 3ch.

The 3rd and 4th rows form the pattern.

Zig-zag mesh stitch

Make a number of chain divisible by 4 plus 1 and 4 extra turning chain.

1st row (RS) Into 7th ch from hook work 1dc, 2ch, miss 1ch, 1tr into next ch, *2ch, miss 1ch, 1dc into next ch, 2ch, miss 1ch, 1tr into next ch, rep from * to end.

2nd row 1ch to count as first dc, miss first tr, *3ch, 1dc into next tr, rep from * to end, working last dc into 4th of first 6ch.

3rd row 3ch to count as first tr, *2ch, 1dc into 2nd of next 3ch, 2ch, 1tr into next dc, rep from * to end, working last tr into first 1ch.

4th row As 2nd row but working last dc into 3rd of first 3ch.

The 3rd and 4th rows form the pattern.

Picot mesh stitch

Make a number of chain divisible by 4 plus 1 and 5 extra turning chain.

1st row (RS) Into 10th ch from hook work 1dc, 3ch, 1dc into same ch as before, *5ch, miss 3ch, (1dc, 3ch, 1dc) into next ch —called 1 picot—, rep from * to last 4ch, 5ch, miss 3ch, 1dc into last ch.

2nd row 5ch, 1 picot into 3rd of first 5ch loop, *5ch, 1 picot into 3rd ch of next loop, rep from * to last loop, 5ch, 1 picot into 6th of first 9ch, 2ch, miss 2ch, 1tr into next ch.

3rd row 6ch, *1 picot into 3rd ch of next 5ch loop, 5ch, rep from * to last loop, 1 picot into 3rd of first 5ch.

4th row As 2nd row but ending with 5ch, 1 picot into 4th ch of last 6ch loop, 2ch, 1tr into first 1ch.

The 3rd and 4th rows form the pattern.

Fancy grill

Make a number of chain divisible by 4 plus 1 and 5 extra turning chain.

1st row (RS) Into 10th ch from hook work 1tr, *3ch, miss 3ch, 1tr into next ch, rep from * to end.

2nd row 3ch to count as first tr, miss first tr, *2ch, 1dc into 2nd of 3ch, 2ch, 1tr into next tr, rep from * to end, ending with 2ch, 1dc into 7th of first 9ch, 2ch, miss 1ch, 1tr into next ch.

3rd row 3ch to count as first tr, miss first tr, *3ch, 1tr into next tr, rep from * to end, working last tr into 3rd of first 3ch.

4th row As 2nd row but ending with 1dc into 2nd of 3ch, 2ch, 1tr into 3rd of first 3ch.

The 3rd and 4th rows form the pattern.

Mesh and clusters

Make a number of chain divisible by 8 plus 5 and 4 extra turning chain.

1st row (RS) Into 7th ch from hook work 1dc, *5ch, miss 3ch, 1dc into next ch, rep from * to last 2ch, 2ch, miss 1ch, 1tr into last ch.

2nd row 5ch, 1dc into first 5ch loop, *4ch, **yrh, insert hook into next loop, yrh and draw a loop through, yrh and draw through 2 loops on hook (2 loops now rem on hook), rep from ** 3 times more into same loop, noting that there will be one more loop on hook at end of each rep, (5 loops now on hook), yrh and draw through all loops on hook—called 1Cl —, 4ch, 1dc into next loop, rep from * to end, ending with 1dc into last 5ch loop, 2ch, 1tr into 4th of first 6ch.

3rd row 3ch, 1dc into 2ch loop, 5ch, *1dc into next 4ch loop, 5ch, rep from * to last loop, 1dc into last loop, 2ch, 1tr into first of first 5ch.

4th row 5ch, *1Cl into next 5ch loop, 4ch, 1dc into next 5ch loop, 4ch, rep from * to last 5ch loop, 1Cl into last 5ch loop, 2ch, 1tr into 3rd ch loop.

5th row As 3rd.

6th row As 2nd but ending with 1dc into last 5ch loop, 2ch, 1tr into 3ch loop.

The 3rd to 6th rows form the pattern.

Open V mesh

Make a number of chain divisible by 6 plus 1 and 3 extra turning chain.

1st row (RS) Into 7th ch from hook work (1tr, 2ch, 1tr)—called 1V—, *3ch, miss 2ch, 1dc into next ch, 3ch, miss 2ch, 1V into next ch, rep from * to last 3ch, 3ch, miss 2ch, 1dc into last ch.

2nd row 6ch, *1dc into 2ch sp of V, 3ch, 1tr into next dc, 3ch, rep from * to last V, 1dc into 2ch sp of V, 3ch, 1tr into 4th of first 6ch.

3rd row 4ch, *1V into next dc, 3ch, 1dc into next tr, 3ch, rep from * to end, ending with 1V into last dc, 3ch, 1dc into 3rd of first 6ch.

4th row As 2nd but ending with 1tr into first of first 4ch.

The 3rd and 4th rows form the pattern.

Straight mesh

Make a number of chain divisible by 6 plus 1 and 5 extra turning chain.

1st row (RS) Into 12th ch from hook work (1dc, 1ch, 1dc)—called 1V—, *5ch, miss 5ch, 1V into next ch, rep from * to last 6ch, 5ch, miss 5ch, 1dc into last ch.

2nd row 6ch, *1V into 1ch sp of V, 5ch, rep from * to end, ending with 1V into 1ch sp of V, 5ch, 1dc into 6th of first 11ch.

3rd row As 2nd but ending with 1dc into first of first 6ch.

The 3rd row forms the pattern.

Solomon's knot

There is no foundation chain for this stitch, which begins with a slip loop on the hook, 1ch.

1st row *Draw the loop on the hook up to 1.5cm ($\frac{1}{2}$in), yrh and draw a loop through, insert hook into the back loop only of the loop just made, yrh and draw a loop through, (2 loops now on hook), yrh and draw through 2 loops on hook—one knot has been made—, rep from * for required length, making an even number of knots.

2nd row Miss the knot on the hook and the next 3 knots, insert hook into centre of next knot and work 1dc, *make 2 knots, miss 1 knot along first row, 1dc into next knot, rep from * to end, working last dc into first ch at beg of first row.

3rd row Make 3 knots, 1dc into next unjoined knot of last row, *make 2 knots, 1dc into next unjoined knot of last row, rep from * to end. The 3rd row forms the pattern.

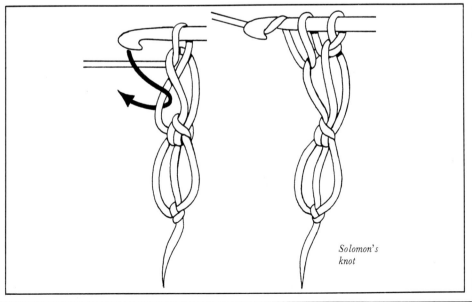

Solomon's knot

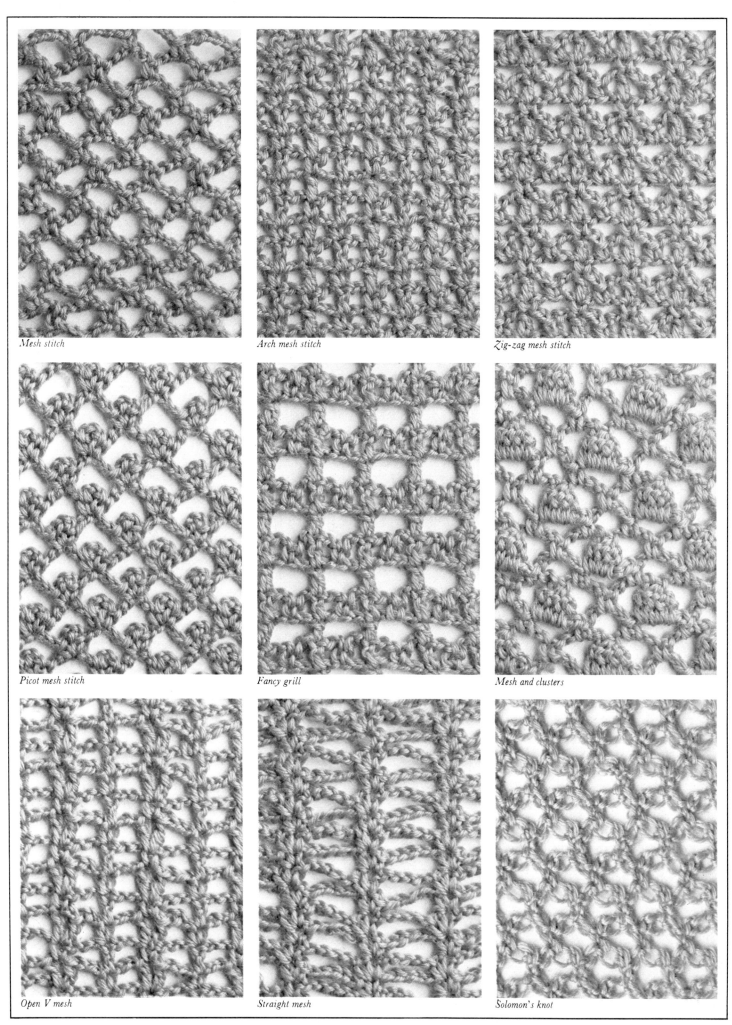

Mesh stitch

Arch mesh stitch

Zig-zag mesh stitch

Picot mesh stitch

Fancy grill

Mesh and clusters

Open V mesh

Straight mesh

Solomon's knot

35

Shell stitches

Plain shell
Make a number of chain divisible by 6 plus 1.
1st row (RS) Into 4th ch from hook work 5tr, *miss 2ch, 1dc into next ch, miss 2ch, 5tr into next ch, rep from * to last 3ch, miss 2ch, 1dc into last ch.
2nd row 3ch to count as first tr, 2tr into first dc (edge st), *1dc into 3rd of 5tr, 5tr into next dc, rep from * to last shell, 1dc into 3rd of 5tr, 3tr into 3rd of first 3ch.
3rd row 1ch to count as first dc, *5tr into next dc, 1dc into 3rd of 5tr, rep from * to end working last dc into 3rd of first 3ch.
4th row As 2nd, working last 3tr into first 1ch.
The 3rd and 4th rows form the pattern.

Spaced shell
Make a number of chain divisible by 6 plus 1.
1st row (RS) Into 4th ch from hook work 5tr, *miss 2ch, 1dc into next ch, miss 2ch, 5tr into next ch, rep from * to last 3ch, miss 2ch, 1dc into last ch.
2nd row 3ch to count as first tr, *2ch, 1dc into 3rd of 5tr, 2ch, 1tr into next dc, rep from * to last shell, 2ch, 1dc into 3rd of 5tr, 2ch, 1tr into 3rd of first 3ch.
3rd row 1ch to count as first dc, *5tr into next dc, 1dc into next tr, rep from * to end working last dc into 3rd of first 3ch.
4th row As 2nd, working last tr into first ch.
The 3rd and 4th rows form the pattern.

Open work shell
Make a number of chain divisible by 9 plus 1 and 4 extra turning chain.
1st row (WS) Into 8th ch from hook work 1dc, 3ch, miss 2ch, 1dc into next ch, 2ch, miss 2ch, 1tr into next ch, *2ch, miss 2ch, 1dc into next ch, 3ch, miss 2ch, 1dc into next ch, 2ch, miss 2ch, 1tr into next ch, rep from * to end.
2nd row 1ch to count as first dc, *1ch, miss 2ch sp, work (2tr, 1ch, 2tr, 1ch, 2tr) into 3ch sp, 1ch, miss 2ch sp, 1dc into next tr, rep from * to end working last dc into 5th of first 7ch.
3rd row 3ch to count as first tr, *2ch, 1dc into 1ch sp between first 2 pairs of tr, 3ch, 1dc into 1ch sp between next 2 pairs of tr, 2ch, 1tr into next dc, rep from * to end working last tr into first ch.
4th row As 2nd, working last dc into 3rd of first 3ch.
The 3rd and 4th rows form the pattern.

Open work double treble shell
Make a number of chain divisible by 8 plus 1 and 4 extra turning chain.
1st row (WS) Into 5th ch from hook work 1tr, *miss 3ch, work (1tr, 3ch, 1tr) into next ch, miss 3ch, work (1tr, 1ch, 1tr) into next ch, rep from * to end.
2nd row 3ch to count as first tr, 1ch, 1tr into first 1ch sp, *6dtr into 3ch sp, work (1tr, 1ch, 1tr) into 1ch sp, rep from * to end working last (1tr, 1ch, 1tr) into sp between the turning ch and first tr.
3rd row 3ch to count as first tr, 1ch, 1tr into 1ch sp, *work (1tr, 3ch, 1tr) between 3rd and 4th of 6dtr, work (1tr, 1ch, 1tr) into 1ch sp, rep from * to end working last (1tr, 1ch, 1tr) into 1ch sp between the turning ch and first tr.
The 2nd and 3rd rows form the pattern.

Openwork spaced shell
Make a number of chain divisible by 10 plus 1 and 5 extra turning chain.
1st row (RS) Into 6th ch from hook work 1tr, *3ch, miss 3ch, 1dc into each of next 3ch, 3ch, miss 3ch, work (1tr, 3ch, 1tr) into next ch, rep from * to end, ending with (1tr, 2ch, 1tr) into last ch.
2nd row 3ch to count as first tr, 3tr into first 2ch sp, *3ch, 1dc into 2nd of 3dc, 3ch, 7tr into next 3ch sp between tr, rep from * to end, ending with 4tr into sp between turning ch and first tr.
3rd row 1ch to count as first dc, 1dc into each of next 3tr, *5ch, 1dc into each of next 7tr, rep from * to last shell, 5ch, 1dc into each of next 3tr, 1dc into 3rd of first 3ch.
4th row 1ch to count as first dc, 1dc into next dc, *3ch, work (1tr, 3ch, 1tr) into 3rd of 5ch, 3ch, miss 2dc, 1dc into each of next 3dc, rep from * to end, ending with miss 2dc, 1dc into next dc, 1dc into first ch.
5th row 1ch to count as first dc, *3ch, 7tr into 3ch sp between tr, 3ch, 1dc into 2nd of 3dc, rep from * to end working last dc into first ch.
6th row 1ch to count as first dc, 2ch, *1dc into each of next 7tr, 5ch, rep from * to last shell, 1dc into each of next 7tr, 2ch, 1dc into first ch.
7th row 3ch to count as first tr, 2ch, 1tr into first dc (edge st), *3ch, miss 2dc, 1dc into each of next 3dc, 3ch, work (1tr, 3ch, 1tr) into 3rd of 5ch, rep from * to end, ending with (1tr, 2ch, 1tr) into first ch.
The 2nd to 7th rows form the pattern.

Large shell
Make a number of chain divisible by 10 plus 1 and 1 extra turning chain.
1st row (RS) Into 3rd ch from hook work 1dc, *2ch, miss 3ch, 5tr into next ch, 2ch, miss 3ch, 1dc into each of next 3ch, rep from * to end, ending with 2dc instead of 3dc.
2nd row 1ch to count as first dc, *2ch, 1tr into first tr, (2tr into next tr, 1tr into next tr) twice, 2ch, miss 1dc, 1dc into next dc, rep from * to end working last dc into turning ch.
3rd row 3ch to count as first tr, *yrh, insert hook into first tr and draw a loop through, yrh and draw through 2 loops on hook, rep from * twice into same tr, (4 loops on hook), yrh and draw through all 4 loops on hook—called 3tr tog—, (2ch, miss 1tr, 3tr tog into next tr) 3 times, rep from * to end, 1tr into first tr.
4th row 1ch to count as first dc, 2ch, *1dc into next 2ch sp, 3ch, work (1dc, 3ch, 1dc) into next 2ch sp, 3ch, 1dc into next 2ch sp, 3ch, rep from * to end, omitting last 3ch and ending with 2ch, 1dc into 3rd of first 3ch.
5th row 1ch to count as first dc, 1dc into first 2ch sp, *2ch, miss next 3ch sp, 5tr into next 3ch sp, 2ch, miss next 3ch sp, 1dc into each of next 3ch, rep from * to end, omitting last 3dc and ending with 1dc into last 2ch sp, 1dc into first ch.
The 2nd to 5th rows form the pattern.

Off-centre shell
Make a number of chain divisible by 6 plus 1 and 1 extra turning chain.
1st row (RS) Into 5th ch from hook work (1tr, 2ch, 2tr), *1ch, miss 2ch, 1dc into next ch, 1ch, miss 2ch, work (1tr, 2ch, 2tr) into next ch, rep from * to last 3ch, 1ch, miss 2ch, 1dc into last ch.
2nd row 4ch, 2tr into first dc (edge st), *1ch, 1dc into 2ch sp, 1ch, work (1tr, 2ch, 2tr) into next dc, rep from * to end working last (1tr, 2ch, 2tr) into 3rd of first 4ch.
3rd row Ss into 2ch sp, 1ch to count as first dc, *1ch, work (1tr, 2ch, 2tr) into next dc, 1ch, 1dc into next 2ch sp, rep from * to end working last dc into the loop of turning ch.
4th row As 2nd, working last (1tr, 2ch, 2tr) into first ch.
The 3rd and 4th rows form the pattern.

Shell pattern in panels
Make a number of chain divisible by 13 plus 2 and 2 extra turning chain.
1st row (RS) Into 4th ch from hook work 1tr, 1tr into each ch to end.
2nd row 3ch to count as first tr, 1tr into each of next 3tr, *3ch, miss 3tr, 1dc into next tr, 3ch, miss 3tr, 1tr into each of next 6tr, rep from * to end, ending with 1tr into each of next 3tr, 1tr into 3rd of first 3ch.
3rd row 3ch to count as first tr, 1tr into each of next 3tr, *1ch, 1dc into next 3ch sp, 3ch, 1dc into next 3ch sp, 1ch, 1tr into each of next 6tr, rep from * to end, ending with 1tr into each of next 3tr, 1tr into 3rd of first 3ch.
4th row 3ch to count as first tr, 1tr into each of next 3tr, *7tr into 3ch sp, 1tr into each of next 6tr, rep from * to end, ending as given for previous rows.
The 2nd to 4th rows form the pattern.

Ribbon pattern
Make a number of chain divisible by 10 plus 1 and 2 extra turning chain.
1st row (RS) Into 4th ch from hook work 1tr, *3ch, miss 3ch, work (2tr, 2ch, 2tr) into next ch, 3ch, miss 3ch, 1tr into each of next 3ch, rep from * to end, ending with 1tr into each of last 2ch.
2nd row 3ch to count as first tr, 1tr into next tr, *3ch, work (2tr, 2ch, 2tr) into 2ch sp, 3ch, 1tr into each of next 3tr, rep from * to end, ending with 1tr into next tr, 1tr into 3rd of first 3ch.
The 2nd row forms the pattern.

Plain shell

Spaced shell

Openwork shell

Openwork double treble shell

Openwork spaced shell

Large shell

Off-centre shell

Shell pattern in panels

Ribbon pattern

Bobble & cluster stitches

Long bobble stitch

Make a number of chain divisible by 4 plus 1 and 1 extra turning chain.

1st row (RS) Into 3rd ch from hook work 1dc, 1dc into each ch to end.

2nd row 1ch to count as first dc, 1dc into next dc, *(yrh, insert hook into next dc and draw up a loop, yrh and draw through 2 loops on hook) 5 times into same dc, yrh and draw through all 6 loops on hook—called Mb or make bobble—, 1dc into each of next 3dc, rep from * to last 3dc, Mb into next dc, 1dc into next dc, 1dc into 2nd of first 2ch.

3rd row 1ch to count as first dc, 1dc into each st to end working last dc into first ch.

4th row 1ch to count as first dc, *1dc into each of next 3dc, Mb into next dc, rep from * to last 4 sts, 1dc into each of next 3dc, 1dc into first ch.

5th row As 3rd.

6th row As 2nd, ending with 1dc into first ch. The 3rd to 6th rows form the pattern. Different effects can be obtained by working more rows between each bobble row, noting that it must always be an odd number of rows, such as 3, 5, etc.

Short bobble stitch

Make a number of chain divisible by 4 plus 1 and 1 extra turning chain.

1st row (RS) Into 3rd ch from hook work 1dc, 1dc into each ch to end.

2nd row 1ch to count as first dc, 1dc into next dc, *(yrh, insert hook into next st and draw up a loop) 5 times into same dc, yrh and draw through 10 loops on hook, yrh and draw through rem 2 loops on hook—called Mb or make bobble—, 1dc into each of next 3dc, rep from * to last 3dc, Mb into next dc, 1dc into next dc, 1dc into 2nd of first 2ch.

3rd row 1ch to count as first dc, 1dc into each st to end working last dc into first ch.

4th row 1ch to count as first dc, *1dc into each of next 3dc, Mb into next dc, rep from * to last 4 sts, 1dc into each of next 3dc, 1dc into first ch.

5th row As 3rd.

6th row As 2nd, ending with 1dc into first ch. The 3rd to 6th rows form the pattern. The number of rows between bobble rows may be varied as given for long bobble stitch.

Raised bobble stitch

Make a number of chain divisible by 4 plus 1 and 1 extra turning chain.

1st row (RS) Into 3rd ch from hook work 1dc, 1dc into each ch to end.

2nd row 1ch to count as first dc, 1dc into each dc to end, ending with 1dc into 2nd of first 2ch.

3rd row 1ch to count as first dc, 1dc into next dc, *work 5tr into the st below the next dc 1 row down, take hook out of the working loop, insert hook from front to back under the top loop of the first of these 5tr, insert hook into the working loop and draw it through, 1ch, miss next dc noting that this is the one worked into the row below—called Mb or make bobble—, 1dc into each of next 3dc, rep from * to last 3dc, Mb into st below next dc, 1dc into next dc, 1dc into first ch.

4th row 1ch to count as first dc, 1dc into each st to end missing each 1ch, working last dc into first ch.

5th row 1ch to count as first dc, *1dc into each of next 3dc, Mb into st below next dc, rep from

* to last 4 sts, 1dc into each of next 3dc, 1dc into first ch.

6th row As 4th.
The 3rd to 6th rows form the pattern.

Bobbles forming a diamond pattern

The bobble in this pattern can be made by either the long or short bobble method. Make a number of chain divisible by 12 plus 3 and 1 extra turning chain.

1st row (RS) Into 3rd ch from hook work 1dc, 1dc into each ch to end.

2nd row 1ch to count as first dc, *Mb into next dc, 1dc into each of next 11dc, rep from * to last 2dc, Mb into next dc, 1dc into 2nd of first 2ch.

3rd and every alt row 1ch to count as first dc, 1dc into each st to end working last dc into first ch.

4th row 1ch to count as first dc, 1dc into each of next 2dc, *Mb into next dc, 1dc into each of next 7dc, Mb into next dc, 1dc into each of next 3dc, rep from * to end, ending with 1dc into each of next 2dc, 1dc into first ch.

6th row 1ch to count as first dc, *Mb into next dc, 1dc into each of next 3dc, rep from * to last 2 sts, Mb into next dc, 1dc into first ch.

8th row As 4th.

10th row As 2nd.

12th row 1ch to count as first dc, 1dc into each of next 5dc, *Mb into next dc, 1dc into each of next 11dc, rep from * to last 8 sts, Mb into next dc, 1dc into each of next 6dc, 1dc into first ch.

14th row 1ch to count as first dc, 1dc into each of next 4dc, *Mb into next dc, 1dc into each of next 3dc, Mb into next dc, 1dc into each of next 7dc, rep from * to last 10 sts, Mb into next dc, 1dc into each of next 3dc, Mb into next dc, 1dc into each of next 4dc, 1dc into first ch.

16th row 1ch to count as first dc, 1dc into each of next 2dc, *Mb into next dc, 1dc into each of next 3dc, rep from * to end, ending with 1dc into each of next 2dc, 1dc into first ch.

18th row As 14th.

20th row As 12th.

21st row As 3rd.
The 2nd to 21st rows form the pattern.

Shuttle stitch

Make a number of chain divisible by 4 plus 3 and 2 extra turning chain.

1st row (RS) Into 4th ch from hook work 1tr, 1tr into each ch to end.

2nd row 1ch to count as first dc, 1dc into each tr to end working last dc into 3rd of first 3ch.

3rd row 3ch to count as first tr, 1tr into each of next 2dc, *(yrh, insert hook from right to left behind the next st one row below, yrh and draw a loop through drawing it up to the same height as the tr on the row being worked) twice into the same st, (5 loops on hook), yrh and draw through 4 loops on hook, yrh and draw through rem 2 loops on hook, miss next dc noting that this is the one worked into the row below—called Cl or cluster—, 1tr into each of next 3dc, rep from * to end, ending with 1tr into each of next 2dc, 1tr into first ch.

4th row 1ch to count as first dc, 1dc into each st to end working last dc into 3rd of first 3ch.

5th row 3ch to count as first tr, *Cl into st below next dc (the tr on 3rd row), 1tr into each of next 3dc, rep from * to last 2 sts, Cl into st below next dc, 1tr into first ch.

6th row As 4th. The 3rd to 6th rows form the pattern.

Pineapple stitch

Make a number of chain divisible by 3 plus 2 and 1 extra turning chain.

1st row (RS) Into 3rd ch from hook work 1dc, 1dc into each ch to end.

2nd row 1ch, 1dc into first dc (edge st), 1ch, draw this ch up to 1.5cm ($\frac{1}{2}$in), (yrh, insert hook into the vertical loop of the dc, yrh and draw a loop through drawing it up to 1.5cm ($\frac{1}{2}$in) 4 times into same place, miss 2dc, insert hook from front to back into the next dc, yrh and draw loop through the dc and all 9 loops on hook—called Cl or cluster—, *2ch, draw the 2nd ch up to 1.5cm ($\frac{1}{2}$in), (yrh, insert hook into the vertical loop at the side of the last Cl, yrh and draw loop through drawing it up to 1.5cm ($\frac{1}{2}$in)) 4 times into same place, miss 2dc, insert hook into next dc and complete Cl as before, rep from * ending with 1ch, 1tr into 2nd of first 2ch.

3rd row 3ch to count as first tr, work 3tr into each Cl to end, inserting the hook under the top 2 loops of each Cl, ending with 1tr into first ch.

4th row 1ch, 1dc into first tr (edge st), work Cl to end as given for 2nd row but miss 2tr instead of 2dc, ending with 1tr into 3rd of first 3ch. The 3rd and 4th rows form the pattern.

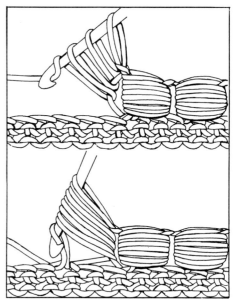

Double treble cluster stitch

Make a number of chain divisible by 4 plus 1 and 1 extra turning chain.

1st row (RS) Into 3rd ch from hook work 1dc, 1dc into each ch to end.

2nd row 4ch to count as first dtr, 1dtr into first dc (edge st), *miss 3dc, 4dtr into next dc, rep from * to last 4dc, miss 3dc, 2dtr into 2nd of first 2ch.

3rd row 1ch to count as first dc, *4ch, work 1dc between 2nd and 3rd dtr of next gr of 4dtr, rep from * to end, ending with 4ch, 1dc into 4th of first 4ch.

4th row 4ch to count as first dtr, 1dtr into first dc (edge st), *4dtr into next dc, rep from * to end, ending with 2dtr into first ch. The 3rd and 4th rows form the pattern.

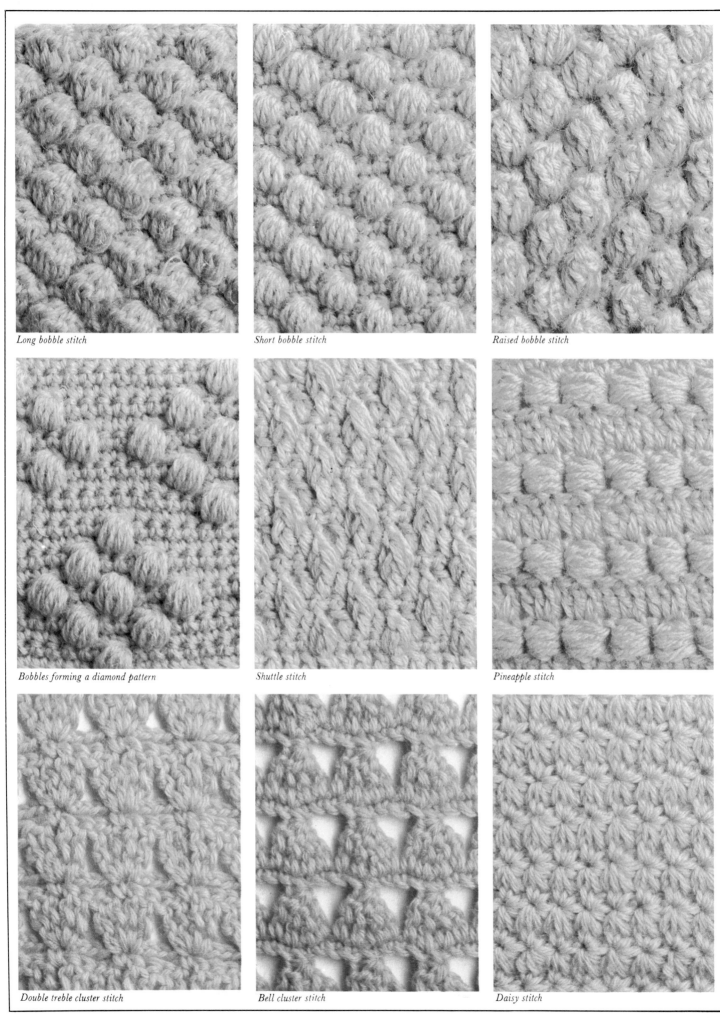

Long bobble stitch

Short bobble stitch

Raised bobble stitch

Bobbles forming a diamond pattern

Shuttle stitch

Pineapple stitch

Double treble cluster stitch

Bell cluster stitch

Daisy stitch

Bell cluster stitch
Make a number of chain divisible by 4 plus 2 and 1 extra turning chain.
1st row (RS) Into 3rd ch from hook work 1dc, 1dc into each ch to end.
2nd row 4ch to count as first dtr, 2ch, *keeping the last loop of each st on hook work 1dtr into each of next 4dc, yrh and draw through all 5 loops on hook—called Cl or cluster—, 4ch, rep from * to last 5dc, work Cl over next 4dc, 2ch, 1dtr into 2nd of first 2ch.
3rd row 1ch to count as first dc, 1dc into each of next 2ch, *miss Cl, 1dc into each of next 4ch, rep from * to end, ending with miss Cl, 1dc into each of next 2ch, 1dc into 4th of first 4ch.
4th row As 2nd, working last dtr into first ch.
The 3rd and 4th rows form the pattern.

Daisy stitch
Make a number of chain divisible by 2 plus 1 and 4 extra turning chain.
1st row (RS) Insert hook into 2nd ch from hook, yrh and draw a loop through, (insert hook into next ch, yrh and draw a loop through) 4 times, yrh and draw through all 6 loops on hook, 1ch, *insert hook into hole at top of daisy just made, yrh and draw a loop through, insert hook into back of last loop of same daisy, yrh and draw a loop through, insert hook into same ch as last loop of same daisy, yrh and draw a loop through, (insert hook into next ch, yrh and draw a loop through) twice, yrh and draw through all 6 loops on hook, 1ch, rep from * to last ch, 1dc into last ch.
2nd row 2ch, 1dc into hole of first daisy, *1ch, 1dc into hole of next daisy, rep from * to end, 1dc into first ch.

3rd row 3ch, insert hook into 2nd ch from hook, yrh and draw a loop through, insert hook into next ch, yrh and draw a loop through, insert hook into next dc, yrh and draw a loop through, insert hook into next dc, yrh and draw a loop through, insert hook into 1ch sp, yrh and draw a loop through, yrh and draw through all 6 loops on hook, 1ch, *insert hook into hole at top of daisy just made, yrh and draw a loop through, insert hook into back of last loop of same daisy, yrh and draw a loop through, insert hook into same 1ch sp as before, yrh and draw a loop through, insert hook into next dc, yrh and draw a loop through, insert hook into next 1ch sp, yrh and draw a loop through, yrh and draw through all 6 loops on hook, 1ch, rep from * to end, 1dc into first 1ch.
The 2nd and 3rd rows form the pattern.

Large patterns

Basket stitch
Make a number of chain divisible by 10 plus 7 and 2 extra turning chain.
1st row (RS) Into 4th ch from hook work 1tr, 1tr into each ch to end.
2nd row 3ch to count as first tr, yrh, insert hook from the back round stem of next tr, yrh and draw loop through, yrh and draw through 2 loops, yrh and draw through rem 2 loops—called RtB or raised treble from the back, see diagram B—, 1RtB round each of next 4tr, *1tr into each of next 5tr, 1RtB round each of next 5tr, rep from * to last st, 1tr into 3rd of first 3ch.
3rd row 3ch to count as first tr, yrh, insert hook from the front round stem of next tr, yrh and draw loop through, yrh and draw through 2 loops, yrh and draw through rem 2 loops—called RtF or raised treble from the front, see diagram A—, 1RtF round each of next 4tr, *1tr into each of next 5tr, 1RtF round each of next 5tr, rep from * to last st, 1tr into 3rd of first 3ch.
4th row As 2nd.
5th row 3ch to count as first tr, 1tr into each of next 5tr, *1RtF round each of next 5tr, 1tr into each of next 5tr, rep from * to last st, 1tr into 3rd of first 3ch.
6th row 3ch to count as first tr, 1tr into each of next 5tr, *1RtB round each of next 5tr, 1tr into each of next 5tr, rep from * to last st, 1tr into 3rd of first 3ch.
7th row As 5th.
8th row As 6th.
9th row As 3rd.
10th row As 2nd.
The 3rd to 10th rows form the pattern.

Open work squares
Make a number of chain divisible by 17 plus 2 and 2 extra turning chain
1st row (RS) Into 4th ch from hook work 1tr, 1tr into each ch to end.
2nd row 3ch to count as first tr, 1tr into each tr to end working last tr into 3rd of first 3ch.
3rd row 3ch to count as first tr, 1tr into each of next 3tr, *3ch, miss 2tr, 1dc into next tr, (5ch, miss 2tr, 1dc into next tr) twice, 3ch, miss 2tr, 1tr into each of next 6tr, rep from * to end, ending with 1tr into each of next 3tr, 1tr into 3rd of first 3ch.
4th row 3ch to count as first tr, 1tr into each of next 3tr, *5ch, (yrh, insert hook into next

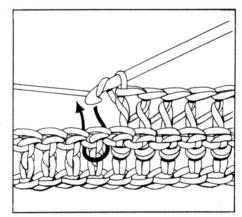

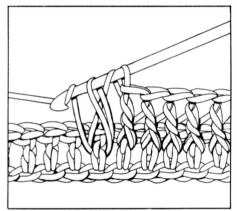

5ch loop and draw up a loop) 3 times, yrh and draw through all 7 loops on hook—called 1Cl or cluster—, 5ch, 1Cl into next 5ch loop, 5ch, 1tr into each of next 6tr, rep from * to end, ending as given for 3rd row.
5th row 3ch to count as first tr, 1tr into each of next 3tr, *3ch, (1Cl into next 5ch loop, 5ch) twice, 1Cl into next 5ch loop, 3ch, 1tr into each of next 6tr, rep from * to end, ending as given for 3rd row.
6th row 3ch to count as first tr, 1tr into each of next 3tr, *(5ch, 1Cl into next 5ch loop) twice, 5ch, 1tr into each of next 6tr, rep from * to end, ending as given for 3rd row.
7th row 3ch to count as first tr, 1tr into each of next 3tr, *3ch, (1dc into next 5ch loop, 5ch) twice, 1dc into next 5ch loop, 3ch, 1tr into each of next 6tr, rep from * to end, ending as given for 3rd row.
8th row 3ch to count as first tr, 1tr into each of next 3tr, *2tr into 3ch loop, 1tr into next dc, (2tr into 5ch loop, 1tr into next dc) twice, 2tr into 3ch loop, 1tr into each of next 6tr, rep from * to end, ending as given for 3rd row.
The 2nd and 8th rows form the pattern.

Open work butterflies
Make a number of chain divisible by 12 plus 1 and 1 extra turning chain.
1st row (RS) Into 3rd ch from hook work 1dc, 1dc into each ch to end.
2nd row 3ch to count as first tr, 3tr into first dc (edge st), *4ch, miss 4dc, 7tr into next dc, rep from * to last 12 sts, 4ch, miss 4dc, 1dc into each of

next 3dc, 4ch, miss 4dc, 4tr into 2nd of first 2ch.
3rd row 2ch to count as first htr, 1htr into each of next 3tr, *4ch, 1dc into 2nd of 3dc, 4ch, 1htr into each of next 7tr, rep from * to end, ending with 1htr into each of next 3tr, 1htr into 3rd of first 3ch.
4th row 3ch to count as first tr, 1tr into each of next 3htr, *3tr into 4ch loop, 3tr into next 4ch loop, 1tr into each of next 7htr, rep from * to end, ending with 1tr into each of next 3htr, 1tr into 2nd of first 2ch.
5th row 1ch to count as first dc, 1dc into each of next 5tr, *3ch, miss 2tr, 1dc into each of next 11tr, rep from * to end, ending with 1dc into each of next 5tr, 1dc into 3rd of first 3ch.
6th row 3ch to count as first tr, 3tr into first dc (edge st), *4ch, miss 5dc, 1dc into each of of next 3dc, 4ch, miss 5dc, 7tr into next dc, rep from * to end, ending with 4tr into first ch.
The 3rd to 6th rows form the pattern.

Diamond pattern
Make a number of chain divisible by 14 plus 1 and 1 extra turning chain.
1st row (RS) Into 3rd ch from hook work 1dc, 1dc into next ch, *4ch, miss 3ch, 1tr into next ch, 2tr into next ch, 1tr into next ch, 4ch, miss 3ch, 1dc into each of next 5ch, rep from * to end, ending with 1dc into each of last 3ch.
2nd row 1ch to count as first dc, 1dc into next dc, *3ch, 4tr into 4ch loop, 1ch, 4tr into next 4ch loop, 3ch, miss 1dc, 1dc into each of next 3dc, rep from * to end, ending with miss 1dc, 1dc into next dc, 1dc into 2nd of first 2ch.
3rd row 3ch to count as first tr, *3ch, 4tr into

Basket stitch

Openwork squares

Openwork butterflies

Diamond pattern

Large diamond pattern

Pyramid pattern

3ch sp, 3ch, 1dtr into single 1ch, 3ch, 4tr into next 3ch sp, 3ch, 1tr into 2nd of 3dc, rep from * to end working last tr into first ch.
4th row 3ch to count as first tr, *4tr into 3ch sp, 3ch, 1dc into next 3ch sp, 1dc into dtr, 1dc into next 3ch sp, 3ch, 4tr into next 3ch sp, 1ch, rep from * to end omitting last 1ch and ending with 1tr into 3rd of first 3ch.
5th row 3ch to count as first tr, 1tr into first tr (edge st), *4ch, 1dc into each of next 3dc, 1dc into each of next 3dc, 1dc into next 3ch sp, 4ch, 4tr into 1ch sp, rep from * to end, ending with 2tr into 3rd of first 3ch.
6th row 3ch to count as first tr, *4tr into 4ch sp, 3ch, miss 1dc into each of next 3dc, 3ch, 4tr into next 4ch sp, 1ch, rep from * to end, omitting last 1ch and ending with 1tr into 3rd of first 3ch.
7th row 4ch to count as first dtr, *3ch, 4tr into 3ch sp, 3ch, 1tr into 2nd of 3dc, 3ch, 4tr into next 3ch sp, 3ch, 1dtr into single 1ch, rep from * to end working last dtr into 3rd of first 3ch.
8th row 1ch to count as first dc, 1dc into 3ch sp, *3ch, 4tr into next 3ch sp, 1ch, 4tr into next 3ch sp, 3ch, 1dc into next 3ch sp, 1dc into dtr, 1dc into next 3ch sp, rep from * to end, ending with 1dc into 3ch sp, 1dc into 4th of first 4ch.
9th row 3ch to count as first tr, 1dc into next dc, *1dc into 3ch sp, 4ch, 4tr into 1ch sp, 4ch, 1dc into next 3ch sp, 1dc into each of next 3dc, rep from * to end, ending with 1dc into 3ch sp, 1dc into next dc, 1dc into first ch.
The 2nd to 9th rows form the pattern.

Large diamond pattern
Make a number of chain divisible by 15 plus 1 and 3 extra turning chain.
1st row (RS) Into 5th ch from hook work 1tr, 1tr into each of next 5ch, *2ch, miss 1ch, 1tr into each of next 6ch, 3ch, miss 2ch, 1tr into each of next 6ch, rep from * to last 9ch, 2ch, miss 1ch, 1tr into each of next 6ch, 1ch, miss 1ch, 1tr into last ch.
2nd row 2ch, noting that these and ch on subsequent rows do not count as a st, 1dc into 1ch sp, *3ch, miss 2tr, 1tr into each of next 4tr, 2ch, 1tr into each of next 4tr, 3ch, 1dc into 3ch sp, rep

from * to end working last dc into turning ch loop at beg of 1st row.
3rd row 4ch, 1dc into 3ch sp, *3ch, miss 2tr, 1tr into each of next 2tr, 2ch, 1tr into each of next 2tr, 3ch, 1dc into 3ch sp, 3ch, 1dc into 3ch sp, rep from * to end working last dc into turning ch loop.
4th row 3ch, 1dc into first 3ch sp, *3ch, 1dc into next 3ch sp, 3ch, 2tr into 2ch sp, (3ch, 1dc into next 3ch sp) twice, rep from * to end working last dc into turning ch loop.
5th row 4ch, 1dc into first 3ch sp, *3ch, 2tr into next 3ch sp, 2ch, 2tr into next 3ch sp, (3ch, 1dc into next 3ch sp) twice, rep from * to end working last dc into turning ch loop.
6th row 3ch, 1dc into first 3ch sp, *3ch, 2tr into next 3ch sp, 1tr into each of next 2tr, 2ch, 1tr into each of next 2tr, 2tr into next 3ch sp, 3ch, 1dc into next 3ch sp, rep from * to end working last dc into turning ch loop.
7th row 4ch, *2tr into next 3ch sp, 1tr into each of next 4tr, 3ch, 1tr into each of next 4tr, 2tr into next 3ch sp, 2ch, rep from * to end omitting last 2ch and ending with 1ch, 1tr into turning ch loop.
8th row 4ch, *1tr into each of next 4tr, 3ch, 1dc into 3ch sp, 3ch, miss 2tr, 1tr into each of next 4tr, 2ch, rep from * to end omitting last 2ch and ending with 1ch, 1tr into turning ch loop.
9th row 4ch, *1tr into each of next 2tr, (3ch, 1dc into next 3ch sp) twice, 3ch, miss 2tr, 1tr into each of next 2tr, 2ch, rep from * to end omitting last 2ch and ending with 1ch, 1tr into turning ch loop.
10th row 3ch, 1tr into 1ch sp, *(3ch, 1dc into next 3ch sp) 3 times, 3ch, 2tr into 2ch sp, rep from * to end working last 2tr into turning ch loop.
11th row 4ch, *2tr into next 3ch sp, (3ch, 1dc into next 3ch sp) twice, 3ch, 2tr into next 3ch sp, 2ch, rep from * to end omitting last 2ch and ending with 1ch, 1tr into turning ch loop.
12th row 4ch, *1tr into each of next 2tr, 2tr into 3ch sp, 3ch, 1dc into next 3ch sp, 3ch, 2tr into next 3ch sp, 1tr into each of next 2tr, 2ch, rep from * to end omitting last 2ch and ending with 1ch, 1tr into turning ch loop.

13th row 4ch, *1tr into each of next 4tr, 2tr into 3ch sp, 2ch, 2tr into next 3ch sp, 1tr into each of next 4tr, 3ch, rep from * to end omitting last 3ch and ending with 1ch, 1tr into turning ch loop.
The 2nd to 13th rows form the pattern.

Pyramid pattern
Make a number of chain divisible by 10 plus 1 and 3 extra turning chain.
1st row (WS) Into 4th ch from hook work 1tr, *4ch, miss 4ch, 1dc into next ch, 4ch, miss 4ch, 3tr into next ch, rep from * to end, ending with 2tr into last ch.
2nd row 3ch to count as first tr, *2tr into next tr, 3ch, 1dc into dc, 3ch, 2tr into next tr, 1tr into next tr, rep from * to end working last tr into 3rd of first 3ch.
3rd row 3ch to count as first tr, 1tr into next tr, *2tr into next tr, 2ch, 1dc into next dc, 2ch, 2tr into next tr, 1tr into each of next 3tr, rep from * to end, ending with 2tr into next tr, 1tr into next tr, 1tr into 3rd of first 3ch.
4th row 3ch to count as first tr, 1tr into each of next 2tr, *2tr into next tr, 1ch, 2tr into next tr, 1tr into each of next 5tr, rep from * to end, ending with 2tr into next tr, 1tr into each of next 2tr, 1tr into 3rd of first 3ch.
5th row 1ch to count as first dc, *4ch, 3tr into 1ch sp, 4ch, 1dc into 5th of 9tr, rep from * to end working last dc into 3rd of first 3ch.
6th row 1ch to count as first dc, *3ch, 2tr into next tr, 1tr into next tr, 2tr into next tr, 3ch, 1dc into next dc, rep from * to end working last dc into first ch.
7th row 1ch to count as first dc, *2ch, 2tr into next tr, 1tr into each of next 3tr, 2tr into next tr, 2ch, 1dc into next dc, rep from * to end working last dc into first ch.
8th row 3ch to count as first tr, 1ch, *2tr into next tr, 1tr into each of next 5tr, 2tr into next tr, 1ch, rep from * to end, 1tr into first ch.
9th row 3ch to count as first tr, 1tr into first tr (edge st), *4ch, 1dc into 5th of 9tr, 4ch, 3tr into 1ch sp, rep from * to end, ending with 2tr into 3rd of first 3ch.
The 2nd to 9th rows form the pattern.

His & hers crochet cardigan

Sizes
To fit 81.5 [86.5:91.5:96.5:101.5]cm (32[34:36:38:40]in) chest
Length to shoulder, 63.0 [64.0:65.0:66.0:67.0]cm (24¾[25¼:25½:26:26½]in)
Sleeve seam, 43.0[44.0:45.0:46.0:47.0]cm (17[17¼:17¾:18:18½]in)
The figures in brackets [] refer to the 86.5 (34), 91.5 (36), 96.5 (38) and 101.5cm (40in) sizes respectively
Tension
16 sts and 9 rows to 10cm (3.9in) over tr worked on No.4.50 (ISR) crochet hook
Materials
10[11:11:12:13] x 50grm balls Jaeger Spiral Spun Double Knitting
One No.4.50 (ISR) crochet hook
One No.4.00 (ISR) crochet hook
6 buttons

Back
Using No.4.50 (ISR) hook make 69[73:77:81:85] ch.
1st row Into 3rd ch from hook work 1dc, 1dc into each ch to end. Turn. 68[72:76:80:84] sts.
2nd row 3ch to count as first tr, 1tr into each dc to end. Turn.
Rep 2nd row 39 times more.
Shape armholes
Next row Ss across first 5 sts, patt to last 5 sts, turn.
Break off yarn and leave work for time being.

Left front
Using No.4.50 (ISR) hook make 34[36:38:40:42] ch.
Work first 2 rows as given for back. 33[35:37:39:41] sts. Rep 2nd row 39 times more, ending with a RS row.
Shape armhole

Next row Patt to last 5 sts, turn.
Break off yarn and leave for time being.

Right front
Using No.4.50 (ISR) hook make 34[36:38:40:42] ch.
Work 41 rows as given for left front.
Shape armhole
Next row Ss across first 5 sts, patt to end.
Do not break off yarn but leave for time being.

Back and fronts worked in one piece
Optional method
Using No.4.50 (ISR) hook make 135[143:151:159:167] ch. Work first 2 rows as given for back. 134[142:150:158:166] sts. Rep 2nd row 39 times more, ending with a RS row.
Divide for armholes
Next row 3ch to count as first tr, 1tr into each of next 27[29:31:33:35]tr, ss across next 10tr

to form underarm, 1tr into each of next 58[62:66:
70:74] tr, ss across next 10tr to form 2nd underarm, 1tr into each of next 28[30:32:34:36] tr.
Do not break off yarn but leave for time being.

Sleeves

Using No.4.50 (ISR) hook make 34[36:38:40:42]
ch.
Work first 2[2:4:4:4] rows as given for back.
33[35:37:39:41] sts. Cont in patt as given for
back, inc one st at each end of next and every foll
4th row until there are 51[53:55:57:59] sts. Cont
without shaping until sleeve measures 43.0
[44.0:45.0:46.0:47.0]cm (17[17¼:17¾:18:18½]in)
from beg, or required length to underarm ending
with a RS row. Mark each end of last row with
coloured thread. Work a further 3 rows, noting
that these 3 rows are set into armhole shaping.
Break off yarn and leave for time being.

Yoke

Using No.4.50 (ISR) hook and with RS of work
facing, return to right front where yarn was left
and work across all pieces as foll:-
1st row 3ch, 1tr into each of next 24[26:28:30:
32] tr, yrh, insert hook into next st and draw up
a loop, yrh and draw through 2 loops on hook,
yrh, insert hook into next st and draw up a loop,
yrh and draw through 2 loops on hook, yrh and
draw through rem 3 loops on hook — called 2tr
tog —, 1tr into next tr noting that this is the last
tr of right front, cont across one sleeve, 1tr into
first st, 2tr tog, 1tr into each of next 45[47:49:51:
53] tr, 2tr tog, 1tr into next tr, cont across back,
1tr into first tr, 2tr tog, 1tr into each of
next 52[56:60:64:68] tr, 2tr tog, 1tr into next
tr, work across 2nd sleeve as given for first
sleeve, cont across left front, 1tr into first tr, 2tr
tog, 1tr into each tr to end. Turn.
208[:220:232:244:256] sts.
2nd row 3ch to count as first tr, 2tr tog, 1tr into
each of next 21[23:25:27:29] tr, 2tr tog, 1tr
into each of next 2tr, 2tr tog, 1tr into each of
next 43[45:47:49:51] tr, 2tr tog, 1tr into each of
next 2tr, 2tr tog, 1tr into each of next 50[54:58:
62:66] tr, 2tr tog, 1tr into each of next 2tr,
2tr tog, 1tr into each of next 43[45:47:49:51]
tr, 2tr tog, 1tr into each of next 2tr, 2tr tog, 1tr
into each of next 21[23:25:27:29] tr, 2tr tog, 1tr
into last st. Turn. 198[210:222:234:246] sts.
3rd row 3ch, work 21[23:25:27:29] tr, 2tr tog,
2tr, 2tr tog, 41[43:45:47:49] tr, 2tr tog, 2tr, 2tr
tog, 48[52:56:60:64] tr, 2tr tog, 2tr, 2tr tog,
41[43:45:47:49] tr, 2tr tog, 2tr, 2tr tog,
22[24:26:28:30] tr. Turn.
4th row 3ch, 2tr tog, work 18[20:22:24:26] tr,
2tr tog, 2tr, 2tr tog, 39[41:43:45:47] tr, 2tr tog,
2tr, 2tr tog, 46[50:54:58:62] tr, 2tr tog, 2tr, 2tr
tog, 39[41:43:45:47]tr, 2tr tog, 2tr, 2tr tog,
18[20:22:24:26] tr, 2tr tog, 1tr into last st.
Turn.
5th row Work as given for 3rd row, allowing for
sts dec and shaping each raglan seam by working
2tr tog, 2tr, 2tr tog. Turn.
6th row Work as given for 4th row, allowing for
sts dec and dec as before at each raglan seam and
at each end of row. Turn.
7th row as 5th. 154[166:178:190:202] sts.
8th row 3ch, 2tr tog, work 12[14:16:18:20] tr,
2tr tog, 2tr, 2tr tog, *across sleeve work 13[14:15:
16:17] tr, 2tr tog, 1tr, 2tr tog, 13[14:15:16:17]
tr, *, 2tr tog, 2tr, 2tr tog, work 38[42:46:50:54]
tr, 2tr tog, 2tr, 2tr tog, rep from * to * across
other sleeve, 2tr tog, 2tr, 2tr tog, work
12[14:16:18:20] tr, 2tr tog, 1tr into last st.
Turn. 140[152:164:176:188] sts.
Mark 1tr between the dec at centre of each sleeve.
Cont dec at front edges at each end of every
alt row until 6[7:8:9:10] sts in all have been dec
and dec at each side of centre marked st on each
sleeve on every 3rd[3rd:3rd:4th:4th] row 3
times more, *at the same time* dec as before at each

raglan seam on every row until 36[38:40:42:44]
sts rem. Fasten off.

Front band (for man)

Using No.4.00 (ISR) hook and with RS of work
facing, rejoin yarn at lower edge of right front,
work approx 3dc into every 2 rows up front edge,
1dc into each st across sleeve tops and back neck,
then 3dc into every 2 rows down left front.
Turn. Work 2 more rows dc.
4th row 1ch, 1dc into each of next 2dc, *2ch,
miss 2dc, 1dc into each of next 9dc, rep from * 5
times more, work in dc to end. Turn.
5th row Work in dc to end, working 2dc into
each 2ch buttonhole. Turn.

Work 2 more rows dc. Fasten off.

Front band (for woman)

Work first 3 rows as given for man.
4th row 1ch, 1dc into each dc to last 60dc, *2ch,
miss 2dc, 1dc into each of next 9dc, rep from *
4 times more, 2ch, miss 2dc, 1dc into each of next
3dc. Turn.
Complete as given for front band for man.

To make up

Do not press. Sew last 3 rows of sleeve seams to
cast off sts at underarm. Join side seams if worked
separately. Join sleeve seams. Press seams under
a damp cloth with a warm iron. Sew on buttons.

Miscellaneous patterns

Brick pattern
Make a number of chain divisible by 4 and 2 extra turning chain.

1st row (RS) Into 4th ch from hook work 1tr, 1tr into each ch to end.

2nd row 1ch to count as first dc, 3ch, miss next 3tr, 1dc between next 2tr *3ch, miss 4tr, 1dc between next 2tr, rep from * to end working last dc into 3rd of first 3ch.

3rd row Ss into first 3ch loop, 3ch to count as first tr, 3tr into same loop, *4tr into next 3ch loop, rep from * to last loop, 3tr into last loop, 1tr into first ch.

4th row 1ch to count as first dc, 1ch, miss 1tr, 1dc between next 2tr, *3ch, miss 4tr, 1dc between next 2tr, rep from * to last 2tr, 1ch, miss 1tr, 1dc into 3rd of first 3ch.

5th row Ss into 1ch sp, 3ch to count as first tr, 1tr into 1ch sp, *4tr into next 3ch loop, rep from * to end, ending with 1tr into 1ch sp, 1tr into first ch.

The 2nd to 5th rows form the pattern.

Brick pattern in panels
Make a number of chain divisible by 9 plus 2 and 2 extra turning chain.

1st row (RS) Into 4th ch from hook work 1tr, 1tr into each of next 2ch, *2ch, miss 1ch, 1dc into next ch, 2ch, miss 1ch, 1tr into each of next 6ch, rep from * to end, ending with 1tr into each of next 4ch.

2nd row Ss into sp between first 2tr, work 1dc into same sp, *(3ch, 1dc into next 2ch sp) twice, 3ch, 1dc between 3rd and 4th of next 6tr, rep from * to end working last dc between last tr and first 3ch.

3rd row 3ch to count as first tr, *3tr into next 3ch loop, 2ch, 1dc into next 3ch loop, 2ch, 3tr into next 3ch loop, rep from * to end, 1tr into last dc.

The 2nd and 3rd rows form the pattern.

Crazy pattern
Make a number of chain divisible by 4 plus 1 and 3 extra turning chain.

1st row (RS) Into 4th ch from hook work 3tr, *miss 3ch, work (1dc, 2ch, 3tr) into next ch, rep from * to last 4ch, miss 3ch, 1dc into last ch.

2nd row 3ch, 3tr into first dc (edge st), *work (1dc, 2ch, 3tr) into next 2ch sp, rep from * to last group, 1dc into 3rd of first 3ch.

The 2nd row forms the pattern. If a straight edge is required to complete this pattern, work the last row as foll:-

Last row 3ch, 1tr into first dc (edge st), *1ch, 1dc into 2ch sp, 2tr into next dc, rep from * to end, ending with 1dc into 3rd of first 3ch.

Florette pattern
Make a number of chain divisible by 3 plus 1 and 3 extra turning chain.

1st row (RS) Into 4th ch from hook work 2tr, *miss 2ch, 3tr into next ch, rep from * to end.

2nd row 1ch, *miss 2tr, 3dc into next tr, rep from * to last 3tr, miss 2tr, 1dc into 3rd of first 3ch.

3rd row 3ch to count as first tr, 2tr into first dc (edge st), *miss 2dc, 3tr into next dc, rep from * to end.

The 2nd and 3rd rows form the pattern.

Close fabric stitch
Make a number of chain divisible by 2 and 3 extra turning chain.

1st row (RS) Into 5th ch from hook work 1dc and 1tr, *miss 1ch, work (1dc and 1tr) into next ch, rep from * to last 2ch, miss 1ch, 1dc into last ch.

2nd row 3ch to count as first tr, *work (1dc and 1tr) into next dc, rep from * to end, 1dc into 4th of first 4ch.

3rd row As 2nd row but ending with 1dc into 3rd of first 3ch.

The 3rd row forms the pattern.

Forget-me-not stitch
Make a number of chain divisible by 3 plus 1 and 4 extra turning chain.

1st row (RS) Into 5th ch from hook work (2tr, 2ch, 1dc), *miss 2ch, work (2tr, 2ch, 1dc) into next ch, rep from * to last 3ch, miss 2ch, 1dc into last ch.

2nd row 3ch to count as first tr, *into next 2ch sp work (2tr, 2ch, 1dc), rep from * to end, 1dc into 4th of first 4ch.

3rd row As 2nd but ending with 1dc into 3rd of first 3ch.

The 3rd row forms the pattern.

Spaced treble groups
Make a number of chain divisible by 2 plus 1 and 2 extra turning chain.

1st row (RS) Into 4th ch from hook work 1tr, 1tr into each ch to end.

2nd row 3ch to count as first tr, 1ch, yrh, insert hook into next tr and draw a loop through, yrh and draw through 2 loops — called trh or treble half —, miss 1tr, work trh into next tr, yrh and draw through all 3 loops on hook, 1ch, *work trh into same st as before, miss 1tr, work trh into next tr, yrh and draw through all 3 loops on hook, 1ch, rep from * to end, 1tr into 3rd of first 3ch.

3rd row 3ch to count as first tr, 1ch, work trh into next 1ch sp, trh into next 1ch sp, yrh and draw through all 3 loops on hook, 1ch, *work trh into same 1ch sp as before, trh into next 1ch sp, yrh and draw through all 3 loops on hook, 1ch, rep from * to end, 1tr into 3rd of first 3ch.

The 3rd row forms the pattern.

Checked and diagonal pattern
Make a number of chain divisible by 3 plus 2 and 2 extra turning chain.

1st row (WS) Into 4th ch from hook work 1tr, 1tr into each ch to end.

2nd row 3ch to count as first tr, *1tr into each of next 3tr, yrh twice, insert hook from right to left round the stem of the tr below the first of these 3tr and complete as for dtr, rep from * to end, 1tr into 3rd of first 3ch.

3rd row 4ch to count as first dtr, *miss 1dtr, 1dtr into each of next 3tr, rep from * to end, 1dtr into 3rd of first 3ch.

4th row 3ch, *miss next 2dtr, work 1dtr round stem of next dtr then keeping hook behind this dtr work 1tr into each of the 2 missed dtr and 1tr into top of same dtr as the one worked round, rep from * to end, 1tr into 4th of first 4ch.

5th row 4ch to count as first dtr, *1dtr into each of next 3tr, miss next dtr, rep from * to end, 1dtr into 3rd of first 3ch.

6th row 3ch to count as first tr, *1tr into each of next 3dtr, 1dtr round stem of the first of these 3dtr, rep from * to end, 1tr into 4th of first 4ch.

The 3rd to 6th rows form the pattern.

Raised flower pattern
Make a number of chain divisible by 6 plus 1 and 1 extra turning chain.

1st row (RS) Into 3rd ch from hook work 1htr, 1htr into each ch to end.

2nd row 2ch to count as first htr, 1htr between each htr to end.

Rep 2nd row twice more.

5th row 2ch to count as first htr, work (1htr between htr) 3 times, *work 6tr round the stem of the next htr on 4th row, turn and work 6tr round stem of preceding htr on 4th row, join with a ss to first tr, turn again and cont along row, work (1htr between htr) 6 times, rep from * to end, ending with (1htr between htr) 3 times.

6th to 10th rows As 2nd.

11th row 2ch to count as first htr, work (1htr between htr) 6 times, *work 6tr round the stem of the next htr on 10th row, turn and work 6tr round stem of preceding htr on 10th row, join with a ss to first tr, turn again and cont along row, work (1htr between htr) 6 times, rep from * to end.

12th and 13th rows As 2nd.

The 2nd to 13th rows form the pattern.

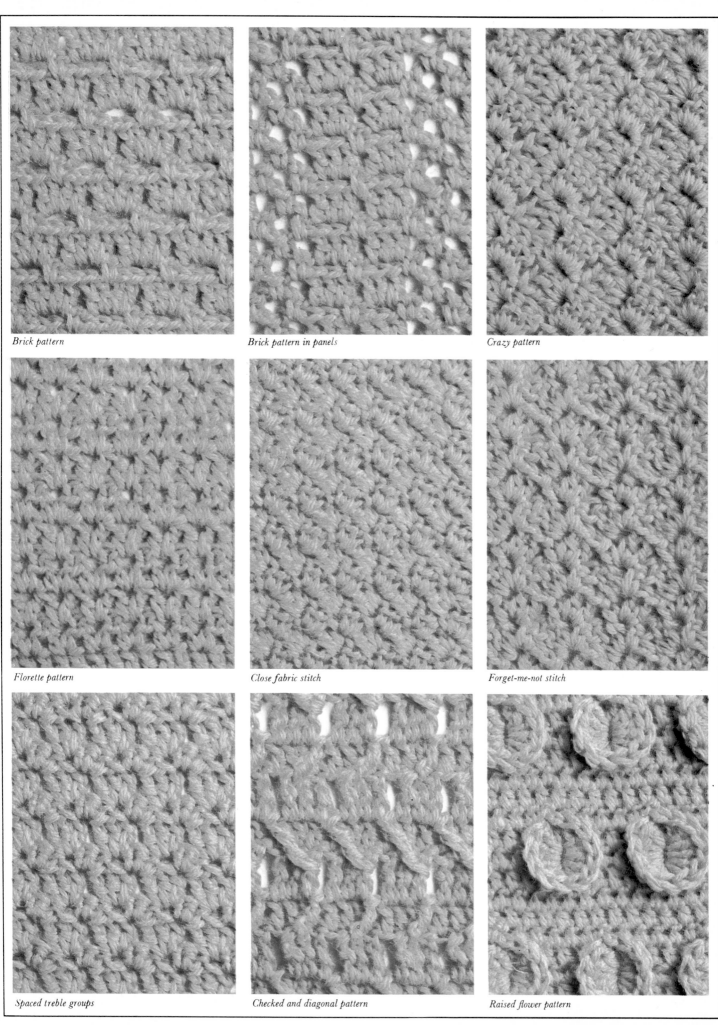

Brick pattern

Brick pattern in panels

Crazy pattern

Florette pattern

Close fabric stitch

Forget-me-not stitch

Spaced treble groups

Checked and diagonal pattern

Raised flower pattern

Coloured patterns

Raised trebles in two colours
Using A, make a number of chain divisible by 2 plus 1 and 2 extra turning chain.
1st row (RS) Into 4th ch from hook work 1tr, 1tr into each ch to end.
2nd row 1ch to count as first dc, 1dc into each tr to end working last dc into 3rd of first 3ch

and joining in B as given in Chapter 9.
3rd row Using B, 1ch to count as first dc, *work 1RtF round stem of next tr on first row as given in Chapter 20, miss 1dc of 2nd row, 1dc into next dc, rep from * to end working last dc into first ch
4th row Using B, 1ch to count as first dc, 1dc into each st to end working last dc into first ch

and joining in A.
5th row Using A, as 3rd, working RtF round stem of RtF.
6th row Using A, as 4th.
The 3rd to 6th rows form the pattern.

Chevron pattern in two colours
Using A, make a number of chain divisible by 13 plus 1 and 2 extra turning chain.
1st row (RS) Into 3rd ch from hook work 1dc, *1dc into each of next 5ch, miss 2ch, 1dc into each of next 5ch, 3dc into next ch, rep from * to end working only 2dc into last ch.

2nd row 1ch to count as first dc, 1dc into first dc (edge st), *1dc into each of next 5dc, miss 2dc, 1dc into each of next 5dc, 3dc into next dc, rep from * to end, ending with 2dc into turning ch and changing colour on last st as given in Chapter 9.
3rd row Using B, as 2nd row but do

not change colour.
4th row Using B, as 2nd row.
5th row Using A, as 3rd row.
6th row Using A, as 2nd row.
The 3rd to 6th rows form the pattern.

Shell pattern in two colours
Using A, make a number of chain divisible by 6 plus 1 and 3 extra turning chain.
1st row (RS) Into 4th ch from hook work 2tr, *miss 2ch, 1dc into next ch, miss 2ch, 5tr into next ch, rep from * to end, ending with 3tr into last ch and changing colour on last st as given in Chapter 9. *Turn.*

2nd row Using B, 1ch to count as first dc, *5tr into next dc, 1dc into 3rd of 5tr, rep from * to end working last dc into 3rd of first 3ch. *Do not turn.* Leave loop of B for time being.
3rd row Return to beg of 2nd row, using A pull yarn through first ch on to hook, 3ch to count as first tr, 2tr into first 1ch, *1dc into 3rd of 5tr, 5tr into next dc, rep from * to end, ending

with 3tr into last dc and changing colour on last st. *Turn.*
The 2nd and 3rd rows form the pattern.

Fish-scale pattern in two colours
Using A, make a number of chain divisible by 6 plus 1 and 3 extra turning chain.
1st row (RS) Into 4th ch from hook work 2tr, *miss 2ch, 1dc into next ch, miss 2ch, 5tr into next ch, rep from * to end, ending with 3tr into last ch and changing colour on last st as given in Chapter 9. *Turn.*
2nd row Using B, 1ch to count as first dc, *2ch,

yrh, insert hook into next tr and draw a loop through, yrh and draw through 2 loops on hook — called trh —, work trh into next tr, into next dc then into each of next 2tr, (6 loops on hook), yrh and draw through all 6 loops on hook, 2ch, 1dc into next tr, rep from * to end working last dc into 3rd of first 3ch. *Do not turn.* Leave loop of B for time being.
3rd row Return to beg of 2nd row, using A pull

yarn through first ch on to hook, 3ch to count as first tr, 2tr into first 1ch (edge st), *1dc into top of group, 5tr into next dc, rep from * to end, ending with 3tr into last dc and changing colour on last st. *Turn.*
The 2nd and 3rd rows form the pattern.

Three-clour check pattern
Using A, make a number of chain divisible by 4 plus 2 and 2 extra turning chain.
1st row (RS) Into 4th ch from hook work 1tr, *2ch, miss 2ch, 1tr into each of next 2ch, rep from * to end, joining in B on last st as given in Chapter 9.
2nd row Using B, *2ch, miss first 2tr, 1tr into each of the 2 missed ch of commencing ch, rep from * to end, ending with 2ch, miss next tr, ss

into 3rd of first 3ch joining in C.
3rd row Using C, 3ch to count as first tr, 1tr into next tr of first row, *2ch, miss 2tr of 2nd row, 1tr into each of next 2tr of 1st row, rep from * to end joining in A on last st.
4th row Using A, *2ch, miss first 2tr, 1tr into each of next 2tr on 2nd row, rep from * to end, ending with 2ch, miss 1tr, ss into 3rd of first 3ch joining in B.
The 3rd and 4th rows form the pattern, working

1 row in each colour throughout. To avoid a row of holes in the final casting off row, use the next colour and either a 3rd or 4th row but instead of working '2ch, miss 2tr', work 1dc into each of these 2tr then 1tr into each of the next 2tr on previous row.

Three-colour broken stripe pattern
Using A, make a number of chain divisible by 2 plus 1 and 2 extra turning chain.
1st row (RS) Into 3rd ch from hook work 1htr, * miss 1ch, 2htr into next ch, rep from * to end joining in B on last st as given in Chapter 9.

2nd row Using B, 2ch to count as first htr, *work 2htr between next 2 pairs of htr, rep from * to end, ending with 2htr between last 2 pair, 1htr into 2nd of first 2ch, joining in C.
3rd row Using C, 2ch to count as first htr, 1htr between first htr and next pair, *2htr between

next 2 pairs of htr, rep from * to end working last 2htr between last pair and first 2ch, joining in A. The 2nd and 3rd rows form the pattern, working 1 row in each colour throughout.

Two-colour openwork pattern
Using A, make a number of chain divisible by 5 plus 3 and 2 extra turning chain.
1st row (RS) Into 6th ch from hook work 2tr, 2ch, 2tr into next ch, *miss 3ch, 2tr into next ch, 2ch, 2tr into next ch, rep from * to last 3ch, miss 2ch, 1tr into last ch.

2nd row 3ch to count as first tr, *work (2tr, 2ch, 2tr) into 2ch sp, rep from * to end working 1tr into 3rd of first 5ch, joining in B on last st as given in Chapter 9.
3rd row Using B, as 2nd row but working last tr into 3rd of first 3ch and do not change colour.
4th row Using B, as 3rd row, joining in A.

The 3rd row forms the pattern, working 2 rows in each colour throughout and using more colours if required, always making sure that you leave the yarn at the end you want for next time, to avoid breaking off the yarn.

Two-colour broken stripe pattern
Using A, make a number of chain divisible by 4 plus 1 and 1 extra turning chain.
1st row (RS) Into 3rd ch from hook work 1dc, 1dc into each ch to end.
2nd row 1ch to count as first dc, 1dc into each dc to end working last dc into 2nd of first 2ch

and joining in B on last st as given in Chapter 9.
3rd row Using B, 1ch to count as first dc, 1dc into next dc, *1dc into next dc inserting hook 1 row below, 1dc into each of next 3dc, rep from * to last 3dc, 1dc into next dc inserting hook 1 row below, 1dc into next dc, 1dc into first ch.
4th row Using B, as 2nd row working last dc

into first ch and joining in A.
5th row Using A, 1ch to count as first dc, *1dc into each of next 3dc, 1dc into next dc inserting hook 1 row below, rep from * to last 4dc, 1dc into each of next 3dc, 1dc into first dc.
The 2nd to 5th rows form the pattern.

Three-colour speckle pattern
Using A, make a number of chain divisible by 2 plus 1 and 2 extra turning chain.
1st row (RS) Into 3rd ch from hook work 1tr, *miss 1ch, work 1dc and 1tr into next ch, rep

from * to last 2ch, miss 1ch, 1dc into last ch joining in B as given in Chapter 9.
2nd row Using B, 1ch to count as first dc, 1tr into edge st, *work 1dc and 1tr into next dc, rep from * to end, ending with 1dc into 2nd of first

2ch, joining in C.
3rd row Using C, as 2nd row working last dc into first ch and joining in A.
The 2nd row forms the pattern, working one row in each colour throughout.

Raised trebles in two colours

Chevron pattern in two colours

Shell pattern in two colours

Fish-scale pattern in two colours

Three-colour check pattern

Three-colour broken stripe pattern

Two-colour openwork pattern

Two-colour broken stripe pattern

Three-colour speckle pattern

47

More large patterns

Window panes
Make a number of chain divisible by 18 plus 10 and 2 extra turning chain.

1st row (RS) Into 4th ch from hook work 1tr, 1tr into each of next 8ch, *8ch, miss 8ch, 1tr into each of next 10ch, rep from * to end.

2nd row 3ch to count as first tr, 1tr into next tr, (2ch, miss 2tr, 1tr into each of next 2tr) twice, *8ch, (1tr into each of next 2tr, 2ch, miss 2tr) twice, 1tr into each of next 2tr, rep from * to end working last tr into 3rd of first 3ch.

3rd row 3ch to count as first tr, 1tr into next tr, (2tr into 2ch sp, 1tr into each of next 2tr) twice, *8ch, (1tr into each of next 2tr, 2tr into 2ch sp) twice, 1tr into each of next 2tr, rep from * to end working last tr into 3rd of first 3ch.

4th row 3ch to count as first tr, 1tr into next tr, (2ch, miss 2tr, 1tr into each of next 2tr) twice, *4ch, insert hook under 3 strands of 8ch and work 1dc linking the 3 strands tog, 4ch, (1tr into each of next 2tr, 2ch, miss 2tr) twice, 1tr into each of next 2tr, rep from * to end working last tr into 3rd of first 3ch.

5th row As 3rd.

6th row 3ch to count as first tr, 8ch, miss 8tr, 1tr into next tr, *1tr into each of next 8ch, 1tr into next tr, 8ch, miss 8tr, 1tr into next tr, rep from * to end working last tr into 3rd of first 3ch.

7th row 3ch to count as first tr, 8ch, *(1tr into each of next 2tr, 2ch, miss 2tr) twice, 1tr into each of next 2tr, 8ch, rep from * to last st, 1tr into 3rd of first 3ch.

8th row 3ch to count as first tr, 8ch, *(1tr into each of next 2tr, 2tr into 2ch sp) twice, 1tr into each of next 2tr, 8ch, rep from * to last st, 1tr into 3rd of first 3ch.

9th row 3ch to count as first tr, 4ch, insert hook under 3 strands of 8ch and work 1dc linking the 3 strands tog, 4ch, *(1tr into each of next 2tr, 2ch, miss 2tr) twice, 1tr into each of next 2tr, 4ch, 1dc linking 3 strands of 8ch tog, 4ch, rep from * to last st, 1tr into 3rd of first 3ch.

10th row As 8th.

11th row 3ch to count as first tr, 1tr into each of next 8ch, 1tr into next tr, *8ch, miss 8tr, 1tr into next tr, 1tr into each of next 8ch, 1tr into next tr, rep from * to end working last tr into 3rd of first 3ch.

The 2nd to 11th rows form the pattern.

Japanese fans
Make a number of chain divisible by 14 plus 1 and 1 extra turning chain.

1st row (WS) Into 3rd ch from hook work 1dc, 1dc into each ch to end.

2nd row 1ch to count as first dc, *miss 6dc, yrh, insert hook into next dc and draw loop through pulling the loop up to a height of 1.5cm ($\frac{1}{2}$in), yrh and draw through 2 loops, yrh and draw through rem 2 loops — called 1 long tr —, work 12 more long tr into same dc, miss 6dc, 1dc into next dc, rep from * to end working last dc into 2nd of first 2ch.

3rd row 4ch to count as first long tr, 1 long tr into first dc (edge st), *5ch, 1dc into 7th of 13 long tr, 5ch, 2 long tr into next dc, rep from * to end working last 2 long tr into first ch.

4th row 1ch to count as first dc, *13 long tr into next dc, 1dc between next 2 long tr, rep from * to end working last dc between last long tr and first 4ch.

The 3rd and 4th rows form the pattern.

Flower pattern
Make a number of chain divisible by 20 plus 1 and 5 extra turning chain.

1st row (RS) Into 10th ch from hook work 1tr, * 3ch, (yrh twice, insert hook into top of last tr worked and draw loop through, (yrh and draw through 2 loops) twice, (2 loops rem on hook) — called half dtr —, work another half dtr into same place, yrh and draw through all 3 loops on hook — called 1ClA or 1 Cluster A —, miss 3ch, work 3 half dtr into next ch, yrh and draw through all 4 loops on hook — called 1ClB or 1 Cluster B —, miss 3ch, 1ClB into next ch, 1ClA into top of Cl just worked, miss 3ch, 1tr into next ch, 5ch, miss 3ch, 1dc into next ch, 5ch, miss 3ch, 1tr into next ch, rep from * to end, omitting last 5ch and 1tr.

2nd row 1ch to count as first dc, *5ch, 1tr into tr, 3ch, work (1ClB, 3ch and 1ClB) into top of 2ClB of previous row, 3ch, 1tr into next tr, 5ch, 1dc into next dc, rep from * to end working last dc into 4th of first 9ch.

3rd row 3ch to count as first, tr, *miss 1ch, 1ClB into next ch, 1ClA into top of Cl just worked, 1tr into next tr, 5ch, 1dc into 3ch sp between 2Cl, 5ch, 1tr into next tr, 1ClA into top of tr just worked, miss 3ch, 1ClB into next ch, miss 1ch and 1dc, rep from * to end but after last ClB work 1tr into first ch.

4th row 3ch to count as first tr, 1ch, 1ClB into top of first 1ClB, *3ch, 1tr into next tr, 5ch, 1dc into next dc, 5ch, 1tr into next tr, 3ch, (1ClB, 3ch, 1ClB) into top of 2 ClB of previous row, rep from * to end, ending with 1ClB into top of last 1ClB, 1ch, 1tr into 3rd of first 3ch.

5th row 1ch to count as first dc, *5ch, 1tr into next tr, 1ClA into top of tr just worked, miss 3ch, 1ClB into next ch, miss 1ch, 1dc and 1ch, work 1ClB into next ch, 1ClA into top of Cl just workrd, 1tr into next tr, 5ch, 1dc into 3ch sp between 2 Cl, rep from * to end working last dc into 3rd of first 3ch.

The 2nd to 5th rows form the pattern, ending 2nd row by working last dc into first ch.

Diagonal raised pattern
Make a number of chain divisible by 8 plus 6 and 2 extra turning chain.

1st row (WS) Into 4th ch from hook work 1tr, 1tr into each ch to end.

Note: Before working next row refer to Basket stitch in Chapter 20, for working method of RtF and RtB.

2nd row 3ch to count as first tr, 1RtF round each of next 4tr, *1RtB round each of next 4tr, 1RtF round each of next 4tr, rep from * to end, 1tr into 3rd of first 3ch.

3rd row 3ch to count as first tr, work 4RtB, *4RtF, 4RtB, rep from * to last st, 1tr into 3rd of first 3ch.

4th row 3ch to count as first tr, work 3RtF, *4RtB, 4RtF, rep from * to last 2 sts, 1RtB, 1tr into 3rd of first 3ch.

5th row 3ch to count as first tr, work 1RtF, *4RtB, 4RtF, rep from * to last 4 sts, 3RtB, 1tr into 3rd of first 3ch.

6th row 3ch to count as first tr, work 2RtF, *4RtB, 4RtF, rep from * to last 3 sts, 2RtB, 1tr into 3rd of of first 3ch.

7th row As 6th.

8th row As 5th.

9th row As 4th.

10th row As 3rd.

11th row As 2nd.

12th row 3ch to count as first tr, work 3RtB, *4RtF, 4RtB, rep from * to last 2 sts, 1RtF, 1tr into 3rd of first 3ch.

13th row 3ch to count as first tr, work 1RtB, *4RtF, 4RtB, rep from * to last 4 sts, 3RtF, 1tr into 3rd of first 3ch.

14th row 3ch to count as first tr, work 2RtB, *4RtF, 4RtB, rep from * to last 3 sts, 2RtF, 1tr into 3rd of first 3ch.

15th row As 14th.

16th row As 13th.

17th row As 12th.

The 2nd to 17th rows form the pattern.

Openwork chevron pattern
Make a number of chain divisible by 14 and 2 extra turning chain.

1st row (RS) Into 4th ch from hook work 1tr, 1tr into each of next 5ch, *2ch, 1tr into each of next 14ch, rep from * to last 7ch, 2ch, 1tr into each of next 7ch.

2nd row Miss first tr (edge st), ss into next tr, 3ch to count as first tr, 1ch, miss 1tr, (1tr into next tr, 1ch, miss 1tr) twice, *(1tr, 3ch, 1tr) into 2ch sp, (1ch, miss 1tr, 1tr into next tr) 3 times, miss 2tr, (1tr into next tr, 1ch, miss 1tr) 3 times, rep from * to last 2ch sp, (1tr, 3ch, 1tr) into 2ch sp, (1ch, miss 1tr, 1tr into next tr) 3 times but do not work into turning chain, turn.

3rd row Miss first tr (edge st), ss into 1ch sp, 3ch to count as first tr, * (1tr into next tr, 1tr into 1ch sp) twice, (2tr, 2ch, 2tr) into 3ch sp, (1tr into 1ch sp, 1tr into next tr) twice, 1tr into next 1ch sp, miss 2tr, (1tr into next 1ch sp, 1tr into next tr) twice, 1tr into next 1ch sp, rep from * to last 3ch sp, (2tr, 2ch, 2tr) into 3ch sp, miss next tr, (1tr into 1ch sp, 1tr into next tr) twice, 1tr into next 1ch sp but do not work into turning ch, turn.

The 2nd and 3rd rows form the pattern.

Star pattern in panels
Make a number of chain divisible by 22 plus 1 and 2 extra turning chain.

1st row (RS) Into 4th ch from hook work 1tr, 1tr into each of next 2ch, *(5ch, miss 2ch, 1dc into each of next 3ch, 5ch, miss 2ch, 1tr into next ch) twice, 1tr into each of next 6ch, rep from * to end, ending with 1tr into each of last 3ch.

2nd row 1ch to count as first dc, 1dc into each of next 3tr, *(1dc into first ch of 5ch loop, 4ch, 1dc into 2nd of 3dc, 4ch, 1dc into last ch of 5ch loop, 1dc into next tr) twice, 1dc into each of next 6tr, rep from * to end, ending with 1dc into each of last 2tr, 1dc into 3rd of first 3ch.

3rd row 1ch to count as first dc, 1dc into each of next 4dc, *(5ch, 1tr into next tr, 5ch, 1dc into each of next 3dc) twice, 1dc into each of next 5dc, rep from * to end, ending with 1dc into last

Window panes

Japanese fans

Flower pattern

Diagonal raised pattern

Openwork chevron pattern

Star pattern in panels

dc, 1dc into first ch.

4th row 3ch to count as first tr, 1tr into each of next 3dc, *(4ch, 1dc into last ch of 5ch loop, 1dc into next tr, 1dc into first ch of next 5ch loop, 4ch, 1tr into 2nd of 3dc) twice, 1tr into each of next 6dc, rep from * to end, ending with

1tr into each of last 2dc, 1tr into first ch.

5th row 3ch to count as first tr, 1tr into each of next 3tr, *(5ch, 1dc into each of next 3dc, 5ch, 1tr into next tr) twice, 1tr into each of next 6tr, rep from * to end, ending with 1tr into each of last 2tr, 1tr into 3rd of first 3ch.

The 2nd and 5th rows form the pattern. The panels could be varied in width by rep the figures in brackets more times, noting that 6 extra ch are required for each extra rep, or fewer or more tr could be worked between each panel.

Spiral motifs

Spiral motif

Make 6ch. Join with a ss to first ch to form circle.

1st round 1ch, work 12dc into circle. Do not join this or subsequent rounds.

2nd round Work 2dc into each dc to end. 24dc.

3rd round *1dc into each of next 3dc, 3ch, miss 1dc, rep from * 5 times more.

4th round *1dc into each of next 3dc, 2dc into 3ch sp, 3ch, rep from * 5 times more.

5th round *Miss 1dc, 1dc into each of next 4dc, 2dc into 3ch sp, 4ch, rep from * 5 times more.

6th round *Miss 1dc, 1dc into each of next 5dc, 2dc into 4ch sp, 4ch, rep from * 5 times more.

7th round *Miss 1dc, 1dc into each of rem dc of group, 2dc into ch loop, 5ch, rep from * 5 times more.

Rep 7th round 5 times more.

13th round Miss 1dc, ss into next dc, 2ch to count as next dc, 1dc into each of next 10dc, 5tr

into next dc, 2dc into ch loop, *miss 1dc, 1dc into each of next 11dc, 5tr into next dc, 2dc into ch loop, rep from * 4 times more. Join with a ss to 2nd of first 2ch. Fasten off.

This motif can be increased in size by working the 7th round as many times as necessary, noting that when working the edging there will be one more dc in each group for every extra repeat of the 7th round.

Six-sided motif

Make 10ch. Join with a ss to first ch to form circle.

1st round 3ch to count as first tr, work 23tr into circle. Join with a ss to 3rd of first 3ch. 24tr.

2nd round 3ch to count as first tr, 3tr into ss at base of 3ch, *miss 1tr, 1dc into next tr, miss 1tr, 7tr into next tr, rep from * 4 times more, miss 1tr, 1dc into next tr, miss 1tr, 3tr into ss at end of 1st round. Join with a ss to 3rd of first 3ch.

3rd round 3ch, 1dc into ss at base of 3ch, *7ch, work (1dc, 3ch, 1dc) into 4th of next 7tr, rep from * 4 times more, 7ch, ss into 3ch loop at beg of round.

4th round 3ch, 3tr into first 3ch loop, *5ch, 1dc into 7ch loop, 5ch, 7tr into 3ch loop, rep from * 4 times more, 5ch, 1dc into 7ch loop, 5ch, 3tr into 3ch loop at beg of round. Join with a ss to 3rd of first 3ch.

5th round 3ch, 3tr into ss at base of 3ch, *(5ch, 1dc into next 5ch loop) twice, 5ch, 7tr into 4th

of 7tr, rep from * 4 times more, (5ch, 1dc into next 5ch loop) twice, 5ch, 3tr into ss at end of round. Join with a ss to 3rd of first 3ch.

6th round As 5th, working the instructions in brackets 3 times instead of twice.

7th round As 5th, working the instructions in brackets 4 times. Fasten off.

To increase the size of the motif, continue repeating the 5th round, working the instructions in brackets once more for each round.

Rose square

This motif is worked in 4 colours. Using A, make 6ch. Join with a ss to first ch to form circle.

1st round 3ch to count as first tr, *2ch, 1tr into circle, rep from * 6 times more, 2ch. Join with a ss to 3rd of first 3ch.

2nd round Into each 2ch sp work (1dc, 1htr, 3tr, 1htr, 1dc). Join with a ss to ss at end of 1st round.

3rd round *4ch, 1dc into back of next tr of 1st round, rep from * 6 times more, 4ch. Join with a ss to ss at end of 2nd round, keeping each 4ch loop behind the petals of the 2nd round.

4th round Into each 4ch loop work (1dc, 1htr, 5tr, 1htr, 1dc). Join with a ss to ss at end of 3rd round.

5th round As 3rd working into the back of the dc of 3rd round. Break off A.

6th round Join in B to ss at end of last round, into each 4ch loop work (1dc, 1htr, 7tr, 1htr, 1dc). Join with a ss to ss at end of 5th round.

7th round Using B, as 3rd working into the back of the dc of 5th round.

8th round Using B, into each 4ch loop work (1dc, 1htr, 2tr, 5dtr, 2tr, 1htr, 1dc). Join with a ss to ss at end of 7th round. Break off B.

9th round Join C to centre dtr of any petal, 1ch to count as first dc, 7ch, keeping last loop of each dtr on hook work 3dtr into centre dtr of next petal, yrh and draw through all 4 loops on hook — called 1Cl or cluster —, (4ch, 1Cl) twice into same dtr, *7ch, 1dc into centre dtr of next petal, 7ch, (1Cl, 4ch, 1Cl, 4ch, 1Cl) into centre dtr of next petal, rep from * twice more, 7ch. Join with a ss to first ch. Break off C.

10th round Join D to centre 1Cl of one corner,

3ch to count as first tr, 3ch, 3tr into top of same 1Cl, *1ch, 3tr into next 4ch loop, 1ch, (3tr, 1ch, 3tr) into next 7ch loop, 1ch, (3tr, 1ch, 3tr) into next 7ch loop, 1ch, 3tr into next 4ch loop, 1ch, **, (3tr, 3ch, 3tr) into centre 1Cl at corner, *, rep from * to * twice more then from * to ** once more, 2tr into top of 1Cl at first corner. Join with a ss to 3rd of first 3ch.

11th round Using D, ss into first 3ch sp, 3ch to count as first tr, 3ch, 3tr into 3ch sp, *(1ch, 3tr into next 1ch sp) 7 times, 1ch, **, (3tr, 3ch, 3tr) into 3ch sp at corner, *, rep from * to * twice more, then from * to ** once more, 2tr into last 3ch sp. Join with a ss to 3rd of first 3ch.

12th round Using D, as 11th, working (1ch, 3tr into next 1ch sp) 8 times instead of 7. Fasten off.

Square motif with bobbles

Make 6ch. Join with a ss to first ch to form circle.

1st round 1ch to count as first dc, work 11dc into circle. Join with a ss to first ch. 12dc.

2nd round 3ch to count as first tr, 1tr into same place, (yrh, insert hook into next dc and draw a loop through, yrh and draw through 2 loops on hook) 6 times into same dc, yrh and draw through 6 loops on hook, yrh and draw through rem 2 loops on hook — called Bl or bobble —, *2tr into each of next 2dc, Bl into next dc, rep from * twice more, 2tr into next dc. Join with a ss to 3rd of first 3ch.

3rd round 3ch to count as first tr, 1tr into same place, *1tr into each of next 3 sts, 2tr into next st, 1ch, 2tr into next st, rep from * twice more, 1tr into each of next 3 sts, 2tr into next st, 1ch. Join with a ss to 3rd of first 3ch.

4th round 3ch to count as first tr, 1tr into same place, *(1tr into next tr, Bl into next tr) twice, 1tr into next tr, 2tr into next tr, 2ch, 2tr into next tr, rep from * 3 times more omitting last 2tr. Join with a ss to 3rd of first 3ch.

5th round 3ch to count as first tr, 1tr into same place, *1tr into each of next 7 sts, 2tr into next st, 3ch, 2tr into next st, rep from * 3 times more omitting last 2tr. Join with a ss to 3rd of first 3ch.

6th round 3ch to count as first tr, 1tr into same place, *1tr into each of next 2tr, (Bl into next tr, 1tr into next tr) 3 times, 1tr into next tr, 2tr into next tr, 4ch, 2tr into next tr, rep from * 3 times more omitting last 2tr. Join with a ss to 3rd of first 3ch.

7th round 3ch to count as first tr, 1tr into same place, *1tr into each of next 11 sts, 2tr into next st, 5ch, 2tr into next st, rep from * 3 times more omitting last 2tr. Join with a ss to 3rd of first 3ch. Fasten off.

Danish square

This motif is worked in 3 colours. Using A, make 10ch. Join with a ss to first ch to form circle.

1st round 1ch to count as first dc, work 19dc into circle. Join with a ss to first ch. 20dc.

2nd round 1ch to count as first dc, *7ch, miss 4dc, 1dc into next dc, rep from * 3 times more omitting last dc. Join with a ss to first ch.

3rd round 1ch to count as first dc, *9dc into

7ch loop, 1dc into next dc, rep from * 3 times more omitting last dc. Join with a ss to first ch. Break off A.

4th round Join B to 5th of 9dc at any corner, 1ch to count as first dc, 2dc into same dc, *1dc into each of next 9dc, 3dc into next dc, rep from * 3 times more omitting last 3dc. Join with a ss to first ch. Break off B.

5th round Join C to 2nd of 3dc at any corner,

3ch to count as first tr, 2ch, 1tr into same dc, *(1ch, miss 1dc, 1tr into next dc) 5 times, 1ch, miss 1dc, (1tr, 2ch, 1tr) into next dc, rep from * twice more, (1ch, miss 1dc, 1tr into next dc) 5 times, 1ch. Join with a ss to 3rd of first 3ch. Break off C.

6th round Join A to 2ch sp at any corner, 1ch to count as first dc, 2dc into same sp, *(1dc into next tr, 1dc into 1ch sp) 6 times, 1dc into next

tr, 3dc into 2ch sp, rep from * 3 times more omitting last 3dc. Join with a ss to first ch.
7th round Using A, ss into next dc, 3ch to count as first tr, 2ch, 1tr into same dc, *(1ch, miss 1dc, 1tr into next dc) 7 times, 1ch, miss 1dc, (1tr, 2ch, 1tr) into next dc, rep from * twice more, (1ch, miss 1dc, 1tr into next dc) 7 times, 1ch. Join with

a ss to 3rd of first 3ch. Break off A.
8th round Join B to 2ch sp at any corner, work as 6th round, repeating the instructions in brackets 8 times instead of 6.
9th round Using B, as 7th, working the instructions in brackets 9 times. Break off B.
10th round Join C to 2ch sp at any corner, work

as 6th round, repeating instructions in brackets 10 times.
11th round Using C, as 7th, working instructions in brackets 11 times. Break off C.
12th round Using A, as 6th round, working instructions in brackets 12 times. Fasten off.

Norwegian motif
Make 4ch. Join with a ss to first ch to form circle.
1st round 1ch to count as first dc, work 7dc into circle. Join with a ss to first ch, 8dc.
2nd round 4ch to count as first dtr, *2ch, 1dtr into next dc, 5ch, 1dtr into next dc, rep from * 3 times more omitting last dtr. Join with a ss to 4th of first 4ch.
3rd round 1ch to count as first dc, *2dc into 2ch sp, 1dc into next dtr, (3dc, 2ch, 3dc) into 5ch loop, 1dc into next dtr, rep from * 3 times more omitting last dc. Join with a ss to first ch.
4th round 4ch,(yrh twice, insert hook into next

dc and draw loop through, yrh and draw through 2 loops, yrh and draw through 2 loops — called dtrh —) into each of next 3dc, yrh and draw through all 4 loops on hook, *7ch, 1dc into next 2ch sp, 7ch, miss 3dc, work dtrh into each of next 4dc, yrh and draw through all loops on hook, rep from * twice more, 7ch, 1dc into 2ch sp, 7ch. Join with a ss to top of first cluster.
5th round 1ch to count as first dc, 2dc into top of same cluster, *1dc into each of next 7ch, 1dc into next dc, 1dc into each of next 7ch, 3dc into top of next cluster, rep from * 3 times more omitting last 3dc. Join with a ss to first ch.
6th round Ss into each of next 2dc, *1dc into

next dc, 5ch, miss 4dc, 1dc into next dc, 5ch, miss 3dc, 1dc into next dc, 5ch, miss 4dc, 1dc into next dc, 7ch, miss 3dc, rep from * 3 times more. Join with a ss to first dc.
7th round Ss into first 5ch loop, 3ch to count as first tr, (2tr, 3ch, 3tr) into same loop, (3tr, 3ch, 3tr) into each of next two 5ch loops, *(3tr, 3ch, 3tr, 3ch, 3tr) into 7ch loop, (3tr, 3ch, 3tr) into each of next three 5ch loops, rep from * twice more, (3tr, 3ch, 3tr, 3ch, 3tr) into 7ch loop. Join with a ss to 3rd of first 3ch. Fasten off.

Spiders web motif
Make 8ch. Join with a ss to first ch to form circle.
1st round 3ch to count as first tr, work 23tr into circle. Join with a ss to 3rd of first 3ch. 24tr.
2nd round 3ch to count as first tr, 1tr into each of next 2tr, 3ch, *1tr into each of next 3tr, 3ch, rep from * 6 times more. Join with a ss to 3rd of first 3ch.
3rd round 3ch to count as first tr, 1tr into each of next 2tr, 8ch, *1tr into each of next 3tr, 8ch, rep from * 6 times more. Join with a ss to 3rd of first 3ch.
4th round 3ch to count as first tr, 1tr into each of next 2tr, *4ch, 1dc into 8ch loop, 4ch, 1tr into each of next 3tr, rep from * 7 times more omitting last 3tr. Join with ss to 3rd of first 3ch.
5th round 3ch to count as first tr, 1tr into each of next 2tr, *4ch, 1dc into 4ch loop, 1dc into next dc, 1dc into 4ch loop, 4ch, 1tr into each of next 3tr, rep from * 7 times more omitting last 3tr. Join with a ss to 3rd of first 3ch.
6th round 3ch to count as first tr, 1tr into each of next 2tr, *4ch, 1dc into 4ch loop, 1dc into each of next 3dc, 1dc into 4ch loop, 4ch, 1tr into each of next 3tr, rep from * 7 times more omitting last 3tr. Join with a ss to 3rd of first 3ch.
7th round 3ch to count as first tr, 1tr into each of next 2tr, *5ch, miss 1dc, 1dc into each of next 3dc, miss 1dc, 5ch, 1tr into each of next 3tr, rep from * 7 times more omitting last 3tr. Join with a ss to 3rd of first 3ch.
8th round 3ch to count as first tr, 1tr into each of next 2tr, *4ch, miss 1dc, (1dtr, 4ch, 1dtr) into next dc, miss 1dc, 4ch, 1tr into each of next 3tr, rep from * 7 times more omitting last 3tr. Join with a ss to 3rd of first 3ch.
9th round 1ch to count as first dc, 1dc into each of next 2tr, *5dc into each of next three 4ch loops, 1dc into each of next 3tr, rep from * 7 times more omitting last 3dc. Join with a ss to first ch. Fasten off.

Star of Eve motif
Make 4ch. Join with a ss to first ch to form circle.
1st round 3ch to count as first tr, work 11tr into circle. Join with a ss to 3rd of first 3ch.
2nd round *6ch, ss into 3rd ch from hook, 4ch, ss into next tr, rep from * to end working last ss into ss at end of 1st round. Fasten off.

Small round motif
This motif is useful as a filler between larger motifs. Make 12ch. Join with a ss to first ch to form circle.
1st round 3ch, (yrh, insert hook into circle and draw a loop through, yrh and draw through 2 loops on hook — called trh —) twice, yrh and

draw through all 3 loops on hook, *3ch, work trh 3 times into circle, yrh and draw through all 4 loops on hook — called 1Cl —, rep from * 6 times more, 3ch. Join with a ss to top of first 1Cl.
2nd round 3ch to count as first tr, 2ch, 1tr into top of same 1Cl, *(1tr, 2ch, 1tr) into 3ch sp, (1tr, 2ch, 1tr) into top of next 1Cl, rep from * 6 times more, (1tr, 2ch, 1tr) into 3ch sp. Join with a ss to 3rd of first 3ch. Fasten off.

Top row, left : Spiral motif
Top row, centre : Spider's web motif
Top row, right : Six-sided motif
Centre : Danish square
Centre left : Norwegian motif
Centre right : Square motif with bobbles
Bottom left : Star of Eve motif
Bottom centre : Rose motif
Bottom right : Small round motif

Filet crochet patterns

Filet crochet is normally worked from a chart and before beginning any of these patterns, you should study the following explanations of the working methods for each symbol shown on these charts.

Block
A block is shown as a cross on the charts and consists of 3tr. When 1 block stands alone there will be 4tr in the group, the first of which belongs to the previous space. When 2 blocks stand alone there will be 7tr in the group, 3 for each block and 1 for the previous space. Therefore, all groups of blocks will have 3 times as many trebles as there are crosses, plus 1 treble. When working the block into a space, work the first 2tr into the space and the 3rd tr into the next tr.

Space
A space is shown as an open square on the charts and consists of 2ch, miss 2ch or 2tr, 1tr into next tr for each space.

Lacet
A lacet is shown as a 'V' on the charts, taking up 2 squares, and consists of 3ch, miss 2ch or 2tr, 1dc into next st, 3ch, miss 2ch or 2tr, 1tr into next st.

Bar
A bar is shown as a line taking up 2 squares in width on the charts and consists of 5ch, miss 1 lacet or 5 sts, 1tr into next st.
Note On all the charts, the first row is worked in the direction of the arrow.

Lover's knot
This design can be used as an all-over pattern. Make a number of chain divisible by 132 plus 1 and 2 extra turning chain.

1st row Into 4th ch from hook work 1tr, 1tr into each of next 2ch, *(2ch, miss 2ch, 1tr into next ch) 5 times, 1tr into each of next 6ch, (2ch, miss 2ch, 1tr into next ch) 6 times, 1tr into each of next 6ch, (2ch, miss 2ch, 1tr into next ch) 5 times, 1tr into each of next 6ch, rep from * to end, ending with 1tr into each of last 3ch instead of 6ch. This row on the chart will read, *1 blk, 5 sps, 2 blks, 6 sps, 2 blks, 5 sps, 1 blk, rep from * to end.
2nd row 3ch to count as first tr, 1tr into each of next 3tr, *(2ch, 1tr into next tr) 5 times, 1tr into each of next 6tr, (2ch, 1tr into next tr) 6 times, 1tr into each of next 6tr, (2ch, 1tr into next tr) 5 times, 1tr into each of next 6tr, rep from * to end, ending with 1tr into each of next 2tr, 1tr into 3rd of first 3ch. This row on the chart is the same as the 1st row.
3rd row *9 sps, 4 blks, 9 sps, rep from * to end.
4th row *2 sps, 2 blks, 3 sps, 2 blks, 4 sps, 2 blks, 3 sps, 2 blks, 2 sps, rep from * to end.
Continue working from the chart, rep 42 rows as required. This pattern can be alternated for an all-over fabric, beginning alternate reps at point marked 'A' on chart.

Oak leaf insertion
Make 108ch.

1st row Into 4th ch from hook work 1tr, 1tr into each of next 2ch, (3ch, miss 2ch, 1dc into next ch, 3ch, miss 2ch, 1tr into next ch) twice, (2ch, miss 2ch, 1tr into next ch) 18 times, 1tr into each of next 3ch, (2ch, miss 2ch, 1tr into next ch) 6 times, (3ch, miss 2ch, 1dc into next ch, 3ch, miss 2ch, 1tr into next ch) twice, 1tr into each of next 3ch. This row on the chart will read, 1 blk, 2 lacets, 18 sps, 1 blk, 6 sps, 2 lacets, 1 blk.
2nd row 3ch to count as first tr, 1tr into each of next 3tr, (5ch, 1tr into next tr) twice, (2ch, 1tr into next tr) 6 times, 1tr into each of next 3tr, (2ch, 1tr into next tr) 18 times, (5ch, 1tr into next tr) twice, 1tr into each of next 2tr, 1tr into 3rd of first 5ch. This row on the chart will read 1 blk, 2 bars, 6 sps, 1 blk, 18 sps, 2 bars, 1 blk.
3rd row 3ch to count as first tr, 1tr into each of next 3tr, (3ch, 1dc into 3rd of 5ch, 3ch, 1tr into next tr) twice, (2ch, 1tr into next tr) 12 times, (2tr into next sp, 1tr into next tr) twice, (2ch, 1tr into next tr) 4 times, 1tr into each of next 3tr, (2ch, 1tr into next tr) 6 times, (3ch, 1dc into 3rd of 5ch, 3ch, 1tr into next tr) twice, 1tr into each of next 2tr, 1tr into 3rd of first 3ch. This row on the chart will read, 1 blk, 2 lacets, 12 sps, 2 blks, 4 sps, 1 blk, 6 sps, 2 lacets, 1 blk.
4th row 1 blk, 2 bars, 6 sps, 1 blk, 3 sps, 4 blks,

1 sp, 4 blks, 6 sps, 2 bars, 1 blk.
Continue working from the chart, rep 42 patt rows as required.

Rose motif or insertion
Make 108ch.

1st row Into 4th ch from hook work 1tr, 1tr into each of next 2ch, *2ch, miss 2ch, 1tr into next ch, rep from * to last 3ch, 1tr into each of next 3ch. This row on the chart will read, 1 blk, 33 sps, 1 blk.
2nd row 3ch to count as first tr, 1tr into each of next 3tr, (2ch, 1tr into next tr) 10 times, 2tr into next sp, 1tr into next tr, (2ch, 1tr into next tr) 11 times, 2tr into next sp, 1tr into next tr, (2ch, 1tr into next tr) 10 times, 1tr into each of next 2tr, 1tr into 3rd of first 3ch. This row on the chart will read, 1 blk, 10 sps, 1 blk, 11 sps, 1 blk, 10 sps, 1 blk.
3rd row 3ch to count as first tr, 1tr into each of next 3tr, (2ch, 1tr into next tr) 9 times, 2tr into next sp, 1tr into next tr, 2ch, miss 2tr, 1tr into next tr, (2ch, 1tr into next tr) 11 times, 2ch, miss 2tr, 1tr into next tr, 2tr into next sp, 1tr into next tr, (2ch, 1tr into next tr) 9 times, 1tr into each of next 2tr, 1tr into 3rd of first 3ch. This row on the chart will read, 1 blk, 9 sps, 1 blk, 13 sps, 1 blk, 9 sps, 1 blk.
4th row 1 blk, 9 sps, 4 blks, 9 sps, 1 blk, 1 sp, 1 blk, 8 sps, 1 blk.
Continue working from chart, rep 2nd to 41st rows to form patt.

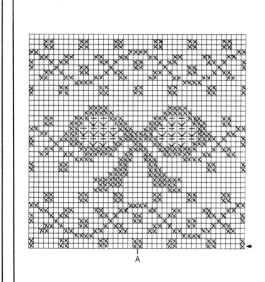

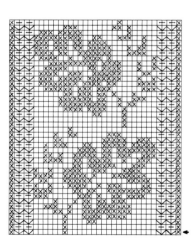

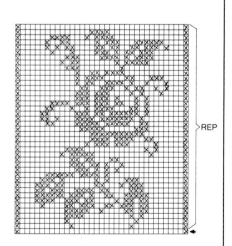

REP

Butterfly motif

Make 75ch.

1st row Into 4th ch from hook work 1tr, 1tr into each ch to end. 73tr.

2nd row 3ch to count as first tr, 1tr into each of next 3tr, (2ch, miss 2tr, 1tr into next tr) 22 times, 1tr into each of next 2tr, 1tr into 3rd of first 3ch. 1 blk, 22 sps and 1 blk.

3rd row 3ch to count as first tr, 1tr into each of next 3tr, (2ch, 1tr into next tr) 4 times, 2tr into next sp, 1tr into next tr, (2ch, 1tr into next tr) 9 times, 2tr into next sp, 1tr into next tr, (2ch, 1tr into next tr) 5 times, 2tr into next sp. 1tr into next tr, 2ch, 1tr into each of next 3tr, 1tr into 3rd of first 3ch. This row on the chart will read, 1 blk, 4 sps, 1 blk, 9 sps, 1 blk, 5 sps, 1 blk, 1 sp, 1 blk.

4th row Reading from the chart, 1 blk, 6 sps, 3 blks, 8 sps, 3 blks, 2 sps, 1 blk.
Continue working from the chart.

Acorn pattern

This design can be used as an all-over pattern. Make a number of chain divisible by 36 plus 11, e.g. 83ch.

1st row Into 8th ch from hook work 1tr, *2ch, miss 2ch, 1tr into next ch, rep from * to end. Multiples of 12 sps plus 2.

2nd row 5ch to count as first tr and 2ch, *1tr into next tr, 2ch, rep from * to end, 1tr into 5th of first 7ch.

3rd row 5ch to count as first tr and 2ch, (1tr into next tr, 2ch) 8 times, *(1tr into next tr, 2tr into next sp) 3 times, (1tr into next tr, 2ch) 9 times, rep from * to last 5 sts, (1tr into next tr, 2tr into next sp) 3 times, (1tr into next tr, 2ch) twice, 1tr into 3rd of first 5ch. This row on the chart will read, *9 sps, 3 blocks, rep from * to last 2 sps, 2 sps.

4th row 2 sps, *4 blks, 8 sps, rep from * to end. Continue working from the chart, rep 2nd to 13th rows to form the patt.

Star motif

Make 62ch.

1st row Into 8th ch from hook work 1tr, *2ch, miss 2ch, 1tr into next ch, rep from * to end. 19 sps.

2nd row 5ch to count as first tr and 2ch, (1tr into next tr, 2ch) 4 times, 1tr into next tr, 2tr into next sp, (1tr into next tr, 2ch) 7 times, 1tr into next tr, 2tr into next sp, (1tr into next tr, 2ch) 5 times, 1tr into 5th of first 7ch. This row on the chart will read, 5 sps, 1 blk, 7 sps, 1 blk, 5 sps.

3rd row 5ch to count as first tr and 2ch, (1tr into next tr, 2ch) 4 times, 1tr into each of next 4tr, 2tr into next sp, (1tr into next tr, 2ch) 5 times, 1tr into next tr, 2tr into next sp, 1tr into each of next 4tr, (2ch, 1tr into next tr) 5 times working last tr into 3rd of first 5ch. This row on the chart will read, 5 sps, 2 blks, 7 sps, 2 blks, 5 sps.

4th row 5 sps, 3 blks, 3 sps, 3 blks, 5 sps. Continue working from the chart.

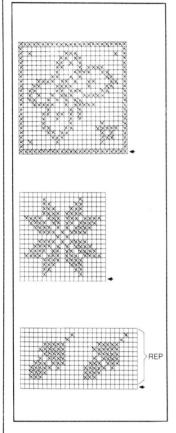

From top to bottom : Lover's knot ; Oak leaf insertion ; Rose motif ; Butterfly motif ; Acorn pattern ; Star motif.

Patchwork slip-on

Sizes
To fit 81.5/86.5 [91.5/96.5]cm (*32/34[36/38]in*)
bust
Length to shoulder, 58.5[59.5]cm (*23[23½]in*)
The figures in brackets [] refer to the 91.5/96.5cm
(*36/38in*) size only

Tension
24 sts and 12 rows to 10cm (*3.9in*) over tr worked
on No.3.00 (ISR) crochet hook

Materials
1 x 50 grm ball each of Jaeger Celtic-Spun 4 ply
in 6 contrast colours, A, B, C, D, E and F
One No.3.00 (ISR) crochet hook

Note
Slip-on is made in 10 separate panels. Twist
yarns at back of work and change colours as
given in Chapter 10

Slip-on
1st patch
Using No.3.00 (ISR) hook and A, make 22[24]ch.
1st row (RS) Into 4th ch from hook work 1tr,
1tr into each ch to end. 20[22]tr.
2nd row 3ch to count as first tr, 1tr into each tr
to end.
Break off A. Rep 2nd row 10 times more, working
2 rows each in B, C, D, E and F. These 12 rows
form 1st patch.
2nd patch
Using No.3.00 (ISR) hook and A, make 22[24]ch.

Work 1st and 2nd rows as given for 1st patch.
Using A only, rep 2nd row 10 times more. These
12 rows form 2nd patch, varying colours as
required for each subsequent rep of this patch.
3rd patch
Using No.3.00 (ISR) hook and C, make 22[24]ch.
Work 1st and 2nd rows as given for 1st patch. Rep
2nd row 4 times more. Break off C. Join in D.
7th row Using D, 3ch to count as first tr, 1tr
into each of next 9[10]tr, join in E on last tr,
using E, 1tr into each of next 10[11]tr.
8th row Using E, 3ch to count as first tr, 1tr
into each of next 9[10]tr, join in D on last tr,
using D, 1tr into each of next 10[11]tr.
Rep 7th and 8th rows twice more. These 12 rows
form 3rd patch.
4th patch
Using No.3.00 (ISR) hook and B, make 10[11]ch,
join in F on last ch, using F, make 12[13]ch.
1st row Using F, into 4th ch from hook work 1tr,
1tr into each of next 8[9]ch, join in B on last
tr, using B, 1tr into each of next 10[11]ch.
20[22]tr.
2nd row Using B and F, work as given for 8th
row of 3rd patch.
Rep these 2 rows 5 times more. These 12 rows
form 4th patch.
5th patch
Using No.3.00 (ISR) hook and A, make 22[24]ch.
Work 1st and 2nd rows as given for 1st patch.

Rep 2nd row 3 times more. Break off A. Join in
E. Rep 2nd row twice more. Break off E. Join in
C. Rep 2nd row 5 times more. These 12 rows
form 5th patch.

Centre front and back panels
Using colours and patches as required, work 48
continuous patt rows. Fasten off. Work 3 more
panels in same way.

Underarm panels
Using colours and patches as required, work as
given for centre panels. Work 1 more panel in
same way.

Shoulder panels
Using colours and patches as required, work
70[72] continuous patt rows. Fasten off. Work
3 more panels in same way.

To make up
Press each panel under a damp cloth with a warm
iron. Join panels as shown in diagram.

Edging Using No.3.00 (ISR) hook, any colour
and with RS of work facing, work 3 rounds dc
round lower edge. Work in same way round neck
and armholes, dec one st in each corner on every
round. Press edging.

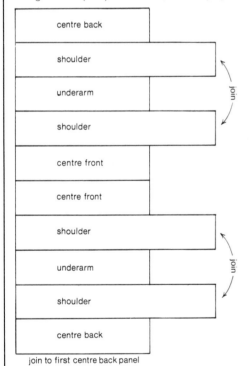

*Cosy slip-on worked in simple strips of colourful
patchwork crochet. The diagram (above) shows how
the strips are joined to form a one-piece garment.*

Edgings

Edging No.1
Make 14ch.

1st row (WS) Into 8th ch from hook work 1tr, 2ch, miss 2ch, work (2tr, 2ch, 2tr) into next ch, 2ch, miss 2ch, 1tr into last ch.

2nd row 5ch to count as first tr and 2ch, miss first 2ch sp, work (2tr, 2ch, 2tr) into next 2ch sp, 1tr into each of next 2tr, 2ch, 1tr into next tr, 2ch, 1tr into 5th of first 7ch.

3rd row 5ch, miss first tr, 1tr into next tr, 2ch, 1tr into each of next 4tr, wotk (2tr, 2ch, 2tr) into 2ch sp, 2ch, 1tr into 3rd of first 5ch.

4th row 5ch to count as first tr and 2ch, miss first 2ch sp, work (2tr, 2ch, 2tr) into next 2ch sp, 1tr into each of next 6tr, 1tr into next tr, 2ch, 1tr into 5ch loop, work (2ch, 1tr) 6 times into same loop, 2ch, ss into base of tr at end of 2nd row, turn.

5th row 5ch, 1dc into first 2ch sp, work (1dc, 5ch, 1dc) into each of next seven 2ch sp, 3ch, 1tr into first tr of 8tr gr, 2ch, miss 3tr, 1tr into next tr, 2ch, work (2tr, 2ch, 2tr) into next 2ch sp, 2ch, 1tr into 3rd of first 5ch.

The 2nd to 5th rows form the pattern, ending 2nd rows by working last tr into 1st tr of previous row.

Edging No.2
Make 19ch.

1st row (RS) Into 3rd ch from hook work 1htr, 1htr into each ch to end. 18 sts.

2nd row 4ch to count as first dtr, *yrh 3 times, insert hook into next htr and draw a loop through, (yrh and draw through 2 loops) twice, (3 loops on hook), yrh, miss 2htr, insert hook into next htr and draw a loop through, (yrh and draw through 2 loops on hook) 4 times, (1 loop on hook), 2ch, 1tr into centre point of cross just made, rep from * 3 times more, 1dtr into 2nd of first 2ch.

3rd row 2ch to count as first htr, *1htr into next st, 2htr into 2ch sp, 1htr into next st, rep from * to end, 1htr into 4th of first 4ch.

Rep 2nd and 3rd rows for the required length, ending with a 3rd row. Do not break off yarn but turn work sideways and work along edge, as foll:

1st row 1ch, 1dc into edge of htr, *4dc into 4ch edge, 2dc into edge of next htr, rep from * to end.

2nd row 6ch to count as first dtr and 2ch, miss edge st and next dc, *work a cross st as on 2nd row of edging over next 4dc, 2ch, miss 2dc, rep from * to end, ending with miss 1dc, 1dtr into first 1ch. Note that the cross sts should come over the 4dc worked into the 4ch each time.

3rd row 5ch, 1dc into first leg of cross, 5ch, 1dc into next leg of cross, rep from * to end, ending with 5ch, 1dc into 4th of first 6ch.

Fasten off.

Edging No.3
Make a number of chain diviisble by 27 plus 25 and 4 extra turning chain.

1st row (RS) Into 8th ch from hook work 1tr, *2ch, miss 2ch, 1tr into next ch, rep from * to end. This makes a number of tr divisible by 9, or sps divisible by 9 plus 8.

2nd row 5ch to count as first tr and 2ch, miss first tr and 2ch, 1tr into next tr, *2ch, 1tr into next tr, rep from * to end working last tr into 5th of first 7ch.

3rd row 4ch, keeping last loop of each dtr on hook work 2dtr into the first tr (edge st), yrh and draw through all 3 loops on hook, *4ch, miss 1tr, work (1tr, 2ch, 1tr) into next tr, 4ch, miss 1tr, work (1dtr, 3ch, 1dtr) into next tr, 4ch, miss 1tr, work (1tr, 2ch, 1tr) into next tr, 4ch, miss 1tr, keeping last loop of each dtr on hook work 3dtr into next tr, yrh and draw through all 4 loops on hook — called 1Cl or cluster —, 2ch, 1Cl into next tr, rep from * to end omitting last 2ch and 1Cl and working last 1Cl into 3rd of first 5ch.

4th row 4ch, keeping last loop of each dtr on hook work 2dtr into top of first 1Cl at edge, yrh and draw through all 3 loops on hook, *4ch, work (1tr, 2ch, 1tr) into next 2ch sp, 4ch, work (1dtr, 3ch, 1dtr, 3ch, 1dtr) into 3ch sp, 4ch, work (1tr, 2ch, 1tr) into next 2ch sp, 4ch, 1Cl into top of 1Cl, 2ch, 1Cl into top of next 1Cl, rep from * to end omitting last 2ch and 1Cl.

5th row 1ch to count as first dc, *2ch, work (1tr, 2ch, 1tr) into 2ch sp, 4ch, work (1dtr, 3ch, 1dtr) into next 3ch sp, 4ch, work (1dtr, 3ch, 1dtr) into next 3ch sp, 4ch, work (1tr, 2ch, 1tr) into next 2ch sp, 2ch, 1dc into top of 1Cl, 2dc into 2ch sp between Cl, 1dc into top of next 1Cl, rep from * to end omitting last 3dc.

6th row 1ch to count as first dc, *2ch, work (1tr, 2ch, 1tr) into 2ch sp between tr, 5ch, work (1dtr, 3ch, 1dtr) into next 3ch sp, 4ch, work (1dtr, 3ch, 1dtr) into next 4ch sp, 4ch, work (1dtr, 3ch, 1dtr) into next 3ch sp, 5ch, work (1tr, 2ch, 1tr) into next 2ch sp, 2ch, miss 1dc, 1dc into each of next 2dc, rep from * to end, ending with 2ch, 1dc into first ch.

7th row 1ch to count as first dc, *work (1tr, 2ch, 1tr) into 2ch sp between tr, (5ch, 5tr into next 3ch sp) 3 times, 5ch, work (1tr, 2ch, 1tr) into next 2ch sp, miss next 2ch sp, 2dc and 2ch sp, rep from * to end, ending with (1tr, 2ch, 1tr) into 2ch sp, 1dc into first ch. Fasten off.

Edging No.4
Make 14ch.

1st row (RS) Into 7th ch from hook work 1tr, 2ch, 1tr into next ch, 3ch, miss 2ch, 1dc into next ch, 3ch, miss 2ch, work (1tr, 2ch, 1tr) into last ch.

2nd row 5ch to count as first tr, 1tr into first 2ch sp, 3ch, 5tr into next 2ch sp, turn.

3rd row 5ch, miss first 2tr, work (1tr, 2ch, 1tr) into next tr, 3ch, 1dc into 2nd of next 3ch, 3ch, 4th row 3ch to count as first tr, 2ch, 1tr into first 2ch sp, 3ch, 5tr into next 2ch sp, 3ch, 1tr into 5ch loop, (2ch, 1tr) 4 times into same 5ch loop, 3ch, miss next row end, 1ss into 3rd of 6ch at beg of 1st row, turn.

5th row 1ch to count as first dc, 3dc into 3ch sp, work (1dc, 3ch, 1dc) into each of next four 2ch sp, 3dc into next 3ch sp, 3ch, miss 2tr, work work (1tr, 2ch, 1tr) into 2ch sp at end.

(1tr, 2ch, 1tr) into next tr, 3ch, 1dc into 2nd of 3ch, 3ch, work (1tr, 2ch, 1tr) into 2ch sp at end.

The 2nd to 5th rows form the pattern, noting that when working a repeat of the 4th row, the last ss is worked into the dc before the 3ch loop of the previous 5th row.

Edging No.5
Make 8ch.

1st row (RS) Into 8th ch from hook work (2tr, 3ch, 2tr), turn.

2nd row 9ch, work (2tr, 10ch, 2tr) into 3ch sp, turn.

3rd row 5ch, work 17tr into 10ch sp, 1dc into 9ch loop, turn.

4th row (5ch, miss 1tr, 1dc into next tr) 5 times, turn.

5th row 7ch, work (2tr, 3ch, 2tr) into first 5ch loop, turn.

Rep the 2nd to 5th rows for the required length, ending with a 4th row. Do not break off yarn but turn work sideways and work along edge, as foll:

1st row 7ch, 1dc into next 5ch loop, 5ch, keeping last loop of each tr on hook work 3tr into next 7ch loop, yrh and draw through all 4 loops on hook — called 1Cl or cluster —, *5ch, 1dc into next 5ch loop, 5ch, 1Cl into next 7ch loop, rep from * to end working last 1Cl into commencing 7ch loop.

2nd row 3ch to count as first tr, work 6tr into each 5ch loop to end, 6tr into first 7ch loop, turn.

3rd row 4ch to count as first tr and 1ch, miss first 2tr, 1tr into next tr, *1ch, miss 1tr, 1tr into next tr, rep from * to end. Fasten off.

Edging No.6
Make 10ch. Join with a ss to first ch to form circle.

1st row (WS) 3ch to count as first tr, 14tr into circle, turn.

2nd row 5ch to count as first tr and 2ch, miss edge st and next tr, 1tr into next tr, *2ch, miss 1tr, 1tr into next tr, rep from * 5 times more, working last tr into 3rd of first 3ch.

3rd row *3ch, 7tr into next 2ch sp, take hook out of last working loop and insert from front to back into 3rd of 3ch, then into the working loop and draw the loop through, rep from * 6 times more, turn.

4th row 10ch, miss two 3ch sp, work (1dc, 5ch, 1dc) into next 3ch sp, turn.

5th row 3ch to count as first tr, 13tr into 5ch loop, 1dc into 10ch loop, turn.

Rep the 2nd to 5th rows for the required length, ending with a 3rd row. Do not break off yarn but turn work sideways and work as foll:

Next row *10ch, 1dc into next 10ch loop, 5ch, 1dc into 3rd of 3ch at beg of next row, rep from * to end. Fasten off.

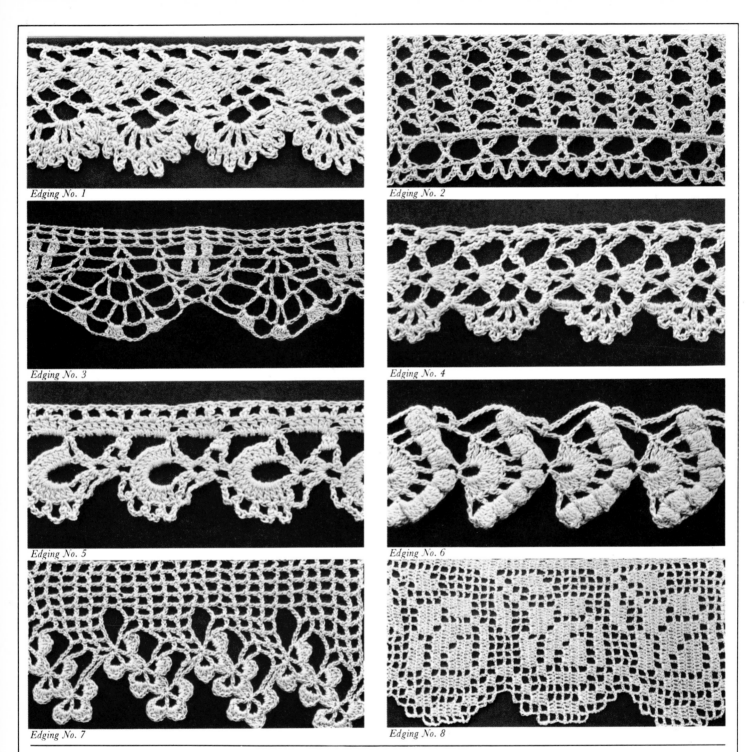

Edging No. 1

Edging No. 2

Edging No. 3

Edging No. 4

Edging No. 5

Edging No. 6

Edging No. 7

Edging No. 8

Edging No.7

Make 21ch.

1st row (WS) Into 8th ch from hook work 1tr, (2ch, miss 2ch, 1tr into next ch) 3 times, 5ch, miss 3ch, 1tr into last ch, (3ch, 1tr into same ch) 3 times, turn.

2nd row Into each of three 3ch loops work (1dc, 1htr, 1tr, 1dtr, 1tr, 1htr, 1dc—called 1 shamrock), 5ch, 1tr into 5ch sp, (2ch, 1tr into next tr) 4 times, 2ch, 1tr into 5th of first 7ch.

Edging No.8

Make 53ch.

1st row (RS) Into 8th ch from hook work 1tr, 2ch, miss 2ch, 1tr into each of next 4ch, (2ch, miss 2ch, 1tr into next ch) 5 times, 1tr into each of next 12ch, (2ch, miss 2ch, 1tr into each of next 4ch) twice. This row on the chart will read, 2 sps, 1 blk, 5 sps, 4 blks, 1 sp, 1blk, 1 sp, 1 blk.

2nd row 3ch to count as first tr, 1tr into each of next 3tr, 2ch, 1tr into next tr, 2ch, miss 2tr,

3rd row 5ch to count as first tr and 2ch, 1tr into next tr, (2ch, 1tr into next tr) 4 times, 2ch, 1tr into 5ch sp, 7ch, 1tr into dtr in centre of shamrock, (3ch, 1tr into same dtr) 3 times, turn.

4th row Make a shamrock as on 2nd row, 5ch, 1tr into 7ch loop, (2ch, 1tr into next tr) 6 times, 2ch, 1tr into 3rd of first 5ch.

5th row As 3rd but work (2ch, 1tr into next tr) 6 times instead of 4 times.

6th row As 4th but working (2ch, 1tr into next tr)

1tr into next tr, 2tr into sp, 1tr into next tr, (2ch, miss 2tr, 1tr into next tr) twice, 1tr into each of next 6tr, 2tr into sp, 1tr into next tr, (2ch, 1tr into next tr) 4 times, 1tr into each of next 3tr, 2ch, 1tr into next tr, 2ch, 1tr into 5th of first 7ch. This row on the chart will read, 1 blk, 2 sps, 1 blk, 2 sps, 3 bks, 4 sps, 1 blk, 2 sps.

3rd row 7ch, 1tr into first tr (edge st) — one sp inc —, then work 1 sp, 1 blk, 9 sps, 1 blk, 1 sp, 1 blk, 1 sp, 1 blk.

8 times instead of 6 times.

7th row 5ch to count as first tr and 2ch, miss first tr and 2ch, 1tr into next tr, (2ch, 1tr into next tr) 3 times, 7ch, miss four 2ch sp, 1tr into next 2ch sp, (3ch, 1tr into same sp) 3 times, turn.

Rep the 2nd to 7th rows for the required length, ending with a 6th row.

4th row 1 blk, 1 sp, 1 blk, 2 sps, 1 blk, 3 sps, 4 blks, 2 sps, 1 blk, 1 sp working last tr of this sp into 5th of first 7ch of 1st row, 5ch, 1tr into same place as last tr, turn and work 1ss into each of the first 3ch — 1 sp inc.

Beg with a 5th row cont in patt from chart, inc 1 sp at end of 6th row as given in 4th row. To dec at end of 12th and 14th rows, work to last sp, turn, and to dec 1 sp at beg of 15th (or 1st) row, ss over first sp, 5ch to count as first tr and 2ch, cont in patt to end.

Edging No.9

Make 150ch and work in patt from chart, working 1st row from A to B, as foll:

1st row Into 4th ch from hook work 1tr, 1tr into each of next 2ch, (2ch, miss 2ch, 1tr into next ch) 29 times, 1tr into each of next 3ch, (2ch, miss 2ch, 1tr into next ch) 17 times, 1tr into each of next 3ch. 1 blk, 29 sps, 1 blk, 17 sps 1 blk.

2nd row 1 blk, 18 sps, 2 blks, 6 sps, 3 blks, 18 sps, 1 blk.

Cont in patt from chart until 55th row has been worked, shown as C on chart.

56th row Patt to last 2 sps, turn.

57th row Patt to end.

58th row Patt to last 2 sps, turn.

Cont to dec 2 sps or blks on every alt row until 101st row has been worked, noting that this row will read, 2 sps, 1 blk.

Next row 1 blk, turn.

Next row 1 blk, ending at outside edge, turn and ss across the 4tr of this blk to inside edge.

Turn work through 90 degrees and cont along 2nd side, beg at point marked D on chart.

1st row 3ch, 3tr into side of last blk, 2ch, ss into the tr between 2 sps on 101st row.

2nd row Ss over the next 3ch of first sp on 101st row, turn and cont back along row just worked, 1 sp, 1 blk, turn.

3rd row 2 blks, 2 sps, ss into tr between sps on 99th row.

4th row Ss over the next 3ch of first sp on 99th row, turn and cont back along row just worked, 1 sp, 3 blks, turn.

5th row 4 blks, 2 sps, ss into tr between sps on 97th row.

Cont in this way until 48 rows have been completed, ending at outside edge.

49th row Patt to end, then work 3tr into side of blk on 55th row at point marked C on chart. This completes corner shaping. Cont in patt from chart until 151st row has been completed, point marked EF, then beg again at point marked AB. If a longer edging is required the rep of the patt is from row 70 on the side after the corner to row 30 on the first side, 122 rows in all.

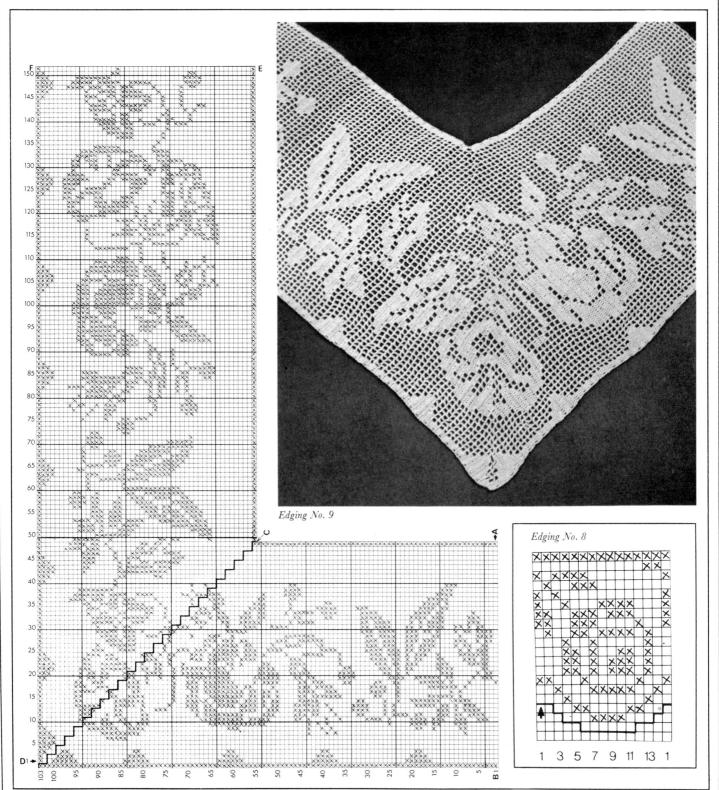

Edging No. 9

Edging No. 8

57

Aran patterns

Aran rib
Make the required number of chain and 1 extra turning chain.
1st row (RS) Into 3rd ch from hook work 1htr, 1htr into each ch to end.

2nd row 2ch to count as first htr, miss first htr, work 1htr into horizontal loop in front of each htr to end, 1htr into 2nd of first 2ch.
3rd row 2ch to count as first htr, miss first htr, work 1htr into back loop only of each htr to end,

1htr into 2nd of first 2ch.
The 2nd and 3rd rows form the pattern.

Mock cable pattern
Make a number of chain divisible by 6 plus 2 and 2 extra turning chain.
1st row (WS) Into 4th ch from hook work 1tr, 1tr into each ch to end.
2nd row 3ch to count as first tr, miss first tr, 1tr into next tr, *miss 2tr, 1dtr into each of next

2tr, keeping hook at back of work work 1dtr into each of the 2 missed tr, 1tr into each of next 2tr, rep from * to end working last tr into 3rd of first 3ch.
3rd row 3ch to count as first tr, miss 1tr, 1tr into next tr, *miss 2dtr, 1dtr into each of next 2dtr, keeping hook at front of work work 1dtr

into each of the 2 missed dtr, 1tr into each of next 2tr, rep from * to end working last tr into 3rd of first 3ch.
4th row As 2nd but working the dtr into dtr of 3rd row.
The 3rd and 4th rows form the pattern.

Cable panel
Worked over 17 stitches and 1 stitch at each end. Make 20 chain.
1st row (RS) Into 3rd ch from hook work 1htr, 1htr into each ch to end.
2nd row 2ch to count as first htr, miss first htr, work 1htr into each htr to end working last htr into 2nd of first 2ch.
3rd row 2ch to count as first htr, miss first htr, *work 1RtF round each of next 2htr, see Chapter 15, 1htr into next htr, rep from * to end working last htr into 2nd of first 2ch.
4th and every alt row 2ch to count as first htr, miss first htr, 1htr into each st to end working last htr into 2nd of first 2ch.
5th row 2ch to count as first htr, miss first htr,

(1RtF round each of next 2RtF on 3rd row, 1htr into next htr) twice, (miss next 2RtF and 1htr, yrh twice, insert hook round stem of next RtF from front to back and complete as for dtr — called RdtF —, 1RdtF into next RtF, keeping hook at back of work 1htr into the missed htr, then keeping hook in front of work but *behind* the 2RdtF just worked, work 1RdtF into each of the 2 missed RtF — called Cr5B —), (1htr into next htr, 1RtF round each of next 2RtF) twice, 1htr into 2nd of first 2ch.
7th row 2ch to count as first htr, miss first htr, work 1RtF round each of next 2RtF, 1htr into next htr, (miss 2RtF and next 1htr, work 1RdtF round each of next 2RtF, keeping hook at back of work 1htr into the missed htr, then keeping

hook at front of work and *in front* of the 2RdtF just worked, work 1RdtF round each of the 2 missed RtF — called Cr5F —), 1htr into next htr, Cr5F, 1htr into next htr, 1RtF round each of next 2RrF, 1htr into 2nd of first 2ch.
9th row 2ch to count as first htr, miss first htr, (Cr5B, 1htr into next htr) twice, Cr5B, 1htr into 2nd of first 2ch.
11th row As 7th.
13th row As 5th.
15th and 17th rows As 3rd but working RtF round RtF and not round htr.
18th row As 4th.
The 5th to 18th rows form the pattern.

Lattice panel
Worked over 26 stitches. Make 27 chain.
1st row (RS) Into 3rd ch from hook work 1htr, 1htr into each ch to end.
2nd row 2ch to count as first htr, miss first htr, 1htr into each htr to end working last htr into 2nd of first 2ch.
3rd row 2ch to count as first htr, miss first htr, 1htr into next htr, work 1RtF round each of next 2htr, see Chapter 15, 1htr into each of next 2htr, rep from * to end working last htr into 2nd of first 2ch.
4th and every alt row 2ch to count as first htr, miss first htr, 1htr into each st to end working last htr into 2nd of first 2ch.

5th row 2ch to count as first htr, miss first htr, 1htr into next htr, *(miss 2RtF and 2htr, work 1RdtF round each of next 2RtF, see cable panel, keeping hook at back of work 1htr into each of the 2 missed htr, then keeping hook at front of work and *in front* of the 2RdtF just worked, work 1RdtF round each of the 2 missed RtF — called Cr6F —), 1htr into each of next 2htr, rep from * to end working last htr into 2nd of first 2ch.
7th row 2ch to count as first htr, miss first htr, 1htr into next htr, 1RtF round each of next 2RdtF, *1htr into each of next 2htr, (miss 2RdtF and 2htr, work 1RdtF round each of the next 2RdtF, keeping hook at back of work 1htr into

each of the 2 missed htr, then keeping hook in front of work but *behind* the 2RdtF just worked, work 1RdtF round each of the 2 missed RdtF — called Cr6B —), rep from * once more, 1htr into each of next 2htr, 1RtF round each of next 2RdtF, 1htr into next htr, 1htr into 2nd of first 2ch.
9th row As 5th, reading RdtF instead of RtF where appropriate.
10th row As 4th.
The 7th to 10th rows form the pattern.

Diamond panel
Worked over 14 stitches. Make 15 chain.
1st row (RS) Into 3rd ch from hook work 1dc, 1dc into each ch to end.
2nd row 1ch to count as first dc, miss first dc, 1dc into each dc to end working last dc into 2nd of first 2ch.
3rd row 1ch to count as first dc, miss first dc, 1dc into next dc, 1RtF round next dc on 1st row, see Chapter 15, miss the same 1dc on 2nd row, 1dc into each of next 8dc, 1RtF round next dc on 1st row, miss the same 1dc on 2nd row, 1dc into next dc, 1dc into first ch.
4th and every alt row 1ch to count as first dc, miss first dc, 1dc into each st to end working last dc into first ch.
5th row 1ch to count as first dc, miss first dc, 1dc into each of next 2dc, 1RtF round next RtF,

miss 1dc, 1dc into each of next 6dc, 1RtF round next RtF, miss 1dc, 1dc into each of next 2dc, 1dc into first ch.
7th row 1ch to count as first dc, miss first dc, 1dc into each of next 3dc, 1RtF round next RtF, miss 1dc, 1dc into each of next 4dc, 1RtF round next RtF, miss 1dc, 1dc into each of next 3dc, 1dc into first ch.
9th row 1ch to count as first dc, miss first dc, 1dc into each of next 4dc, 1RtF round next RtF, miss 1dc, 1dc into each of next 2dc, 1RtF round next RtF, miss 1dc, 1dc into each of next 4dc, 1dc into first ch.
11th row 1ch to count as first dc, miss first dc, 1dc into each of next 5dc, 1RtF round each of next 2RtF, miss 2dc, 1dc into each of next 5dc, 1dc into first ch.

13th row 1ch to count as first dc, 1dc into each of next 5dc, miss 1RtF, 1RtF round next RtF, 1RtF round the missed RtF, miss 2dc, 1dc into each of next 5dc, 1dc into first ch.
15th row As 9th.
17th row As 7th.
19th row As 5th.
21st row 1ch to count as first dc, miss first dc, 1dc into next dc, 1RtF round next RtF, miss 1dc, 1dc into each of next 8dc, 1RtF round next RtF, miss 1dc, 1dc into next dc, 1dc into first ch.
22nd row As 4th.
The 5th to 22nd rows form the pattern.

Chevron pattern
Make a number of chain divisible by 6 plus 2 and 1 extra turning chain.
1st row (RS) Into 3rd ch from hook work 1dc, 1dc into each ch to end.
2nd row 1ch to count as first dc, miss first dc, 1dc into each dc to end working last dc into 2nd of first 2ch.

3rd and 4th rows As 2nd working last dc into first ch.
5th row 1ch to count as first dc, miss first dc, 1dc into each of next 2dc, 1RtF round 2nd dc of 2nd row, see Chapter 15, *miss 4dc on 2nd row, 1RtF round next dc on 2nd row, miss 2dc on 4th row, 1dc into each of next 4dc on 4th row, 1RtF round dc on 2nd row next to last RtF, rep from *

to last 5 sts on 4th row, miss 4dc on 2nd row, 1RtF round next dc on 2nd row, miss 2dc on 4th row, 1dc into next dc on 4th row, 1dc into first ch.
The 2nd to 5th rows form the pattern.

Aran rib

Chevron pattern

Mock cable pattern

Cable panel

Lattice panel

Diamond panel

59

Tunisian crochet stitches

Simple two-colour pattern
Using A, make the required number of chains.
1st row As 1st row of basic Tunisian stitch, see Chapter 14. Join in B.

2nd row Using B, as 2nd row of basic Tunisian stitch.
3rd row Using B, as 3rd row of basic Tunisian stitch. Change to A.

4th row Using A, as 2nd row.
The 3rd and 4th rows form the pattern, working 2 rows in each colour throughout and always changing colour to work the even numbered rows.

Slip stitch pattern in two colours
Using A, make an odd number of chain.
1st row As 1st row of basic Tunisian stitch, see Chapter 14. Join in B.
2nd row Using B, as 2nd row of basic Tunisian stitch.

3rd row Using B, *insert hook behind vertical thread of next st and draw up a loop, yfwd, insert hook behind vertical thread of next st and sl it on to the hook without drawing up a loop — called sl 1 —, ybk, rep from * to last 2 sts, draw up a loop on each of last 2 sts. Change to A.

4th row Using A, as 2nd row.
5th row Using A, *yfwd, sl 1, ybk, draw up a loop in next st, rep from * to end. Change to B.
The 2nd to 5th rows form the pattern, ending with a 2nd or 4th row.

Two-colour check pattern
Using A, make a number of chain divisible by 6 plus 3.
1st row Using A, insert hook into 2nd ch from hook and draw a loop through, insert hook into next ch and draw a loop through ,*using B, (insert hook into next ch and draw a loop through)

3 times, using A, (insert hook into next ch and draw a loop through) 3 times, rep from * to end.
2nd row As 2nd row of basic Tunisian stitch, see Chapter 14, working 3 sts in A, *3 sts in B, 3 sts in A, rep from * to end.
3rd row As 3rd row of basic Tunisian stitch, working 3 sts in A, *3 sts in B, 3 sts in A, rep

from * to end.
4th row As 2nd.
5th to 8th rows As 3rd and 4th rows but reading A for B and B for A.
9th to 12th rows As 3rd and 4th rows.
The 5th to 12th rows form the pattern.

Two-coloured mock rib
Using A, make an even number of chain and work 1st row as given for basic Tunisian stitch, see Chapter 14. Join in B.
2nd row Using B, as 2nd row of basic Tunisian stitch.
3rd row Using B, *insert hook from right to left behind vertical thread of next st and draw a loop through, insert hook from left to right behind vertical thread of next st and draw a loop through, rep from * to last st, insert hook into last st and draw a loop through. Change to A.
4th row Using A, as 2nd.
5th row Using A, *insert hook from left to right behind vertical thread of next st and draw a loop through, insert hook from right to left behind vertical thread of next st and draw a loop through, rep from * to last st, insert hook into last st and draw a loop through. Change to B.
6th row As 2nd.
The 3rd to 6th rows form the pattern.

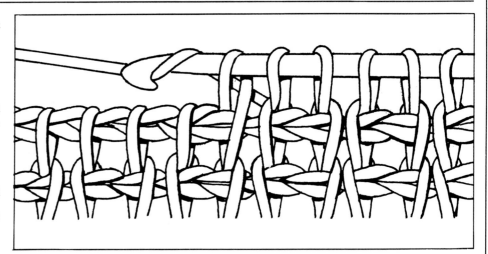

Brick pattern
Using A, make a number of chain divisible by 4 plus 1. Work first 2 rows of basic Tunisian stitch, see Chapter 14, joining in B on last st of 2nd row, see Chapter 9.
3rd and 4th rows Using B, work in basic Tunisian stitch. Change to A on last st of 4th row.
5th row Using A, insert hook behind vertical thread of next st and draw a loop through, *yrh,

insert hook from right to left behind vertical threads of next st but on the row below (i.e. the 1st row) and draw a loop through, yrh and draw through 2 loops on hook — called 1 long tr —, draw a loop through each of next 3 sts in basic pattern, rep from * to end, ending with 1 long tr and 2 basic stitches.
6th row Using A, as 2nd row. Change to B on last st.

7th and 8th rows Using B, as 3rd and 4th rows. Change to A on last st.
9th row Using A, draw up a loop in each of next 3 sts, *1 long tr working into the 5th row, 3 basic stitches, rep from * to last st, 1 basic st in last st.
10th row As 6th.
The 3rd to 10th rows form the pattern, ending with a 6th or 10th row.

Two-colour wave pattern
Using A, make a number of chain divisible by 10 plus 2. Work first 2 rows of basic Tunisian stitch, see Chapter 14, joining in B on last stitch of 2nd row, see Chapter 9.
3rd row Using B, insert hook from right to left behind vertical thread of next st and sl it on to the hook — called 1 sl st —, *work 2 basic stitches, work 4tr (see Chapter 14), 2 basic stitches, 2 sl sts, rep from * to end.
4th row Using B, as 2nd row of basic Tunisian stitch. Change to A on last st.
5th and 6th rows Using A, work in basic pattern. Change to B on last st.
7th row Using B, 1ch, work 1tr into each of next 2 sts, *2 basic stitches, 2 sl sts, 2 basic sts, 4tr, rep from * to end, ending with 3tr instead of 4tr.
8th row As 4th.
9th and 10th rows As 5th and 6th rows.
The 3rd to 10th rows form the pattern, ending with a 6th or 10th row.

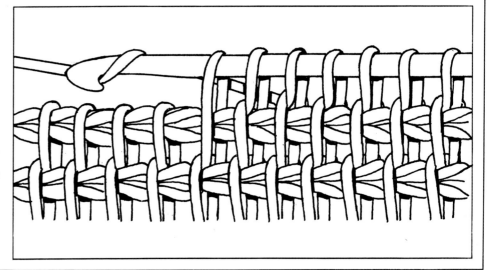

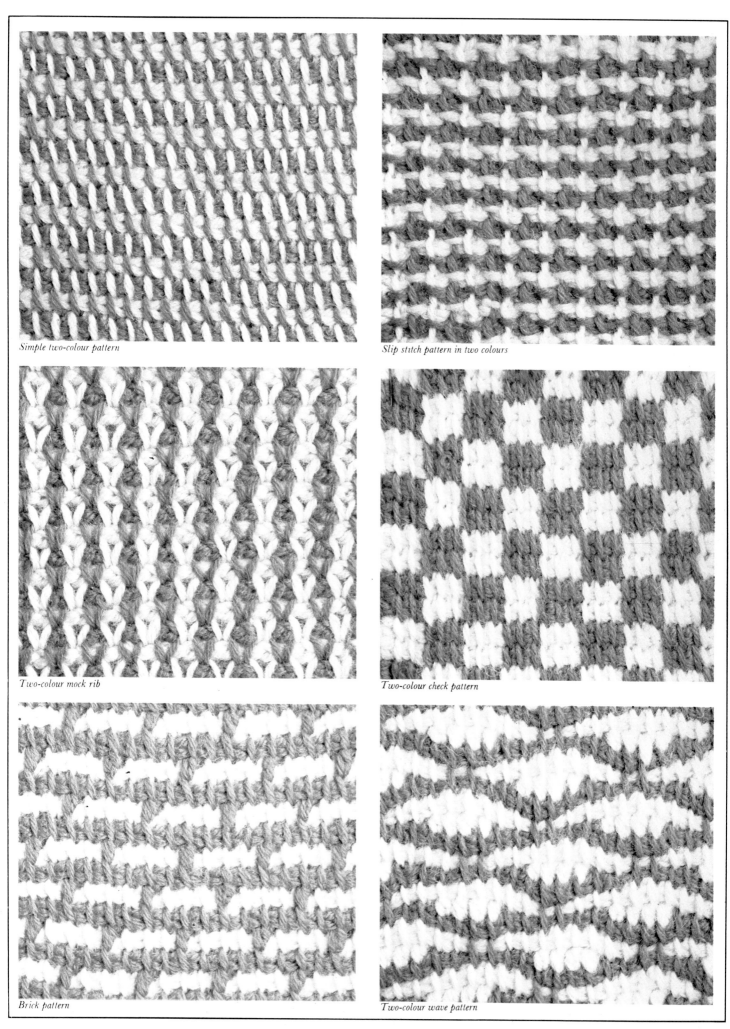

Simple two-colour pattern

Slip stitch pattern in two colours

Two-colour mock rib

Two-colour check pattern

Brick pattern

Two-colour wave pattern

61

Five simple designs

Mohair muffler

Size
25cm (9¾in) wide by 167.5cm (66in) long, adjustable

Tension
2 patts and 10 rows to 15cm (6in) worked on No.6.00 (ISR) crochet hook

Materials
6 x 25grm balls of Lister Tahiti or Lee Target Mohair
One No.6.00 (ISR) crochet hook

Muffler
Using No.6.00 (ISR) hook make 37ch. Work in mesh and cluster patt as given in Chapter 17, until work measures 167.5cm (66in), or required length, ending with a 3rd or 5th patt row. Fasten off. Trim each end with knotted fringe, if required.

Loopy tea-cosy

Size
23cm (9in) high by 32cm (12½in) wide

Tension
16 sts and 20 rows to 10cm (3.9in) over patt worked on No.4.00 (ISR) crochet hook

Materials
7 x 25grm balls of Wendy Random Double Knitting
One No.4.00 (ISR) crochet hook
Length of card 2cm (¾in) wide

Tea-cosy
Using No.4.00 (ISR) hook make 53ch.
1st row (RS) Into 3rd ch from hook work 1dc, 1dc into each ch to end. 52 sts.
2nd row 1ch to count as first dc, *holding strip of card at back of work, insert hook into next st so that it comes above the card, wind yarn towards you round the hook and the card twice, then round the hook again, draw this loop through the first 2 loops and the st, (2 loops on hook), yrh and draw through rem 2 loops, rep from * to end, moving the card along as necessary, ending with 1dc into 2nd of first 2ch.
3rd row 1ch to count as first dc, 1dc into each st to end, ending with 1dc into first ch.
4th row As 2nd, ending with 1dc into first ch.
Rep 3rd and 4th rows until work measures 15cm (6in) from beg, ending with a 4th row.
Shape top
Next row Ss over first 2 sts, 1ch, 1dc into each st to last 2 sts, turn.
Next row Patt to end.
Rep last 2 rows 3 times more. Dec in same way, dec 3 sts at each end of next and foll alt row, then 4 sts at each end of foll 2 alt rows, ending with a WS row. 8 sts. Fasten off. Make another piece in same way
To make up
Join 2 pieces tog. Cut 12 lengths of yarn 244cm (96in) long and make a twisted cord as given on page 11. St cord round seam, with a loop at top.

Crochet carpet bag

Size
38cm (15in) wide by 38cm (15in) deep

Tension
Each motif measures 12.5cm (5in) by 12.5cm (5in) worked on No. 4.00 (ISR) crochet hook

Materials
Approximately 10 x 25grm balls of Double Knitting yarn in assorted colours, or oddments

One No.4.00 (ISR) crochet hook
Pair of wooden handles 25.5cm (*10in*) across
lower edge

1st motif
Using No.4.00 (ISR) hook and any colour, make
8ch. Join with a ss to first ch to form circle.
1st round 3ch, (yrh, insert hook into circle and
draw a loop through, yrh and draw through 2
loops on hook) twice, yrh and draw through all 3
loops on hook, 2ch, work instructions in brackets
3 times more, yrh and draw through all 4 loops on
hook — called 1Cl —, (5ch, 1Cl, 2ch, 1Cl) 3
times, 5ch. Join with a ss to top of first Cl or 3rd
of first 3ch.
2nd round Ss into next 2ch sp, 3ch to count as
first tr, 2tr into same 2ch sp, 2ch, (1Cl, 3ch,
1Cl) into next 5ch sp, 2ch, *3tr into next 2ch
sp, 2ch (1Cl, 3ch, 1Cl) into 5ch sp, 2ch, rep from
* twice more. Join with a ss to 3rd of first 3ch.
3rd round 3ch to count as first tr, 1tr into each
of next 2tr, *2tr into 2ch sp, 2ch, (1Cl, 3ch, 1Cl)
into 3ch sp, 2ch, 2tr into 2ch sp, 1tr into each
of next 3tr, rep from * 3 times more, omitting
last 3tr. Join with a ss to 3rd of first 3ch.
4th round 3ch to count as first tr, 1tr into each
of next 4tr, *2tr into 2ch sp, 2ch, (1Cl, 3ch,
1Cl) into 3ch sp, 2ch, 2tr into 2ch sp, 1tr into
each of next 7tr, rep from * 3 times more, ending
with 1tr into each of last 2tr. Join with a ss to
3rd of first 3ch.
5th round 3ch to count as first tr, 1tr into each
of next 6tr, *2tr into 2ch sp, 2ch, (1Cl, 3ch,
1Cl) into 3ch sp, 2ch, 2tr into 2ch sp, 1tr into
each of next 11tr, rep from * 3 times more,
ending with 1tr into each of last 4tr. Join with a ss
to 3rd of first 3ch. Fasten off.
Using colours as required, make 17 more motifs
in same way.
To make up
Join 3 motifs to form each row, then join 6 rows.
Fold work in half and join 2 motifs at each side,
using dc through both thicknesses of 2 motifs,
then through one thickness of next motif, across
top edge and down first motif of other side,
then through both thicknesses of rem 2 motifs. Complete rem edges in dc. Fold top edge over handle
and sl st down.

Lampshade cover
Size
Approximately 25cm (*9¾in*) diameter by 19cm
(*7½in*) deep
Tension
14 V sts and 15 rows to 10cm (*3.9in*) worked on
No.1.50 (ISR) crochet hook
Materials
2 x 20 grm balls of Coat's Mercer-Crochet
No.20 for main section
2 x 20 grm balls of Coat's Mercer-Crochet
No.10 for edging and trimmings
One No.1.50 (ISR) crochet hook
Length of buckram or parchment for mounting

Lampshade
Using No.1.50 (ISR) hook and No. 20 cotton,
make 139ch and beg at top. Join with a ss first
ch to form circle.
1st round 5ch, miss 1ch, 1tr into next ch, (2ch,
miss 1ch, 1tr into next ch) 68 times, miss 1ch,
2ch. Join with a ss to 3rd of first 5ch. 70 sps.
2nd round 5ch, 1tr into next tr, (2ch, 1tr into
next tr) 68 times, 2ch. Join with a ss to 3rd of
first 5ch.
3rd round 5ch, 1dtr into base of 5ch, (1dtr, 1ch,
1dtr) into each tr to end. Join with a ss to 4th
of first 5ch.
4th round 5ch, 1dtr into base of 5ch, (1dtr, 1ch,

Left: Warm, quick-to-make mohair muffler
Top right: Loopy tea-cosy, using scraps of yarn
Right: Capacious carpet bag made from motifs

1dtr) into ch sp between each dtr — called V st —, to end. Join with a ss to 4th of first 5ch.
Rep 4th round twice more.

7th round 6ch, 1dtr into base of 6ch, (1dtr, 2ch, 1dtr) into each V st to end. Join with a ss to 4th of first 6ch.
Rep 7th round 5 times more.

13th round (inc round) *Work 9 V st as 7th round, between next 2 V sts work a double V of (1dtr, 2ch, 1dtr, 2ch, 1dtr), rep from * to end. Join with a ss to 4th of first 6ch.

14th round Work 1 V st into each V st, working 1 V st into centre dtr of each double V st. Join as before.
Work 2 rounds V st without shaping.

17th round (inc round) *Work 10 V st, between next 2 V sts work a double V, rep from * to end. Join as before.

18th round As 14th.
Work 2 rounds V st without shaping.

21st round (inc round) *Work 11 V sts, between next 2 V sts work a double V, rep from * to end. Join as before.

22nd round As 14th.
Work 2 rounds V st without shaping.

25th round (inc round) *Work 12 V sts, between next 2 V sts work a double V, rep from * to end. Join as before.

26th round As 14th. Fasten off.

Borders
Using No.1.50 (ISR) hook and No.10 cotton, rejoin yarn to join of 26th round.
1st round *2dc into 2ch sp of V st, 1dc into sp between V sts, rep from * to end. Join with a ss to first dc.
Work 3 more rounds dc.
5th round *1dc into each of next 6dc, 5ch, take hook out of working loop and insert it into the first of the 6dc, draw the working loop through and complete a dc, into the 5ch loop make 12dc, rep from * to end. Join with a ss to first dc. Fasten off.
Using No.1.50 (ISR) hook and No.10 cotton, rejoin yarn to join of 1st round at top edge.
1st round Work 2dc into each ch sp to end. Join with a ss to first dc.
2nd round As 5th round of border for lower edge.

Rose spray trimming
Using No.1.50 (ISR) hook and No.10 cotton make a length of ch 35.5cm (*14in*) long for stem. Work a row of dc into each side of ch. Fasten off.

Large rose
Using No.1.50 (ISR) hook and No.10 cotton, work 2 Irish rose motifs as given in Chapter 13, but starting with 24dc instead of 18 and making 8 petals.

Medium rose
Work 2 motifs as given for large rose, working first 5 rounds only.

Leaf
Using No.1.50 (ISR) hook and No.10 cotton make 22ch.
1st row Into 7ch from hook work 1tr, *2ch, miss 2ch, 1tr into next ch, rep from * 3 times more, 2ch, miss 2ch, 1dc into last ch. Turn.
Next round 2ch, 3dc into first ch sp, 1dc into next tr, *3tr into next ch sp, 1tr into next tr, rep from * twice more, 3dc into next ch sp, 1dc into next tr, 7dc into first 6ch, cont down 2nd side of leaf, 1dc into next tr, 3dc into next ch sp, **1tr into next tr, 3tr into next ch sp, rep from ** twice more, 1dc into next tr, 3dc into last ch sp. Join with a ss to 2nd of first 2ch.
Next round Work 1dc into each dc and tr, working 3dc into 4th dc at top of leaf. Join with a ss to first dc, make 8ch, turn and work 1dc into 3rd ch from hook, 1dc into each of next 4ch, to form stalk. Fasten off.
Make another leaf in same way.

To make up
Press each piece under a damp cloth with a warm

Top: Delicate Irish crochet lampshade cover
Above: Glittery evening belt for a touch of class

iron. Arrange rose spray on background and st in place. Mount cover on buckram or parchment, or st on to ready made lampshade.

Evening belt
Size
4cm (*1½in*) wide by 76cm (*30in*) long, adjustable
Tension
18 sts to 10cm (*3.9in*) over dc worked on No.4.00 (ISR) crochet hook using yarn double
Materials
1 x 100 metres (*110yd*) ball of Twilley's Gold-fingering in each of 3 colours, A, B and C
One No.4.00 (ISR) crochet hook
One 4cm (*1½in*) buckle

Using No.4.00 (ISR) hook and 2 strands of A, make a ch the required length, having multiples of 3 ch plus 1 extra turning ch, e.g. 136ch.
1st row (RS) Into 3rd ch from hook work 1dc, 1dc into each ch to end, joining in 2 strands of B on last dc. Break off A.
2nd row Using B, 4ch, *yrh, insert hook into next

dc and draw a loop through, yrh and draw through 2 loops on hook, *, rep from * to * into same dc, miss 2dc, rep from * to * twice into next dc, yrh and draw through all 5 loops on hook — called 1Cl —, **2ch, rep from * to * twice into same dc as 2nd half of last 1Cl, miss 2dc, rep from * to * twice into next dc and complete 1Cl, rxp from ** to last dc, 1ch, 1tr into last dc joining in 2 strands of A. Break off B.
3rd row Using A, 1ch, 2dc into first 1ch sp, *1dc into top of 1Cl, 2dc into 2ch sp, rep from * to end, working last 2dc into turning ch loop. Break off A.
4th row With RS of work facing join in 2 strands of C to beg of 3rd row, 1ch, 1dc into first st (edge st), 1dc into each dc to end, 2dc into turning ch, do not turn but cont across short end of belt, 1dc into end of 3rd row, 2dc into end of 2nd row, 1dc into end of 1st row, cont along starting ch, 2dc into first ch, 1dc into each ch to end, 2dc into last ch, work across other short end as before. Join with a ss to first ch. Do not turn.
5th row Using 1 strand of C only, work in crab st round all edges, as given in Chapter 7. Fasten off.

Sew buckle to one end of belt.

CROCHET COLLECTION

50 patterns for home & family

1

Striking chevron striped golfer and hat with a 'twenties look.

Sizes: to fit 81.5[86.5:91.5: 101.5]cm (32[34:36: 38:40]in) bust

JAMES WEDGE

2

Aran crochet
cardigan which looks
just as good on
a man!

Sizes: to fit
96.5[106.5]cm (38
[42]in) bust/chest

3,4

A bright shoulder
bag with an
unusual fastening
and plenty of room
inside, with a
jaunty matching
cap.

Size: cap to fit an
average head

5

Glamorous and flattering—a short halter neck evening dress.

Sizes : to fit 86.5[91.5:96.5]cm (32[34:36:38]in) bust

6

Stunning full-length evening dress, aswirl with frills and trimmed with butterflies in glitter yarn.

Size : to fit 86.5 cm (34in) bust

JAMES WEDGE

1 Chevron golfer and matching hat

Sizes
To fit 81.5[86.5:91.5:96.5:101.5]cm (32[34:36: 38:40]in) bust
Length to shoulder, 51.5[54.0:54.0:56.0:57.0]cm 20¼[21¼:21¼:22:22½]in)
The figures in brackets [] refer to the 86.5 (34), 91.5 (36), 96.5 (38) and 101.5cm (40in) sizes respectively

Tension
22 sts and 24 rows to 10.0cm (3.9in) over dc worked on No.3.50 (ISR) crochet hook

Materials
Jaeger Sheriden 4 ply
Golfer 3[3:3:4:4] x 50 grm balls in main shade, A
1[1:1:1:1] ball each of contrast colours, B. C and D
Hat 1[1:1:1:1] ball in main shade, A
1[1:1:1:1] ball each of contrast colours, B, C and D
One No.3.50 (ISR) crochet hook

Golfer
Using No.3.50 (ISR) hook and A, make 94ch and beg at right side seam.
1st row (RS) Into 3rd ch from hook work 1dc, 1dc into each of next 8ch, *work 3dc into next ch, 1dc into each of next 10ch, insert hook into next ch and draw loop through, miss 1ch, insert hook into next ch and draw loop through, yrh and draw through all 3 loops on hook, 1dc into each of next 10ch, rep from * to last 11ch, work 3dc into next ch, 1dc into each of last 10ch. Turn. 93 sts.
2nd row 1ch to count as first dc, insert hook into next dc and draw loop through, insert hook into next dc and draw loop through, yrh and draw through all 3 loops on hook — called dec 1 —, 1dc into each of next 8dc, *3dc into next dc, 1dc into each of next 10dc, insert hook into next dc and draw loop through, miss 1dc, insert hook into next dc and draw loop through, yrh and draw through all 3 loops on hook — called dec 2 —, 1dc into each of next 10dc, rep from * to last 12dc, 3dc into next dc, 1dc into each of next 8dc, dec 1, 1dc into first turning ch. Turn.
The 2nd row forms patt. Join in B. Cont in patt working (2 rows A, 2 rows B, 2 rows C and 2 rows D) throughout. Rep 8 striped patt rows 9[10:11:12:13] times in all. Mark each end of last row with coloured thread to form left side seam. Rep 8 striped patt rows 8[9:10:11:12] times more, then first 7 rows once more, ending with 1st row in D. With RS facing, fold work in half at left side seam.
**Next row (joining row) 1ch, ss into first ch of commencing ch, work in patt to end working through each dc of last row and each matching ch of first row. Fasten off.
Mark each end of last row with coloured thread, ******, to form right side seam.

Back yoke
Using No.3.50 (ISR) hook, A and with RS of work facing, miss first 8 rows ends on top edge from right side seam to form back underarm, rejoin yarn to next row end, 2ch to count as first dc, 1dc into each of next 55[63:71:79:87] row ends, turn, noting that next 8 row ends are missed to form other back underarm. 56[64:72: 80:88]dc. Cont in dc, dec one st at each end of next and every row until 50[56:62:68:74] sts rem. Cont without shaping until armholes measure 19.0[20.5:20.5:21.5:23.0]cm (7½[8:8: 8½:9]in) from beg, ending with a WS row.
Shape shoulders and neck
Next row 1ch to count as first dc, 1dc into each of next 16[18:20:22:24]dc, turn.

Next row Dec one st, patt to last 5[6:7:8:9] sts, turn.
Next row Ss across first 5[6:7:8:9] sts, patt to last 2 sts, dec one. Fasten off.
With RS of work facing, miss first 16[18:20:22: 24] sts, rejoin yarn to rem sts and patt to end. Complete to match first side, reversing shaping.
Front yoke
Using No.3.50 (ISR) hook, A and with RS of work facing, miss first 8 row ends on top edge from left side seam to form front underarm, rejoin yarn to next row end, 2ch to count as first dc, 1dc into each of next 24[28:32:36:40] row ends, turn, 25[29:33:37:41]dc. Cont in dc, dec one st at armhole edge on next 3[4:5:6:7] rows, at the same time dec one st at neck edge on every foll 4th row until 15[17:19:21:23] sts rem. Cont without shaping until armhole measures same as back to shoulder, ending at armhole edge.
Shape shoulder
Next row Ss across first 5[6:7:8:9] sts, patt to end. Turn.
Next row Patt to last 5[6:7:8:9] sts, turn. Fasten off.
With RS of work facing, miss next 6 row ends for centre front neck, rejoin yarn to next row end, 2ch to count as first dc, 1dc into each of next 24[28:32:36:40] row ends, noting that next 8 rows ends are missed to form other front underarm. Complete to match first side, reversing shaping.
Welt
Using No.3.50 (ISR) hook, A and with RS of work facing, rejoin yarn to lower edge at right side seam.
Next round 2ch to count as first dc, *work 1dc into next row end, rep from * to end. Join with a ss to 2nd of first 2ch.
Work 17[19:19:21:21] more rounds dc. Fasten off.
Neckband
Join shoulder seams. Using No.3.50 (ISR) hook, A and with RS of work facing, rejoin yarn to lower edge of right front neck, 2ch to count as first dc, work 1 row dc up right front neck, round back neck and down left front neck. Turn. Break off A. Join in B. Work in dc, working (2 rows B, 2 rows C, 2 rows D and 2 rows A). Fasten off.
Armbands
Using No.3.50 (ISR) hook, A and with RS of work facing, rejoin yarn to marked underarm row end, work 1 round dc round armhole. Join in B. Work 2 rounds dc, dec one st at underarm on first round. Rep last 2 rounds using, C, D and A. Fasten off.
To make up
Press under a damp cloth with a warm iron. Overlap right front neckband over left front neckband and st down to centre front row ends.
Hat
Using No.3.50 (ISR) hook and A, make 46ch and beg at centre back of crown. Work first 2 rows and cont in striped patt as given for golfer. Rep 8 striped patt rows 11 times, then first 7 rows once more, ending with a 1st row in D. Join as given for golfer from ** to **, to form centre back seam.
Shape crown
Using No.3.50 (ISR) hook, A and with RS of work facing, rejoin yarn to centre back seam.
1st round 2ch to count as first dc, work 1dc into each of next 95 row ends. Join with a ss to 2nd of first 2ch. 96 sts.
Next round 1ch, 1dc into each of next 9dc, work 2dc tog, *1dc into each of next 10dc, work 2dc tog, rep from * to end. Join with a ss to first ch. 88 sts.
Work 2 rounds dc without shaping.
Next round 1ch, 1dc into each of next 8dc, work 2dc tog, *1dc into each of next 9dc, work 2dc tog, rep from * to end. Join with a ss to first ch. 80 sts.

Work 2 rounds without shaping. Cont dec in this way on next and every foll 3rd round until 56 sts rem, then on every round until 8 sts rem. Break off yarn, thread through rem sts, draw up and fasten off.

To make up
Press as given for golfer. Turn in 1.5cm (½in) hem at lower edge to WS and sl st down.
Front loop Using No.3.50 (ISR) hook and A, make 29 ch.
1st row Into 3rd ch from hook work 1dc, 1dc into each ch to end. Turn.
Work 9 more rows dc. Fasten off. Fold in half with RS facing and join long edge. Sew one short end to centre front of RS of crown, level with crown shaping, and other end to sl st seam of turned under hem to gather up front crown.

2 Aran crochet cardigan

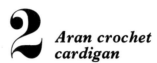

Sizes
To fit 96.5[106.5]cm (38[42]in) chest
Length to shoulder, 63.5[66.0]cm (25[26]in)
Sleeve seams, 45.5cm (18in)
The figures in brackets [] refer to the 106.5cm (42in) size only

Tension
12dc and 16 rows to 10cm (3.9in) over patt worked on No.6.00 (ISR) crochet hook

Materials
20 [22] x 50 grm balls Templetons Ardfinnan
One No.6.00 (ISR) crochet hook
One No.5.50 (ISR) crochet hook
6 buttons

Back
Using No.5.50 (ISR) hook make 7ch for welt.
1st row Into 3rd ch from hook work 1dc, 1dc into each ch to end. Turn. 6 sts.
2nd row 1ch, *1dc into horizontal loop below next dc, rep from * to end. Turn.
Rep 2nd row 59[65] times more. 61[67] rows. Do not break off yarn. Change to No.6.00 (ISR) hook, turn and work along long edge of welt, 1ch, 1dc into each row end. Turn. 61[67] sts.
Next row (WS) 1ch, (1htr into next dc, 1ss into next dc) 4[5] times, 1dc into each of next 10dc, 1ss into next dc, (1htr into next dc, 1ss into next dc) 11[12] times, 1dc into each of next 10dc, 1ss into next dc, (1htr into next dc, 1ss into next dc) 4[5] times. Turn.
Next row 2ch, (1ss into htr, 1htr into ss) 4[5] times, 1dc into each of next 10dc, 1htr into next ss, (1ss into htr, 1htr into ss) 11[12] times, 1dc into each of next 10dc, 1htr into next ss, (1ss into htr, 1htr into ss) 4[5] times. Turn.
Next row 1ch, (1htr into ss, 1ss into htr) 4[5] times, 1dc into each of next 10dc, 1ss into htr, (1htr into ss, 1ss into htr) 11[12] times, 1dc into each of next 10dc, 1ss into htr, (1htr into ss, 1ss into htr) 4[5] times. Turn.
Rep last 2 rows until work measures 40.5cm (16in) from beg, ending with a WS row.
Shape armholes
Next row Ss over first 4 sts, and into 5th st, 2ch, patt to last 4 sts, turn.
Keeping patt correct, dec one st at each end of next 3[4] rows. 47[51] sts.
Cont without shaping until armholes measure 20.5 [23.0]cm (8[9]in) from beg, ending with a WS row.
Shape neck and shoulders
Next row Ss over first 5 sts and into next st, 1ch, patt over next 10[11] sts, turn.
Complete this side first.
Next row Ss over first 2 sts and into 3rd st, 1ch, patt over next 3[4] sts, turn. 4[5] sts. Fasten off.
Return to where work was left, miss first 15[17]

sts, using No.6.00 (ISR) hook rejoin yarn into next st, 1ch, patt to last 5 sts, turn.
Next row Ss over first 5 sts and into next st, 1ch, patt to last 2 sts, turn. 4[5] sts. Fasten off.

Left front

Using No.5.50 (ISR) hook make 7ch for welt and work first 2 rows as given for back. 6 sts. Rep 2nd row 27[30] times more. 29[32] rows. Change to No.6.00 (ISR) hook, turn and work along top of welt as given for back. 29[32] sts. **.
Next row (WS) 2ch[1ch, 1htr into next dc], 1ss into next dc, (1htr into next dc, 1ss into next dc) 4 times, 1dc into each of next 10dc, 1ss into next dc, (1htr into next dc, 1ss into next dc) 4[5] times. Turn.
Cont in patt as now set until work measures same as back to underarm, ending at armhole edge.
Shape armhole and front edge
Next row Ss over first 4 sts and into 5th st, 2ch, patt to last st, turn.
Dec one st at armhole edge on next 3[4] rows, *at the same time* cont dec one st at front edge on every 4th row 7[8] times more. 14[15] sts. Cont without shaping until armhole measures same as back to shoulder, ending at armhole edge.
Shape shoulder
Next row Ss over first 5 sts and into next st, 1ch, patt to end. Turn.
Next row Patt to last 5 sts, turn. 4[5] sts. Fasten off.

Right front

Work as given for left front to **.
Next row (WS) 1ch, (1htr into next dc, 1ss into next dc) 4[5] times, 1dc into each of next 10dc, 1ss into next dc, (1htr into next dc, 1ss into next dc) 4[5] times, 1htr into last st on first size only. Turn.
Complete to match left front, reversing all shaping.

Sleeves

Using No.5.50 (ISR) hook make 13ch and work first 2 rows as given for back. 12 sts. Rep 2nd row 25[29] times more. 27[31] rows. Change to No.6.00 (ISR) hook and work along top edge of cuff as given for back inc one st in centre. 28[32] sts.
Next row (WS) 1ch, (1htr into next dc, 1ss into next dc) 4[5] times, 1dc into each of next 10dc, 1ss into next dc, (1htr into next dc, 1ss into next dc) 4[5] times. Turn.
Cont in patt as now set, inc one st at each end of 7th and every foll 6th row, working extra sts into edge patt, until there are 44[48] sts. Cont without shaping until sleeve measures 45.5cm (*18in*) from beg, ending with a WS row.
Shape top
Next row Ss over first 4 sts and into 5th st, 2ch, patt to last 4 sts, turn.
Dec one st at each end of next and foll 5[6] alt rows, then at each end of next 8 rows. 8[10] sts. Fasten off.

Front band

Using No.5.50 (ISR) hook make 7ch and work first 2 rows as given for back. Rep 2nd row twice more. 6 sts.
5th row (buttonhole row) 1ch, 1dc, 2ch, miss 2dc, 1dc into last 2dc. Turn.
6th row 1ch, 1dc, 2dc into 2ch sp, 1dc into last 2dc. Turn.
Cont in patt, making 5 more buttonholes at intervals of 6.5cm (*2½in*), then cont until band is long enough to reach up front edge, round back neck and down other front. Fasten off.

To make up

Press under a damp cloth with a warm iron. Join shoulder seams. Using No.5.50 (ISR) hook work surface crochet over each panel of 10dc as

shown in diagram. Join side and sleeve seams. Set in sleeves. Sew on front band. Press seams. Sew on buttons.

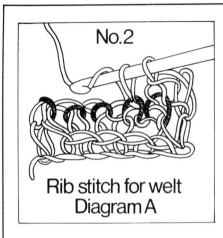

Rib stitch for welt
Diagram A

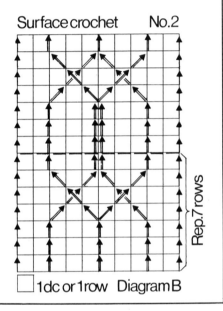

Surface crochet   No.2

Rep.7 rows

□ 1dc or 1row   Diagram B

 Lady's bag and matching hat

Size
Cap to fit an average head
Tension
Motif measures 11.5cm (*4½in*) over patt worked on No.4.00 (ISR) crochet hook
Materials
Wendy Courtelle Double Crepe
Bag 4 x 20 grm balls in main shade, A
2 balls each of contrast colours, B, C and D
1 ball of contrast colour, E
Cap 1 ball in main shade, A
1 ball each of 4 contrast colours, B, C, D and E
One No.4.00 (ISR) crochet hook
One No.3.50 (ISR) crochet hook
Vilene and lining for bag

Bag
First motif
Using No.4.00 (ISR) hook and C, make 5ch. Join with a ss to first ch to form circle.
1st round 3ch to count as first tr, 2tr into circle, 2ch, *3tr, 2ch, rep from * twice more. Join with a ss to 3rd of first 3ch. Break off C. Join in A to any 2ch sp.
2nd round Using A, (3ch, 2tr, 2ch, 3tr) into

first 2ch sp, *(1ch, 3tr, 2ch, 3tr) into next 2ch sp, rep from * twice more, 1ch. Join with a ss to 3rd of first 3ch. Break off A. Join in B to any 2ch sp.
3rd round Using B, (3ch, 2tr, 2ch, 3tr) into first 2ch sp, *1ch, 3tr into next 1ch sp, (1ch, 3tr, 2ch, 3tr) into 2ch sp at corner, rep from * twice more, 1ch, 3tr into next 1ch sp, 1ch. Join with a ss into 3rd of first 3ch. Break off B. Join in C to any 2ch sp.
4th round Using C, (3ch, 2tr, 2ch, 3tr) into first 2ch sp, *(1ch, 3tr into next 1ch sp) twice, (1ch, 3tr, 2ch, 3tr) into 2ch sp, rep from * twice more, (1ch, 3tr into next 1ch sp) twice, 1ch. Join with a ss to 3rd of first 3ch. Break off C. Join in A to any 2ch sp.
5th round Using A, 3ch, 2tr into first 2ch sp, 1tr into each of next 3tr, *1tr into next 1ch sp, 1tr into each of next 3tr, rep from * twice more, 3tr into corner 2ch sp, 1tr into each of next 3tr, rep from * to last 1ch sp, 1tr into 1ch sp, 1tr into each of last 3tr. Join with a ss to 3rd of first 3ch. Fasten off.
Work 8 more motifs in same way.

Second motif
Work as given for first motif, working colours as foll: 1st round in A, 2nd round in B, 3rd round in D, 4th round in A and 5th round in B. Fasten off.
Make 3 more motifs in same way.

Third motif
Work as given for first motif, working colours as foll: 1st round in E, 2nd round in D, 3rd round in B, 4th round in E and 5th round in D. Fasten off.
Make 3 more motifs in same way.

Half motif
Using No.4.00 (ISR) hook and A, make 5ch. Join with a ss to first ch to form circle.
1st round Using A, 4ch to count as first tr and 1ch sp, (3tr, 2ch, 3tr) into circle, 1ch, 1tr into circle. Break off A. Join in B and work in rows beg at same edge on every row.
2nd row Using B, join yarn into 3rd of first 4ch, 4ch, 3tr into 1ch sp, 1ch, (3tr, 2ch, 3tr) into 2ch sp, 1ch, 3tr into next 1ch sp, 1ch, 1tr into last tr. Break off B. Join in D.
3rd row Using D, join yarn to 3rd of first 4ch, 4ch, 3tr into 1ch sp, 1ch, 3tr into next 1ch sp, 1ch, (3tr, 2ch, 3tr) into corner 2ch sp, 1ch, 3tr into next 1ch sp, 1ch, 3tr into next 1ch sp, 1ch, 1tr into last tr. Break off D. Join in A.
4th row Using A, join yarn to 3rd of first 4ch, 4ch, 3tr into 1ch sp, 1ch, (3tr, 2ch, 1ch) twice, (3tr, 2ch, 3tr) into corner 2ch sp, (1ch, 3tr into 1ch sp) 3 times, 1ch, 1tr into last tr. Break off A. Join in B.
5th row Using B, join yarn to 3rd of first 4ch, 3ch, *1tr into next ch, 1tr into each of next 3tr, rep from * to corner, 3tr into corner 2ch sp, **1tr into each of next 3tr, 1tr into next ch, rep from ** to end, 1tr into last tr. Fasten off.
Work one more half motif, working colours as given for 3rd motif.

To make up
Press on RS under a dry cloth with a cool iron. Pin motifs into position as shown in diagram and sew back loops only by top sewing.
Shoulder strap Using No.3.50 (ISR) hook and A, make 8ch.
1st row Into 2nd ch from hook work 1dc, 1dc into each ch to end. Turn.
Cont in dc until work measures 152.5cm (*60in*) from beg. Fasten off.
Place strap into position round sides and lower edge of bag and sew down. Using No.3.50 (ISR) hook and A, work one row tr round edge of flap. Fasten off.
Loop Using No.3.50 (ISR) hook and A, make 6ch.
Next row Into 2nd ch from hook work 1dc, 1dc

into each ch to end. Turn. 5 sts.
Cont in dc until work measures 6.5cm (2½in)
from beg. Fasten off.
Strap Using No.3.50 (ISR) hook and A, make 9ch.
Next row Into 2nd ch from hook work 1dc,
1dc into each ch to end. Turn.
Cont in dc until work measures 10.0cm (4in)
from beg.
Next row Miss first dc, 1dc into each dc to last
2 sts, miss 1dc, 1dc into last dc. Turn.
Rep last row until 2 sts rem. Fasten off.
Ss loop to front of bag and straight edge of
strap to flap, sl strap through loop. Press seams
lightly. Cut lining and Vilene to same size as
bag. Join side seams and sl st to inside of bag
and flap.

Cap

Work 2 motifs as given for first motif, one motif
as given for second motif and one motif as
given for third motif.

To make up

Press as given for bag.
Join motifs in sequence A, B, A and C by top
sewing and leaving back seam open.
Shape crown Using No.3.50 (ISR) hook and A,
rejoin yarn and work one row dc along row of
tr at top of 4 motifs. Turn.
1st row *1dc, miss 1dc, 1dc, rep from * to end.
Turn.
2nd row 1ch, *1dc into each st to end. Turn.
3rd row 1ch, *1dc, miss 1dc, rep from * to end.
Turn.
Rep last row twice more. Fasten off. Join back
seam by top sewing. Using No.3.50 (ISR) hook
and A, work 2 rows dc round lower edge. Fasten
off.

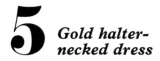

5 *Gold halter-necked dress*

Sizes
To fit 81.5 [86.5:91.5:96.5]cm (32[34:36:38]in)
bust
Length to shoulder, 94.0[90.5:96.5:98.0]cm
(37[37½:38:38½]in)
The figures in brackets [] refer to the 96.5 (34)
91.5 (36) and 96.5cm (38in) sizes respectively
Materials
8 blocks and 10 rows to 10cm (3.9in) over patt
worked on No.3.00 (ISR) crochet hook
Tension
10[11:12:12] x 20 grm balls Emu Candlelite
One No.4.00 (ISR) crochet hook
One No.3.50 (ISR) crochet hook
One No.3.00 (ISR) crochet hook
12 buttons

Skirt
Using No.3.00 (ISR) hook make 163[175:187:
199]ch, and beg at waist.
1st row Into 4th ch from hook work 1tr, *1ch,
miss 1ch, 1tr into each of next 2ch, rep from *
to end. Turn. 54[58:62:66] blocks.
2nd row 3ch to count as first tr, 1tr into next
tr, *1ch, miss 1ch, 1tr into each of next 2tr, rep
from * to end. Turn.
The 2nd row forms patt and is rep throughout.
Work 2 rows patt.
5th row (inc row) Patt over first 6[7:8:9]
blocks, *2tr into first tr of next block, 1ch, 1tr
into next tr of block, patt over next 6 blocks, *,
rep from * to * once more, inc as before over next
block, patt over next 12[14:16:18] blocks, rep
from * to * twice, inc next block as before,
patt over rem 6[7:8:9] blocks. Turn.
6th row Patt over first 6[7:8:9] blocks, *2tr into
single tr, patt over next 7 blocks, *, rep from * to

* once more, 2tr into single tr, patt over next
13[15:17:19] blocks, rep from * to * twice, 2tr
into single tr, patt over next 7[8:9:10] blocks.
Turn. 60[64:68:72] blocks.
Work 4 rows patt.
11th row Patt over first 6[7:8:9] blocks, *2tr
into first tr of next block, 1ch, 1tr into next tr of
block, patt over next 7 blocks, *, rep from * to *
once more, inc as before over next block, patt
over next 14[16:18:20] blocks, rep from * to *
twice, inc as before over next block, patt over
rem 6[7:8:9] blocks. Turn.
12th row Patt over first 6[7:8:9] blocks, *2tr into
single tr, patt over next 8 blocks, *, rep from *
to * once more, 2tr into single tr, patt over next
15[17:19:21] blocks, rep from * to * twice, 2tr
into single tr, patt over rem 7[8:9:10] blocks.
Turn. 66[70:74:78] blocks.
Work 4 rows without shaping. Keeping inc in
line, inc on next 2 rows. 72[76:80:84] blocks.
Work 2 rows without shaping. Change to No.3.50
(ISR) hook and work 2 rows without shaping.
(Keeping inc in line, inc over next 2 rows. Work 4
rows without shaping) twice. 84[88:92:96] blocks.
Inc on next 2 rows, then work 2 rows without
shaping. 90[94:98:102] blocks. Change to No.4.00
(ISR) hook and work 2 rows without shaping.
(Inc on next 2 rows. Work 4 rows without
shaping) 3 times. 108[112:116:120] blocks. Inc
on next 2 rows. 114[118:122:126] blocks.
Fasten off.

Bodice
Using No.3.00 (ISR) hook and with RS of work
facing, rejoin yarn to starting ch at waist.
1st row 3 ch to count as first tr, 1tr into next tr,
*1ch, miss 1ch, 1tr into each of next 2tr, rep
from * to end. Turn. 54[58:62:66] blocks.
2nd row As 1st.
3rd row (inc row) Patt over first 6[7:8:9] blocks,
2tr into first tr of next block, 1ch, 1tr into next
tr of block, patt over next 13 blocks, inc in next
block, patt over next 12[14:16:18] blocks, inc in

next block, patt over next 13 blocks, inc in next
block, patt over rem 6[7:8:9] blocks. Turn.
4th row Patt to end, working 2tr into each of the
single tr of inc blocks. Turn. 58[62:66:70] blocks.
Work 2 rows without shaping. Commence centre
front panel patt.
7th row *Patt over first 6[7:8:9] blocks, 2tr into
first tr of next block, 1ch, 1tr into next tr of
block, patt over next 14 blocks, inc in next block,
patt over next 6[7:8:9] blocks, *, 1ch, 1tr into
first tr of next block, 3ch, miss next tr of block
and first tr of next block, 1tr into next tr of
block, 1ch, rep from * to * once. Turn.
8th row *Patt over first 6[7:8:9] blocks, 2tr into
single tr, patt over next 15 blocks, 2tr into single
tr, patt over next 7[8:9:10] blocks, *, 1ch, 1tr
into next tr, 3ch, 1tr into next tr, 1ch, rep from
* to * once more. Turn. 62[66:70:74] blocks,
noting that single tr in centre front panel are
counted as one block.
Keeping patt correct throughout as now set,
work 3 rows without shaping.
12th row Patt over first 29[31:33:35] blocks, 1ch,
1tr into first tr of next block, miss next tr, 2ch,
1tr into next tr, 3ch, 1tr into next tr, 2ch, miss
first tr of next block, 1tr into next tr, 1ch, patt
to end. Turn.
13th row Patt over first 29[31:33:35] blocks, 1ch,
1tr into next tr, 2ch, 1tr into next tr, 3ch, 1tr
into next tr, 2ch, 1tr into next tr, 1ch, patt to
end. Turn.
Rep last row 3 times more. Break off yarn.
Shape top
1st row With RS of work facing, miss first
6[7:8:9] blocks, rejoin yarn to first tr of next
block, 3ch, 1tr into next tr, patt over next 21[22:
23:24] blocks, 1tr into first tr of next block,
miss next tr, (2ch, 1tr into next tr) twice, 3ch,
(1tr into next tr, 2ch) twice, miss first tr of next
block, 1tr into next tr, 1ch, patt to last 6[7:8:9]
blocks, turn. Break off yarn.
2nd row With WS of work facing, miss first 7
blocks, rejoin yarn to first tr of next block, 3ch,

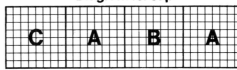

Diagram for cap

Nos.3&4

| C | A | B | A |

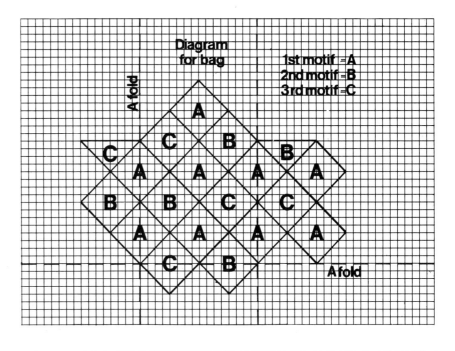

Diagram for bag

A fold

1st motif = A
2nd motif = B
3rd motif = C

A fold

1tr into next tr, patt over next 14[15:16:17] blocks, 1ch, (1tr into next tr, 2ch) twice, 1tr into next tr, 3ch, 1tr into next tr, (2ch, 1tr into next tr) twice, 1ch, patt to last 7 blocks, turn.

3rd row Ss over first block, patt to last block. turn.

Rep 3rd row twice more.

6th row Ss over first block, patt over next 10[11:12:13] blocks, 1ch, 1tr into first tr of next block, miss next tr, (2ch, 1tr into next tr) 3 times, 3ch, (1tr into next tr, 2ch) 3 times, miss first tr of next block, 1tr into next tr, 1ch, patt to last block, turn.

7th row Ss over first block, patt over next 9[10:11:12] blocks, 1ch, (1tr into next tr, 2ch) 3 times, 1tr into next tr, 3ch, 1tr into next tr, (2ch, 1tr into next tr) 3 times, 1ch, patt to last block, turn.

Keeping patt correct as now set, dec 1 block at each end of next 3 rows. 20[22:24:26] blocks.

11th row Ss over first block, patt over next 4 blocks, 1tr into first tr of next block, miss next tr, (2ch, 1tr into next tr) 4 times, 3ch, (1tr into next tr, 2ch) 4 times, miss next tr, 1tr into next tr, 1ch, patt to last block, turn.

12th row Ss over first block, patt over next 3 blocks, 1ch, (1tr into next tr, 2ch) 4 times, 1tr into next tr, 3ch, 1tr into next tr, (2ch, 1tr into next tr) 4 times, 1ch, patt to last block, turn. 16[18:20:22] blocks.

Keeping patt correct as now set, dec one block at each end of next 0[1:1:2] rows, then work 5[5:6:6] rows without shaping. 16[16:18:18] blocks.

Shape neck

1st row Patt over first 3[3:4:4] blocks, turn. Complete this side first. Work 2 rows without shaping.

4th row 1ch, 1dc into next tr, 1ch, patt over next 2[2:3:3] blocks. Turn.

5th row Patt to end. Turn.

Rep 4th and 5th rows 5 times more. Fasten off. Return to where work was left, rejoin yarn to 3rd [3rd:4th:4th] block from other end, patt to end. Complete to match first side, reversing shaping.

To make up

Press work under a damp cloth with a cool iron. Join back seam leaving 30.5cm (*12in*) open at top. Using No.3.00 (ISR) hook and with RS of work facing, work 60dc down right side of back opening.

Next row (buttonhole row) 1ch, 1dc into next dc, (2ch, miss 2dc, 1dc into each of next 4dc) 9 times, 2ch, miss 2dc, 1dc into each of last 2dc. Turn.

Next row Work in dc to end, working 2dc into each 2ch sp. Turn.

Work 1 more row in dc. Fasten off.

Work 2 rows in dc along other edge of opening. Sew on buttons. Sew buttonhole edge over other edge at bottom. Using No.3.00 (ISR) hook and with RS of work facing, work 1 round dc round lower edge.

Next round (picot round) *3ch, ss into first of these 3ch, 1dc into each of next 3dc, rep from * to end, ss into first ch. Fasten off.

Work in same way round top and neck edge. Press seams. Sew 2 rem buttons to one end of strap at neck, using holes in patt on other end for buttonholes.

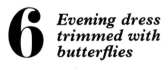
Sizes

To fit 86.5cm (*34in*) bust
Length to shoulder, 132.0cm (*52in*)

Tension

1 patt to 4.0cm (*1½in*) worked on No.4.00 (ISR) crochet hook

Materials

48 x 20grm balls Emu Tricel Nylon Double Knitting in main shade, A
1 x 20grm ball each of Emu Candelite in contrast colours, B, C and D
One No.4.50 (ISR) crochet hook
One No.4.00 (ISR) crochet hook
One No.3.50 (ISR) crochet hook
One No.3.00 (ISR) crochet hook
One No.2.50 (ISR) crochet hook
91.5cm (*1yd*) grosgrain ribbon
40.5cm (*16in*) zip fastener

Skirt

Using No.4.00 (ISR) hook and A, make 133ch and work in one piece, and beg at waist.

***Base row** Into 5th ch from hook work 2dtr, miss 3ch, 1dc into next ch, *3ch, 5dtr into next ch, miss 3ch, 1dc into next ch, rep from * 14 times, miss next 3ch, 3dtr into last ch. Turn.

Next row 1ch to count as first dc, 1dc into top of first dtr, 5dtr into next dc, *1dc into top of next group of 5dtr, 5dtr into next dc, rep from * ending last rep with 1dc into top of last dtr. Turn.

Next row (inc row) 4ch, 2dtr into first dc, *1dc into 3rd of 5dtr group, 5dtr into next dc, 1dc into top of next group, (3dtr, 1dc, 3dtr) into next dc, *, rep from * to * twice, (1dc into next group, 5dtr into next dc) twice, rep from * to * 3 times, patt to end. Turn.

Next row 1ch, patt to end working 1dc into 2nd of 3dtr group of inc. Turn.

Next row 4ch, 2dtr into first dc, 1dc into next group, patt to end, ending with 3dtr into last dc. Turn.

Work 2 more rows patt. ***.

Next row (inc row) 1ch, 1dc into top of first dtr, ** (*5dtr into next dc, 1dc into 3rd dtr of next 5dtr group, rep from * once, (3dtr, 1dc, 3dtr into next dc, 1dc into next group)**, 3 times, (5dtr into next dc, 1dc into next group) twice, rep from ** to ** 3 times, patt to end. Turn.

Work 8 more rows patt, working over inc as before.

Next row (inc row) 4ch, 2dtr into first dc, **(1dc into next group, *5dtr into next dc, 1dc into next group, rep from * once, (3dtr, 1dc, 3dtr) into next dc, 1dc into top of next group, 5dtr into next dc)**, 3 times, (1dc into next group, 5dtr into next dc) twice, rep from ** to ** 3 times, patt to end. Turn.

Work 10 rows, working over inc as before. Change to No.4.50 (ISR) hook and work 2 rows.

Next row (inc row) 1ch, 1dc into first dtr, **(*5dtr into next dc, 1dc into next group, rep from * twice, (3dtr, 1dc, 3dtr) into next group, 5dtr into next dc, 1dc into next group)**, 3 times, (5dtr into next dc, 1dc into next group) twice, rep from ** to ** 3 times, patt to end. Turn.

Work 16 rows in patt, working over inc as before.

Divide for front slit

Next row 4ch, 2dtr into first dc, 1dc into next group, *5dtr into next dc, 1dc into next group, rep from * twice, (3dtr, 1dc, 3dtr into next dc, 1dc into next group, **, 5dtr into next dc, 1dc into next group, **, rep from ** to ** 4 times) twice, 3dtr, 1dc, 3dtr into next dc, 1dc into next group, (5dtr into next dc, 1dc into next group) 3 times, turn.

Complete this side first. Work 10 rows patt, working over inc as before.

Next row 1ch, 1dc into top of next 5dtr, patt to end. Turn.

Next row Patt to last 5dtr group, 1dc into top of this group. Fasten off.

Return to where work was left.

Next row Miss next dc, rejoin yarn into 3rd dtr of next group, 1dc into this dtr, *5dtr into next dc, 1dc into top of next group, rep from * twice, (3dtr, 1dc, 3dtr into next dc, 1dc into next

group, **, 5dtr into next dc, 1dc into next group, **, rep from ** to ** 4 times) twice, 3dtr, 1dc, 3dtr into next dc, 1dc into next group, (5dtr into next dc, 1dc into next group) 3 times, 3dtr into last dc. Turn.

Work 10 rows, working over inc as before.

Next row Patt to last dc, 1dc into this dc. Turn.

Next row 3ch, 1dc into top of next group, patt to end. Fasten off.

Waist band

Sew back seam, leaving 25.5cm (*10in*) at waist open for zip. Using No.3.50 (ISR) hook and A, make 102 dc round waist of skirt. Work 6 more rows dc. Fasten off.

Bodice

Using No.3.50 (ISR) hook and A, make 133ch. Work in one piece as given for skirt from *** to ***. 7 rows. Change to No.4.00 (ISR) hook and work 5 more rows in patt.

Join bodice

Join last row with a ss to first dc at beg of row to form circle. Fasten off.

Next row Mark 12th dc from back seam with coloured thread and work 3ch, 2dtr into same dc, patt to end, ending with 3dtr into same first dc to form base of V neck opening. Turn.

Next row 1ch, 5dtr into next dc, patt to end, ending last patt with 1dc into top of turning ch. Turn.

Next row 3ch, 1dc into top of next group, patt to end, ending with 1dc into top of last dtr group. Turn.

Next row 4ch, 2dtr into first dc, patt to end, ending with 3dtr into last dc. Turn.

Left front

Next row 1ch, 3dtr into first dc, 1dc into top of next group, (5dtr into next dc, 1dc into top of next group) 3 times, turn.

Next row 4ch, 2dtr into first dc, 1dc into top of next group, (5dtr into next dc, 1dc into top of next group) twice, 5dtr into next dc, 1dc into top of last dtr. Turn.

Next row 4ch, 2dtr into first dc, patt to end. Turn.

Next row 4ch, patt to end, ending with 1dc into last dtr. Turn.

Next row 4ch, 1dc into top of next group, patt to end. Turn.

Next row 4ch, 2dtr into first dc, patt to end, ending with 3dtr into last dc. Turn.

Work 6 rows more.

Next row Patt to last dc, 1tr into this dc. Fasten off.

Back

Return to where work was left, miss first 5dtr for underarm, rejoin yarn to top of next 5dtr group, 1dc into same dtr, (5dtr into next dc, 1dc into top of next 5dtr group) 9 times, turn.

Next row 4ch, 2dtr into first dc, 1dc into top of next group, (5dtr into top of next group) 8 times, 3dtr into next dc. Turn.

Work 10 rows patt. Fasten off.

Right front

Return to where work was left, miss first 5dtr for underarm, rejoin yarn to top of next 5dtr group, 1dc into same dtr, (5dtr into next dc, 1dc into next group) 3 times, 3dtr into next dc, 1dc into last group. Turn.

Complete as given for left front, reversing shaping.

To make up

Do not press. Join shoulder seams. Join skirt to bodice. Work 1 row of dc along both sides of back opening for zip. Insert zip. Sew ribbon to inside of waist band.

Armbands Using No.3.50 (ISR) hook and A, work 1 row of patt of 1dc, 5dtr round armhole. Fasten off.

Neck edging Using No.4.00 (ISR) hook and A,

make 8ch.

Next row Into 5th ch from hook work 1tr, 1ch, miss 1ch, 1tr into last ch. Turn.

Next row 4ch, 1tr into next tr, 1ch, 1tr into 3rd ch of turning ch. Turn.

Rep last row until work is long enough to fit across back neck, down left front and up right front neck. Fasten off.

Using No.4.00 (ISR) hook, A and with RS of neck edging facing, rejoin yarn in first sp, *1dc into first sp, 5dtr into next sp, rep from * along one side of edge. Fasten off.

Next row *5dtr into next dc, 1dc into 5dtr group, rep from * to end. Fasten off.

Next row *1dc into 5dtr group, 5dtr into next dc, rep from * to end. Fasten off.

Change to No.3.50 (ISR) hook. Join in B.

Next row (picot row) Using B, 1dc into first dc, *1dc into each of next 3dtr, 3ch, ss into last dc, 1dc into each of next 2dtr, 1dc into next dc, rep from * to end. Break off B.

Rep last row using C and D. Stitch edging round neck. Work same edging and frill for hem and front slit of skirt.

Butterflies (optional)

Using No.3.00 (ISR) hook and B, make 4ch for first wing.

Next row Into 3rd ch from hook work 1dc, 1dc into last ch. Turn. 3dc.

Next row 3ch, 1tr into first dc, 2tr into next dc, 2tr into turning ch. Fasten off.

Next row Using C, 3ch, 1dtr into first tr, 2dtr into each tr to end. 12dtr. Fasten off.

Next row Using D and beg at cast on edge, work 1ch, 3dc into side edge of B, 4dc into side edge of C, 3dc into corner, 1dc into each of next 3dtr, 2dc into next dtr, 1dc into each of next 2dtr, 2dc between 4th and 5th tr of 2nd row of B, miss next dtr, 1dc into next dtr, 2dc into corner, 3dc into side edge of C, 2dc into side edge of B, ending at end of 2nd row of B. Fasten off.

Make another wing in same way.

Body

Using No.2.50 (ISR) hook and A, make 9ch.

Next row Into 3rd ch from hook 1dc, 1dc into each ch to end. Turn.

Next row 1ch, 1dc into each dc to end. Turn. 8dc. Rep last row once more.

Next row *Ss first st of last row tog with first ch on first row to form roll, rep from * to end. Sew pair of wings tog at commencing ch, place body over seam and sew on. Work 2 eyes in B on body using French knots.

Make 20 butterflies in this way, using different colours for each pair of wings. Sew on butterflies to skirt.

7 Long sleeved lacy smock

Sizes
To fit 81.5[86.5:91.5]cm (*32[34:36]in*) bust
Length to shoulder, 68.5[70.0:71.0]cm (*27[27½: 28]in*)
Sleeve seam, 51.0cm (*20in*)
The figures in brackets [] refer to the 86.5 (*34*) and 91.5cm (*36in*) sizes respectively

Tension
24 sts and 13 rows to 10cm (*3.9in*) over trebles worked on No.3.00 (ISR) crochet hook

Materials
10[10:11] x 50 grm balls Patons Cameo Crepe
One No.3.00 (ISR) crochet hook
One No.2.50 (ISR) crochet hook
3 buttons

Back
**Using No.3.00 (ISR) hook make 99[105:111]ch and beg at yoke. Place coloured marker in 97th[103rd:109th]ch.

1st row (WS) Into 4th ch from hook work 1tr, 1tr into each ch to end. 97[103:109] sts. Fasten off.

Shape armholes
Next row (RS) Miss first 16[17:18] sts, rejoin yarn into next 3ch, 1tr into each of next 64[68:72]sts, turn. 65[69:73]sts.

Next row 3ch, miss first st, 1tr into each st to end, 1tr into top of 3 turning ch. Turn. **.

Rep last row until work measures 18.0[19.0: 20.5]cm (*7[7½:8]in*) from beg, ending with a RS row.

Shape shoulders
Next row Ss over first 4 sts, 1dc into each of next 4 sts, 1htr into each of next 4[4:5]sts, 1tr into each of next 4[5:5]sts. Fasten off.

Miss first 33[35:37]sts, rejoin yarn to rem sts, 3ch, 1tr into each 3[4:4]sts, 1htr into each of next 4[4:5]sts, 1dc into each of next 4 sts. Fasten off.

***Using No.3.00 (ISR) hook and with RS of work facing, rejoin yarn into marked ch of starting ch.

Base row 3ch, 3tr into first ch, *2ch, miss 5ch, 7tr into next ch, rep from * ending last rep with 4tr into last ch. Turn. 15[16:17] groups of 7tr with 4tr at each end.

1st row 4ch, miss first tr, *1tr into next tr, 1ch, rep from * ending last rep with 1tr into top of 3ch. Turn.

2nd row 4ch, 1dc into first 1ch sp, 3ch, 1dc into next 1ch sp, *miss next tr, 1dc into next tr, 1ch, 1dc into next tr, 3ch, miss next 1ch sp, (1dc into next 1ch sp, 3ch, 4 times, rep from * ending last rep with miss next tr, 1dc into next tr, 1ch, 1dc into next tr, 3ch, miss next 1ch sp, 1dc into next 1ch sp, 3ch, 1dc into last 1ch sp, 2ch, 1htr into 3rd of 4ch. Turn.

3rd row 1ch, 1dc into first st, (3ch, 1dc into next 3ch sp) twice, *2ch, (1dc into next 3ch sp, 3ch) 4 times, 1dc into next 3ch sp, rep from * ending last rep with 2ch, (1dc into next 3ch sp, 3ch) twice, 1dc into 2nd of 4ch. Turn.

4th row 4ch, 1dc into first 3ch sp, *3ch, 1dc into next 3ch sp, rep from * ending last rep with 2ch, 1htr into last dc. Turn.

5th row 1ch, 1dc into first st, 3ch, 1dc into next 3ch sp, *5ch, miss next 3ch sp, (1dc into next 3ch sp, 3ch) twice, 1dc into next 3ch sp, rep from * ending last rep with 5ch, miss next 3ch sp, 1dc into next 3ch sp, 3ch, 1dc into 2nd of 4ch. Turn.

6th row 4ch, 1dc into first 3ch sp, *7ch, 1dc into next 3ch sp, 3ch, 1dc into next 3ch sp, rep from * ending last rep with 7ch, 1dc into last 3ch sp, 2ch, 1htr into last dc. Turn.

7th row 1ch, 2dc into 2ch sp, *1ch, 7tr into 4th of next 7ch, 1ch, 3dc into next 3ch sp, rep from * ending last rep with 1dc into last ch sp, 1dc into 2nd of 4ch. Turn.

8th row 3ch, *1tr into next tr, 1ch, rep from * ending last rep with 1tr into last tr, 1tr into last dc. Turn.

9th row 1ch, 1dc into first tr, *1dc into next tr, 3ch, miss 1ch sp, (1dc into next 1ch sp, 3ch) 4 times, miss next tr, 1dc into next tr, 1ch, rep from * ending last rep with 1dc into last tr, 1dc into top of 3ch. Turn.

10th row 3ch, *(1dc into next 3ch sp, 3ch) 4 times, 1dc into next 3ch sp, 2ch, rep from * ending with 2ch, 1htr into last dc. Turn.

11th row 4ch, *1dc into next 3ch sp, 3ch, rep from * ending last rep with 1dc into last 3ch sp, 2ch, 1htr into 2nd of 3ch. Turn.

12th row 5ch, *(1dc into next 3ch sp, 3ch) twice, 1dc into next 3ch sp, 5ch, miss next 3ch sp, rep from * ending last rep with 3ch, 1htr into 2nd of 4ch. Turn.

13th row 6ch, miss first 3ch sp, *1dc into next 3ch sp, 3ch, 1dc into next 3ch sp, 7ch, rep from * ending last rep with 4ch, 1htr into 2nd of 5ch. Turn.

14th row 3ch, 3tr into first st, 1ch, *3dc into next 3ch sp, 1ch, 7tr into 4th of next 7ch, 1ch, rep from * ending last rep with 4tr into 2nd of 6ch. Turn.

These 14 rows form patt. Rep patt 3 times more, then rows 1-13 once more.

Edging
Next row 1ch, 1dc into first st, 4ch, *ss into next 3ch sp, (5ch, ss into same 3ch sp) 3 times, 4ch, 1dc into 7ch sp, 4ch, rep from * ending last rep with 1dc into first of 6ch. Fasten off***

Front
Work as given for back from ** to **. Rep last row until work measures 11.5[12.5:14.0] cm (*4½[5: 5½]in*) from armhole shaping, ending with a RS row.

Shape neck
Next row 3ch, miss first st, 1tr into each of next 17[18:19] sts, (yrh, draw loop through next st, yrh, draw loop through first 2 loops on hook) twice, yrh, draw loop through 3 loops on hook— called dec 1 —, 1tr into next st, turn. 20[21:22] sts. Complete this side first.

Next row 3ch, miss first st, dec 1, 1tr into each st to end, 1tr into top of 3ch. Turn.

Next row 3ch, miss first st, 1tr into each st to last 3 sts, dec 1, 1tr into top of 3ch. Turn.

Rep last 2 rows once more. 16[17:18]sts. Cont without shaping until work measures same as back to shoulder, ending with a WS row.

Shape shoulder
Next row Ss over first 4 sts, 1dc into each of next 4 sts, 1 htr into each of next 4[4:5]sts, 1tr into each of next 3[4:4] sts, 1tr into top of 3ch. Fasten off.

Return to where work was left, with RS of work facing, miss first 23[25:27]sts, rejoin yarn into next st, 3ch, dec 1, 1tr into each st to end, 1tr into top of 3ch. Complete to match first side, reversing shaping.
Work as given for back from *** to ***.

Sleeves
Using No.3.00 (ISR) hook make 76[82:88]ch and beg at top.

Base row Into 4th ch from hook work 3tr, *2ch, miss 5ch, 7tr into next ch, rep from * ending last rep with 4tr into last ch. 11[12:13] groups of 7tr and 4tr at each end. Turn.

Cont in skirt patt as given for back until sleeve measures same as missed sts for underarm on back and fronts. Place markers at each end of last row. Cont without shaping until sleeve measures 51.0cm (*20in*) from markers, ending with a 13th patt row. Work edging as given for back.

To make up
Press each piece under a damp cloth with a warm iron. Join right shoulder seam, then join left shoulder seam for 1.5cm (*½in*) from armhole. Join side and sleeve seams to markers. Set in sleeves between markers to underarm sts left on back and front, then sew sleeve top in position.

Neck border Using No.2.50 (ISR) hook and with RS of work facing, work 3 rows dc all round neck. Fasten off.

Shoulder border back Using No.2.50 (ISR) hook and with RS of work facing, work 2 rows dc along back shoulder. Fasten off.

Shoulder border front Using No.2.50 (ISR) hook and with RS of work facing, work 2 rows dc along front shoulder, making 3 buttonholes on last row, by working 1ch, miss 2 sts. Fasten off. Press seams. Sew on buttons. Make 2 twisted cords and thread through last row of sleeves before edging, draw up and tie.

8 Cap sleeved waistcoat

Sizes
To fit 81.5[86.5:91.5:96.5]cm (32[34:36:38]in) bust
Length to shoulder, 94.0[95.0:96.5:98.0]cm (37[37½:38:38½]in)
The figures in brackets [] refer to the 86.5 (34), 91.5 (36) and 96.5cm (38in) sizes repectively

Tension
4 patt and 15 rows to 12.5cm (5in) over patt worked on No.3.50 (ISR) crochet hook

Materials
11[12:13:14] x 25 grm balls Patons Limelight Crepe
One No.4.00 (ISR) crochet hook
One No.3.50 (ISR) crochet hook
One No.3.00 (ISR) crochet hook
6 buttons

Back and fronts
Using No.3.00 (ISR) hook make 195[209:223:237]ch. Work in one piece to underarm.
1st row Into 2nd ch from hook work 1dc, 1dc into each ch to end. Turn. 194[208:222:236]sts.
2nd row 1ch, 1dc into first st, 1dc into each st to end. Turn.
3rd row As 2nd.
Change to No.4.00 (ISR) hook. Commence patt.
Base row 1ch, 1dc into first st, *4ch, miss 3 sts, 1dc into next st, 4ch, miss 2 sts, 1dc into next st, rep from * to last 4 sts, 4ch, miss 3 sts, 1dc into last st. Turn.
1st row (RS) 3ch, 3tr into first ch sp, *3ch, 1dc into next ch sp, 3ch 3tr into next ch sp, rep from * to end, 1tr into last dc. Turn.
2nd row 1ch, 1dc into first tr, *4ch, 1dc into next ch sp, rep from * ending last rep with 1dc into top of 3ch. Turn.
3rd row 5ch, 1dc into first ch sp, * 3ch, 3tr into next ch sp, 3ch, 1dc into next ch sp, rep from * to end, 3ch, 1tr into last dc. Turn.
4th row 1ch, 1dc into first tr, miss first ch sp, *4ch, 1dc into next ch sp, rep from * ending last rep with 1dc into 3rd of 5ch. Turn.
These 4 rows form patt and are rep throughout.
Cont in patt until work measures 53.5cm (21in) from beg. Change to 3.50 (ISR) hook. Cont in patt until work measures 75.0cm (29½)in from beg, ending with a 1st patt row.

Divide for armholes and shape neck
1st row Ss over first 4 sts, 1ch, 1dc into next ch sp, (4ch, 1dc into next ch sp) 11[11:13:13] times, turn.
Complete this side first.
2nd row Ss over first dc and 2ch, 3ch, 1tr into same ch sp, *3ch, 1dc into next ch sp, 3ch, 3tr into next ch sp, rep from * ending last rep with 2tr into last ch sp, turn.
3rd row Ss over first 2 sts, 1ch, 1dc into next ch sp, *4ch, 1dc into next ch sp, rep from * to end. Turn.
Rep last 2 rows 1[1:2:2] times more.
Next row 3ch, 3tr into first ch sp, *3ch, 1dc into next ch sp, 3ch, 3tr into next ch sp, rep from * ending last rep with 2tr into last ch sp. Turn.
Next row Ss over first 2 sts, 1ch, *1dc into next ch sp, 4ch, rep from * ending last rep with 1dc into top of 3ch. Turn.
Next row 5ch, 1dc into first ch sp, *3ch, 3tr into next ch sp, 3ch, 1dc into next ch sp, rep from * ending last rep with 2tr into last ch sp. Turn.
Next row Ss over first 2 sts, 1ch, 1dc into first ch sp, *4ch, 1dc into next ch sp, rep from * ending last rep with 1dc into 3rd of 5ch. Turn.
Next row 3ch, 3tr into first ch sp, *3ch, 1dc into next ch sp, 3ch, 3tr into next ch sp, rep from * ending last rep with 1tr into last dc. Turn.
Cont without shaping until armhole measures

19.0[20.5:21.5:23.0]cm (7½[8:8½:9]in) from beg, ending with a 1st of 3rd patt row. Fasten off.
Return to where work was left, with WS of work facing miss first 2[3:2:3] groups of 3tr, rejoin yarn into next ch sp, 1ch, 1dc into same ch sp, (4ch, 1dc into next ch sp) 25[25:29:29] times, turn.
Complete back first. Rep 2nd and 3rd rows as given for left front 2[2:3:3] times.
Next row 3ch, 3tr into first ch sp, *3ch, 1dc into next ch sp, 3ch, 3tr into next ch sp, rep from * ending last rep with 1tr into last dc. Turn.
Cont without shaping until back measures same as front to shoulder, ending with a 1st or 3rd patt row. Fasten off.
Return to where work was left, miss first 2[3:2:3] groups of 3tr, with WS of work facing, work 1ch, 1dc into same ch sp, (4ch, 1dc into next ch sp) 11[11:13:13] times, turn. Complete to match first front, reversing shaping.

Sleeves
Using No.3.00 (ISR) hook make 76[83:90:97] ch.
1st row Into 2nd ch from hook work 1dc, 1dc into each ch to end. Turn. 75[82:89:96] sts.
2nd row 1ch, 1dc into first st, 1dc into each st to end. Turn.
3rd row As 2nd.
Change to No.3.50 (ISR) hook. Work base row as given for back and fronts. Work 2nd and 3rd rows as given for left front shaping 5 times. Fasten off.

To make up
Press each piece under a dry cloth with a cool iron, omitting dc borders. Join shoulder seams. Set shaped edges of sleeves into armholes.
Front border Using No.3.00 (ISR) hook and with RS of work facing, work 3 rows dc up right front, round neck and down left front, working 6 buttonholes on right front on 2nd row, first to come at beg of neck shaping and last to come 35.5cm (14in) from lower edge, with 4 more evenly spaced between.
Next row (buttonhole row) Work in dc to first marker, *2ch, miss 2 sts, work in dc to next marker, rep from * to end.
Press seams. Sew on buttons.

9 Suit with matching hat

Sizes
Jacket to fit 81.5[86.5:91.5:96.5]cm (32[34:36:38]in) bust
Length to shoulder, 65.0[66.0:67.5:68.5]cm (25½[26:26½:27]in)
Sleeve seam, 14.0cm (5½in)
Skirt to fit 86.5[91.5:96.5:101.5]cm (34[36:38:40]in) hips
Length to waist, 57.0[58.5:59.5:61.0]cm (22½[23:23½:24]in)
The figures in brackets [] refer to the 86.5 (34), 91.5 (36) and 96.5cm (38in) bust sizes respectively

Tension
24 sts and 12 rows to 10 m (3.9in) over tr worked on No.3.00 (ISR) crochet hook; 22 sts and 34 rows to 10cm (3.9in) over patt worked on No.3.50 (ISR) crochet hook

Materials
Jacket 5[6:6:7] x 50 grm balls Patons Cameo Crepe in main shade, A
3[3:4:4] balls each of contrast colours, B and C
Skirt 6[7:7:8] balls in main shade, A
Hat 2 balls in main shade, A
Oddments of B and C

One No.3.50 (ISR) crochet hook
One No.3.00 (ISR) crochet hook
One No.2.50 (ISR) crochet hook
Waist length of petersham
20.5 cm (8in) zip
2 hook and eyes

Jacket
Pocket linings (make 2)
Using No.3.00 (ISR) hook and A, make 31ch.
1st row Into 2nd ch from hook work 1dc, 1dc into each ch to end. Turn. 30 sts.
2nd row 1ch, 1dc into first dc, 1dc into each dc to end. Turn.
Rep 2nd row until work measures 11.5cm (4½in) from beg. Fasten off.

Back and fronts
Using No.3.00 (ISR) hook and A, make 186[198:210:222]ch and work in one piece to underarm.
1st row (WS) Into 2nd ch from hook work 1dc, 1dc into each ch to end. Turn 185[197:209:221] sts.
2nd row 1ch, 1dc into first st, 1dc into each st to end. Turn.
Rep last row 5 times more. Change to No.3.50 (ISR) hook. Commence patt.
Base row 1ch, 1dc into first st, 1dc into each of next 10[11:13:10] sts, (miss next st, 1dc into each of next 17[18:19:21] sts) 9 times, miss next st, 1dc into each of next 11[13:14:11] sts. 175[187:199:211] sts. Turn.
**1st row 1ch, 1dc into first st, 1dc into each st to end. Turn.
2nd row As 1st.
3rd row As 1st. Join in B.
4th row Using B, 1ch, 1dc into first st, *1dc into next st 1 row below, 1dc into next st 2 rows below, 1dc into next st 3 rows below, 1dc into next st 2 rows below, 1dc into next st 1 row below, 1dc into next st, rep from * to end. Turn.
5th—7th rows Using B, as 1st. Join in C.
8th—11th rows Using C, as 4th—7th rows.
12th—15th rows Using A, as 4th—7th rows. **
The 4th—15th rows form patt. Cont in patt until work measures 14.0cm (5½in) from beg, ending with a 4th, 8th or 12th patt row.

Place pockets
Next row (WS) 1ch, 1dc into first st, 1dc into each of next 6[7:9:10] sts, miss next 30 sts and work across 30 sts of pocket, 1dc into each of next 101[111:119:129] sts, miss next 30 sts and work across 30 sts of other pocket, 1dc into each of last 7[8:10:11] sts. Turn.
Cont in patt until work measures 45.5cm (18in) from beg, ending with a WS row.

Divide for armholes
Keeping patt correct, work right front first.

Shape armhole and front edge
1st row Ss over first st, 1ch, patt across next 39[42:45:48] sts. turn.
Complete this side first.
2nd row Ss over 2 sts, 1ch, patt to end. Turn.
3rd row Patt to last 2 sts, turn.
4th row Ss over first st, 1ch, patt to end. Turn.
5th row Ss over first st, 1ch, patt to last st, turn.
6th row As 4th.
7th row Patt to last st, turn.
Rep 4th[4th and 5th:4th—6th:4th—7th rows] once more. 29[30:32:34] sts.
Keeping armhole edge without shaping, cont dec one st at front edge on every 4th row until 17[18:19:20] sts rem. Cont without shaping until work measures 65.0[66.0:67.5:68.5] cm (25½[26:26½:27]in) from beg, ending with a WS row.

Shape shoulder
1st row Patt to last 4[4:5:5] sts, turn.
2nd row Ss over 4[4:5:5] sts, 1ch, patt to end. Turn.
3rd row As 1st. Fasten off.

Return to where work was left, miss first 6 sts, rejoin yarn to rem sts, patt 83[89:95:101] sts, turn.
Complete back first.
Next row Ss over first 2 sts, 1ch, patt to last 2 sts, turn.
Rep last row once more.
Next row Ss over first st, 1ch, patt to last st, turn.
Rep last row 4[5:6:7] times more. 65[69:73:77] sts. Cont without shaping until back measures same as front to shoulder, ending with a WS row.
Shape shoulders
1st row Ss over 4[4:5:5] sts, 1ch, patt to last 4 [4:5:5] sts, turn.
Rep last row twice more. Fasten off.
Return to where work was left, miss first 6 sts, rejoin yarn to rem sts, patt to last st, turn.
Complete to match right front, reversing shaping.

Sleeves
Using No.3.00 (ISR) hook and A, make 62[62:68:68] ch.
Base row (WS) Into 4th ch from hook work 1tr, 1tr into each ch to end. Turn. 60[60:66:66] sts.
1st row 3ch, miss first st, 1tr into each tr to end, 1tr into top of 3ch. Turn.
2nd-4th rows As 1st.
5th and 6th rows 3ch, 1tr into first tr, 1tr into each tr to end, 2tr into top of 3ch. Turn.
7th row As 1st.
Rep last 3 rows until there are 72[74:78:80] sts. Cont without shaping until sleeve measures 14.0cm (5½in) from beg.
Shape top
1st row Ss over first 4tr and into next tr, 3ch, 1tr into each tr to last 4 sts, turn.
2nd row 3ch, miss first tr, (yrh, draw loop through next st, draw loop through first 2 loops on hook) twice, draw loop through all 3 loops on hook—called dec 1—, 1tr into each tr to last 3 sts, dec 1, 1tr into top of 3ch. Turn.
Rep last row until 34[34:38:38] sts rem.
Next row 3ch, miss first tr, (dec 1) twice, 1tr into each tr to last 5 sts, (dec 1) twice, 1tr into top of 3ch. Turn.
Rep last row until 22 sts rem. Fasten off.
Cuff
Using No.3.50 (ISR) hook, A and with WS of work facing, rejoin yarn into first ch of starting ch and work cuff.
1st row Using A, 1ch, 1dc into first ch, 1dc into each of next 5[5:6:6] ch, (miss next ch, 1dc into each of next 11[11:12:12] ch) 4 times, miss next ch, 1dc in to each of last 5[5:6:6] ch. 55[55:61:61] sts.
Work in patt from ** to ** as given for back. Fasten off.

To make up
Press each piece under a damp cloth with a warm iron. Join shoulder and sleeve seams. Set in sleeves. Turn back cuffs.
Pocket tops Using No.3.00 (ISR) hook, A and with RS of work facing, work 6 rows dc across 30 pocket top sts. Fasten off. Sew pocket top neatly to RS of work and sew pocket linings to WS.
Front and neck borders Using No.3.00 (ISR) hook, A and with RS of work facing, beg at lower edge of right front and work 1 row dc up right front, round back of neck and down left front. Turn. Work 7 more rows dc. Fasten off. Press seams.

Skirt back
Using No.2.50 (ISR) hook and A, make 149 155:161:167] ch.
Base row (WS) Into 2nd ch from hook work 1dc, 1dc into each ch to end. Turn. 148[154:160:

166] sts. Change to No.3.00 (ISR) hook.
Next row 3ch, miss first st, 1tr into each st to end. Turn.
Next row 3ch, miss first st, 1tr into each st to end, 1tr into top of 3ch. Turn.
Rep last row until work measures 7.5[9.0:10.0: 11.5]cm (3[3½:4:4½]in) from beg.
Shape skirt
Next row 3ch, miss first st, 1tr into each of next 13[14:15:16] tr, dec 1, 1tr into each of next 14[15:16:17] tr, dec 1, 1tr into each tr to last 32[34:36:38] tr, dec 1, 1tr into each of next 14[15:16:17] tr, dec 1, 1tr into each of next 13[14:15:16] tr, 1tr into top of 3ch. Turn.
Work 2 rows without shaping. Rep last 3 rows until 76[82:88:94] sts rem. Cont without shaping until work measures 54.5[56.0:57.0 58.5]cm (21½[22:22½:23]in) from beg. Change to No.2.50 (IRS) hook. Work 2.5cm (1in) dc. Fasten off.

Skirt front
Work as given for skirt back.

To make up
Press as given for jacket. Join side seams, leaving 20.5cm (8in) open at top of one side edge for zip. Sew in zip. Sew in petersham using casing st. Sew on hooks and eyes. Press seams.

Hat
Using No.3.00 (ISR) hook and A, make 6ch. Join with a ss to form circle.
1st round 3ch, work 15tr into circle. Join with a ss to top of first 3ch. 16tr.
2nd round 3ch, 1tr into base of 3ch, 2tr into each st to end. Join with a ss to top of first 3ch. 32 sts.
3rd round 3ch, 2tr into next tr, *1tr into next tr, 2tr into next tr, rep from * to end. Join with a ss to top of first 3ch. 48 sts.
4th round 3ch, 1tr into each of next 2tr, 2tr into next tr, *1tr into each of next 3tr, 2tr into next tr, rep from * to end. Join with a ss to top of first 3ch. 60 sts.
5th round 3ch, 1tr into each of next 4tr, 2tr into next tr, *1tr into each of next 5tr, 2tr into next tr, rep from * to end. Join with a ss to top off first 3ch. 70 sts.
6th round 3ch, 1tr into each of next 5tr, 2tr into next tr, *1tr into each of next 6tr, 2tr into next tr, rep from * to end. Join with a ss to top of first 3ch. 80 sts.
7th round 3ch, 1tr into each of next 6tr, 2tr into next tr, *1tr into each of next 7tr, 2tr into next tr, rep from * to end. Join with a ss to top of first 3ch. 90 sts.
8th round 3ch, 1tr into each of next 13tr, 2tr into next tr, *1tr into each of next 14tr, 2tr into next tr, rep from * to end. Join with a ss to top of first 3ch. 96 sts.
9th round 3ch, 1tr into each of next 14tr, 2tr into next tr, *1tr into each of next 15tr, 2tr into next tr, rep from * to end. Join with a ss to top of first 3ch. 102 sts.
10th round 3ch, 1tr into each of next 15tr, 2tr into next tr, *1tr into each of next 16tr, 2tr into next tr, rep from * to end. Join with a ss to top of first 3ch. 108 sts.
11th round 3ch, 1tr into each of next 16tr, 2tr into next tr, *1tr into each of next 17tr, 2tr into next tr, rep from * to end. Join with a ss to top of first 3ch. 114 sts.
12th round 3ch, 1tr into each of next 17tr, 2tr into next tr, *1tr into each of next 18tr, 2tr into next tr, rep from * to end. Join with a ss to top of first 3ch. 120 sts.
13th round 3ch, 1tr into each of next 18tr, 2tr into next tr, *1tr into each of next 19tr, 2tr into next tr, rep from * to end. Join with a ss to top of first 3ch. 126 sts.
14th round 3ch, 1tr into each tr to end. Join

with a ss to top of first 3ch.
Rep last round until work measures 18.0cm (7in) from beg. Change to No.2.50 (ISR) hook and work 4 rounds dc, turning at end of last round. Change to No.3.50 (ISR) hook.
Next row (WS) 1ch, 1dc into first st, 1dc into each of next 7 sts, (miss next st, 1dc into each of next 10 sts) 10 times, miss next st, 1dc into each of last 7 sts. Turn. 115 sts.
Work from ** to ** as given for jacket back. Fasten off.

To make up
Press as given for jacket. Join brim seam. Press seam. Turn back brim.

10,11 *Sleeveless cardigan and hat*

Sizes
To fit 84.0/86.5[89.0/91.5:94.0/96.5:99.0/101.5] cm (33/34[35/36:37/38:39/40]in) bust
Length to shoulder, 71.0[72.5:73.5:75.0]cm (28 [28½:29:29½]in)
The figures in brackets [] refer to the 89.0/91.5 (35/36), 94.0/96.5 (37/38) and 99.0/101.5cm (39/40in) sizes respectively
Tension
20 sts and 8 rows to 10cm (3.9in) over patt worked on No.4.00 (ISR) crochet hook
Materials
Jaeger Dappelwul
Cardigan 7[7:8:8] x 1 oz balls in main shade, A
5[5:5:6] balls each of contrast colours, B and C
Hat 1 x 1oz ball each of A, B and C
One No.4.00 (ISR) crochet hook
One No.3.50 (ISR) crochet hook
One No.3.00 (ISR) crochet hook
9 buttons.

Cardigan back and fronts
Using No.3.50 (ISR) hook and A, make 190 [202:210:222] ch and work in one piece to underarm.
1st row (WS) Into 2nd ch from hook work 1dc, 1dc into each ch to end. Turn. 189[201:209:221] sts.
2nd row 1ch, 1dc into first st, 1dc into each dc to end. Turn.
Rep last row 5 times more. Break off A. Change to No.4.00 (ISR) hook and join in colours as required. Commence patt.
1st row (RS) Using C, 3ch, 1tr into first st, *1ch, miss 3 sts, 3tr into next st, rep from * ending last rep with 2tr into last st. Turn.
2nd row Using A, *1ch, 3tr into next centre st of 3 sts missed on previous row, rep from * ending with ss into top of 3ch. Turn.
3rd row Using B, 3ch, 1tr into top of 3ch just worked into, *1ch, 3tr into 2nd of next 3tr of row in C, rep from * ending last rep with 2tr into last tr of row in C. Turn.
4th row Using C, *1ch, 3tr into 2nd of next 3tr of row in A, rep from * ending last rep with ss into top of 3ch. Turn.
5th row Using A, 3ch, 1tr into top of 3ch just worked into, *1ch, 3tr into 2nd of next 3tr of row in B, rep from * ending last rep with 2tr into last tr of row in B. Turn.
6th row Using B, *1ch, 3tr into 2nd of next 3tr of row in C, rep from * ending last rep with ss into top of 3ch. Turn.
7th row Using C, 3ch, 1tr into top of 3ch just worked into, *1ch, 3tr into 2nd of next 3tr of row in A, rep from * ending last rep with 2tr into last tr of row in A. Turn.

8th row Using A, *1ch, 3tr into 2nd of next 3tr of row in B, rep from * ending last rep with ss into top of 3ch. Turn.

The 3rd to 8th rows inclusive form patt. Work 2 more rows patt.

Shape darts

Next row Using A, 3ch, 1tr into top of 3ch just worked into, (1ch, 3tr into 2nd of next 3tr of row in B) 11[12:12:13] times, 1ch, 1tr into 2nd of next 3tr of row in B, (1ch, 3tr into 2nd of next 3tr of row in B) 22[23:25:26] times, 1ch, 1tr into 2nd of next 3tr of row in B, (1ch, 3tr into 2nd of next 3tr of row in B) 11[12:12:13] times, 1ch, 2tr into last tr of row in B. Turn.

Next row Using B, (1ch, 3tr into 2nd of next 3tr of row in C) 11[12:12:13] times, *1ch, 1tr into 2nd of next 3tr of row in C, yrh, draw loop through st just worked into, draw loop through first 2 loops on hook, yrh, draw loop through 2nd of next 3tr of row in C, draw loop through first 2 loops on hook, draw loop through all 3 loops on hook, 1tr into st just worked into, *, (1ch, 3tr in to 2nd of next 3tr of row in C) 21[22:24:25] times, rep from * to * once, (1ch, 3tr into 2nd of next 3tr of row in C) 11[12:12:13] times, ss in to top of 3ch. Turn. 181[193:201:213] sts. Work 6 rows patt without shaping.

Next row Using C, 3ch, 1tr into top of 3ch just worked into, (1ch, 3tr into 2nd of next 3tr of row in A) 11[11:12:12] times, 1ch, 1tr into 2nd of next 3tr of row in A, (1ch, 3tr into 2nd of next 3tr of row in A) 20[23:23:26] times, 1ch, 1tr into 2nd of next 3tr of row in A, (1ch, 3tr into 2nd of next 3tr of row in A) 11[11:12:12] times, 1ch, 2tr into last tr of row in A. Turn.

Next row Using A, (1ch, 3tr into 2nd of next 3tr of row in B) 11[11:12:12] times, *1ch, 1tr into 2nd of next 3tr of row in B, yrh, draw loop through st just worked into, draw loop through first 2 loops on hook, yrh, draw loop through 2nd of next 3tr of row in B, draw loop through first 2 loops on hook, draw loop through all 3 loops on hook, 1tr into st just worked into, *, (1ch, 3tr into 2nd of next 3tr of row in B) 19[22:22:25] times, rep from * to * once, (1ch, 3tr into 2nd of next 3tr of row in B) 11[11:12:12] times, ss into top of 3ch. Turn. 173[185:193:205] sts. Cont in patt without shaping until work measures 51.0cm (20in) from beg, ending with a WS row.

Divide for armholes

Keeping continuity of patt correct work right front first.

1st row Using colour of previous row, ss over ss, 1tr and into next tr, using correct colour, 1ch, patt across 8[9:9:9] groups, ss into 2nd of next 3tr, turn.

****2nd row** Using colour of previous row, ss over ss, 1tr and into next tr, using correct colour, 1ch, patt to last group, ss into 2nd of these 3tr, turn.

Rep last row 4 times more. **. 3[4:4:4] groups.

7th row Using colour of previous row, ss over ss, 1tr and into next tr, using correct colour, 1ch, patt to end. Turn.

8th row Patt to last group, ss into 2nd of these 3tr. turn.

Rep last 2 rows 0[1:1:1] time more. 2 groups.

Cont in patt without shaping until work measures 71.0[72.5:73.5:75.0]cm (28[28½:29:29½]in) from beg. Fasten off.

With RS of work facing miss first 3[3:4:5] groups for underarm, using correct colour rejoin yarn to 2nd of next 3tr, 1ch, patt 18[19:19:20] groups, ss into 2nd of next 3tr, turn.

Work as given for right front from ** to **. 13[14:14:15] groups. Cont in patt without shaping until back measures same as front to shoulder. Fasten off.

With RS of work facing miss first 3[3:4:5] groups for underarm, using correct colour rejoin yarn to 2nd of next 3tr, 1ch, patt to last groups,

ss into 2nd of last 3tr, turn.

Complete to match right front, reversing shaping.

To make up

Press under a damp cloth with a warm iron. Join shoulder seams.

Armbands Using No.3.00 (ISR) hook, A and with RS of work facing, work 5 rounds dc round armholes. Fasten off.

Front border Using No.3.00 (ISR) hook, A and with RS of work facing, beg at lower edge of right front and work 5 rows dc up right front, round neck and down left front, working 9 buttonholes on 3rd row of right front by working 2ch and missing 2dc, inc and dec in corners as required. Fasten off.

Pockets (make 2) Using No.3.00 (ISR) hook and A, make 31ch. Work 12.5cm (5in) dc. Fasten off. Sew on pockets and buttons. Press seams.

Hat

Using No.3.50 (ISR) hook and A, make 5ch. Join with a ss to first ch to form circle.

1st round 3ch, 15tr into circle. Join with a ss to top of first 3ch. 16 sts.

2nd round 3ch, 1tr into base of 3ch, 2tr into each st to end. Join with a ss to top of first 3ch. 32 sts.

3rd round 3ch, 1tr into each of next 2 sts, 2tr into next st, *1tr into each of next 3 sts, 2tr into next st, rep from * to end. Join with a ss to top of first 3ch. 40 sts.

4th round As 3rd. 50 sts.

5th round 3ch, 1tr into each of next 3 sts, 2tr into next st, (1tr into each of next 4 sts, 2tr into next st) 9 times. Join with a ss to top of first 3ch. 60 sts.

6th round 3ch, 1tr into each of next 4 sts, 2tr into next st, (1tr into each of next 5 sts, 2tr into next st) 9 times. Join with a ss to top of first 3ch. 70 sts.

Cont inc in this way on next 3 rounds. 100 sts. Change to No.4.00 (ISR) hook and join in colours as required. Commence patt.

1st round Using C, 3ch, 1tr into base of 3ch, *1ch, miss 3 sts, 3tr into next st, rep from * ending last rep with 1tr into base of 3ch. Join with a ss to top of first 3ch.

2nd round Using A, *1ch, 3tr into next centre st of 3 missed sts of previous round, rep from * to end. Join with a ss to first ch.

3rd round Using B, 3ch, 1tr into base of 3ch, 1ch, *3tr into 2nd of next 3tr of round in C, 1ch, rep from * ending with 1tr into base of 3ch. Join with a ss to top of first 3ch.

4th round Using C, *1ch, 3tr into 2nd of next 3tr of round in A, rep from * to end. Join with a ss to first ch.

5th round Using A, as 3rd but working into round of B.

6th round Using B, as 4th but working into round of C.

7th round Using C, as 3rd but working into round of A.

8th round Using A, as 4th but working into round of B.

The 3rd to 8th rounds form patt. Cont in patt until work measures 18.0cm (7in) from beg, ending with a 4th, 6th or 8th round. Break off B and C. Cont using A only. Change to No.3.00 (ISR) hook.

Headband

Next round 1ch, 1dc into base of 1ch, *1dc into each of next 3tr, 1dc into 2nd of next 3tr 2 rounds down, rep from * ending last rep with 1dc into each of last 3tr. Join with a ss to first dc. 100 sts.

Work 4 more rounds dc. Fasten off.

To make up

Press as given for cardigan.

12 *Long-line sleeveless waistcoat*

Sizes

To fit 84.0/86.5[89.0/91.5:94.0/96.5]cm (33/34[35/36:37/38]in) bust
Length to shoulder, 71.0[72.5:73.5]cm (28[28½: 29]in) excluding border
The figures in brackets [] refer to the 89.0/91.5 (35/36) and 94.0/96.5 (37/38in) sizes respectively

Tension

6 patt to 12.0cm (4¾in) and 8 rows to 9.0cm (3½in) worked on No.5.00 (ISR) crochet hook

Materials

6[7:8] x 50 grm balls of Patons Double Knitting in main shade, A
2[2:2] balls of contrast colour, B
One No.5.00 (ISR) crochet hook
One No.4.00 (ISR) crochet hook

Back

Using No.5.00 (ISR) hook and A, make 68[74:80] ch.

Base row Into 4th ch from hook work 2tr, *1ch, miss 2ch, 3tr into next ch, rep from * 19[21:23] times more, 1ch, miss 2ch, 2tr into next ch, 1tr into last ch. Turn. 22[24:26] blocks. Commence patt. Join in B.

****1st row** Using A, 3ch to count as first tr, *using B work 1ch, 3tr into next sp, using A work 1ch, 3tr into next sp, rep from * ending with 3tr in B in last sp, 1ch in A, 1tr in A in last st. Turn. Break off A.

2nd row Using B, 3ch, 2tr into first sp, *1ch, 3tr into next sp, rep from * to end. Turn. Join in A.

3rd row As 1st. Break off B.

4th row Using A, 3ch, 2tr into first sp, *1ch, 3tr into next sp, rep from * to end. Turn.

5th row Using A, 4ch to count as first tr and 1ch sp, *3tr into next sp, 1ch, rep from * ending with 3tr into last sp, 1ch, 1tr into last st. Turn.

6th and 7th rows As 4th and 5th.

8th row As 4th.

These 8 rows form the pattern. Work patt rows 4 times more, then work 1st-4th rows once more.

Shape armholes

Keep 2 colour patt correct throughout.

1st row Ss into 2nd[2nd:3rd] sp, 3ch, 2tr in same sp, *1ch, 3tr in next sp, rep from * until 3tr have been worked in 2nd[2nd:3rd] sp from end, turn.

2nd row Ss over first 2 sts, 3ch, 2tr in first sp, *1ch, 3tr in next sp, rep from * until 3tr have been worked in last sp, turn.

Rep 2nd row 4[5:4] times more. Keeping patt correct work without shaping until 8th band in B has been completed, then work 2[3:4] rows A.

Shape neck

1st size only

1st row Using A, 3ch, 2tr in first sp, (1ch, 3tr in next sp) twice, 1ch, 3tr in next sp, turn.

2nd row Using A, ss over first st, 3ch, 2tr in first sp, (1ch, 3tr in next sp) twice, 1ch, 1tr in last st. Fasten off.

2nd and 3rd sizes only

1st row Using A, 3ch, 2tr in first sp, (1ch, 3tr in next sp) 3 times, miss 2tr, 1tr in next tr, turn.

2nd row Using A, ss over first st, 4ch, (3tr in next sp, 1ch) 3 times, 1tr in last st. Fasten off.

1st size only

Return to where work was left, miss first 6 sp, rejoin yarn to next sp, 3ch, 1tr in same sp, patt to end. Complete to match first side, reversing shaping.

2nd and 3rd sizes only

Return to where work was left, miss first 7[8] sp, (Continued on next text page.)

7,8

Attractive, long sleeved, lacy smock (left) and (right) a long, button-through jacket with cap sleeves.

Sizes: (left) to fit 81.5[86.5:91.5]cm (32[34:36]in) bust; (right) as above plus 96.5cm (38in) bust

PATONS

9

Pretty threesome comprising a short sleeved, unbuttoned jacket, neatly shaped skirt and matching beret.

Sizes: to fit 81.5[86.5:91.5: 96.5]cm (32[34:36: 38]in) bust

10,11

Striking sleeveless cardigan with round neck and trimmed with patch pockets, plus a pretty pull-on hat.

Sizes: to fit 84.0/ 86.5[89.0/91.5: 94.0/96.5:99.0/ 101.5]cm (33/34 [35/36:37/38: 39/40]in) bust Hat to fit an average head

12

Casual, edge-to-edge, sleeveless waistcoat, worked in two colours, Long-line to team with trousers, with a neat round neckline.

Sizes: to fit 84.0/86.5[89.0/91.5: 94.0/96.5]cm (33/34 [35/36:37/38]in) bust

13

Unusual striped jersey with dolman sleeves and a shirt front opening

Sizes: to fit 86.5 [91.5:96.5:101.5]cm (34[36:38:40]in) bust

JAMES WEDGE

SIRDAR

14

*Jazzy beach wrap
for anytime.*

*Sizes: to fit
81.5|86.5[91.5|96.5]
cm (32|34[36|38]in)
bust*

15

*Bright, summer
halter top with
flower motif.*

*Sizes: to fit 86.5
[91.5:96.5]cm (34[36:
38]in) bust*

16

Superbly styled,
belted, wrapover coat,
for town or country
wear. Worked in
three colours with
a shawl collar and
deep square armholes.

Sizes : to fit 86.5
[91.5:96.5:101.5]cm
34[36:38:40]in) bust

PATONS

(Continued from last text page.)
rejoin yarn to next tr, 3ch, 3tr in next sp, patt to end. Complete to match first side, reversing shaping.

Left front
Using No.5.00 (ISR) hook and A, make 32[35:38] ch.
Base row Into 4th ch from hook work 2tr, *1ch, miss 2ch, 3tr in next ch, rep from * 7 [8:9] times more, 1ch, miss 2ch, 2tr in next ch, 1tr in last ch. Turn. 10[11:12] blocks.
1st and 3rd sizes only
1st and 3rd rows As 1st row of back.
2nd row As 2nd row of back.
4th row As 4th row of back.
2nd size only
1st and 3rd rows Using A, 4ch, 3tr in first sp, *using B, 1ch, 3tr in next sp, using A, 1ch, 3tr in next sp, rep from * ending with 3tr in B in last sp, 1ch in A, 1tr in A in last st. Turn.
2nd row As 2nd row of back.
4th row As 4th row of back.
All sizes
Keeping continuity of patt as on back, cont without shaping until front measures same as back to underarm, ending with same patt row.
Shape armhole
Keep 2 colour patt correct throughout.
1st row Ss to 2nd[2nd:3rd] sp, 3ch, 2tr in same sp, 1ch, 3tr in next sp, patt to end. Turn.
2nd row Work in patt until 3tr have been worked in last sp, turn.
3rd row Ss over first 2 sts, 3ch, 2tr in next sp, 1ch, 3tr in next sp, patt to end. Turn.
Work 3[4:3] more rows, dec at armhole edge as before on every row. Work 4[3:4] rows without shaping, ending at armhole edge.
Shape neck
Keep 2 colour patt correct as given for back.
1st row Work in patt until 3tr have been worked in last sp, turn.
2nd row Ss over first 2 sts, 3ch, 2tr in next sp, 1ch, 3tr in next sp, patt to end. Turn.
Work 3[3:4] more rows dec at neck edge as before on every row. Work 4[5:5] rows without shaping. Fasten off.

Right front
Work as given for left front, reversing shaping and noting that on 2nd size only the 1st and 3rd patt rows will read as foll:
1st and 3rd rows Using A, 3ch, (using B 1ch, 3tr in next sp, using A 1ch, 3tr in next sp) 5 times, using A 1ch, 1tr in last st. Turn.

To make up
Press each piece under a damp cloth with a warm iron. Join shoulder and side seams.
Edging Using No.4.00 (ISR) hook, A and with RS of work facing, beg at lower edge of right side seam and work a row of dc all round edges. Turn. Work another row of dc, inc in corner sts as required. Turn. Work a row of tr all round, inc in corner sts as before. Fasten off. Work edging round armholes in same way.
Press seams and edgings.

13 Striped jersey with dolman sleeves

Sizes
To fit 86.5[91.5:96.5:101.5]cm (34[36:38:40]in) bust
Length to shoulder, 62.0[63.5:65.0:65.0]cm (24½[25:25½:25½]in)
Sleeve seam from neck edge, 63.5[63.5:65.0:66.0]cm (25[25:25½:26]in)
The figures in brackets [] refer to the 91.5 (36in), 96.5 (38) and 101.5cm (40in) sizes respectively

Tension
16 sts to 7.5cm (3in) and 32 rows to 10cm (3.9in) over patt worked on No.3.50 (ISR) crochet hook
Materials
5[5:5:6] x 50 grm balls Patons Cameo Crepe in main shade, A
4[4:4:5] balls each of contrast colours, B and C
One No.3.50 (ISR) crochet hook
One No.3.00 (ISR) crochet hook
6 buttons

Back
Using No.3.50 (ISR) hook and A, make 104 [108:116:120]ch.
1st row Into 2nd ch from hook work 1dc, 1dc into each ch to end. Turn. 103[107:115:119] sts.
2nd row 1ch, 1dc into each st to end. Turn.
3rd row As 2nd. Join in B.
4th row Using B and with RS of work facing, 1ch, 1dc into each of next 3 sts, *insert hook into next st 2 rows below, yrh and draw through a loop, yrh and draw through 2 loops — called 1Ldc —, 1dc into each of next 3 sts, rep from * to end. Turn.
5th row Using B, 1ch, 1dc into each st to end. Turn. Join in C.
6th row Using C, 1ch, 1dc into first dc, *1Ldc into centre dc of 3dc, 1dc into each of next 3 sts, rep from * to last 2 sts, 1Ldc into centre dc of next 3dc, 1dc into last st. Turn.
7th row Using C, 1ch, 1dc into each dc to end. Turn.
The last 4 rows form patt and are rep throughout. Keeping patt correct, work striped patt as foll: (2 rows A, 2 rows B and 2 rows C) throughout. Cont in patt as now set, dec one st at each end of next and every foll 8th row until 91[95:103:107] sts rem. **. Cont without shaping until work measures 42.0cm (16½in) from beg, ending with a WS row.
Shape sleeves
Keeping patt correct as now set, inc one st at each end of next 8 rows. 107[111:119:123] sts.
9th row 5ch, into 2nd ch from hook work 1dc, 1dc into each of next 3ch, patt to end. Turn.
Rep last row 7 times more. 139[143:151:155] sts.
17th row 13ch, into 2nd ch from hook work 1dc, 1dc into each of next 11ch, patt to end. Turn.
Rep last row 7 times more. 235[239:247:251] sts.
25th row Work 13[11:10:11]ch, into 2nd ch from hook work 1dc, 1dc into each of next 11[9:8:9] ch, patt to end. Turn.
Rep last row once more. 259[259:265:271] sts.
Keeping patt as now set, cont without shaping until back measures 59.5[61.0:62.0:62.0]cm (23½[24:24½:24½]in)from beg, ending with a WS row.
Shape sleeve top and shoulders
1st row Ss over first 8[8:10:12] sts, patt to last 8[8:10:12] sts, turn.
2nd row Ss over first 12 sts, patt to last 12 sts, turn.
Rep last row 8 times more. Fasten off.

Front
Work as given for back to **. Cont without shaping until front measures 31.5[33.0:33.0:33.0] cm (12½[13:13:13]in) from beg, ending with a WS row.
Divide for front opening
1st row Patt 42[44:48:50] sts, turn.
Complete this side first. Cont without shaping until side edge measures same as back to sleeve shaping, ending with a WS row.
Shape sleeve
Keeping patt as now set, inc one st at side edge on next 8 rows. 50[52:56:58] sts.
9th row 5ch, into 2nd ch from hook work 1dc, 1dc into each of next 3ch, patt to end. Turn.
10th row Patt to end. Turn.
Rep last 2 rows 3 times more. 66[68:72:74] sts.
17th row 13ch, into 2nd ch from hook work 1dc,

1dc into each of next 11ch, patt to end. Turn.
18th row Patt to end. Turn.
Rep last 2 rows 3 times more. 114[116:120:122]sts.
25th row Work 13[11:10:11] ch, into 2nd ch from hook work 1dc, 1dc into each of next 11[9:8: 9] ch, patt to end. Turn. 126[126:129:132] sts. Cont without shaping until front measures 54.5[56.0:56.0:56.0] cm (21½[22:22:22]in) from beg, ending with a WS row.
Shape neck
Next row Patt to last 3[3:4:5] sts, turn. Dec one st at neck edge on next 7 rows. 116[116:118:120] sts. Cont without shaping until sleeve edge measures same as back to shoulder, ending with a WS row.
Shape top and shoulder
Next row Ss over first 8[8:10:12] sts, patt to end. Turn.
Next row 1ch, patt to last 12 sts, turn.
Next row Ss over first 12 sts, patt to end. Turn.
Rep last 2 rows 3 times more. Fasten off.
Using No.3.50 (ISR) hook, with RS of work facing and using colour required, miss first 7 sts, rejoin yarn to next st, patt to end. Complete to match first side, reversing shaping.

To make up
Press under a damp cloth with a warm iron. Join sleeve tops and shoulders.
Neckband Using No.3.00 (ISR) hook, A and with RS of work facing, beg at top of right front and work 13 rows dc all round neck edge. Fasten off.
Left front border Using No.3.00 (ISR) hook, A and with RS of work facing, beg at top of left front and work 9 rows dc along left side of opening. Fasten off.
Right front border Mark position for 6 buttons on left front, first to come 1.5cm (½in) above lower edge and last to come in centre of neckband, with 4 more evenly spaced between. Work right front border as given for left front border, working buttonholes when markers are reached on 5th row by working 2ch, miss 2dc, then work 2dc into each 2ch sp on next row. Sew down base of borders.
Cuffs Using No.3.00 (ISR) hook, A and with RS of work facing, work in dc along lower edge of sleeve. Turn. Cont in dc for a further 6.5cm (2½in). Fasten off. Join side and sleeve seams. Press seams. Sew on buttons.

14 Jazzy beach wrap

Sizes
To fit 81.5/86.5[91.5/96.5]cm (32/34[36/38]in) bust
Length to shoulder, 61.0[71.0cm] (26[28]in)
Sleeve seam, 35.5[38.0]cm (14[15]in)
The figures in brackets [] refer to the 91.5/96.5 cm (36/38in) size only
Tension
18 sts to 10cm (3.9in) over tr worked on No.4.00 (ISR) crochet hook; 16 sts to 10cm (3.9in) over tr worked on No.4.50 (ISR) crochet hook
Materials
Sirdar Wash 'n' Wear Double Crepe
3 x 40 grm balls in main shade, A
2 balls each of contrast colours, B, C, D, E, F and G
One No.4.50[5.00] (ISR) crochet hook
One No.4.00[4.50] (ISR) crochet hook

Yoke
Using No.4.00[4.50] (ISR) hook and B, make 156ch loosely.
1st row (RS) Into 4th ch from hook work 1tr, 1tr into each ch to end. Turn. 154tr. Break off B. Join in C.

Divide for left front

1st row Using C, *3ch, 1tr into each of next 26tr, turn. Break off C.
Rep last row 11 times more, using D, E, B, A, F, G, D, C, E, F and B in turn. Fasten off at end of last row.

Shape neck
Using No.4.00[4.50] (ISR) hook, A and with WS of work facing, miss first 8tr and leave for neck, rejoin yarn to next tr, 3ch, 1tr into end. Break off A. Rep last row 7 times more, using C, G, D, B, F, C, and E. Fasten off.

Divide for back
Using No.4.00[4.50] (ISR) hook, C and with WS of work facing, miss first 22tr for armhole, rejoin yarn to next tr, 3ch, 1tr into each of next 55tr, turn. Break off C. Work 19 more rows in tr, using colours as given for left front in same order. Fasten off.

Divide for right front
Using No.4.00[4.50] (ISR) hook, C and with WS of work facing, miss first 22tr for armhole, rejoin yarn to next tr, 3ch, 1tr into each of next 26tr. Turn. Break off C. Complete to match left front, reversing neck shaping.

Bodice

Using No.4.50[5.00] (ISR) hook, E and with RS of yoke facing, rejoin yarn to first commencing ch.
1st row 3ch, miss 1ch, (1tr, 1ch, 1tr) all into next ch, *(miss 1ch, (1tr, 1ch, 1tr) all into next ch) 7 times, (1tr, 1ch, 1tr) all into next ch, *, rep from * to * 8 times, (miss 1ch, (1tr, 1ch, 1tr) all into next ch) 7 times, miss 1ch, 1tr into first of 3ch. Turn. Break off E. 80 1ch sp.
2nd row Using D, 3ch, *(1tr, 1ch, 1tr) all into next 1ch sp, rep from * to end, 1tr into 3rd of first 3ch. Turn. Break off D.
3rd row Using B, 4ch, *(1dtr, 1ch, 1dtr) all into next 1ch sp, rep from * to end, 1dtr into 3rd of first 3ch. Turn. Break off B.
4th row Using A, 4ch, *(1dtr, 1ch, 1dtr) all into next 1ch sp, rep from * to end, 1dtr into 4th of first 4ch. Turn. Break off A.
5th row Using D, 6ch, *1dtr into next 1ch sp, 2ch, rep from * to end, 1dtr into 4th of first 4ch. Turn. Break off D.
6th row Using G, 4ch, *(1dtr, 1ch, 1dtr) all into next dtr, rep from * to end, 1dtr into 4th of first 6ch. Turn. Break off G.
7th row Using E, 9ch, *miss 3dtr, 1dc in next dtr, 8ch, rep from * ending with miss 4dtr, 1dc into 4th of first 4ch. Turn.
8th row Using E, 1ch, *7tr into next ch loop, 1dc into next dc, rep from * to end, working last dc into first of first 9ch. Turn. Break off E.
9th row Using F, 6ch, *(1dtr, 3ch, 1dtr) all into centre tr of 7tr, 3ch, rep from * ending with (1dtr, 3ch, 1dtr) all into centre tr of 7tr, 2ch, 1dtr into first 1ch. Turn.
10th row Using F, 4ch, *(1dtr, 1ch) 4 times into next 3ch sp, 1dtr into same sp, miss next 3ch sp, rep from * ending with (1dtr, 1ch) 4 times into last 3ch sp, 1dtr into same sp, 1dtr into 4th of first 6ch. Turn. Break off F.
11th row Using B, 6ch, *(1dtr, 3ch, 1dtr) all into centre dtr of 5dtr, 3ch, rep from * ending with (1dtr, 3ch, 1dtr) all into centre dtr of 5dtr, 2ch, 1dtr into 4th of first 4ch. Turn. Break off B.
12th row Using D, 3ch, *2tr into next ch sp, 3tr into next ch sp, rep from * to last ch sp, 2tr into last ch sp, 1tr into 4th of first 6ch. Turn. Break off D.
13th row Using A, 4ch, *(1dtr, 1ch) 4 times into centre tr of next 3tr gr, 1dtr into same tr, rep from * to end, 1dtr into 3rd of first 3ch. Turn. Break off A.
14th row Using G, 6ch, work as given for 11th row.
15th row Using D, 3ch, work as given for 12th row.
16th row Using C, 6ch, *(1dtr, 1ch, 1dtr,

1dtr) all into centre tr of 3tr gr, 2ch, rep from * to end, 1dtr into 3rd of first 3ch. Turn. Break off C.
17th row Using E, 6ch, *(1dc, 5ch, 1dc) all into centre dtr of 3dtr gr, 5ch, rep from * to end, 1dc into 4th of first 6ch. Turn. Break off E.
18th row Using B, 3ch, miss next ch sp, *7tr into next ch sp, 1dc into next ch sp, rep from * to last 2 ch sps, 7tr into next ch sp, miss next sp, 1dc into first of first 6ch. Turn. Break off B.
19th row Using F, 5ch, *miss 1tr, 1tr into next tr, 1ch, miss 1tr, 1dc into next tr, 1ch, miss 1tr, 1tr into next tr, miss 1tr, 1dtr into next dc, rep from * ending with 1dtr into 2nd of first 3ch. Turn. Break off F.
20th row Using A, 2ch, *7tr into next dc, 1ch, 1dc into next dtr, 1ch, rep from * to last dc, 7tr into last dc, 1ch, 1dc into 5th of first 5ch. Turn. Break off A.
21st row Using D, 5ch, work as given for 19th row.
22nd row Using G, 10ch, 1dc into next dtr, *8ch, 1dc into next dtr, rep from * ending with 1dc into 4th of first 5ch. Turn.
23rd row Using G, 3ch, *9tr into next ch loop, 1dc into next dc, rep from * ending with 1tr into 2nd of first 10ch. Turn. Break off G.
24th row Using E, 6ch, *1dc into centre tr of 9tr gr, 8ch, rep from * ending with 6ch, 1dc into 3rd of first 3ch. Turn.
25th row Using E, 3ch, 4tr into next ch loop, 1dc into next dc, *9tr into next ch loop, 1dc into next dc, rep from * to last ch loop, 4tr into last ch loop, 1tr into 2nd of first 6ch. Turn. Break off E.
26th row Using B, 7ch, 1dtr into next tr, *4ch, (1dtr, 3ch, 1dtr) all into centre tr of 9tr gr, rep from * ending with 4ch, 1dtr into last tr, 3ch, 1dtr into 3rd of first 3ch. Turn. Break off B.
27th row Using F, 3ch, 2tr into 3ch sp, *3tr into 4ch sp, 3tr into 3ch sp, rep from * ending with 2tr into last ch sp, 1tr into 4th of first 7ch. Turn. Break off F.
28th row Using C, 4ch, 1dtr into each tr to end, 1dtr into 3rd of first 3ch. Turn. Break off C.
29th row Using A, 1dtr into next dtr, 4ch, 1dc into top of dtr just worked, 2ch, miss 3dtr, *2dtr into next dtr, 4ch, 1dc into dtr just worked, 2ch, miss 2dtr, rep from * ending with miss 3dtr, 1dtr into next dtr, 4ch, 1dc into top of dtr just worked, miss 1dtr, 1dtr into 4th of first 4ch. Fasten off.

Sleeves

Using No.4.00[4.50] (ISR) hook and G, make 69ch loosely and beg at top.
1st row (RS) Into 4th ch from hook work 1tr, 1tr into each ch to end. Turn. Break off G. 67tr.
2nd row Using C, *3ch, 1tr into each tr to end, 1tr into 3rd of first 3ch. Turn. Break off C.
Rep last row 11 times more, using F, B, E A B, C, D, F, G, A and C in turn. Change to No.4.50[5.00] (ISR) hook.
1st row Using E, 3ch, *miss 1tr, (1tr, 1ch, 1tr) all into next tr, rep from * to last 2tr, miss 1tr, 1tr into 3rd of first 3ch. Break off E. 32 1ch sp.
Rep 2nd-20th rows inclusive as given for bodice. Fasten off.

To make up
Press each piece under a damp cloth with a cool iron. Join shoulder seams. Join sleeve seams leaving 7.0[7.5]cm (2¾[3]in) free at underarm. Sew rem of sleeve seam to tr at armholes. Set in sleeves.
Edging Using No.4.00[4.50] (ISR) hook, A and with RS of work facing, rejoin yarn at lower edge of right front, 2ch to count as first dc, work 1 row dc along front edge having multiples of 3 sts plus 1, work 9dc across front neck, work 50dc evenly across right neck, back neck and left neck,

work 9dc across front neck and work 1 row dc along front edge as given for right front. Fasten off. Using No.4.00[4.50] (ISR) hook, A and with RS of work facing, rejoin yarn at lower edge of right front to first dc.
Next row 7ch, 1dc into 3rd of 7ch, *1ch, miss 2dc, 1tr into next dc, 4ch, 1dc into top of tr just worked, *, rep from * to * until neck shaping is reached, (1ch, 1tr in next dc, 4ch, 1dc into top of tr just worked) twice, (1ch, miss 2dc, 1tr in next dc, 4ch, 1dc into top of tr just worked) twice, miss 3dc, 1tr into next dc, rep from * to * 15 times, miss 3dc, 1tr into next dc, (1ch, miss 2dc, 1tr into next dc, 4ch, 1dc into top of tr just worked) twice, 1ch, 1tr into next dc, 4ch, 1dc into top of tr just worked noting that neck edging is now completed, 1ch, 1tr into next dc, 4ch, 1dc into top of tr just worked, rep from * to * ending at lower edge of left front. Fasten off.

15 Bright, summer halter top with motif

Sizes
To fit 86.5[91.5:96.5]cm (*34[36:38]in*) bust
The figures in brackets [] refer to the 91.5 (*36*) and 96.5cm (*38in*) sizes respectively

Tension
24 sts and 12 rows to 10cm (*3.9in*) over tr worked on No.3.50 (ISR) crochet hook

Materials
5[5:6] x 25grm balls Twilleys Cortina in main shade, A
Oddments of contrast colours, B, C, D and E
One No.4.00 (ISR) crochet hook
One No.3.50 (ISR) crochet hook
7 small buttons

Front
Using No.4.00 (ISR) hook and B, beg at centre of motif and make 5ch. Join with a ss to first ch to form circle.
1st round (RS) 4ch to count as first dtr, 4dtr into circle, *2ch, 5dtr into circle, rep from * twice more, 2ch. Join with a ss to 4th of first 4ch. Turn to WS.
2nd round (WS) *4ch over back of next dtr petal, ss over each of next 2ch between petals, rep from * 3 times more. Turn.
3rd round Using C, work 3ch, 2tr, 5dtr, 3tr into 4ch loop at back of petal, *2ch, 3tr, 5dtr, 3tr into next 4ch loop, rep from * twice more, 2ch. Join with a ss to 3rd of first 3ch. Turn to WS.
4th round *9ch over back of next petal, ss over each of next 2ch between petals, rep from * 3 times more. Turn.
5th round Using D, 3ch, 3tr, 9dtr, 4tr into first loop, *2ch, 4tr, 9dtr, 4tr into next loop, rep from * twice more, 2ch. Join with a ss to 3rd of first 3ch. Turn to WS.
6th round *11ch over back of next petal, ss over each of next 2ch between petals, rep from * 3 times more. Turn.
7th round Using E, 3ch, 3tr, 11dtr, 4tr into first loop, *2ch, 4tr, 11dtr, 4tr into next loop, rep from * twice more, 2ch. Join with a ss to 3rd of first 3ch. Turn.
8th round Using E, 1ch, 1dc into each of next 9 sts, (1dc, 1ch, 1dc) into each of next 9 sts, 1dc into 2ch sp, *1dc into each of next 9 sts, (1dc, 1ch, 1dc) into next dtr, 1dc into each of next 9 sts, 1dc into 2ch sp, rep from * twice more. Join with a ss to first ch. Break off yarn.
Using No.3.50 (ISR) hook and A, beg in any 1ch sp of last round of motif, work 4ch to count as first tr and 1ch sp, 1tr into 1ch sp, work 1tr into each of next 21dc to 1ch sp, *(1tr, 1ch, 1tr) into 1ch sp, 1tr into each dc to next 1ch sp, rep

from * twice more. Join with a ss to 3rd of first 4ch

Next round 3ch, 1tr, 1ch, 2tr into 1ch sp of corner, 1tr into each tr to next 1ch sp of corner, *2tr, 1ch, 2tr into 1ch sp of corner, 1tr into each tr to next corner, rep from * twice more. Join with a ss to 3rd of first 3ch.
Rep last round 3[4:5] times more.

Shape square
Complete each side of square separately.
Next row 3ch, 1tr into each of next 2tr leaving last loop of each tr on hook, yrh and draw through all loops on hook — called dec 1 —, 1tr into each tr to last 2tr before next corner, 1tr into each of next 2tr leaving last loop on hook, yrh and draw through all loops, turn.
Next row 3ch, dec 1, 1tr into each tr to last 2tr before next corner, dec 1, turn.
Rep last row until all sts are worked off.
Complete each side in same way.

Side edge
Using No.4.00 (ISR) hook, A and with RS of work facing, work 60[64:68]tr along one side of square for right back edge. Work 6[7:8] more rows tr.

Shape back
Cont in tr, keeping waist edge without shaping and dec one st at back edge at beg of next and every alt row 12 times in all. Fasten off.
Using No.4.00 (ISR) hook, A and with RS of work facing, rejoin yarn to opposite side of square and work left back to match right back, reversing shaping.

Top edge
Using No.4.00 (ISR) hook, A and with RS of work facing, rejoin yarn to centre 1ch sp of top of square and work right front neck.
Next row 3ch, work 1tr into each tr along top of square, 2tr into each of next 6 row ends of back, dec 1 over next row end, turn.
Next row 3ch, dec 1, 1tr into each tr to last 2tr, dec 1. Turn.
Next row 3ch, 1tr into each tr to last 2tr, dec 1. Turn.
Rep last 2 rows until 5tr rem. Work 28.0cm (11in) on these sts or required length of strap. Fasten off.
Using No.4.00 (ISR) hook, A and with WS of work facing, rejoin yarn to centre 1ch sp at top of square and work left front neck to match right front neck, reversing shaping.

Waist edging
Using No.4.00 (ISR) hook, A and with RS of work facing, rejoin yarn at waist and work 1 row dc along waist edge. Turn.
Next row 5ch to count as 1dtr and 1ch, *miss 1dc, 1dtr into next dc, 1ch, rep from * to end. Fasten off.
Fold row of dtr in half to WS and sl st down.

Button band
Using No.3.50 (ISR) hook, A and with RS of work facing, work 4 rows dc along left side of centre back. Fasten off. Mark positions for 7 buttons on this edge.

Buttonhole band
Using No.3.50 (ISR) hook, A and with RS of work facing, work 2 rows dc along right side edge of centre back.
Next row (buttonhole row) 1dc into each of next 2dc, *4ch, miss 4dc, work in dc to next marker, rep from * to end.
Next row Work in dc to end, working 4dc into each 4ch sp of previous row.
Work 1 more row dc. Fasten off.

To make up
Press each piece lightly under a damp cloth with a warm iron omitting centre motif. Using No.4.00 (ISR) hook, and respective colours, work 1dc

into each tr, dtr and 2ch sp of each petal on every layer of petals working (1dc, 1ch, 1dc) into centre dtr of each petal. Fasten off.
Edging Using No.4.00 (ISR) hook, A and with RS of work facing, beg at top of right back and work as given for waist edging to top of strap. Work other side of back in same way.
Beg at inner edge of strap and work in same way down strap, round neck and along inner edge of other strap. Fasten off. Complete as given for waist edging. Sew on buttons.

16 Smart, belted wrapover coat

Sizes
To fit 86.5[91.5:96.5:101.5]cm (34[36:38:40]in) bust
Length to shoulder, 99.0[100.5:101.5:103.0]cm (39[39½:40:40½]in)
Sleeve seam, 45.5cm (18in)
The figures in brackets [] refer to the 91.5 (36), 96.5 (38) and 101.5cm (40in) sizes respectively

Tension
15½ sts and 12 rows to 10cm (3.9in) over htr worked on No.4.50 (ISR) crochet hook

Materials
Patons Capstan
6[6:7:7] x 50 grm balls in main shade, A
12[13:13:14] balls of contrast colour, B
12[12:13:14] balls of contrast colour, C
One No.4.50 (ISR) crochet hook

Back
Using No.4.50 (ISR) hook and A, make 92[96: 100:104]ch loosely.
Base row (RS) Into 3rd ch from hook work 1htr, 1 htr into each ch to end. Turn. 91[95:99:103]sts.
1st row 2ch, miss first st, 1htr into each st to end. Turn.
Rep 1st row twice more.

Shape darts
4th row (dec row) 2ch, miss first st, 1htr into of next 8 sts, yrh, insert hook into next st and draw yarn through, insert hook into next st and draw yarn through, yrh and draw through all 4 loops on hook — called dec 1 —, 1htr into each st to last 11 sts, dec 1, 1htr into each st to end. Turn.
Rep 1st-4th rows 3 times more, then 1st row once more. Break off A. Join in C.
18th row Using C, 5ch, miss first 2 sts, *(yrh loosely, insert hook into next st and draw yarn through, pull loop up to height of 2.5cm (1in) 4 times all into same st, yrh and draw through all 9 loops on hook — called 1cl —, 2ch, miss one st, rep from * to last st, 1dtr in turning ch. Turn. Break off C. Join in A.
19th row Using A, 2ch, 1htr in first sp, work 2htr into each sp ending with 2htr in last sp, 1htr into 3rd of first 5ch. Turn.
20th and 21st rows As 1st.
Break off A. Join in C.
22nd row As 18th.
Break off C. Join in B.
23rd to 25th rows Using B, as 19th to 21st rows.
26th row Using B, as 4th.
27th to 29th rows Using B, as 1st.
Rep 26th to 29th rows 3 times more. 75[79:83: 87] sts.
42nd and 43rd rows Using B, as 1st.
Break off B. Join in A.
44th row Using A, as 18th.
Break off A. Join in B.
45th row Using B, as 19th.
Using B, cont in htr without shaping until work measures 73.5cm (29in) from beg, ending with a WS row. Break off B. Join in A.

Next row Using A, as 18th
Break off A. Join in C.
Next row As 19th. **.
Shape armholes
Cont using C throughout.
Next row Ss into each of next 10[11:12:13] sts, 2ch, do not miss a st, 1htr into each st to last 9[10:11:12] sts, turn.
Cont without shaping until work measures 99.0[100.5:101.5:103.0]cm (39[39½:40:40½]in) from beg, ending with a RS row. Fasten off.

Right front
***Using No.4.50 (ISR) hook and A, make 56[58:60:62]ch loosely.
Base row (RS) Into 3rd ch from hook work 1htr, 1htr into each ch to end. Turn. 55[57:59:61] sts. ***.
Work as given for back from ** to **, shaping dart as foll:
4th row (dec row) Patt to last 11 sts, dec 1, patt to end. Turn.
Shape armhole
Cont using C throughout.
Next row 2ch, miss first st, 1htr into each st to last 9[10:11:12] sts, turn.
Cont without shaping until front measures same as back to shoulder, ending at armhole edge. Fasten off.

Left front
Work as given for right front from *** to ***, then work as given for back from ** to **, shaping dart as foll;
4th row (dec row) 2ch, miss first st, 1htr into each of next 8 sts, dec 1, patt to end. Turn.
Shape armhole
Cont using C throughout.
Next row Ss into each of next 10[11:12:13] sts, 2ch, do not miss a st, 1htr into each st to end. Turn.
Cont without shaping until front measures same as back to shoulder, ending at front edge. Do not break off yarn. Sew 17[18:18:19] sts of fronts to corresponding sts of back to form shoulders.

Collar
Return to where work was left, using No.4.50 (ISR) hook, 2ch, miss first st, 1htr into each of next 20[20:21:21] sts, work 23[23:25:25] htr across back then 1htr into each of next 21[21:22: 22] sts across top of right front. 65[65:69:69] sts. Cont in htr until collar measures 19.0cm (7½in) from beg. Fasten off.

Sleeves
Using No.4.50 (ISR) hook and C, make 40[42: 44:46] ch loosely.
Base row Into 3rd ch from hook work 1htr, 1htr into each ch to end. Turn. 39[41:43:45] sts.
Cont in htr, inc one st at each end of every foll 5th row until there are 57[59:61:63] sts. Cont without shaping until sleeve measures 45.5cm (18in) from beg. Break off C. Join in A.
Next row Using A, as 18th row of back.
Break off A. Join in B.
Next row Using B, as 19th row of back.
Using B, work 2 rows htr. Break off B. Join in A.
Next row Using A, as 18th row of back.
Next row Using A, as 19th row of back. Fasten off.

Belt
Using No.4.50 (ISR) hook and B, make 200 [203: 206:209]ch loosely. Work 5 rows htr. Work 1 round of htr all round edges of belt, working 2htr into each corner. Join with a ss. Fasten off.

To make up
Press each piece lightly under a damp cloth with a warm iron. Join side seams. Join sleeve seams

for 45.5cm (*18in*). Set in sleeves, sewing rows at top of sleeves to armhole shaping of back and and fronts.

Edging Using No.4.50 (ISR) hook, C and with RS of work facing beg at lower edge of right front, work 2 rows dc all round front and collar edges. Fasten off.

Press seams and edging.

17 Gossamer-light stole

Size
Width 56.0cm (*22in*), length 157.5cm (*62in*)
Tension
1 patt to 18.5cm (*7¼in*) and 14 rows to 20.0cm (*7¾in*) over patt worked on No.4.00 (ISR) crochet hook
Materials
7 x 50 grm balls Patons Kismet
One No.4.00 (ISR) crochet hook
One No.3.00 (ISR) crochet hook

Stole
Using No.4.00 (ISR) hook make 126ch. Mark 2nd ch from hook with coloured thread.

1st row (RS) Into 2nd ch from hook work 1dc, 3ch, *1dc into next ch, 5ch, miss next 7ch, 5tr into next st — called 1 shell —, (miss 2ch, 1dc into next ch, miss 2ch, 1 shell into next ch) 4 times, 5ch, miss 7ch, 1dc into next ch, 5ch, rep from * ending last rep with 3ch, 1dc into last ch. Turn.

2nd row Ss into first dc, 4ch, 2tr into next 3ch sp, *5ch, (1dc into 3rd tr of next shell, 1 shell into next dc) 4 times, 1dc into 3rd tr of next shell, 5ch, miss next 5ch sp, 1 shell into next 5ch sp, rep from * ending last rep with 2tr into last 3ch sp, 1ch, 1tr into last ch. Turn.

3rd row 5ch, miss first tr, 3tr into next 1ch sp, *5ch, (1dc into 3rd tr of next shell, 1 shell into next dc) 3 times, 1dc into 3rd tr of next shell, 5ch, (3tr, 3ch, 3tr) into 3rd tr of next shell, rep from * ending last rep with 3tr in sp between last tr and 4ch, 1ch, 1dtr into 3rd of 4ch. Turn.

4th row 1ch, 1dc into first dtr, *3ch, miss next tr, 1 shell into next tr, 5ch, (1dc into 3rd tr of next shell, 1 shell into next dc) twice, 1dc into 3rd tr of next shell, 5ch, miss next 5ch sp and next tr, 1 shell into next tr, 3ch, 1dc into next 3ch sp, rep from * ending last rep with 1dc into 4th of 5 turning ch. Turn.

5th row 3ch, 1dc into first 3ch sp, *3ch, 1 shell into 3rd tr of next shell, 5ch, 1dc into 3rd tr of next shell, 1 shell into next dc, 1dc into 3rd tr of next shell, 5ch, 1 shell into 3rd tr of next shell, (3ch, 1dc into next 3ch sp) twice, rep from * ending last rep with 1dc into last 3ch sp. Turn.

6th row 4ch, 4dtr into first 1ch sp, *3ch, 1 shell into 3rd tr of next shell, 5ch, (1dc, 10ch) 5 times and 1dc all into 3rd tr of next shell, 5ch, 1 shell into 3rd tr of next shell, 3ch, miss next 3ch sp, 9dtr into next 3ch sp, rep from * ending last rep with 3ch, 5dtr into last sp between last dc and turning ch. Turn.

7th row 5ch, miss first dtr, (1dtr into next dtr, 1ch) 3 times, 1dtr into next dtr, *1 shell into 3rd tr of next shell, (1dc into next 10ch sp, 3ch) 4 times, 1dc into next 10ch sp, 1 shell into 3rd tr of next shell, (1dtr into next dtr, 1ch) 8 times, 1dtr into next dtr, rep from * ending last rep with (1dtr into next dtr, 1ch) 4 times, 1dtr into top of turning ch. Turn.

8th row 3ch, 2tr into first dtr, (1dc into next dtr, 1 shell into next dtr) twice, *5ch, miss next shell and next 3ch sp, (1dc into next 3ch sp, 5ch) twice, (1 shell into next dtr, 1dc into next dtr) 4 times, 1 shell into next dtr, rep from * ending last rep with (1 shell into next dtr, 1dc into next dtr) twice, 3tr into 4th of 5 turning ch. Turn.

9th row 1ch, 1dc into first tr, (1 shell into next dc, 1dc into 3rd tr of next shell) twice, *5ch, miss next 5ch sp, 1 shell into next 5ch sp. 5ch, (1dc into 3rd tr of next shell, 1 shell into next dc) 4 times, 1dc into 3rd tr of next shell, rep from * ending last rep with (1dc into 3rd tr of next shell, 1 shell into next dc) twice, 1dc into top of turning ch. Turn.

10th row 3ch, 2tr into first dc, 1dc into 3rd tr of next shell, 1 shell into next dc, 1dc into 3rd tr of next shell, *5ch, (3tr 3ch, 3tr) into 3rd tr of next shell, 5ch, (1dc into 3rd tr of next shell, 1 shell into next dc) 3 times, 1dc into 3rd tr of next shell, rep from * ending last rep with 1dc into 3rd tr of next shell, 1 shell into next dc, 1dc into 3rd tr of next shell, 3tr into last dc. Turn.

11th row 1ch, 1dc into first tr, 1 shell into next dc, 1dc into 3rd tr of next shell, *5ch, miss next 5ch sp and next tr, 1 shell into next tr, 1dc into next 3ch sp, 3ch, miss next tr, 1shell into next tr, 5ch, (1dc into 3rd tr of next shell, 1 shell into next dc) twice, 1dc into 3rd tr of next shell, rep from * ending last rep with 1dc into 3rd tr of next shell, 1 shell into next dc, 1dc into top of turning ch. Turn.

12th row 3ch, 2tr into first dc, *1dc into 3rd tr of next shell, 5ch, 1 shell into 3rd tr of next shell, (3ch, 1dc into next 3ch sp) twice, 3ch, 1 shell into 3rd tr of next shell, 5ch, 1dc into 3rd tr of next shell, 1 shell into next dc, rep from * ending last rep with 1dc into 3rd tr of next shell, 3tr into last dc. Turn.

13th row 10ch, (1dc into first tr, 10ch) twice, 1dc into same tr, *5ch, miss next 5ch sp, 1 shell into 3rd tr of next shell, 3ch, miss next 3ch sp, 9dtr into next 3ch sp, 3ch, miss next 3ch sp, 1 shell into 3rd tr of next shell, 5ch, (1dc, 10ch) 5 times all into 3rd tr of next shell, 1dc into same tr, rep from * ending last rep with (1dc, 10ch) twice into top of turning ch, 1dc into same ch, 5ch, 1tr tr into same ch as last dc. Turn.

14th row 1ch, miss tr tr, 1dc into 5ch sp, (3ch, 1dc into next 10ch sp) twice, *1 shell into 3rd tr of next shell, (1dtr into next dtr, 1ch) 8 times, 1dtr into next dtr, 1 shell into 3rd tr of next shell, 1dc into next 10ch sp, (3ch, 1dc into next 10ch sp) 4 times, rep from * ending last rep with (3ch, 1dc into next 10ch sp) twice. Turn.

15th row 1ch, 1dc into first dc, 3ch, 1dc into first 3ch sp, *5ch, miss next 3ch sp and next shell, (1 shell into next dtr, 1dc into next dtr) 4 times, 1 shell into next dtr, 5ch, miss next shell and 3ch, 1dc into next 3ch sp, 5ch, 1dc into next 3ch sp, rep from * ending last rep with 1dc into last 3ch sp, 3ch, 1dc into last dc. Turn.

The 2nd — 15th rows form patt and are rep throughout. Rep patt 3 times more. Fasten off. Using No.4.00 (ISR) hook and with RS of work facing, rejoin yarn into first ch of starting ch.

Next row 1ch, 1dc into same ch, 3ch, *1dc into next ch, 5ch, miss 7ch, 1 shell into next ch, (miss 2ch, 1dc into next ch, miss 2ch, 1 shell into next ch) 4 times, 5ch, miss 7ch, 1dc into next ch, 5ch, rep from * ending last rep with 3ch, 1dc into marked ch. Turn.

Work 2nd — 15th rows 4 times more. Fasten off.

To make up
Using No.3.00 (ISR) hook, work 1 row dc along each straight side. Do not press.

18 Patchwork evening skirt

Sizes
To fit 91.5/99.0cm (*36/39in*) hips
Length to waist, 95.0[105.5]cm (*37½[41½in*]) The figures in brackets [] refer to the 105.5cm (*41½in*) length only

Tension
Each square measures 10cm (*3.9in*) by 10cm (*3.9in*) worked on No.3.50 (ISR) crochet hook
Materials
Patons Cameo-Crepe 4-ply
5[6] x 50 grm balls in main shade, A
5[5] balls each of contrast colours, B and C
One No.3.50 (ISR) crochet hook
One No.3.00 (ISR) crochet hook
Waist length of petersham
20.5cm (*8in*) zip fastener
Note
Join in colours as required and carry yarn not in use along back of square

1st square
Using No.3.50 (ISR) hook and B, make 4ch. Join with a ss to first ch to form circle.

1st round Using B, 3ch, 2tr into circle, (1ch, 3tr into circle) 3 times, 1ch. Join with a ss to top of first 3ch.

2nd round Using B, ss into last ch sp of previous round, 3ch, 2tr, 1ch, 3tr into this ch sp, (3tr, 1ch, 3tr into next ch sp) 3 times. Join with a ss to top of first 3ch. Join in A.

3rd round Using A, ss into sp between first and last group of previous round, 3ch, 2tr into this sp, 3tr, 1ch, 3tr into next ch sp—called corner group—, (3tr in sp between 2 groups, 1 corner group) 3 times. Join with a ss to top of first 3ch.

4th round Using B, ss into sp between first and last group of previous round, 3ch, 2tr into this sp, 3tr into each sp between groups and 1 corner group into each corner to end. Join with a ss to top of first 3ch.

5th round Using C, as 4th.

6th round Using A, as 4th. Fasten off.

2nd square
As 1st square reading C for B and B for C.

3rd square
Using No.3.50 (ISR) hook and A, make 4ch. Join with a ss to first ch to form circle.

1st round Using A, 3ch, 2tr into circle, (1ch, 3tr into circle) 3 times, 1ch. Join with a ss to top of first 3ch. Break off A. Join in B.

2nd round Using B, ss into last ch sp of previous round, 3ch, 2tr, 1ch, 3tr into this ch sp, (1ch, 3tr, 1ch, 3tr into next ch sp) 3 times, 1ch. Join with a ss to top of first 3ch.

3rd round Using B, (4tr, 1ch, 4tr into next ch sp, 1dc into next ch sp between groups) 4 times. Join with a ss to ss of previous round. Break off B. Join in C.

4th round Using C, ss into last ch sp of 2 rounds below, 4ch, 2dtr, 1ch, 3dtr into this ch sp, 3tr, 1ch, 3tr into next corner ch sp, (3dtr, 1ch, 3dtr into next ch sp of 2 rounds below, 3tr, 1ch, 3tr into next corner ch sp) 3 times. Join with a ss to top of first 4ch.

5th round Using C, 3ch, 2tr into last sp between groups of previous round, 3tr into next ch sp, 3tr into next sp, 3tr, 1ch, 3tr into next corner ch sp, (3tr into next sp, 3tr into next ch sp, 3tr into next sp, 3tr, 1ch, 3tr into next corner ch sp) 3 times. Join with a ss to top of first 3ch. Break off C. Join in A.

6th round Using A, ss into last sp of previous round, 3ch, 2tr into this sp, 3tr into each sp and 3tr, 1ch, 3tr into each corner ch sp to end. Join with a ss to top of first 3ch. Fasten off.

4th square
As 3rd square reading C for B and B for C.

Skirt
Work 24[30] each of 1st and 4th squares and 30[30] each of 2nd and 3rd squares.

To make up
Press each square under a dry cloth with a cool

iron. Using flat seam join squares as foll:
1st strip Beg with 3rd square and alternating squares join three 3rd squares and three 2nd squares. Join 9 more strips in same way.
2nd strip Beg with 1st square and alternating squares join three 1st squares and three 4th squares. Join 7[9] more strips in same way.
Back short version Beg with 1st strip and alternating strips join 9 strips tog, forming an oblong 6 squares wide and 9 squares long. Make another piece for front in same way.
Back long version Work as for short version beg with 1st strip and alternating strips join 10 strips tog, forming an oblong 6 squares wide and 10 squares long.
Join side seams leaving opening in one side for zip.
Waistband Using No.3.00 (ISR) hook, A and with RS of work facing, beg at side opening and work 168dc along waist edge, working 14dc along each square. Work 4.0cm (1½in) dc. Fasten off.
Lower edge Using No.3.50 (ISR) hook, A and with RS of work facing, work 1dc into each st and 1dc into each seam between squares along lower edge. Join with a ss. Work 1 more round dc. Fasten off. Cut petersham and sew inside waistband. Sew in zip. Press seams.

19 Long sleeved dress

Sizes
To fit 84.0/89.0cm (*33/35in*) bust
89.0/94.0cm (*35/37in*) hips
Length to shoulder, 96.5cm (*38in*)
Sleeve seam, 42.0cm (*16½in*)
Tension
1 lace patt to 7.5cm (*3in*) worked on No.4.50 (ISR) crochet hook; 3 block patts to 6.5cm (*2½in*) worked on No.3.50 (ISR) crochet hook
Materials
21 x 20grm balls Lee Target Duo Double Crepe Tricel Nylon *or*
24 x 25grm balls Lee Target Motoravia Double Knitting
One No.4.50 (ISR) crochet hook
One No.4.00 (ISR) crochet hook
One No.3.50 (ISR) crochet hook
2 buttons

Back
Using No.4.50 (ISR) hook make 94ch and beg at lower edge.
Base row Into 2nd ch from hook work 1dc, 1dc into each of next 2ch, *4ch, miss 3ch, 1tr into each of next 3ch, 4ch, miss 3ch, 1dc into each of next 4ch, rep from * ending last rep with 1dc into each of last 3ch. Turn.
Commence patt.
1st row (WS) 1dc into each of first 2dc, *4ch, 2tr into 4ch sp, 2ch, 2tr into next 4ch sp, 4ch, 1dc into each of 2 centre dc of previous row, rep from * ending last rep with 2dc into end dc, 4ch. Turn.
2nd row 2tr into first 4ch sp, *4ch, 2dc into 2ch sp, 4ch, 2tr into next 4ch sp, 2ch, 2tr into next 4ch sp, rep from * ending last rep with 2ch, 1tr into end dc, 3ch. Turn.
3rd row 1tr into 2ch sp, *4ch, 1dc into next 4ch sp, 1dc into each of next 2dc, 1dc into next 4ch sp, 4ch, 3tr into 2ch sp, rep from * ending last rep with 4ch, 2tr into turning ch sp, 4ch. Turn.
4th row 2tr into first 4ch sp, *4ch, 1dc into each of 2 centre dc of previous row, 4ch, 2tr into 4ch sp, 2ch, 2tr into next 4ch sp, rep from * ending last rep with 2ch, 1tr into top of turning ch. Turn.

5th row 1dc into first tr, 1dc into 2ch sp, *4ch, 2tr into 4ch sp, 2ch, 2tr into next 4ch sp, 4ch, 2dc into 2ch sp, rep from * ending last rep with 2dc into turning ch sp. Turn.
6th row 1dc into each of first 2dc, *1dc into 4ch sp, 4ch, 3tr into 2ch sp, 4ch, 1dc into next 4ch sp, 1dc into each of next 2dc, rep from * to end. Turn.
These 6 rows form patt. Cont in patt until work measures 30.5cm (*12in*) from beg when slightly stretched. Change to No.4.00 (ISR) hook. Cont in patt until work measures 53.5cm (*21in*) from beg, when slightly stretched, ending with a 5th row.
Change to No.3.50 (ISR) hook. Commence block patt.
1st row 3ch, 3tr into first ch sp, *1ch, 3tr into next ch sp, rep from * to last 2dc, 1ch, 1tr into last dc. Turn. 21 blocks.
2nd row 3ch, 2tr into first ch sp, *1ch, 3tr into next ch sp, rep from * to last st, 1ch, 3tr into turning ch sp. Turn.
3rd row 3ch, 3tr into first ch sp, *1ch, 3tr into next ch sp, rep from * to last 3tr, 1ch, 1tr into last tr. Turn.
The 2nd and 3rd rows form patt. Cont in patt until work measures 73.5cm (*29in*) from beg, ending with a 2nd row.
Shape armholes
1st row Ss across first 3tr, miss next block, 3ch, 3tr into next ch sp, patt to last ch sp, 1ch, 1tr into this ch sp, turn.
2nd row 3ch, miss first block, 3tr into next ch sp, patt to turning ch, 1ch, 1tr into turning ch. Turn.
Rep 2nd row 3 times more. 15 blocks. Beg with a 2nd row cont in patt without shaping until armholes measure 10.0cm (*4in*) from beg, ending with a 2nd row.
Divide for back opening
1st row 3ch, 3tr into first ch sp, (1ch, 3tr into next ch sp) 6 times, 1ch, 1tr into next ch sp, turn.
2nd row 3ch, 2tr into first ch sp, *1ch, 3tr into next ch sp, rep from * to turning ch, 1ch, 3tr into turning ch. Turn.
Cont in patt until armhole measures 18.0cm (*7in*) from beg, ending with a 3rd row.
Next row 3ch, 2tr into first ch sp, (1ch, 3tr into next ch sp) 3 times, (1ch, 3dc into next ch sp) 4 times. Fasten off.
Return to where work was left, rejoin yarn to next st.
1st row 3ch, miss one block, 3tr into next ch sp, patt to end. Turn.
Complete to match first side, reversing shaping.

Front
Work as given for back until front measures 5 rows less than back to shoulder, omitting back opening and ending with a 2nd row.
Shape neck
1st row (RS) 3ch, (3tr into next ch sp, 1ch) 6 times, 1tr into next ch sp, turn.
2nd row 3ch, miss first block, 3tr into next ch sp, patt to end. Turn.
3rd row Patt to turning ch, 1ch, 1tr into turning ch. Turn.
Rep 2nd and 3rd rows once more.
Next row Ss across first block, 3dc into next ch sp, (1ch, 3dc into next ch sp) 3 times. Fasten off.
Return to where work was left, miss one ch sp, rejoin yarn to next ch sp.
1st row 3ch, 3tr into next ch sp, patt to end. Turn.
2nd row Patt to turning ch, 1ch, 1tr into turning ch. Turn.
3rd row 3ch, miss first block, 3tr into next ch sp, patt to end. Turn.
Rep 2nd and 3rd rows once more.
Next row 3dc into first ch sp, (1ch, 3dc into next ch sp) 3 times. Fasten off.

Sleeves
Using No.3.50 (ISR) hook make 35ch.
Base row Into 3rd ch from hook work 2tr, *miss 3ch, 1ch, 3tr into next ch, rep from * to end. Turn. 9 blocks.
1st row (WS) 3ch, 3tr into first ch sp, *1ch, 3tr into next ch sp, rep from * to last 3tr, 1ch, 1tr into end tr. Turn..
2nd row 3ch, 2tr into first ch sp, *1ch, 3tr into next ch sp, rep from * to turning ch, 1ch, 3tr into turning ch sp. Turn.
These 2 rows form patt. Rep 1st and 2nd rows once more, then 1st row once more.
Shape sleeve
1st row 3ch, 3tr into first ch sp, patt to turning ch sp, 1ch, 3tr, 1ch, 1tr into turning ch sp. Turn.
2nd row 3ch, 1tr into first ch sp, patt to turning ch sp, 1ch, 2tr into turning ch sp. Turn.
3rd row 3ch, 3tr into first ch sp, patt to last 2tr, 1ch, 1tr into end tr. Turn.
4th row As 2nd patt row.
5th row As 1st patt row.
Rep 1st to 5th shaping rows inclusive 5 times. 14 blocks. Cont in patt without shaping until sleeve measures 40.5cm (*16in*) from beg, ending with a 2nd row.
Shape top
1st row (WS) Ss across first 3tr, miss next block, 3ch, 3tr into next ch sp, patt to last ch sp, 1ch, 1tr into last ch sp. Turn.
2nd row 3ch, miss first block, 3tr into next ch sp, patt to turning ch, 1ch, 1tr into turning ch, turn.
3rd row 3ch, 2tr into first ch sp, patt to turning ch, 3tr into turning ch sp, turn.
4th row As 2nd.
Rep 2nd and 3rd rows once more, then rep 2nd row until 3 blocks rem. Fasten off.

Neck edging
Join shoulder seams. Mark position for 2 buttonholes on right side of neck opening, first to come at top of neck and 2nd 4.0cm (*1½in*) below.
Using No.3.50 (ISR) hook and with RS of work facing, rejoin yarn at right side of back opening and work 1 round of dc down right back opening, up left side of back opening and all round neck. Join with a ss to first dc.
Next round (buttonhole round) Work in dc round back opening, making buttonholes as markers are reached by working (3ch, miss 2dc), work round neck edge as foll: miss 2dc, (1ch, 1tr) 3 times into next dc, miss 2dc, 1ch, 1dc into next dc, to end. Join with a ss to first dc.
3rd round Work 1 round crab st all round, working in dc from left to right instead of from right to left. Fasten off.

Cuff edging
Using No.3.50 (ISR) hook and with RS of sleeve facing, work 1 row dc evenly round lower edge.
2nd row *Miss 2dc, (1ch, 1tr) 3 times into next dc, miss 2dc, 1ch, 1dc into next dc, rep from * all round.
3rd row Work in crab st as given for neck edging. Fasten off.

Belt
Using No.4.50 (ISR) hook make 5ch. Join with a ss to first ch to form circle. Cont in ch until belt measures 112.0cm (*44in*) from beg. Ss back into 5th ch from hook to form circle. Fasten off.

To make up
Press each piece lightly under a damp cloth with a warm iron. Join side seams. Set in sleeves. Join sleeve seams.
Lower edging Using No.3.50 (ISR) hook and with RS of work facing, rejoin yarn at side seam.
1st round 3ch, 1tr into side seam, *1ch, 1dc

89

into ch sp, (1ch, 1tr) 4 times into centre tr of 3tr block, 1ch, 1dc into ch sp, (1ch, 1tr) 4 times into centre of 4dc block, rep from * all round, (1ch, 1tr) twice into side seam. Join with a ss to 3rd of first 3ch.
2nd round Work 1 round of crab st as given for neck edging. Fasten off.
Press seams. Sew on buttons. Thread belt through 1st row of block patt at waist to tie at centre front.

20 *Coat in two versions*

Sizes
To fit 81.5[86.5:94.0:101.5]cm (*32[34:37:40]in*) bust
Length to shoulder, 86.5[86.5:89.0:89.0]cm (*34[34:35:35]in*)
Sleeve seam, 43.0[43.0:44.5:44.5]cm (*17[17:17½ 17½]in*)
The figures in brackets [] refer to the 86.5 (*34*), 94.0 (*37*) and 101.5cm (*40in*) sizes respectively
Tension
3 V sts and 8 rows to 10cm (*3.9in*) over patt worked on No.5.00 (ISR) hook in Bainin and Heatherspun
Materials
Sleeveless coat 15[16:17:19] x 50 grm balls Mahony's Bainin
or 14[15:17:18] x 50 grm balls Mahony's Heatherspun
Coat with sleeves 20[21:23:24] x 50 grm balls Bainin
or 19[20:22:23] x 50 grm balls Heatherspun
One No.6.00 (ISR) crochet hook
One No.5.50 (ISR) crochet hook
One No.5.00 (ISR) crochet hook
5 buttons for coat with sleeves

Back and fronts
Using No.6.00 (ISR) hook make 130[140:150:160]ch and work in one piece to underarm.
Base row Into 4th ch from hook work (yrh, insert hook into st, yrh and draw through, yrh and draw through 2 loops) twice into same st, yrh and draw through 3 loops on hook — called ½ V st —, *miss 4ch, (1tr, 2ch, 1dc) into next st, 2ch, 1tr into same st — called 1 V st —, rep from * to last 6ch, miss 4ch, ½ V st into next ch, 1ch, 1tr into last ch. 24[26:28:30] V sts and ½ V st at each end. Turn.
Commence patt.
1st row 2ch, 1 V st into space after the ½ V st on previous row, 1 V st into each space to end, 1tr into 3rd of turning ch. Turn. 25[27:29:31] V sts.
2nd row 3ch, ½ V st into space between tr and first V st of previous row, 1 V st into each space to end, ending with ½ V st into space after last V st on row below, 1ch, 1tr into 2nd of turning ch. Turn.
Rep last 2 rows until work measures 26.5cm (*10½in*) from beg. Change to No.5.50 (ISR) hook and cont in patt until work measures 47.0cm (*18½in*) from beg. Change to No.5.00 (ISR) hook and work in patt until work measures 68.5cm (*27in*) for coat with sleeves and 63.5cm (*25in*) for sleeveless coat, ending with 1st[2nd:1st:2nd] patt row.
Divide for armholes
1st row Patt across 5½[6:6½:7] V sts, 1tr into next space, 2ch, ss into same place, ss across next V st to next space, 2ch, 1tr into space, patt 10[11:12:13] V sts, ½ V st into next space, turn.
Complete back first.
Next row (dec row) 2ch, 1tr into top of ½ V st, miss first V st, *1 V st into next space, rep from * to last space, work ½ V st into next space, turn. ½ V st dec at each end.
Next row Work as given for 2nd patt row. Turn. 8[9:10:11] V sts and ½ V st at each end of row.
Cont without shaping until armholes measures 23.0[23.0:25.5:25.5]cm (*9[9:10:10]in*) for sleeveless coat and 18.0[18.0:20.5:20.5]cm (*7[7:8:8]in*) for coat with sleeves, ending with 1st patt row.
Shape shoulders and back neck
1st row Ss across first V st to space, 2ch, 1tr into same place, patt 1[1:2:2] V sts, 2ch, ss into next space, ss across next 3[4:3:4] V sts, 2ch, 1 V st into each of next 1[1:2:2] spaces, ½ V st into next space. Fasten off.
Return to where work was left, miss 1 V st, rejoin yarn to next space at armhole edge for left front.
Next row 2ch, 1tr into same space, patt to end.
Keeping patt correct dec ½ V st at armhole edge on next 2 rows. Cont without shaping on these 5[5½:6:6½] V sts until armhole measures 5 rows less than back to shoulder, ending at front edge.
Shape neck
1st row Ss across 1½[2:1½:2] V sts to space, ½ V st into space, 1 V st into next space, patt to end.
Dec ½ V st at end of next row. Work 3 rows without shaping. 2½[2½:3½:3½] V sts.
Shape shoulder
1st row Ss across first V st to space, 2ch, 1tr into same place, patt to end. Fasten off.
Return to where work was left, rejoin yarn to rem sts at armhole edge of right front. Complete to match left front, reversing shaping.

Sleeves
Using No.5.50 (ISR) hook make 27[27:31:31]ch.
Next row Into 2nd ch from hook work 1dc, 1dc into each ch to end. Turn. 26[26:30:30]dc.
Commence patt.
Base row 3ch, ½ V st into first dc, *miss 3dc, 1 V st into next dc, rep from * to last 5 dc, miss 3dc, ½ V st into next dc, 1tr into last dc. Turn. 5[5:6:6] V sts and ½ V st at each end.
Cont in patt as given for back until sleeve measures 18.0cm (*7in*) from beg, ending with 1st patt row.
Next row (inc row) 2ch, 1 V st into space between tr and first V st, 1 V st into each space to end, ending with 1 V st into last space after last V st, 1ch, 1tr under ch. Turn. ½ V st inc at each end.
Next row As 2nd patt row.
Work 11 rows patt without shaping, ending with 1st patt row, then rep inc row. 8[8:9:9] V sts.
Beg with 2nd patt row, cont without shaping until sleeve measures 43.0[43.0 44.5:44.5]cm (*17[17:17½:17½]in*) from beg, ending with 1st[1st:2nd:2nd] patt row.
Shape top
Mark each end of last row with coloured thread.
Work 3[3:4:4] rows patt, ending with 2nd patt row.
Next row Ss into top of first ½ V st, 2ch, 1tr into top of ½ V st, *1 V st into next space, rep from * to last space, ½ V st into space, turn.
Next row 2ch, 1tr into top of ½ V st, miss first V st, *1 V st into next space, rep from * to last space, ½ V st into space, turn.
Rep last row 3 times more. Fasten off.

Collar
Using No.5.00 (ISR) hook make 17[17:21:21]ch.
1st row *Miss 3ch, 1 V st into next ch, rep from * to last ch, 1tr into ch. Turn. 4[4:5:5] V sts.
Change to No.5.50 (ISR) hook.
Next row 8ch, into 4th ch from hook work 1 V st, miss next 3ch, 1 V st into next ch, 1 V st into each space to end, 1 V st under 3ch at beg of previous row. 2 V sts inc at beg of row.
Rep last row 3 times more. 12[12:13:13] V sts.
Next row 3ch, ½ V st into last tr of last V st in row below, 1 V st into each space to end, ending with ½ V st under 3ch at beg of previous row, 1ch, 1tr into same place as ½ V st.
Beg with 1st patt row cont without shaping until collar measures 12.5[12.5:14.0:14.0]cm (*5[5:5½:5½]in*) from beg. Fasten off.

To make up
Press each piece under a damp cloth with a hot iron. Join shoulder seams. Sew shaped edge of collar to neck beg and ending 0.5cm (*¼in*) in from front edge.
Edging Rejoin yarn to lower edge of right front. Using No.5.00 (ISR) hook and with RS of work facing, work 1 row of firm dc up right front edge, round collar and down left front edge. Fasten off for sleeveless coat.
Coat with sleeves
Turn and work 1dc into each dc up left front and round collar to top of right front. Mark positions for 5 buttons, first to come 0.5cm (*¼in*) below beg of neck and last to come 20.5[20.5:21.5:21.5]cm (*8[8:8½:8½]in*) lower, with 3 more evenly spaced between. Cont working 1dc into each dc down right front, *at the same time* making buttonhole loops when markers are reached as foll: 2ch, miss 2 dc, 1dc into next dc. Fasten off.
Set in sleeves. Join sleeve seams. Press seams.
Sleeveless coat
Armbands Using No.5.00 (ISR) hook and with RS of work facing, rejoin yarn and work 1 row dc round armhole, working 4dc to every 2.5cm (*1in*). Work 1 more round. Fasten off. Press seams.

21 *Simple sleeveless top*

Sizes
To fit 84.0/86.5 [91.5:96.5/99.0]cm (*33/34[36:38/39]in*) bust
Length to shoulder, 51.0cm (*20in*)
The figures in brackets [] refer to the 91.5 (*36*) and 96.5/99.0cm (*38/39in*) sizes repectively
Tension
2 shells to 3.0cm (*1¼in*) over patt worked on No.2.50 (ISR) crochet hook
Materials
4[5:5] x 50 grm balls of Mahony Blarney Michele
One No.2.50 (ISR) crochet hook

Back
Using No.2.50 (ISR) hook make 110 [118:126]ch loosely.
1st row Into 2nd ch from hook work 1dc, 1dc into each ch to end. Turn. 109[117:125]dc.
2nd row 1ch to count as first dc, 1dc into each dc to end. Turn.
Commence patt.
1st row 4ch to count as first tr and 1ch sp, 1tr into first dc, *miss 3dc, work (1tr, 1ch, 1tr, 1ch, 1tr) all into next dc — called 1 shell —, *, rep from * to * 25[27:29] times more, miss 3dc, work (1tr, 1ch, 1tr) all into last dc — called ½ shell. Turn. 26[28:30] shells with ½ shell at each end.
2nd row 1ch to count as first dc, 1dc into first 1ch sp, *1dc between next 2tr, 1dc into next 1ch sp, 1dc into centre tr of shell, 1dc into next 1ch sp, *, rep from * to * 25[27:29] times more, 1dc between next 2tr, 1dc into last 1ch sp, 1dc into 3rd of first 4ch. Turn.
These 2 rows form patt. Cont in patt until work measures 31.0cm (*12¼in*) from beg, ending with a 2nd patt row.
Shape armholes
1st row 1ch, miss first dc, ss into each of next 8dc, 3ch, rep from * to * of 1st patt row 22[24:26] times, miss 3dc, 1tr into next dc, turn.
2nd row 1ch, rep from * to * of 2nd patt row,

noting that the first dc is worked between the first 2tr, 22[24:26] times, 1dc into turning ch. Turn.

3rd row 1ch, miss first dc, ss into each of next 2dc, 3ch, rep from * to * of 1st patt row 20[22:24] times, miss 3dc, 1tr into next dc, turn.

4th row 1ch, rep from * to * of 2nd patt row 20[22:24] times, 1dc into turning ch. Turn.

5th row As 3rd armhole row but working 18[20:22] times instead of 20[22:24] times.

6th row As 4th armhole row but working 18[20:22] times instead of 20[22:24] times.

7th row 1ch, miss first dc, ss into each of next 2dc, 3ch, 1tr into same dc as last ss, rep from * to * of 1st patt row 16[18:20] times, miss 3dc, ½ shell into next dc, turn.

8th row As 2nd patt row but rep from * to * 16[18:20] times in all. Turn.

9th row As 1st patt row but working 16[18:20] shells with ½ shell at each end. Turn.

Cont in patt without shaping until armholes measure 12.5cm (*5in*) from beg, ending with a 2nd patt row.

Shape neck

1st row 4ch, 1tr into first dc, rep from * to * of 1st patt row 3[4:4] times, miss 3dc, 1tr into next dc, turn.

Complete this side first.

2nd row 1ch, rep from * to * of 2nd patt row 3[4:4] times, 1dc between next 2tr, 1dc into last ch sp, 1dc into turning ch. Turn.

3rd row 4ch, 1tr into first dc, rep from * to * of 1st patt row 2[3:3] times, miss 3dc, 1tr into next dc, turn.

4th row 1ch, rep from * to * of 2nd patt row 2[3:3] times, 1dc between next 2tr, 1dc into last ch sp, 1dc into turning ch. Turn.

5th row 4ch, 1tr into first dc, rep from * to * of 1st patt row 1[2:2] times, miss 3dc, ½ shell into next dc, turn.

6th row 1ch, 1dc into first tr, 1dc into 1ch sp, rep from * to * of 2nd patt row 1[2:2] times, 1dc between next 2tr, 1dc into 1ch sp, 1dc into turning ch. Turn. Fasten off.

Return to where work was left, miss first 8[8:10] shells for centre back neck, rejoin yarn to dc over centre tr of next shell, 3ch, rep from * to * of 1st patt row 3[4:4] times, miss 3dc, ½ shell into last dc. Turn.

Next row 1ch, 1dc into first tr, 1dc into 1ch sp, rep from * to * of 2nd patt row 3[4:4] times, 1dc into turning ch. Turn.

Next row 1ch, miss first dc, ss into each of next 2dc, 3ch, rep from * to * of 1st patt row 2[3:3] times, miss 3dc, ½ shell into last dc. Turn.

Next row 1ch, 1dc into first tr, 1dc into 1ch sp, rep from * to * of 2nd patt row 2[3:3] times, 1dc into turning ch. Turn.

Next row 1ch, miss first dc, ss into each of next 2dc, 3ch, 1tr into same dc as last ss, rep from * to * of 1st patt row 1[2:2] times, miss 3dc, ½ shell into last dc. Turn.

Next row 1ch, 1dc into first tr, 1dc into 1ch sp, rep from * to * of 2nd patt row 1[2:2] times, 1dc between next 2tr, 1dc into last ch sp, 1dc into turning ch. Fasten off.

Front

Work as given for back until 8th armhole row has been completed.

Shape front neck

1st row 4ch, 1tr into first dc, rep from * to * of 1st patt row 4[5:5] times, miss 3dc, 1tr into next dc, turn.

2nd row 1ch, rep from * to * of 2nd patt row 4[5:5] times, 1dc between next 2tr, 1dc into last ch sp, 1dc into turning ch. Turn.

3rd row 4ch, 1tr into first dc, rep from * to * of 1st patt row 3[4:4] times, miss 3dc, 1tr into next dc, turn.

4th row 1ch, as 2nd neck row but working 3[4:4] times.

5th row As 3rd neck row but working 2[3:3] times.

6th row As 2nd neck row but working 2[3:3] times.

7th row 4ch, 1tr into first dc, rep from * to * of 1st patt row 1[2:2] times, miss 3dc, ½ shell into next dc, turn.

8th row 1ch, 1dc into first tr, 1dc into 1ch sp, rep from * to * of 2nd patt row 1[2:2] times, 1dc between next 2tr, 1dc into last ch sp, 1dc into turning ch. Turn.

Cont without shaping until armhole measures same as back to shoulder, ending with a 2nd patt row. Fasten off.

Return to where work was left, miss first 6[6:8] shells for centre front neck, rejoin yarn to dc over centre tr of next shell, 3ch, rep from * to * of 1st patt row 4[5:5] times, miss 3dc, ½ shell into last dc. Turn.

2nd row 1ch, 1dc into first tr, 1dc into 1ch sp, rep from * to * of 2nd patt row 4[5:5] times, 1dc into turning ch, turn.

3rd row 1ch, miss first dc, ss into each of next 2dc, 3ch, rep from * to * of 1st patt row 3[4:4] times, miss 3dc, ½ shell into last dc. Turn.

4th row As 2nd but working 3[4:4] times.

5th row As 3rd but working 2[3:3] times.

6th row As 2nd but working 2[3:3] times.

7th row 1ch, miss first dc, ss into each of next 2dc, 3ch, 1tr into same dc as last ss, rep from * to * of 1st patt row 1[2:2] times, miss 3dc, ½ shell into last dc. Turn.

8th row 1ch, 1dc into first tr, 1dc into 1ch sp, rep from * to * of 2nd patt row 1[2:2] times, 1dc between next 2tr, 1dc into last ch sp, 1dc into turning ch. Turn.

Complete to match first side.

Armbands

Join shoulder seams. Using No.2.50 (ISR) hook and with RS of work facing, work 1 row dc all round armholes noting that an odd number of sts is required. Turn.

2nd row 1ch, 1dc into first dc, *yrh, insert hook into next st and draw loop through, (yrh, insert hook into same st as before and draw loop through) 3 times, yrh and draw through all 9 loops on hook — called B1 —, 1dc into next dc, rep from * to end. Turn.

3rd row 1ch, 1dc into first dc, *1dc into top of B1, 1dc into next dc, rep from * to end. Turn.

4th row 1ch, ss into first dc, *(1dc, 1ch, 1tr) all into next dc, miss 1dc, ss into next dc, rep from * to end. Fasten off.

Neckband

Using No.2.50 (ISR) hook and with RS of work facing, rejoin yarn at one shoulder seam, work 1 round dc round neck edge. Join with a ss to first dc. Turn.

2nd round As 2nd row of armbands. Join with a ss to first ch. Turn.

3rd round As 3rd row of armbands. Join with a ss to first ch. Turn.

4th round As 4th row of armbands. Join with a ss to first ch. Fasten off.

Lower edges

Using No.2.50 (ISR) hook and with RS of work facing, rejoin yarn to lower edge of back and work 1dc into each ch to end. Turn.

2nd row As 2nd row of armbands.

3rd row As 3rd row of armbands.

4th row Work 1dc into each dc to end. Turn.

Rep last row once more. Rep 2nd, 3rd and 4th rows as given for armbands. Fasten off.

Work along front edge in same way.

To make up

Press each piece under a dry cloth with a warm iron. Join piece seams. Press seams and borders lightly.

22 Chunky buttoned cardigan

Sizes

To fit 81.5[86.5:91.5:96.5:101.5]cm (*32[34:36:38:40]in*) bust
Length to shoulder, 58.5[58.5:58.5:61.0:61.0]cm (*23[23:23:24:24]in*)
Sleeve seam, 43.0cm (*17in*)
The figures in brackets [] refer to the 86.5 (*34*), 91.5 (*36*), 96.5 (*38*) and 101.5cm (*40in*) sizes respectively

Tension

2 patt to 10cm (*3.9in*) and 4 rows to 6.0cm (*2¼in*) over patt worked on No.5.00 (ISR) crochet hook

Materials

13[14:15:16:17] x 50 grm balls Mahony's Blarney Bainin
One No.5.00 (ISR) crochet hook
One No.4.00 (ISR) crochet hook
6 buttons

Back and fronts

Using No.4.00 (ISR) hook make 130[138:146:154:162]ch and work in one piece to underarm.

Next row Into 2nd ch from hook work 1dc, 1dc into each ch to end. Turn. 129[137:145:153:161] sts.

Change to No.5.00 (ISR) hook. Commence patt.

1st row 1dc into first st, 2ch, 1tr into next st, *1ch, miss 2 sts, (1tr, 3ch, 1tr) into next st — called 1 V st —, miss 2 sts, 1ch, 1tr into each of next 3 sts, rep from * to last 7 sts, 1ch, miss 2 sts, 1 V st into next st, 1ch, miss 2 sts, 1tr into each of last 2 sts. Turn.

2nd row (RS) 1dc into first st, 3ch, *7tr into arch of V st, 1ch, 1tr into 2nd of 3tr in row below, 1ch, rep from * working last tr into ch above dc at beg of previous row. Turn. 16[17:18:19:20] shell patts.

3rd row 1dc into first st, 3ch — called ½ V st —, *1ch, miss 2 sts, 1tr into each of next 3 sts, 1ch, miss 2 sts, 1 V st into next st, rep from * ending with 1ch, 3tr, miss 2 sts, 1ch, ½ V st into ch above dc on previous row. Turn.

4th row 1dc into first st, 2ch, 3tr into ½ V st, *1ch, 1tr into 2nd of 3tr in row below, 1ch, 7tr into V st, rep from * ending with 1ch, 1tr into 2nd of 3tr, 1ch, 3tr into ½ V st, 1tr into 2nd ch above dc of previous row. Turn.

5th row 1dc into first st, 2ch, 1tr into next st, *miss 2 sts, 1ch, 1 V st into next st, 1ch, miss 2 sts, 1tr into each of next 3 sts, rep from * ending with 1ch, 1 V st, 1ch, miss 2 sts, 1tr into next st, 1tr into ch above dc in previous row. Turn.

The last 4 rows form patt and are rep throughout.
Cont in patt until work measures 34.5[34.5:37.0:37.0:34.5]cm (*13½[13½:14½:14½:13½]in*) from beg or 5.0cm (*2in*) less than required length to underarm, ending with a 2nd[2nd:4th:4th:2nd] row.

Divide for armholes

1st row Patt across 3½[3½:4:4:4½] V sts, 2tr and 1dc over middle 3tr of shell, ss across next 5 sts for beg of armhole shaping, 1dc into next st, 1tr into each of next 2 sts, patt across 7[8:8:9:9] V sts, 2tr and 1dc over middle 3tr of shell, ss into next st, turn.

Complete back first.

2nd row Ss across dc and first tr, 7tr into V st, cont in patt ending with 7tr into last V st, miss 1 st, ss into next st, turn.

3rd row Ss across first 2tr, 1dc into next st, 1tr into each of next 2 sts, patt to last shell, 2tr and 1dc over middle 3tr of shell, ss into next st, turn. **

4th row Ss across dc and first tr, 1dc into same tr, 2ch, 7tr into V st, patt until 6[7:7:8:8] shells have been worked, 1tr into 2nd tr, turn.

5th row As 3rd row of patt.

Work 7[7:7:9:9] more rows patt without shaping, ending with 2nd[2nd:2nd:4th:4th] row of patt. Fasten off.
With RS of work facing, rejoin yarn to armhole edge of left front.
Next row Ss across dc and first tr, 7tr into V st, patt to end. Turn.
Next row Patt to last shell, 2tr and 1dc over middle 3tr of shell, ss into next st, turn.
Next row Ss across dc and first tr, 1dc into same tr, 2ch, 7tr into V st, patt to end. Turn.
Work 4[4:4:6:6] rows without shaping, ending at front edge.
Shape neck
1st row Miss first st, ss across next 2[2:6:2:6] sts, 1dc into next st, 1tr into each of next 2 sts, patt to end. Turn.
2nd row Patt to last V st, 1ch, 7tr into V st, ss into next st, turn.
3rd row Ss across first 3tr, 1dc into same st as last ss, 2ch, 1tr into each of next 2 sts, patt to end. Turn.
4th row Patt to last V st, 7tr into last V st, 1ch, miss 1 st, 1tr into each of last 2 sts. Turn.
Shape shoulder
1st row Miss first st, 3ch, 1tr into same st, 1ch, 3tr over middle 3tr of shell, 1ch, 1 V st, 1ch, miss 2 sts, 1tr into next st, 1dc into next st, ss into next st, turn.
2nd row Ss across dc and first tr, 3dc and 3tr into V st, 1ch, 1tr into 2nd of next 3tr, 1ch, 3tr into ½ V st, 1tr into last st. Turn.
3rd row 1dc into first st, 2ch, 1tr into each of next 2 sts, 1dc into each of next 2 sts, ss into next st. Fasten off.
With WS of work facing, rejoin yarn to armhole edge of right front. Complete to match left front, reversing shaping.

Sleeves
Using No.4.00 (ISR) hook make 34[34:34:42:42] ch.
Next row Into 2nd ch from hook work 1dc, 1dc into each ch to end. Turn. 33[33:33:41:41]dc.
Change to No. 5.00 (ISR) hook and work 5 rows in patt as given for back and fronts. 4[4:4:5:5] shells. Working inc sts into patt where possible, inc 1tr at each end of next and every alt row 8 times in all. 6[6:6:7:7] shells. Cont without shaping until sleeve measures 38.0cm (*15in*) from beg, or 5.0cm (*2in*) less than required length to underarm, ending with a 5th patt row. Mark each end of last row with coloured thread.
Shape top
Next row Miss first st, 1dc into next st, 7tr into V st, patt to end, ending with 7tr into V st, 1dc into next st, ss into next st, turn.
Next row Miss first st, ss across next 2 sts, 1dc into next st, 1tr into each of next 2 sts, patt until 5[5:5:6:6] V sts have been worked, 1tr into each of next 2 sts, 1dc into next st, ss into next st, turn.
Work as given for back from ** to ** twice, then rep 2nd row once more. Fasten off.

To make up
Press each piece under a damp cloth with a warm iron. Join shoulder seams, leaving 12.0 [14.0:14.5:15.0:16.0]cm (*4¾[5½:5¾:6:6¼]in*) open for back neck.
Edging Using No.4.00 (ISR) hook and with RS of work facing, work 1 row firm dc all round edge of jacket, beg quarter of the way along lower edge, working 1dc into each ch, then working 1dc into corner and marking this st, working 2dc into each end of row, then 1dc into corner. Cont in this way all round edge. Join with a ss.
2nd round *1dc into each dc to corner st, 3dc into corner st, rep from * 3 times more, 1dc into each st to end. Join with a ss.
3rd round *1dc into each dc to corner, 3dc into

first of 3dc at corner, rep from * 3 times more, 1dc into each dc to end. Join with a ss.
Rep last round once more. Mark position for 6 buttons on left front, first to come 1.5cm (*½in*) above lower edge and last to come 1.5cm (*½in*) below top edge with 4 more evenly spaced between.
5th round (buttonhole round) As 3rd round, making buttonholes when markers are reached as foll: 3ch, miss 3dc, 1dc into next dc.
6th round As 3rd round, working 3dc into each 3ch buttonhole.
Work 2 more rounds. Fasten off.
Join sleeve seams. Using No.4.00 (ISR) hook work 8 rounds dc round lower edge of sleeve, working 1dc into each ch st of first row. Fasten off. Set in sleeves. Press seams. Sew on buttons.

 Sleeveless summer slip-on

Sizes
To fit 81.5[86.5:91.5:96.5]cm (*32[34:36:38]in*) bust
Length to shoulder, 44.5[44.5:45.5:45.5]cm (*17½[17½:18:18]in*)
The figures in brackets [] refer to the 86.5 (*34*), 91.5 (*36*) and 96.5cm (*38in*) sizes respectively
Tension
24 sts to 10.0cm (*3.9in*) over tr worked on No.3.00 (ISR) crochet hook
Materials
7[7:8:8] x 25 grm balls of Sirdar Tricel Nylon 4 ply
One No.3.00 (ISR) crochet hook
One No.2.50 (ISR) crochet hook

Back
Using No.2.50 (ISR) hook make 84[90:96:102]ch.
1st row (RS) Into 4th ch from hook work 1tr, 1tr into each ch to end. Turn. 82[88:94:100]tr.
2nd row 3ch to count as first tr, 1tr into each tr to end. Turn.
Rep last row 4 times more. Change to No.3.00 (ISR) hook. Work 2[2:4:4] more rows tr.
Next row (inc next) 3ch, 1tr into first tr, 1tr into each tr to last 2tr, 2tr into next tr, 1tr into last tr. Turn.
Work 3 rows tr without shaping. **. Work 17 more rows tr, inc as before at each end of next and every foll 4th row. 94[100:106:112]tr. Work 7 rows tr without shaping.
Shape armholes
1st row Ss across first 7[7:9:9]tr, 3ch, yrh, (insert hook in next tr, yrh and draw loop through) twice, yrh and draw through 3 loops, yrh and draw through 2 loops — called dec 1 —, work in tr to last 9[9:11:11]tr, dec 1, 1tr into next tr, turn.
2nd row 3ch, dec 1, work in tr to last 3tr, dec 1, 1tr into last tr. Turn.
Rep 2nd row 4[6:6:8] times more. 70[72:74:76] tr. Work 10[8:8:6] rows tr without shaping.
Shape neck
1st row 3ch, 1tr into each of next 9tr, yrh, (insert hook into next tr, yrh and draw through loop) into each of next 3tr, yrh and draw through 4 loops on hook, yrh and draw through 2 loops on hook — called dec 2 —, 1dtr into next tr, turn.
Complete this side first.
2nd row 4ch, dec 2, 1tr into each tr to end. Turn. 10tr.
Work 6 rows tr without shaping. Fasten off.
Return to where work was left, with RS facing rejoin yarn to 14th tr from other end.
1st row 4ch, dec 2, 1tr into each tr to end. Turn.
2nd row 3ch, 1tr into each of next 7tr, dec 2,

1dtr into 4th of first 4ch. Turn. 10tr.
Work 6 rows tr without shaping. Fasten off.

Front
Work as given for back to **.
Next row 3ch, 1tr into first tr, 1tr into each of next 28[31:34:37]tr, *2ch, miss 2tr, 1tr into next tr, *, rep from * to * 8 times more, 1tr into each tr to last 2tr, 2tr into next tr, 1tr into last tr. Turn.
Next row 3ch, 1tr into each of next 29[32:35:38]tr, *2ch, 1tr into next tr, *, rep from * to * 8 times more, 1tr into each tr to end. Turn.
Keeping centre panel of tr and 2ch sps correct throughout, work 15 rows patt inc one st at each end of next and every foll 4th row. 34[37:40:43]tr on each side of centre panel. Work 5 rows patt without shaping.
Next row 3ch, 1tr into each of next 33[36:39:42]tr, *2ch, 1tr into 2ch sp, 1tr into next tr, *, rep from * to * 8 times more, 1tr into each tr to end. Turn. 94[100:106:112]tr.
Next row 3ch, 1tr into each tr to end. Turn.
Shape armholes and divide for neck
1st row Ss across first 7[7:9:9]tr, 3ch, dec 1, 1tr into each of next 34[37:38:41]tr, dec 2, 1dtr into next tr, turn.
2nd row 4ch, dec 2, 1tr into each tr to last 3tr, dec 1, 1tr into last tr. Turn.
3rd row 3ch, dec 1, 1tr into each tr to last 4tr, dec 2, 1dtr into last tr. Turn.
Rep 2nd and 3rd rows 1[2:2:3] times more, then 2nd row once more. 23[20:21:18]tr.
1st row 3ch, 1tr into each tr of last 4tr, dec 2, 1dtr into last tr. Turn.
2nd row 4ch, dec 2, 1tr into each tr to end. Turn. 19[16:17:14]tr.
Rep 1st and 2nd rows 2[1:1:1] times more, then 1st row once more for 2nd and 3rd sizes only. 11[10:11:10]tr.
1st and 3rd sizes only
Next row 3ch, 1tr into each tr to last 3tr, dec 1, 1tr into last tr. Turn. 10[10]tr.
All sizes
Work 11[11:10:10] rows tr without shaping. Fasten off.
Return to where work was left, with RS facing rejoin yarn to next tr and complete to match first side, reversing all shaping.

Neckband
Join shoulder seams. Using No.2.50 (ISR) hook and with RS of work facing, beg at left shoulder seam and work 1 round dc all round neck edge. Join with a ss to first dc.
2nd round 1ch, 1dc into each dc to centre 2dc at front of neck, (insert hook into next dc, yrh and draw loop through) twice, yrh and draw through all loops on hook, 1dc into each dc to end. Join with a ss to first dc.
Rep 2nd round once more, working 3dc tog at centre front. Fasten off.

Armbands
Using No.2.50 (ISR) hook and with RS of work facing, work 3 rows dc round armholes. Fasten off.

Flower motif
Using No.2.50 (ISR) hook make 7ch. Join with a ss to first ch to form circle.
1st round 1ch to count as first dc, work 9dc into circle. Join with a ss to first ch.
2nd round *12ch, ss into 2nd ch from hook, 1dc into next ch, 1tr into each of next 7ch, 1dc into next ch, ss into last ch, ss into each of next 2dc in circle, rep from * 3 times more, 12ch, ss into 2nd ch, 1dc into next ch, 1tr into each of next 7ch, 1dc into next ch, ss into last ch, ss into next dc in circle, work 26ch to form stem, 1dc into 3rd ch from hook, 1dc into each ch to end, ss into dc at beg of stem. Fasten off. 5 half petals and stem.
(Continued on next text page.)

17

Gossamer-light stole for day or evening wear.

Size: width 56.0cm (22in); length 157.0cm (62in)

18

Colourful patchwork skirt made from separate squares, finished with a neat waistband.

Sizes: to fit 91.5/99.0cm (36/39in) hips in short or long version

LEE TARGET

19

Flattering, long sleeved dress to take you anywhere, anytime. It has a neat round neck and tie belt at waist.

Sizes: to fit 84.0/89.0cm (33/35 in) bust; 89.0/94.0cm (35/37in) hips

20

Two versions of a useful full length coat: one sleeveless and unbuttoned, the other has long sleeves and buttons to the neck.

Sizes: to fit 81.5[86.5:94.0:101.5] cm (32[34:37:40] in) bust

21

Simple sleeveless top, cool and pretty enough for day or evening wear.

Sizes: to fit 84.0/86.5[91.5:96.5/99.0]cm (33/34[36:38/39]in) bust

22

Chunky, button-to neck cardigan in simple shell pattern.

Sizes: to fit 81.5 [86.5:91.5:96.5:101.5]cm (32[34:36:38:40]in) bust

MAHONY

23

Cool, sleeveless
summer slip-on
with front pattern
panel and pretty
flower motif.

Sizes: to fit 81.5
[86.5:91.5:96.5]cm
(32[34:36:38]in)
bust

24

A froth of frills
for a special
occasion! Demure
round neck and full
puff sleeves set
off this charming
evening blouse.

Sizes: to fit 81.5/
84.0[86.5/89.0:
91.5/94.0:96.5/99.0]
cm (32/33[34/35:
36/37:38/39]in)
bust

25

Comfortable
raglan sleeved
cardigan for a man,
with a v-neck and
inset pockets.

Sizes: to fit
86.5[91.5:96.5:101.5:
106.5:112.0]cm (34[36:
38:40:42:44]in) chest

26

Easy-to-wear
waistcoat with
ribbed effect.

Sizes: to fit 101.5
[106.5:112.0]cm (40
[42:44]in) chest

WENDY

LISTER

SUNBEAM

27.28

A pretty shawl and a cosy,
pram cover:
ideal for a first baby.

Sizes: shawl 122.0cm (48in) square,
pram cover 51.0cm (20in) wide by
68.5cm (27in) long

(Continued from last text page.)

Complete petals. With RS of work facing, rejoin yarn to first of any 12ch on half petal.

Next round 1dc into next ch, 1tr into each of next 7ch, 1dc into next ch, ss into last ch. Fasten off.
Complete rem 4 petals in same way.

To make up
Press lightly under a dry cloth with a cool iron. Join side seams leaving 4.0cm (*1½in*) open at lower edge. Using No.2.50 (ISR) hook and with RS of work facing, work 1 row dc along each side opening edge. Fasten off. Press seams. Sew flower motif in position in centre front panel.

24 Puff-sleeved evening blouse

Sizes
To fit 81.5/84.0[86.5/89.0:91.5/94.0:96.5/99.0] cm (*32/33[34/35:36/37:38/39]in*) bust
Length to shoulder, 52.0[52.0:56.0:56.0]cm (*20½[20½:22:22]in*)
Sleeve seam, 18.0cm (*7in*)
The figures in brackets [] refer to the 86.5/89.0 (*34/35,*) 91.5/94.0 (*36/37*) and 96.5/99.0cm (*38/39in*) sizes respectively

Tension
8 patt and 12 rows to 10cm (*3.9in*) over patt worked on No.3.50 (ISR) crochet hook

Materials
9]10:10:11] x 50 grm balls Patons Cameo Crepe 4-ply
One No.3.50 (ISR) crochet hook
One No.3.00 (ISR) crochet hook
8 buttons
Length of narrow elastic for cuffs

Back
****Using No.3.00 (ISR) hook make 103 [109:115: 121]ch.

Base row Into 4th ch from hook work 1tr, *miss 2ch, 3tr into next ch, rep from * to last 3ch, miss 2ch, 2tr into last ch. Turn. 32[34:36:38] groups and half group at each end.

1st row 2ch, (1tr, 1ch, 1tr) into sp between half group and next group, * (1tr, 1ch, 1tr) into next sp between 2 groups, rep from * ending last rep with (1tr, 1ch, 1tr) in sp between last group and half group, 1tr into top of 3 turning ch. Turn. 33[35:37:39] triangles.

2nd row 2ch, *3tr into ch sp of next triangle, rep from * to end, 1tr into sp between last triangle and turning ch. Turn.

3rd row 3ch, 1tr into sp between first tr and next group, *3tr into next sp between 2 groups, rep from * ending last rep with 2tr into sp between last group and turning ch. Turn.
The last 3 rows form main patt. Rep patt until work measures 12.5cm (*5in*) from beg. **.
Change to No.3.50 (ISR) hook. Cont in patt until work measures 33.0cm (*13in*) from beg.

Shape armholes
***Next row Ss over first 6[6:9:9]sts, ss into next sp, 3ch, patt to last 2[2:3:3] triangles, 1tr into next sp. ***.

Next row Ss over first 3 sts, ss into next sp, 3ch, 1tr into same sp, patt to last group, 2tr into next sp, turn.

Next row Ss over first 3 sts, ss into next st, 2ch, patt to last st, 1tr into centre tr of next group, turn.

Next row Ss over first 3 sts, ss into next sp, 2ch, patt to last triangle, 1tr into next sp, turn. 23[25:25:27] groups.
Cont without shaping until armholes measure 19.0[19.0:23.0:23.0]cm (*7½[7½:9:9]in*) from beg.

Shape shoulders
Next row Ss over first 6 sts, 2ch, patt to last 6 sts. Fasten off.

Front
Work as given for back from ** to **. Change to No.3.50 (ISR) hook. Cont in patt for a further 12.5cm (*5in*), ending with a 1st patt row.

Divide for inset
Next row (WS) 2ch, 3tr into each of next 10[11:12:13]ch sp, 1tr into next sp before triangle, turn.
Complete this side first. Cont in patt for 8 rows, ending with a 1st row.

Shape armhole
Next row Patt to last 2[2:3:3] triangles, 1tr into sp before next triangle, turn.

Next row Ss over first 3 sts, ss into next sp, 3 ch, 1tr into same sp, patt to end. Turn.

Next row Patt to last sp, 1tr into centre tr of next group, turn.

Next row Ss over first 3 sts, ss into next sp, 2ch, patt to end. Turn. 5[6:6:7] groups.
Work 12[12:16:16] more rows patt without shaping. Place coloured marker at front edge on top of last row. Work a further 7 rows.

Shape shoulder
Next row Ss over first 6 sts, 2ch, patt to end. Fasten off.
Return to where work was left, miss first 13 triangles, rejoin yarn to rem sts, 2ch, patt to end. Work 8 rows without shaping.

Shape armhole
Next row Ss over first 6[6:9:9]sts, ss into next sp, 2ch, patt to end. Turn.

Next row Patt to sp before last group, 2tr into sp, turn.

Next row Ss over first 3 sts, ss into next sp, 2ch, patt to end. Turn.

Next row Patt to sp before last triangle, 1tr into sp, turn. 5[6:6:7] groups.
Complete to match first side, reversing shaping.

Right inset
Using No.3.00 (ISR) hook and with WS of work facing, rejoin yarn to marker at neck edge and work 50[50:56:56]dc down right front edge. Change to No.3.50 (ISR) hook.

Base row 3ch, *miss 2 sts, (1tr, 1ch, 1tr) into next st, rep from * to last 2 sts, miss one st, 1tr into last st. Turn. 16[16:18:18] triangles.

1st row 1dc into sp between tr and next triangle, *4ch, 1dc into next sp between 2 triangles, rep from * ending last rep with 4ch, 1dc into sp between last triangle and 3ch. Turn.

2nd row 1dc into first st, 4ch, 1dc into next ch loop, *9ch, 1dc into 7th ch from hook, 2ch, 1dc into next ch loop, rep from * to last ch loop, 4ch, 1dc into last ch. Turn.
These 2 rows form frill patt.

3rd row 2ch, leave frill at back of work, *(1tr, 1ch) into ch sp of next triangle of base row, rep from * to end, 1tr into 2nd of 3 turning ch. Turn, noting that all 3rd rows are now worked into 4th patt rows instead of base row.

4th row *(1tr, 1ch, 1tr) into ch sp of next triangle, rep from * to end, 1tr into sp between last triangle and 2ch. Turn.
These 4 rows form frill patt. Rep 4 patt rows twice more, then 1st-3rd rows once more. Fasten off.

Left inset
Using No.3.00 (ISR) hook and with WS of work facing, rejoin yarn to beg of opening and work 50[50:56:56]dc up left front edge to marker. Change to No.3.50 (ISR) hook and complete to match right inset.

Sleeves
Using No.3.00 (ISR) hook make 66[66:70:70]ch.
Next row Into 2nd ch from hook work 1dc, 1dc into each ch to end. Turn. 65[65:69:69] sts. Change to No.3.50 (ISR) hook.
Base row 3ch, *miss one st, (1tr, 1ch, 1tr) into next st, rep from * to last st, 1tr into last st.

Turn. 32[32:34:34] triangles.
Work 31 rows frill patt as given for inset, ending with a 3rd patt row.

Shape top
Cont in frill patt working as given for back from *** to ***. 28 triangles. Patt 20[20:24:24] rows. Place marker at each end of last row. Work 3 row without shaping.Work as given for first size of back from *** to ***. Work 3 rows without shaping. Rep last 4 rows once more. Fasten off.

To make up
Join shoulder seams.
Neck border Using No.3.00 (ISR) hook and with RS of work facing, work 4 rows dc round neck edge, leaving a small sp at each corner.
Next row 1dc into first st, *4ch, miss 3 sts, 1dc into next st, rep from * to end. Turn.
Next row As 2nd row of frill patt. Fasten off.
Front border Using No.3.00 (ISR) hook and with RS of work facing, rejoin yarn to right front inset and work 1 row dc up right front edge, round neck and down left front edge.
Next row (buttonhole row) Work in dc round to top of right front edge, mark positions for 8 buttons on left front edge, first to come at top of neck and last to come 0.5cm (*¼in*) from bottom, with 6 more evenly spaced between, cont in dc making button loops as markers are reached by working 2ch and missing 2 sts. Fasten off.
Sleeve borders Using No.3.00 (ISR) hook and with RS of work facing, work 8 rows dc along cuff edges.
Next row 1dc into first st, *4ch, miss one st, 1dc into next st, rep from * to end. Turn.
Next row As 2nd row of frill patt. Fasten off.
Sew insets in position, overlapping right border over left. Join side and sleeve seams. Run a gathering thread along sleeve top between markers and gather to fit armhole. Set in sleeves. Thread elastic through row of holes above cuffs and draw up to fit arm firmly. Sew on buttons.

25 Man's raglan sleeved cardigan

Sizes
To fit 86.5[91.5:96.5:101.5:106.5:112.0]cm (*34[36:38:40:42:44]in*) chest
Length to shoulder, 66.0cm (*26in*)
Sleeve seam, 45.5cm (*18in*)
The figures in brackets [] refer to the 91.5 (*36*), 96.5 (*38*), 101.5 (*40*), 106.5 (*42*) and 112.0cm (*44in*) sizes respectively

Tension
20 sts and 16 rows to 10.0cm (*3.9in*) over patt worked on No.3.50 (ISR) crochet hook

Materials
27[28:29:30:31:32] x 25 grm balls of Lister Lavenda Double Crepe *or*
26[27:28:29:30:31] x 20 grm balls of Lister 2 Spun Double Crepe Tricel/Nylon
One No.3.50 (ISR) crochet hook
One No.3.00 (ISR) crochet hook
5 buttons

Back
Using No.3.50 (ISR) hook make 85[90:95:100: 105:110]ch.

1st row Into 2nd ch from hook work 1htr, 1htr into each ch to end. Turn.

2nd row 1ch to count as first dc, 1dc into each htr to end. Turn.

3rd row 3ch to count as first tr, 1tr into each dc to end. Turn.

4th row 2ch to count as first htr, 1htr into each tr to end. Turn.
The 2nd to 4th rows inclusive form patt and are rep throughout. Cont in patt until work measures 39.5cm (*15½in*) from beg, ending with a WS row.

Shape raglan
Next row Ss across first 2[4:6:7:8:9] sts, patt to last 2[4:6:7:8:9] sts, turn.
Next row Patt to end. Turn.
Next row Ss across first st, patt to last st, turn.
Next row Ss across first st, patt to last st, turn.
Rep last 3 rows until 29[30:31:32:33:34] sts rem. Fasten off.

Left front
Using No.3.50 (ISR) hook make 25ch for pocket lining. Work in patt as given for back until work measures 12.5cm (*5in*) from beg. Fasten off.
Using No.3.50 (ISR) hook make 43[46:49:52:55: 58]ch. Work in patt as given for back until work measures 12.5cm (*5in*) from beg, ending with a WS row. **.
Place pocket
Next row Patt 9[10:12:13:15:16]sts, patt across 25 pocket lining sts, miss next 25 sts of front, patt to end. Turn.
Cont in patt until work measures same as back to underarm, ending with same patt row as back.
Shape raglan and front edge
Next row Ss across first 2[4:6:7:8:9] sts, patt to end. Turn.
Next row Patt to end. Turn.
Next row Ss across first st, patt to last st, turn.
Next row Patt to last st, turn.
Next row Patt to last st, turn.
Next row Patt to last st, turn.
Next row Ss across first st, patt to last st, turn.
Cont in this way, dec one st at neck edge on every alt row, *at the same time* rep last 3 rows of raglan shaping until 7 sts rem. Keeping front edge straight, cont dec at raglan edge as before until all sts are worked off.

Right front
Work as given for left front to **.
Place pocket
Next row Patt 9[11:12:14:15:17] sts, patt across 25 pocket lining sts, miss next 25 sts of front, patt to end.
Complete to match left front, reversing all shaping.

Sleeves
Using No.3.50 (ISR) hook make 50[52:54:56:58: 60]ch. Work 8 rows patt as given for back. Cont in patt, inc one st at each end of next and every foll 6th[6th:6th:4th:4th:4th] row until there are 62[66:70:74:78:82] sts. Cont without shaping until sleeve measures 45.5cm (*18in*) from beg, ending with same patt row as back.
Shape raglan
Work as given for back until 6 sts rem. Fasten off.

Front border
Join raglan seams. Using No.3.00 (ISR) hook and with RS of work facing, rejoin yarn at lower edge of right front, work in dc up right front, across sleeve, round back neck, across sleeve, down left front and round lower edge. Join with a ss to first dc. Work 1 more round dc, working 2dc into each corner. Mark positions for 5 buttons on right front, first to come 2.5cm (*1in*) above lower edge and last to come 1.5cm (*½in*) below neck shaping with 3 more evenly spaced between.
Next round (buttonhole round) Work in dc to end, making buttonholes as markers are reached by working 2ch and missing 2dc.
Next round Work in dc to end, working 2dc into each 2ch buttonhole.
Work 1 more round dc. Fasten off.

Pocket tops
Using No.3.00 (ISR) hook and with RS of work facing, rejoin yarn to pocket top sts. Work 4 rows dc. Fasten off.

To make up
Press each piece on WS under a damp cloth with a warm iron for Lavenda and under a dry cloth with a cool iron for 2 Spun. Join side and sleeve seams. Sew down pocket linings and pocket tops. Sew on buttons. Press seams.

26 Man's v-neck waistcoat

Sizes
To fit 101.5[106.5:112.0]cm (*40[42:44]in*) chest
Length to shoulder, 62.0[63.5:65.0]cm (*24½[25: 25½]in*)
The figures in brackets [] refer to the 106.5 (*42*) and 112.0cm (*44in*) sizes respectively
Tension
18tr to 10cm (*3.9in*) over patt worked on No.4.00 (ISR) crochet hook
Materials
17[18:19] x 20 grm balls Wendy Tricel/Nylon Double Crepe
One No. 4.00 (ISR) crochet hook
One No.3.50 (ISR) crochet hook
6 buttons

Back
Using No.4.00 (ISR) hook make 95[99:107]ch.
1st row Into 4th ch from hook work 1tr, 1tr into each ch to end. Turn. 93[97:105]tr.
Commence patt.
1st row (RS) 3ch to count as first tr, 1tr into each of next 0[2:0]tr, *yrh, insert hook from right to left from front and round stem of next tr on previous row, yrh and work as tr — called trF —, 1tr into each of next 5tr, rep from * to last 2[4: 2]tr, trF, 1tr into each of next 1[3:1]tr. Turn.
2nd row 3ch, 1tr into each of next 0[2:0]tr, *yrh, insert hook from right to left from back and round stem of next tr on previous row, yrh and work as tr — called trB —, 1tr into each of next 5tr, rep from * to last 2[4:2]sts, trB, 1tr into each of next 1[3:1] tr. Turn.
These 2 rows form patt. Cont in patt until work measures 39.5cm (*15½in*) from beg, ending with a WS row.
Shape armholes
Next row Ss over first 5[6:8] sts, patt to last 5[6:8] sts, turn.
Next row Ss over first 4 sts, patt to last 4 sts, turn.
Next row Ss over first 2 sts, patt to last 2 sts, turn.
Rep last row 3 times more. 59[61:65] sts.
Cont without shaping until work measures 62.0[63.5:65.0]cm (*24½[25:25½]in*) from beg, ending with a WS row.
Shape shoulders
Next row Ss over first 10 sts, patt to last 10 sts, turn.
Next row Ss over first 8 sts, patt to last 8 sts. Fasten off.

Pockets (make 2)
Using No.4.00 (ISR) hook make 27ch.
Next row Into 4th ch from hook work 1tr, 1tr into each ch to end. Turn. 25tr.
Next row 3ch to count as first tr, 1tr into each of next 2tr, *trF, 1tr into each of next 5tr, rep from * to last 4 sts, trF, 1tr into each of next 3tr. Turn.
Next row 3ch, 1tr into each of next 2tr, *trB, 1tr into each of next 5tr, rep from * to last 4 sts. trB, 1tr into each of next 3tr. Turn.
Rep last 2 rows for 8.0cm (*3¼in*) from beg, ending with a WS row. Fasten off.

Left front
Using No.4.00 (ISR) hook make 47[49:53]ch.

Next row Into 4th ch from hook work 1tr, 1tr into each ch to end. Turn. 45[47:51]tr.
1st row 3ch to count as first tr, 1tr into each of next 0[2:0]tr, *trF, 1tr into each of next 5tr, rep from * to last 2 sts, trF, 1tr into last tr. Turn.
2nd row 3ch, 1tr into next tr, *trB, 1tr into each of next 5tr, rep from * to last 2[4:2] sts, trB, 1tr into each of next 1[3:1]tr. Turn.
Cont in patt as now set until work measures 15.0cm (*6in*) from beg, ending with a WS row.
Place pocket
Next row Patt across first 10[12:16] sts, (work as tr over next st and first st of pocket, leaving last loop of each tr on hook, yrh and draw through all loops on hook — called tr2 tog —) twice, miss next 21 sts of front, patt across next 21 sts of pocket top, (tr2 tog) twice, patt to end. Turn.
Cont in patt until work measures same as back to underarm, ending with a WS row.
Shape armhole and front edge
Next row Ss over first 5[6:8] sts, patt to last 4 sts, work as tr over next 2 sts, leaving last loop of each st on hook, yrh and draw through all loops on hook — called dec 1 —, trF, 1tr into last tr. Turn.
Next row Patt to last 4 sts, turn.
Next row Ss over first 2 sts, patt to last 4 sts, dec 1, trF, 1tr into last tr. Turn.
Next row Patt to last 2 sts, turn.
Rep last 2 rows once more. Cont dec at front edge only inside border on foll 3[4:7] alt rows then on every foll 3rd row until 18 sts rem. Cont without shaping until work measures same as back to shoulder, ending at armhole edge.
Shape shoulder
Next row Ss over first 10 sts, patt to end. Fasten off.

Right front
Using No.4.00 (ISR) hook make 47[49:53]ch.
Next row Into 4th ch from hook work 1tr, 1tr into each ch to end. Turn. 45[47:51]tr.
1st row 3ch to count as first tr, *trF, 1tr into each of next 5tr, rep from * to last 2[4:2] sts, trF, 1tr into each of next 1[3:1]tr. Turn.
2nd row 3ch, 1tr into each of next 0[2:0]tr, *trB, 1tr into each of next 5tr, rep from * to last 2 sts, trB, 1tr into last tr. Turn.
Cont in patt until work measures 15.0cm (*6in*) from beg, ending with a WS row.
Place pocket
Next row Patt over first 10 sts, (tr2 tog) twice, miss next 21 sts of front, patt across next 21 sts of pocket top, (tr2 tog) twice, patt to end. Turn.
Complete to match left front, reversing all shaping.

To make up
Press under a damp cloth with a warm iron. Join shoulder seams. Join side seams. Using No.4.00 (ISR) hook and with RS of work facing, rejoin yarn at left front edge, work 4 rows dc along lower edge. Fasten off.
Front band Using No.4.00 (ISR) hook and with RS of work facing, rejoin yarn to lower edge of right front, work 73[77:81]dc up right front to beg of front shaping, 58dc to shoulder, 24dc round back neck, 58dc to beg of front shaping and 73[77:81]dc down left front. 286[294:302] sts.
Change to No.3.50 (ISR) hook, work 3 rows dc. Mark position for 6 buttonholes on left front, first to come 1.5cm (*½in*) below beg of front shaping and last to come 1.5cm (*½in*) above lower edge with 4 more evenly spaced between.
Next row (buttonhole row) Work in dc to first marker, miss 2dc, 3ch, *work in dc to next marker, miss 2dc, 3ch, rep from * 4 times more, work in dc to end. Turn.
Next row Work in dc to end, working 2dc into each 3ch sp. Turn.
Work 2 more rows dc.

Next row Work in ss all round front band and round lower edge, working 2ss into each lower corner. Fasten off.

Armbands Using No.4.00 (ISR) hook and with RS of work facing, rejoin yarn and work 113[117:121]dc evenly round armhole edge. Work 3 rounds dc and one round ss. Fasten off.

Pocket tops Using No.4.00 (ISR) hook and with RS of work facing, rejoin yarn and work 23dc across pocket top. Work 5 more rows dc, then one row ss. Fasten off.
S1 st pocket tops and pockets in position. Press seams. Sew on buttons.

27 Baby's shawl

Size
122.0cm (48in) by 122.0cm (48in)
Tension
4 groups to 7.5cm (3in) over patt worked on No.4.00 (ISR) crochet hook
Materials
28 x 1oz balls of Sunbeam St. Ives 4 ply
One No.4.00 (ISR) crochet hook

Shawl
Using No.4.00 (ISR) hook make 262ch loosely.
1st row Into 4th ch from hook work (3tr, 2ch, 1dc), *miss 3ch, (3tr, 2ch, 1dc) into next ch, rep from * to last 2ch, miss 1ch, 1tr into last ch. Turn. 48 groups.
2nd row 2ch, (3tr, 2ch, 1dc) into each 2ch sp to end, ending with 1tr into turning ch. Turn. The 2nd row forms patt. Cont in patt until work measures 122.0cm (48in) from beg, ending last row with (3tr, 2ch, 1dc) into turning ch. Do not break off yarn.

Edging
Cont along side edge, working (3tr, 2ch, 1dc) into every alt row along side edge, then into every 3ch sp along cast on edge, then along second side as given for first side. Fasten off.

To make up
Press under a damp cloth with a warm iron.

28 Warm pram cover

Size
51.0cm (20in) wide by 68.5cm (27in) long
Tension
14 sts to 7.5cm (3in) over patt worked on No.5.00 (ISR) crochet hook
Materials
7 x 20 grm balls of Sunbeam Courtelle/Nylon Baby Quickerknit in main shade, A
6 balls of contrast colour, B
One No.5.00 (ISR) crochet hook

Pram cover
Using No.5.00 (ISR) hook and A, make 86ch.
1st row Into 4th ch from hook work 1tr, 1tr into each ch to end. Turn. 84tr.
2nd row 3ch, yrh, insert hook from back to front between next 2tr, round stem of next tr to back again then work 1tr in usual way — called 1TB —, 1TB, *yrh, insert hook from front to back between next 2tr, round stem of next tr to front again then work 1tr in usual way — called 1TF —, 1TF, 1TB into each of next 2 sts, rep from * to end, 1tr into 3rd of first 3ch. Turn. Join in B.
3rd row Using B, 3ch, 1tr into each of next 2tr, *1TF into each of next 2 sts, 1tr into each of

next 2 sts, rep from * to end, 1tr into 3rd of first 3ch. Turn.
4th row Using B, 3ch, 1TF into each of next 2 sts, *1TB into each of next 2 sts, 1TF into each of next 2 sts, rep from * to end, 1tr into 3rd of first 3ch. Turn.
5th row Using A, 3ch, 1TF into each of next 2 sts, *1tr into each of next 2 sts, 1TF into each of next 2 sts, rep from * to end, 1tr into 3rd of first 3ch. Turn.
6th row As 2nd.
Rows 2-6 form patt and are rep throughout.
Cont in patt until work measures 63.5cm (25in) from beg, ending with a 6th patt row.

Edging
Using No.5.00 (ISR) hook and A, rejoin yarn to commencing ch, 2ch, work 1htr into each ch to end, work 3htr into corner, work along side working 3htr into every 2 row ends, 3htr into corner, then work along other edges in same way. Join with a ss to 2nd of first 2ch. Turn.
Next row 2ch, *2htr into next st, 1htr into each htr to corner st, 2htr into corner st, 1htr into next st, rep from * all round. Join with a ss to 2nd of first 2ch. Turn.
Rep last row twice more. Fasten off.

To make up
Press very lightly under a damp cloth with a cool iron.

29 Round yoked jacket

Sizes
To fit 45.5[51.0:56.0]cm (18[20:22]in) chest
Length to shoulder, 23.0[25.5:28.0]cm (9[10:11]in)
Tension
16 sts to 10.0cm (3.9in) over tr worked on No.5.00 (ISR) crochet hook; 18sts to 10.0cm (3.9in) over tr worked on No.4.50 (ISR) crochet hook; 20 sts to 10.0cm (3.9in) over tr worked on No.4.00 (ISR) crochet hook
Materials
4[5:5] x ¾ oz balls of Hayfield Bri-Nova Perle 4 ply
One No.4.00[4.50:5.00] (ISR) crochet hook
3 buttons

Yoke
Using No.4.00[4.50:5.00] (ISR) hook make 49ch and beg at neck.
Base row (WS) Into 2nd ch from hook work 1dc, 1dc into each ch to end. Turn.
Commence yoke patt.
1st row 2ch, 1tr into first dc, 1tr into each of next 5dc, *3tr into next dc, 1tr into each of next 6dc, rep from * 5 times more. Turn.
2nd row 1ch, 1dc into each tr to end. Turn.
3rd row 2ch, 1tr into each of first 7dc, *3tr into next dc, 1tr into each of next 8dc, rep from * ending with 1tr into each of last 7dc. Turn.
4th row As 2nd.
5th row 2ch, 1tr into each of first 8dc, *3tr into next dc, 1tr into each of next 10dc, rep from * ending with 1tr into each of last 8dc. Turn.
6th row As 2nd.
7th row 2ch, 1tr into each of first 9dc, *3tr into next dc, 1tr into each of next 12dc, rep from * ending with 1tr into each of last 9dc. Turn.
8th row As 2nd.
These 8 rows complete yoke.
Skirt
1st row 1ch, *miss 1dc, (3tr, 2ch, 3tr) into next dc, miss 1dc, 1dc into next dc, rep from * to end. Turn. 24 shells.

2nd row 5ch, 1dc into 2ch sp of shell, *2ch, 1tr into dc of last row, 2ch, 1dc into 2ch sp, rep from * ending with 2ch, 1tr into turning ch. Turn.
3rd row 1ch, miss 2ch, *(3tr, 2ch, 3tr) into next dc, 1dc into top of tr, rep from * ending with 1dc into 3rd of first 5ch. Turn.
4th row As 2nd.
5th row 1ch, miss 2ch, *(4tr, 2ch, 4tr) into next dc, 1dc into top of tr, rep from * ending with 1dc into 3rd of first 5ch. Turn.
6th row 7ch, 1dc into 2ch sp, *3ch, 1dc into next dc, 3ch, 1dc into 2ch sp, rep from * ending with 3ch, 1tr into first 1ch. Turn.
7th row As 5th.
Divide for sleeves
8th row 7ch, 1dc into 2ch sp, *3ch, 1tr into next dc, 3ch, 1dc into 2ch sp, rep from * twice more, 7ch, miss 4 complete shells, 1dc into 2ch sp of next shell, (3ch, 1tr into next dc, 3ch, 1dc into 2ch sp) 7 times, 7ch, miss next 4 shells, 1dc into 2ch sp of next shell, 3ch, 1tr into next dc, **3ch, 1dc into 2ch sp, 3ch, 1tr into next dc, rep from ** ending with 1tr into turning ch. Turn.
9th row 1ch, miss 3ch, (5tr, 3ch and 5tr all into next dc) 3 times, (5tr, 3ch, 5tr) into next dc, 1dc into 4th of 7ch at underarm, (5tr, 3ch and 5tr all into next dc, 1dc into top of tr) 7 times, (5tr, 3ch, 5tr) into next dc, 1dc into 4th of 7ch at underarm, (5tr, 3ch and 5tr all into next dc, 1dc into top of tr) 4 times, ending with 1dc into 4th of first 7ch. Turn.
10th row 7ch, 1dc in 3ch sp, *3ch, 1tr into next dc, 3ch, 1dc into 3ch sp, rep from * ending with 3ch, 1tr into first 7ch. Turn.
11th row 1ch, miss 3ch, *(5tr, 3ch, 5tr) all into next dc, 1dc into top of tr, rep from * ending with 1dc into 4th of first 7ch. Turn. 16 shells.
Rep 10th and 11th rows 3 times more, then 10th row once more.
19th row 1ch, 12tr into first dc, *1dc into top of tr, 12tr into next dc, rep from * ending with 1dc into 4th of first 7ch. Do not fasten off.
Border
Cont along front edge for border, working in dc to beg of neck, work round neck as foll: 3ch, * miss 1ch of foundation ch, 1tr into next ch, 1ch, rep from * all round neck ending with 1tr into last ch, then cont in dc down other front edge to beg of shell at lower edge. Fasten off.
Picot edge
Using No.4.00[4.50:5.00] (ISR) hook and with RS of work facing, rejoin yarn at lower edge of right front, *work 2dc into edge, 4ch, ss into top of last dc, rep from * up right front, round neck, down left front and along lower edge working 6 picots on each shell but omitting dc between shells. Join with a ss to first dc. Fasten off.

Sleeves
Using No.4.00[4.50:5.00] (ISR) hook and with WS of work facing, rejoin yarn to dc at centre of 7ch at underarm, 7ch, 1dc into 2ch sp of next shell, (2ch, 1tr into next dc, 2ch, 1dc into next sp) 4 times, 2ch, 1tr into next dc, 2ch, 1dc into 2ch sp of next shell, 2ch, 1tr into dc at centre of 7ch at underarm. Turn.
1st row 1ch, *(4tr, 2ch, 4tr) into next dc, 1dc into top of next tr, rep from * ending with 1dc into 4th of first 7ch. Turn. 6 shells.
2nd row 7ch, *1dc into 2ch sp, 2ch, 1tr into next dc, 2ch, rep from * ending with 1tr into first ch. Turn.
Rep these 2 rows 4 times more.
Cuff
Next row 1ch, *1dc into ch sp, 1dc into next dc, 1dc into ch sp, 1dc into next tr, rep from * ending with 1dc into 7ch sp, 1dc into 3rd ch of sp. Turn.
Next row 1ch, 1dc into each dc to end. Turn.
Rep last row twice more. Work picot edge as given for fronts and lower edges. Fasten off.

To make up

Press as given for raglan sleeved jacket. Join sleeve seams. Sew on buttons to right front for a boy or left front for a girl, using sps in patt for buttonholes.

 Square yoked jacket

Sizes

As given for round yoked jacket

Tension

12 gr of yoke patt to 10.0cm (*3.9in*) worked on No.4.00 (ISR) crochet hook

Materials

4[5:5] x ¾ oz balls of Hayfield Bri-Nova Perle 4 ply
One No.4.00 (ISR) crochet hook
One No.3.00 (ISR) crochet hook
2 buttons

Yoke

Using No.4.00 (ISR) hook make 107(115:123)ch and beg at waist edge of yoke.
Base row (WS) Into 2nd ch from hook work 1tr, * 1dc into next ch, 1tr into next ch, rep from * ending with 1dc into last ch. Turn. 53[57:61]gr. Commence patt.
1st row 2ch, 1dc into first tr, *1tr into next dc, 1dc into next tr, rep from * to last 3 sts, make buttonhole by working 1ch and missing next dc, 1dc into next tr, 1tr into turning ch. Turn.
2nd row 1ch, 1tr into first dc, 1dc into ch sp of buttonhole, *1tr into next dc, 1dc into next tr, rep from * 9[10:11] times more, yrh, insert hook into next st and draw loop through, yrh, insert hook into next st and draw loop through, yrh and draw through 3 loops on hook, yrh and draw through 2 loops on hook — called dec1 —, turn.
Complete left front first.
Next row 1 ch, 1tr into first dc, * 1dc into next tr, 1tr into next dc, rep from * to end. Turn.
Next row Patt to last tr, 1dc in last tr, turn. 11[12:13]gr.
Work 4[6:6] more rows in patt, then work 2 more rows making buttonhole as before.
Shape neck
Next row Patt to last 4 [4:5]gr, dec 1, turn.
Next row Patt to end. Turn.
Rep last 2 rows once more. Cont without shaping until yoke measures 9.0[9.5:10.0]cm (*3½[3¾:4]in*) from beg. Fasten off.
Return to where work was left, miss 5 sts for underarm, rejoin yarn to next st and complete back.
Next row 1ch, *1tr into next dc, 1dc into next tr, rep from * 22[24:26] times more, turn.
Next row 1ch, dec 1, patt to last 2 sts, dec 1. Turn.
Next row As last row. 21[23:25]gr.
Cont without shaping until back measures same as front to shoulder. Fasten off.
Return to where work was left, miss 5 sts for underarm, rejoin yarn to next st and complete right front.
Next row 1ch, patt to end. Turn.
Next row 2ch, patt to last 2 sts, dec 1. Turn.
Next row 1ch, dec 1, patt to end. Turn.
Cont without shaping until work measures same as left front to neck shaping. Fasten off.
Shape neck
Next row Rejoin yarn on tr of 4th[4th:5th]gr from front edge, 1ch, patt to end. Turn.
Complete to match left front, reversing shaping.

Skirt

Using No.4.00 (ISR) hook and with WS of work facing, rejoin yarn at front edge of right front.

Next row 2ch, 1tr into first ch of base row, *1ch, miss 1ch, 1dc into next ch, 1ch, miss 1ch, (1tr, 2ch, 2tr) all into next ch, rep from * to last 2 sts, 1ch, miss next ch, 1dc into last ch. Turn.
Next row 2ch, 1tr into first st, *1ch, 1dc into 2ch sp, 1ch, (1tr, 2ch, 2tr) all into next dc, rep from * ending with 1ch, 1dc into turning ch. Turn.
Rep last row until skirt measures 14.0[15.0:15.0] cm (*5½[6:6]in*) from beg. Fasten off.

Sleeves

Using No.4.00 (ISR) hook make 27[29:31]ch. Work base row as given for yoke. Work 3 rows patt as given for yoke.
Next row (inc row) 2ch, 1dc into first st, patt to last st, 1dc and 1tr into last st. Turn.
Next row 1ch, 1tr into first dc, patt to end, 1dc into turning ch. Turn.
Work 1 row in patt. Rep these 3 rows 3[4:4] times more. Cont without shaping until sleeve measures 11.5[12.5:14.0]cm (*4½[5:5½]in*) from beg, ending with a WS row.
Shape top
Next row Ss across first 3 sts, 1ch, 1dc into next st, dec 1, patt to last 6 sts, dec 1, 1dc into next st, turn.
Next row 2ch, dec 1, patt to last 2 sts, dec 1, 1dc in turning ch. Turn.
Rep last row 4[4:5] times more. Fasten off.

To make up

Press as given for raglan sleeved jacket. Join shoulder and sleeve seams. Set in sleeves, placing seam to centre of 5 underarm sts. Using No.3.00 (ISR) hook and with RS of work facing, rejoin yarn at top of right front, 4ch, miss 0.5cm (*¼in*) at neck edge, 1tr in next st, *miss 0.5cm (*¼in*) at neck edge, 1tr into next st, rep from * all round neck edge. Fasten off.
Border Using No.3.00 (ISR) hook and with RS of work facing, rejoin yarn on centre back 2ch sp of lower edge, *1dc, 2ch and 2tr all into sp, 1dc, 2ch, 2tr all into next dc, rep from * to corner of right front, cont in same way up front, round neck, down front and along lower edge. Join with a ss to first dc. Fasten off. Work round cuffs in same way.
Press seams. Sew on buttons.

31 Raglan sleeved jacket

Sizes

As given for round yoked jacket.
Sleeve seam, 11.5[12.5:14.0]cm (*4½[5:5½]in*)
The figures in brackets [] refer to the 51.0 (*20*) and 56.0cm (*22in*) sizes respectively

Tension

10 groups to 10cm (*3.9in*) over patt worked on No.4.00 (ISR) crochet hook

Materials

4[5:5] x ¾oz balls Hayfield Bri-Nova Perle 4 ply
One No.4.00 (ISR) crochet hook
One No.3.00 (ISR) crochet hook
3 buttons

Back

Using No.4.00 (ISR) hook make 50[54:58]ch.
Base row Into 4th ch from hook work 2tr, *miss 1ch, 2tr into next ch, rep from * to last 2ch, miss 1ch, 1tr into last ch. Turn.
Commence patt.
1st row 3ch to count as first tr, 1tr into first sp between last tr and 2tr gr, *miss next 2tr gr, 2tr into next sp between 2tr gr, rep from * ending with 2tr into last sp. Turn.
2nd row 3ch to count as first tr, 2tr into first

sp, *miss next 2tr gr, 2tr into next sp, rep from * to last gr, 1tr in sp between last tr and 3ch. Turn. 24[26:28]gr.
Rep last 2 rows 7[8:9] times more, then 1st row once more.
Shape raglans
Next row Ss across first 2 gr, 1dc into next sp, 3ch, *miss next 2tr gr, 2tr into next sp, rep from * to last 3 gr, miss next gr, 1tr into next sp, turn.
Next row 3ch, miss first gr, 2tr into next sp, patt to last gr, 1tr into 3ch sp, turn.
Rep last row 10[11:12] times more. Fasten off.

Left front

Using No.4.00 (ISR) hook make 28[30:32]ch.
Work base row as given for back. Work 17[19:21] rows patt as given for back.
Shape raglan
Next row Ss across first 2 gr, 1dc into next sp, 3ch, *miss next gr, 2tr into next sp, rep from * to last gr, 1tr between last tr and 3ch. Turn.
Next row Patt to last gr, 1tr into 3ch sp. turn.
Next row 3ch, miss first gr, 2tr into next sp, patt to end. Turn.
Rep last 2 rows twice more.
Shape neck
Next row Ss across first 5 sts, 1dc into next sp, 3ch, *miss next gr, 2tr into next sp, rep from * to last gr, 1tr into 3ch sp. turn.
Next row 3ch, miss first gr, 2tr into next sp, patt to last gr, 1tr into 3ch sp, turn.
Rep last row 2[3:4] times more.
Next row 3ch, miss first gr, 2tr into 3ch sp. Fasten off.

Right front

Work as given for left front to raglan shaping.
Shape raglan
Next row Patt to last 3 gr, miss next gr, 1tr into next sp, turn.
Next row 3ch, miss first gr, 2tr into next sp, patt to end. Turn.
Next row Patt to last gr, 1tr into 3ch sp, turn.
Rep last 2 rows twice more
Shape neck
Next row 3ch, miss first gr, 2tr into next sp, patt to last 3 gr and ch at end, miss next gr, 1tr into next sp, turn.
Next row 3ch, miss first gr, *2tr into next sp, miss next gr, rep from * to last gr, miss last gr, 1tr into 3ch sp, turn.
Complete to match left front, reversing shaping.

Sleeves

Using No.3.00 (ISR) hook make 30[32:34]ch.
Base row (RS) Into 2nd ch from hook work 1dc, 1dc into each ch to end. Turn.
Next row 1ch to count as first dc, 1dc into each dc to end. Turn.
Rep last row twice more. Change to No.4.00 (ISR) hook. Commence patt.
Base row 3ch, *miss 1dc, 2tr into next dc, rep from * to last 2dc, 2tr into next dc, 1tr into last dc. Turn.
Work 4 rows patt as given for back.
Next row (inc row) 3ch, 2tr into first sp, patt to end, 3tr into 3ch sp. Turn.
Next row (inc row) 3ch, 1tr between first and 2nd tr, miss 2tr gr, *2tr into next sp, miss 2tr gr, rep from * to last 3tr, miss 2tr, 2tr between last tr and 3ch. Turn.
Work 3 rows patt without shaping, then rep the 2 inc rows again. Work 2[4:6] more rows patt.
Shape raglan
Next row Ss across first 2 gr, 1dc into next sp, 3ch, patt to last 3 gr, miss next gr, 1tr into next sp, turn.
Dec as given for back raglan shaping for 11[12: 13] rows. Fasten off.

To make up

Press each piece under a dry cloth with a cool

iron. Join raglan, side and sleeve seams. Using No.3.00 (ISR) hook and with RS of work facing, rejoin yarn at top of right front. 4ch, miss 0.5cm ($\frac{1}{4}in$) of neck edge, 1tr into neck edge, *1ch, miss 0.5cm ($\frac{1}{4}in$) of neck edge, 1tr into neck edge, rep from * all round neck. Fasten off.

Shell border Using No.3.00 (ISR) hook and with RS of work facing, rejoin yarn at lower edge of side seam, *work 1dc and 3tr all into same st of edge, miss 1.5cm ($\frac{1}{2}in$) of edge, rep from * along lower edge, up front edge, round neck, down front edge and along lower edge. Join with a ss to first dc. Fasten off. Work round cuffs in same way. Press seams. Sew on 3 buttons to right front for a boy or left front for a girl, using sps in patt on other front as buttonholes.

Ribbon trimmed dress

Sizes
To fit 45.5cm (*18in*) chest
Length to shoulder, 33.0cm (*13in*)
Sleeve seam, 2.5cm (*1in*)
Tension
24tr to 10cm (*3.9in*) worked on No.2.50 (ISR) crochet hook; 4 shells to 7.5cm (*3in*) worked on No.3.00 (ISR) crochet hook
Materials
3 x 25 grm balls Patons Baby 3-ply Courtelle
One No.3.00 (ISR) crochet hook
One No.2.50 (ISR) crochet hook
274.5cm (*108in*) of 0.5cm ($\frac{1}{4}in$) wide ribbon
2 buttons

Yoke
Using No.2.50 (ISR) hook make 65ch and beg at neck.

1st row (WS) Into 4th ch from hook work 1tr, 1tr into each of next 10ch, 3tr in next ch, 1tr into each of next 5ch, 3tr in next ch, 1tr into each of next 25ch, 3tr in next ch, 1tr into each of next 5ch, 3tr in next ch, 1tr into each of next 12ch. Turn. 71 sts.

2nd row 3ch, miss first st, 1tr into each of next 12 sts, 3tr in next st, 1tr into each of next 7 sts, 3tr in next st, 1tr into each of next 27 sts, 3tr in next st, 1tr into each of next 7 sts, 3tr in next st, 1tr into each of next 12 sts, 1tr in top of ch. Turn. 79 sts.

3rd row 3ch, miss first st, 1tr in next st, (1ch, miss one st, 1tr in next st) 6 times, 1ch, (1tr, 1ch) twice in next st, 1tr in next st, (1ch, miss one st, 1tr in next st) 4 times, 1ch, (1tr, 1ch) twice in next st, 1tr in next st, (1ch, miss one st, 1tr in next st) 14 times, 1ch, (1tr, 1ch) twice in next st, 1tr in next st, (1ch, miss one st, 1tr in next st) 4 times, 1ch, (1tr, 1ch) twice in next st, 1tr in next st, (1ch, miss one st, 1tr in next st) 6 times, 1tr in top of ch. Turn. 95 sts including ch sp.

4th row 3ch, miss first st, 1tr into each of next 15 sts including ch sp, 3tr into next st, 1tr into each of next 13 sts, 3tr into next st, 1tr into each of next 33 sts, 3tr into next st, 1tr into each of next 13 sts, 3tr into next st, 1tr into each st to end, 1tr in top of ch. Turn. 103 sts.

5th row 3ch, miss first st, 1tr into each of next 16 sts, 3tr in next st, 1tr into each of next 15 sts, 3tr in next st, 1tr into each of next 35 sts, 3tr in next st, 1tr into each of next 15 sts, 3tr in next st, 1tr into each st to end. Turn. 111 sts.

6th row 3ch, miss first st, 1tr into each of next 17 sts, 3tr in next st, 1tr into each of next 17 sts, 3tr in next st, 1tr into each of next 37 sts, 3tr in next st, 1tr into each of next 17 sts, 3tr in next st, 1tr into each st to end. Turn. 119 sts.

7th row 4ch, miss 2 sts, 1tr in next st, (1ch, miss one st, 1tr in next st) 8 times, (1ch, 1tr) twice in next st, place marker in last ch, 1ch,

1tr in next st, (1ch, miss one st, 1tr in next st) 9 times, 1ch, (1tr, 1ch) twice in next st, 1tr in next st, (1ch, miss one st, 1tr in next st) 19 times, 1ch, (1tr, 1ch) twice in next st, 1tr in next st, (1ch, miss one st, 1tr in next st) 9 times, 1ch, (1tr, 1ch) twice in next st, 1tr in next st, (1ch, miss one st, 1tr in next st) 9 times, 1ch. Join with a ss to 3rd of first 4ch to join yoke at centre back. Fasten off.

Back
1st row Using No.3.00 (ISR) hook and with RS of work facing, rejoin yarn to marked st, 3ch, 1tr in same st, (2tr, 1ch, 2tr in next ch sp) 21 times, 2tr in next ch sp, turn. 21 shells with 2tr at each end.

2nd row 4ch, miss 2 sts, 1tr in sp between 2nd st and shell, *1tr, 2ch, 1tr in next ch sp, 1tr in sp between 2 shells, rep from * ending with 1tr in sp between last shell and next st, 1ch, 1tr in top of turning ch. Turn.

3rd row 3ch, 1tr in first ch sp, *2tr, 1ch, 2tr in next ch sp, rep from * ending with 2tr in sp of turning ch. Turn.

4th row As 2nd. Fasten off.

Right front
1st row Using No.3.00 (ISR) hook and with RS of work facing, miss first 23 sts, rejoin yarn to next ch sp, 3ch, 1tr in same ch sp, (2tr, 1ch, 2tr in next ch sp) 7 times, turn.

2nd row Ss over 2 sts, ss into ch sp, 4ch, 1tr in same ch sp, *1tr in sp between 2 shells, 1tr, 2ch, 1tr in next ch sp, rep from * ending with 1tr in sp between last shell and next st, 1ch, 1tr in top of turning ch. Turn.

3rd row 3ch, 1tr in first ch sp, *2tr, 1ch, 2tr in next ch sp, rep from * working last shell in sp of turning ch. Turn.

4th row As 2nd. Fasten off.

Left front
1st row Using No.3.00 (ISR) hook and with RS of work facing, miss 15 sts at centre front, rejoin yarn to next ch sp, 3ch, 1tr, 1ch, 2tr in same sp, (2tr, 1ch, 2tr in next ch sp) 6 times, 2tr in next ch sp, turn.

2nd row 4ch, miss 2 sts, *1tr in sp before next shell, 1tr, 2ch, 1tr in next ch sp, rep from * to end. Turn.

3rd row Ss in first ch sp, 3ch, 1tr, 1ch, 2tr in same sp, 2tr, 1ch, 2tr in each of foll sp, ending with 2tr in sp of turning ch. Turn.

4th row As 2nd.

Do not break off yarn. Join work as foll:

Next row As 3rd row to end, 1ch, work across back as 3rd row, 1ch, work across right front as 3rd row ending with 2tr, 1ch, 2tr in sp of turning ch. Turn.

Cont in patt as foll:

1st row Ss over 2 sts, ss into ch sp, 4ch, 1tr in same sp, *1tr in sp between shells, 1tr, 2ch, 1tr in next ch sp, rep from * to end, working 1tr, 2ch, 1tr in ch sp at points where work was joined. Turn.

2nd row Ss into first sp, 3ch, 1tr, 1ch, 2tr in same sp, *2tr, 1ch, 2tr in next ch sp, rep from * to end. Turn. 37 shells.

Rep last 2 rows until work measures 26.5cm (*10½in*) from end of yoke, ending with a 2nd row. Fasten off.

Inset
1st row Using No.2.50 (ISR) hook and with RS of work facing, rejoin yarn to first unworked st at centre front, 3ch in this st, work 1tr into each st and ch sp, turn. 15 sts.

2nd row 3ch, miss first st, 1tr into each st to end. Turn.

3rd row As 2nd.

4th row 4ch, miss 2 sts, (1tr in next st, 1ch, miss one st) 6 times, 1tr in top of turning ch. Turn.

5th row 3ch, miss first st, 1tr into each st to end. Turn.

The 2nd-5th rows form patt. Cont in patt until inset matches main part. Fasten off.

Sleeves
Using No.2.50 (ISR) hook and with RS of work facing, rejoin yarn to join of right front and back, 3ch, work 9tr up side edge of back, 1tr into each of 23 sts and ch sp left unworked, 10tr down side edge of right front. 43 sts. Work 2 more rows in tr, then work row of holes as before.

Next row (picot row) 1dc into first st, 3ch, ss into same st as dc, *1dc into each of next 2 sts, 3ch, ss into same st as last dc worked, rep from * to end. Fasten off.

Work 2nd sleeve in same way.

Back and neck borders
Using No.2.50 (ISR) hook and with RS of work facing, work 1 row dc up left side of back opening, work picot edge round neck then work 2 rows dc along right side of back opening, making 2 button loops on 2nd row by working 2ch and missing 2 sts.

To make up
Press lightly under a dry cloth with a cool iron. Cut ribbon into suitable lengths and thread through holes of yoke and inset, st ends down on WS. Sew sides of fronts to inset with sides of shells overlapping inset. Join sleeve seams. Thread ribbon through holes on sleeves and tie into bows. Press seams. Sew on buttons.

Baby's pram set

Sizes
Coat to fit 40.5[45.5:51.0]cm (*16[18:20]in*) chest
Length to shoulder, 21.5[23.0:24.0]cm (*8½[9:9½] in*)
Sleeve seam, 8.0[9.0:9.5]cm (*3¼[3½:3¾]in*)
Bonnet round face 28.0[30.5:33.0]cm (*11[12: 13]in*)
From Front to back, 12.5[14.0:15.0]cm (*5[5½:6] in*)
Mitts width of hand, 5.0[5.5:6.5]cm (*2[2¼:2½]in*)
Bootees length of foot, 8.0[9.0:9.5]cm (*3¼[3½: 3¾]in*)
The figures in brackets [] refer to the 45.5 (*18*) and 51.0cm (*20in*) sizes respectively
Tension
32 sts to 10.0cm (*3.9in*) over tr worked on No.3.00 (ISR) crochet hook; 28tr worked on No.3.50 (ISR) crochet hook; 24tr worked on No.4.00 (ISR) crochet hook
Materials
Robin Bri-Nylon 3 ply
Complete set 4[5:5] x 20 grm balls
or
Coat 3[3:3] balls
Bonnet, mitts and bootees, 1 ball each
One No.3.00[3.50:4.00] (ISR) crochet hook
4 small buttons
2½ metres (*2½yds*) 1.5cm (*½in*) wide ribbon

Coat
Using No.3.00[3.50:4.00] (ISR) hook make 65ch fairly loosely, beg at neck edge and work in one piece.

1st row (WS) Into 2nd ch from hook work 1dc, 1dc into each ch to end. Turn. 65dc.

2nd row 3ch to count as first tr, *1tr into each of next 4dc, 3tr into next dc, 1tr into next dc, rep from * ending with 1tr into each of last 5dc. Turn. 85 sts.

3rd row 3ch, miss 1tr, 1dc into next tr, *2ch,

miss 1tr, 1dc into next tr, rep from * ending with 1dc into 3rd of first 3ch. Turn.

4th row 3ch, 2tr into first sp, *2tr into next sp, 3tr into next sp, rep from * ending with 2tr into last sp. Turn. 105 sts.

5th row As 3rd.

6th row 3ch, *2tr into each of next 3 sps, 3tr into each of next 2 sps, rep from * ending with 2tr into each of last 2 sps. Turn. 125 sts.

7th row As 3rd.

8th row 3ch, *2tr into each of next 2 sps, 3tr into next sp, rep from * ending with 2tr into each of last 2 sps. Turn. 145 sts.

9th row As 3rd.

10th row 3ch, *2tr into each of next 4 sps, 3tr into next sp, 2tr into each of next 2 sps, rep from * ending with 2tr into each of last 2 sps. Turn. 155 sts.

11th row As 3rd. 77 sps.

12th row 3ch, 2tr into each of next 3 sps, *3tr into next sp, 2tr into each of next 5 sps, *, rep from * to * once more, 2tr into each of next 14 sps, rep from * to * 4 times more, 2tr into each of next 14 sps, rep from * to * once more, 3tr into next sp, 2tr into each of last 3 sps. Turn. 163 sts.

13th row As 3rd. 81 sps.
Commence skirt.

1st row 3ch, *work (2tr, 2ch, 2tr) into next sp — called 1 shell —, 1dc into next sp, *, rep from * to * 5 times more, 1 shell into next sp, miss 15 sps, rep from * to * 12 times, 1 shell into next sp, miss 15 sps, rep from * to * 6 times, 1 shell into last sp, 1tr into 2nd of first 3ch. Turn.

2nd row 3ch, *1 shell into next 2ch sp, 1ch, rep from * to last sp, 1 shell into last sp, 1tr into 3rd of first 3ch. Turn.

3rd row 3ch, *1 shell into next 2ch sp, 1dc into next 1ch sp. *, rep from * to * to last sp, 1 shell into last sp, 1tr into 3rd of first 3ch. Turn. The 2nd and 3rd rows form patt. Rep patt rows 5 times more, ending last row with 1dc into 3rd of first 3ch. Do not break yarn.

Edging
Cont with shell edging on each front and round neck.

Next row 1 shell into same place as last dc, 1dc into last st of previous row, *1 shell into end of next row, 1dc into end of next row, rep from * to edge of yoke, work 1 shell into end of tr rows and 1dc into end of dc rows ending with 1dc, 1 shell into corner, *, across neck edge, **miss 2 sts, 1dc into next st, miss 2 sts, 1 shell into next st, rep from ** ending with 1 shell, 1dc into corner, work from * to * down left front to corner, ss into 2nd of 3ch at beg of last row of skirt. Fasten off.

Sleeves
Using No.3.00[3.50:4.00] (ISR) hook and with RS of work facing, rejoin yarn at centre of underarm between 2 shells on 1st row of skirt.

1st row 3ch, 1 shell into last tr of row, 1dc in same sp as shell on front or back, *miss 1 sp, 1 shell in next sp, 1dc into next sp, rep from * 4 times more, miss next sp, 1 shell in tr, 1tr in same place as 3ch. Turn. 7 shells.
Rep 2nd and 3rd patt rows of skirt 4 times. Fasten off. Work other sleeve in same way.

To make up
Press lightly under a dry cloth with a cool iron. Join sleeve seams. Press seams. Sew on 4 buttons using sp in which shell edging was worked as buttonholes.

Bonnet
Using No.3.00[3.50:4.00] (ISR) hook make 3ch.

1st row Into 3rd ch from hook work 8dc. Turn.

2nd row 3ch, work 2tr into first dc, work 3tr into each of next 7dc. Turn.

3rd row 3ch, miss 1tr, 1dc into next tr, *2ch,

miss 1tr, 1dc into next tr, rep from * to end. Turn.

4th row 3ch, work 3tr into each sp to end. Turn.

5th row As 3rd.

6th row As 4th.

7th row As 3rd.

8th row As 4th but work 2tr into 1st ch sp only.

9th row As 3rd. 40 sps.

10th row 3ch, *miss 1 sp, 1 shell into next sp, 1dc into next sp, rep from * to last sp, 1 shell into last sp, 1tr into 2nd of first 3ch. Turn.
Rep 2nd and 3rd patt rows of coat skirt 4 times more. Fasten off.

To make up
Press as given for coat. Join back seam to beg of shell patt. Using No.3.00[3.50:4.00] (ISR) hook and with RS of work facing, rejoin yarn at front corner and work 2 rows dc round neck edge. Fasten off. Thread ribbon through holes in patt below dc.

Mittens
Using No.3.00[3.50:4.00] (ISR) hook make 14ch.

1st row Into 2nd ch from hook work 1dc, 1dc into each ch to end. Turn.

2nd row 3ch, *4tr into next dc, 1tr into each of next 3dc, 4tr into next dc, *, 1tr into each of next 2dc, rep from * to * once more, 1tr into last st. Turn.

3rd row 3ch, miss 1tr, 1dc into next tr, *2ch, miss 1tr, 1dc into next tr, rep from * to end. Turn.

4th row 3ch, *3tr into next sp, 2tr into each of next 4 sps, 3tr into next sp, *, 2tr into next sp, rep from * to * once more. Turn.

5th row As 3rd. 15 sps.

6th row 3ch, 2tr into each sp to end. Turn.
Rep last 2 rows twice more, then 5th row once.

12th row 3ch, *1 shell into next sp, 1dc into next sp, rep from * to last sp, 1 shell into last sp, 1tr into 2nd of first 3ch. Turn.

13th row 3ch, *1 shell in next sp, 1ch, rep from * to last sp, 1 shell in last sp, 1tr into 3rd of first 3ch. Turn.

14th row 3ch, *1 shell into next 2ch sp, 1dc into next 1ch sp, rep from * to last sp, 1 shell into last sp, 1tr into 3rd of first 3ch. Turn. Fasten off.

To make up
Press as given for coat. Join seam. Thread ribbon through holes at wrist.

Bootees
Using No.3.00[3.50:4.00] (ISR) hook make 37ch.

1st row Into 2nd ch from hook work 1dc, 1dc into each ch to end. Turn.

2nd row 3ch, 1tr into each of next 17dc, 5tr into each of next 2dc, 1tr into each of next 17dc. Turn.

3rd and 5th rows 3ch, miss 1tr, 1dc into next tr, *2ch, miss 1tr, 1dc into next tr, rep from * to end. Turn.

4th row 3ch, 2tr into each of next 10 sps, 4tr into each of next 2 sps, 2tr into each of next 10 sps. Turn.

6th row 3ch, 2tr into each sp to end. Turn.

7th row Ss across first 4tr, 3ch, miss 1tr, 1dc into next tr, *2ch, miss 1tr, 1dc into next tr, rep from * to last 4tr, turn.

8th row 3ch, 4tr into first sp, 2tr into each of next 5 sps, 1tr into each of next 8 sps, 2tr into each of next 5 sps, 4tr into last sp. Turn.

9th row As 3rd.

10th row 2ch, 2dc into each of next 7 sps, 1dc into each of next 4 sps, 2dc into each of next 7 sps. Fasten off.

Edging
Using No.3.00[3.50:4.00] (ISR) hook and with WS of work facing, rejoin yarn to beg of foundation ch.

1st row 3ch, miss 1ch, 1dc into next ch, *2ch,

miss 1ch, 1dc into next ch, 2ch, miss 2ch, 1dc into next ch, 2ch, miss 1ch, 1dc into next ch, rep from * 3 times more, **2ch, miss 1ch, 1dc into next ch, rep from ** once more, 1dc into last st. Turn.
Rep 12th, 13th and 14th rows of mittens. Fasten off.

To make up
Press as given for coat. Join back and centre foot seams. Sew heel seam to foot. Thread ribbon through holes at ankles.

34 Tank top for a girl

Sizes
To fit 56.0[61.0:66.0:71.0]cm (*22[24:26:28]in*) chest
Length to shoulder, 30.5[30.5:35.5:35.5]cm (*12[12:14:14]in*)
The figures in brackets [] refer to the 61.0 (*24*), 66.0 (*26*) and 71.0cm (*28in*) sizes respectively

Tension
Each motif measures 4.0cm (*1½in*) by 4.0cm (*1½in*) worked on No.3.50 (ISR) crochet hook; 5.0cm (*2in*) by 5.0cm (*2in*) worked on No.4.00 (ISR) crochet hook

Materials
Wendy Courtellon Double Knitting or Courtelle Double Crepe
3[3:4:4] x 20 grm balls in main shade, A
2[2:3:3] balls each of contrast colours, B, C, D and E
One No.3.50[4.00:3.50:4.00] (ISR) crochet hook
One No.3.00[3.50:3.00:3.50] (ISR) crochet hook

1st motif
Using No.3.50[4.00:3.50:4.00] (ISR) hook and B, make 8ch. Join with a ss to first ch to form circle.

1st round 4ch to count as first dtr, work 3dtr into circle, *5ch, work 4dtr into circle, rep from * twice more, 5ch. Join with a ss to 4th of first 4ch. Fasten off.
Using B, make 21[21:27:27] more motifs in same way.
Using C, make 23[23:32:32] more motifs in same way.
Using D, make 21[21:22:22] more motifs in same way.
Using E, make 19[19:27:27] more motifs in same way.

To make up
Press each motif under a dry cloth with a cool iron. Using No.3.00[3.50:3.00:3.50] (ISR) hook, and A, place one motif in C and one motif in E tog, work 3dc through both 5ch sp and 1dc into each dtr along one side. Cont joining motifs in this way as given in diagram.
Edging Using No.3.00[3.50:3.00:3.50] (ISR) hook, A and with RS of work facing, work 1 round dc round lower edge. Do not join. Work 1 more round crab st, working in dc from left to right instead of from right to left. Work round armholes and neck in same way.
Press lightly.

35 Open-sided tabard

Sizes
To fit 56.0[61.0:66.0:71.0]cm (*22[24:26:28]in*) chest

Length to shoulder, 37.0[39.5:42.0:44.5]cm ($14\frac{1}{2}$[$15\frac{1}{2}$:$16\frac{1}{2}$:$17\frac{1}{2}$]in)
The figures in brackets [] refer to the 61.0 (24), 66.0 (26) and 71.0cm (28in) sizes respectively

Tension
22 sts to 10.0cm (3.9in) over patt worked on No.3.50 (ISR) crochet hook

Materials
3[3:4:4] x 40 grm balls of Wendy Marina in main shade, A
1[1:1:1] ball of contrast colour, B
One No.3.50 (ISR) crochet hook

Tank top
Using No.3.50 (ISR) hook and A, make 49[55:61:67]ch and beg at lower edge of back.
Base row Into 2nd ch from hook work 1dc, 1dc into each ch to end. Turn. 48[54:60:66]dc.
Commence patt.
1st row 4ch to count as first tr and 1ch sp, 1tr into next dc, *1ch, miss 1dc, 1tr into next dc, rep from * to last 3dc, 1ch, miss 1dc, 1tr into next dc, 1ch, 1tr into last dc. Turn.
2nd row 1ch, work 3dc into first ch sp, *work 2dc into next ch sp, rep from * to last ch sp, work 3dc into last ch sp. Turn.
3rd row 1ch, 2dc into first dc, *1dc into next dc, rep from * to last dc, 2dc into last dc. Turn.
4th row As 1st.
5th row As 2nd.
6th row 1ch, *1dc into next dc, rep from * to end. Turn.

7th row As 1st. 60[66:72:78]sts.
8th row 1ch, work 2dc into each ch sp to end. Turn.
9th row 1ch, 1dc into each dc to end. Turn.
10th row 3ch, *miss 1dc, 1tr into next dc, 1ch, rep from * to last 2dc, miss 1dc, 1tr into last dc. Turn.
The 8th–10th rows inclusive form patt. Work 6 [9:12:15] more rows in patt.
Next row (dec row) 1ch, 1dc into first ch sp, *2 dc into next ch sp, rep from * to last ch sp, 1dc into last ch sp. Turn. 58[64:70:76]sts. Mark each end of row with coloured thread.
Cont in patt, dec in this way on every foll 9th row and marking each end of dec row with coloured thread, until 4 more dec rows have been worked. 50[56:62:68] sts. Cont without shaping until work measures 34.5[37.0:39.5:42.0]cm ($13\frac{1}{2}$[$14\frac{1}{2}$:$15\frac{1}{2}$:$16\frac{1}{2}$]in) from beg, ending with a 10th patt row.
Shape neck
Next row 1ch, (2dc into next ch sp) 7[8:9:10] times, turn.
Complete this side first. Work 11 more rows in patt. Break off yarn.
Return to where work was left, miss first 11[12:13:14] ch sp for back neck, rejoin yarn to next st, patt to end. Turn. Work 11 more rows in patt.
Join for front neck
Next row Patt across first set of sts, make 22[24:26:28] ch, patt across 2nd set of sts. Turn.
Cont in patt until work measures 45.5[48.5:

51.0:53.5]cm (18[$19:20:21$]in) from beg, ending with a 10th patt row.
Next row (inc row) 1ch, 3dc into first ch sp, *2 dc into next ch sp, rep from * to last ch sp, 3dc into last ch sp. Turn.
Cont in patt, inc in this way on every foll 9th row until 5 inc rows in all have been worked. 60 [66:72:78] sts. Work 9[12:15:18] rows without shaping. Dec one st at each end of next row. Work 1 row without shaping. Dec one st at each end of next 5 rows. Fasten off.

Edging
Using No.3.50 (ISR) hook and B, make 3ch.
1st row Into 3rd ch from hook work 1tr and 1dc. Turn.
2nd row 2ch, work 1tr and 1dc into dc of previous row. Turn.
The 2nd row forms patt. Cont in patt until edging is long enough, when slightly stretched, to fit all round outer edges of garment. Fasten off. Work another piece in same way long enough to fit round neck edge.

Ties (make 4)
Using No.3.50 (ISR) hook and 2 strands of A, make a ch 35.5cm (14in) long. Fasten off.

To make up
Press lightly under a dry cloth with a cool iron. Pin edging round outer edge of garment then sl st in position. Sl st edging round neck. Take out marker threads. Sl st ties to each side at underarm. Press edging lightly.

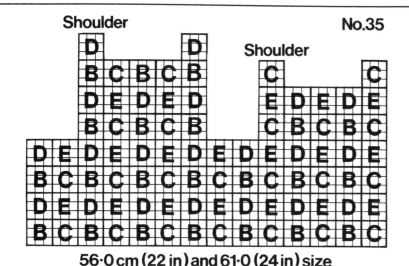

56·0 cm (22 in) and 61·0 (24 in) size

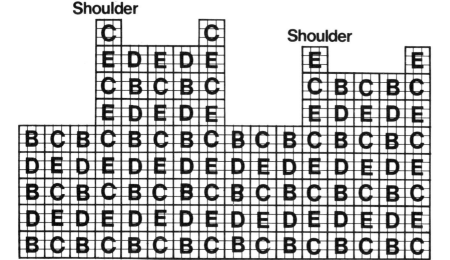

66·0 cm (26 in) and 71·0 cm (28 in) size

36 Four fun hats for children

Cap

Size
To fit 10-14 years
Tension
12dc to 10cm (3.9in) over patt worked on No.5.50 (ISR) crochet hook
Materials
3 x 25 grm balls of Wendy Double Knitting Nylonised in main shade, A
1 ball of contrast colour, B
One No.5.50 (ISR) crochet hook
Note
Yarn is used double throughout
Using No.5.50 (ISR) hook, and with 2 strands of A, make 6ch. Join with a ss to first ch to form circle.
1st round 3ch to count as first tr, work 11tr into circle. Join with a ss to 3rd of first 3ch. 12tr.
2nd round 1ch to count as first dc, 2dc into each of next 2 sts, *1dc into next st, 2dc into each of next 2 sts, rep from * to end. Join with a ss to first ch. 20 sts.
3rd and every alt round 1ch, 1dc into each st to end. Join with a ss to first ch.
4th round 1ch to count as first dc, 1dc into next st, *2dc into each of next 2 sts, 1dc into next st, rep from * to end. Join with a ss to first ch. 28 sts.
6th round 1ch to count as first dc, 1dc into next st, 2dc into next st, *1dc into each of next 3 sts, 2dc into next st, rep from * to end. Join with a ss to first ch. 35 sts.
8th round As 6th. 44 sts.
10th round 1ch to count as first dc, 2dc into next st, *1dc into each of next 3 sts, 2dc into next st, rep from * to end, ending with 1dc into each of last 2 sts. Join with a ss to first ch. 55 sts.
12th round 1ch to count as first dc, 1dc into

each of next 2 sts, 2dc into next st, *1dc into each of next 6 sts, 2dc into next st, rep from * to end, ending with 1dc into each of last 2 sts. Join with a ss to first ch. 63 sts.
Work 9 rounds dc without shaping. Fasten off.

Earflaps (make 2)

Mark join of last round with coloured thread. Using No.5.50 (ISR) hook, A and with RS of work facing, miss first 8 sts from marker, using 2 strands of yarn, rejoin yarn to next st, 2ch, work 1dc into each of next 8 sts. Turn. 9dc. Cont in dc dec one st at each end of next and every alt row until 3 sts rem. Work 3dc tog. Fasten off.

To make up

Press lightly under a damp cloth with a warm iron.
Edging Using No.5.50 (ISR) hook, 2 strands of B and with RS of work facing, rejoin yarn at centre back and work 3 rounds dc all round lower edge, working 3dc into corner sts of earflaps on every round. Work 1 round crab st working in dc from left to right instead of from right to left. Fasten off.
Using 2 strands of B, and with RS of work facing, work in embroidered loop st all round hat as shown in illustration, if required. Using B, make a tassel and sew to top of cap.

Helmet

Sizes
To fit 10-14 years
Tension
5 bobbles to 7.5cm (*3in*) over patt worked on No.6.00 (ISR) crochet hook
Materials
5 x 25 grm balls of Wendy Double Knitting Nylonised
One No.6.00 (ISR) crochet hook
Note
Yarn is used double throughout

Using No.6.00 (ISR) hook and with 2 strands of yarn, make 4ch. Join with a ss to first ch to form circle.
1st round 2ch, *(yrh, insert hook into circle and draw up a loop to 1.5cm (½in),) twice, yrh and draw through all loops on hook — called B1 —, 1ch, rep from * 14 times more. Join with a ss to first of first 2ch. 15 bobbles.
2nd round Ss into first ch sp, 1ch, B1 into first ch sp, 1ch, (B1, 1ch) into each of next 4 ch sp, *(yrh, insert hook into next sp, draw up a loop to 1.5cm (½in),) 3 times into same sp, yrh and draw through all loops on hook — called BB1 —, 1ch, *, rep from * to * once more into same sp, (B1, 1ch) into each of next 8 ch sp, rep from * to * twice into next ch sp. Join with a ss to first ch.
3rd round Ss into first ch sp, 1ch, B1 into first ch sp, 1ch, (B1, 1ch) into each of next 5 ch sp, (BB1, 1ch, into next 1 ch sp between BB1) twice, (B1, 1ch) into each of next 9 ch sp, (BB1, 1ch, into next 1ch sp between BB1) twice. Join with a ss to first ch.
4th-11th rounds Work as given for 3rd round. working one extra B1 and 1ch between each BB1 on back and front on each round. 14 bobbles for back between BB1 and 17 bobbles for front between BB1.
Divide for left strap
12th round Work in patt until second BB1 has been completed, work 1tr into next ch sp, turn.
Next row 4ch to count as first tr and 1ch, (BB1, 1ch, into next 1 ch sp between BB1) twice, 1tr into next sp, turn.
Work 14 more rows as now set over these sts. Fasten off.
Right strap
With RS of work facing, rejoin yarn to 1ch sp

before BB1 on other side.
Next row 4ch to count as first tr and 1ch, (BB1, 1ch, into next 1 ch sp between BB1) twice, 1tr into next sp, turn.
Complete to match left strap. Do not turn work or fasten off.
Edging
Work down side of strap, 1ch 1dc into every row end of strap, along front edge work (1ch, 1dc between each bobble), then work round left strap and back edge in same way. Fasten off.

To make up
Do not press. Darn in ends.

White beret

Size
To fit 10-14 years
Tension
12tr to 10cm (*3.9in*) worked on No.6.00 (ISR) crochet hook
Materials
3 x 50 grm balls of Wendy Diabolo Double Double Knitting
One No.6.00 (ISR) crochet hook

Using No.6.00 (ISR) hook make 5ch. Join with a ss to first ch to form circle.
1st round 1ch to count as first dc, work 9dc into circle. Join with a ss to first ch. 10dc.
2nd round 3ch to count as first tr, 1tr into same st, work 2tr into each dc to end. Join with a ss to 3rd of first 3ch. 20 sts.
3rd round 3ch to count as first tr, 2tr into next st, *1tr into next st, 2tr into next st, rep from * to end. Join with a ss to 3rd of first 3ch. 30 sts.
4th round 4ch to count as first tr and 1ch, 1tr into same st, *miss 1tr, (1tr, 1ch, 1tr) into next tr, rep from * to last st, miss 1tr. Join with a ss to 3rd of first 4ch.
5th round *Into each 1ch sp between tr work (yrh, insert hook into ch sp and draw up a loop) 4 times into same sp, yrh and draw through all loops on hook — called B1 —, 1ch, 1dc into each sp between tr groups, rep from * to end. Join with a ss to top of first B1. 15 bobbles.
6th round 4ch to count as first tr and 1ch, 1tr into same st, 1ch, *(1tr, 1ch) 3 times and 1tr all into top of next B1, 1ch, (1tr, 1ch and 1tr into top of next B1, 1ch) twice, rep from * to last 2 bobbles (1tr, 1ch) 4 times into top of next B1, (1tr, 1ch, 1tr) into next B1, 1ch. Join with a ss to 3rd of first 4ch.
7th round As 5th. 20 bobbles.
8th round Ss to top of first B1, 4ch, 1tr into top of first B1, *(1ch, 1tr) twice into top of next 2 bobbles, 1ch, (1tr, 1ch) 4 times into top of next B1, (1ch, 1tr) into top of next B1, rep from * to last 3 bobbles (1ch, 1tr) twice into top of next 2 bobbles, 1ch, (1tr, 1ch) 4 times into top of last B1. Join with a ss to 3rd of first 4ch.
9th round As 5th. 25 bobbles.
10th round Ss to top of first B1, 4ch, 1tr into top of first B1, *(1ch, 1tr) twice into top of next B1, rep from * to end, 1ch. Join with a ss to 3rd of first 4ch.
11th round As 5th round.
12th round Ss to top of first B1, 4ch, 1tr into top of first B1, *(1ch, 1tr 1ch, 1tr) into top of next 2 B1, (1ch, 1tr) into top of next 2 B1, (1ch, 1tr, 1ch, 1tr) into top of next B1, rep from * to last 4 B1, (1ch, 1tr, 1ch, 1tr) into top of next 2 B1 (1ch, 1tr) into top of next 2 B1, 1ch. Join with a ss to 3rd of first 4ch.
13th round As 5th round. 20 bobbles.
14th round As 12th round.
15th round As 5th round. 16 bobbles.
16th round * 1dc before B1, 1dc into B1, 1dc after B1, rep from * to end. 48dc.

17th and 18th rounds Work in dc all round. Fasten off.

To make up
Press under a damp cloth with a warm iron. Sew in ends.

Jelly bag hat

Size
To fit 10-14 years
Tension
18 sts to 10cm (*3.9in*) over patt worked on No.3.50 (ISR) crochet hook
Materials
3 x 25 grm balls Wendy Double Knitting Nylonised in main shade, A
2 balls of contrast colour, B
1 ball each of contrast colours, C and D
One No.3.50 (ISR) crochet hook

Using No.3.50 (ISR) hook and A, make 82ch and beg at lower edge.
Next row Into 2nd ch from hook work 1dc, 1dc into each ch to end. Turn. 81dc.
Commence patt.
1st row 2ch, 2htr into first dc, miss 1dc, * 2htr into next dc, miss 1dc, rep from * to last st, 1htr into last st. Turn.
2nd row 2ch, miss first htr, *2htr between groups, rep from * to last st, 1htr into last st. Turn.
The last row forms patt and is rep throughout.
Cont in patt working striped patt as foll; 2 rows A, 1 row B, 2 rows D, 1 row B, 4 rows A, 1 row B, 2 rows C, 1 row B, 2 rows A. Cont in striped patt throughout.
Next row (dec row) *Patt over 4 groups, (1htr into next sp) twice, patt over 4 groups, rep from * 3 times more, 1htr into last st. Turn.
Work 15 rows without shaping.
Next row (dec row) *Patt over 3 groups, (1htr into next sp) twice, patt over 4 groups, rep from * 3 times more, 1htr into last st. Turn.
Work 7 rows without shaping.
Next row (dec row) *Patt over 3 groups, (1htr into next sp) twice, patt over 3 groups, rep from * 3 times more, 1htr into last st. Turn.
Work 7 rows without shaping.
Next row (dec row) *Patt over 2 groups, (1htr into next sp) twice, patt over 3 groups, rep from * 3 times more, 1htr into last st. Turn.
Work 7 rows without shaping.
Next row (dec row) *Patt over 2 groups, (1htr into next sp) twice, patt over 2 groups, rep from * 3 times more, 1htr into last st. Turn.
Work 7 rows without shaping.
Next row (dec row) *Patt over one group, (1htr into next sp) twice, patt over 2 groups, rep from * to last st, 1htr into last st. Turn.
Work 7 rows without shaping.
Next row (dec row) *Patt over one group, (1htr into next sp) twice, patt over one group, rep from * 3 times more, 1htr into last st. Turn.
Work 7 rows without shaping.
Next row (dec row) *Patt over one group, (1htr into next sp) twice, rep from * 3 times more, 1htr into last st. Turn.
Work 7 rows without shaping.
Next row (dec row) 1htr into each sp to end, 1htr into last st. Turn.
Work 4 rows without shaping.
Next row Using B, 1htr into each sp, leaving last loop of each st on hook, yrh, pull through all loops on hook. Draw up tightly. Fasten off.

To make up
Press under a damp cloth with a warm iron on WS of work.
Join back seam. Make a pompon using B, C and D and sew to top of hat.

HAYFIELD

29-31

Three useful matinée jackets, suitable for a baby boy or girl: *(top)* round yoked, *(left)* with a square yoke, and *(right)* with raglan sleeves

Sizes: to fit 45.5 [51.0:56.0]cm (18[20: 22]in) chest

PATONS

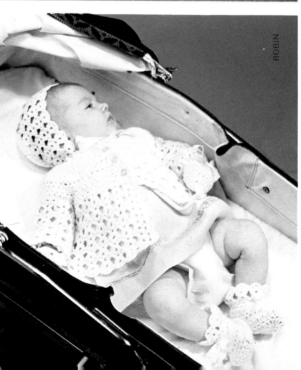

ROBIN

32

Charming baby dress lavishly trimmed with ribbon.

Size: to fit 45.5cm (18in) chest

33

Pram set for a baby.

Sizes: to fit 40.5 [45.5:51.0]cm (16[18: 20]in) chest

109

WENDY

34

Delightful tank top
made from simple
square motifs.

Sizes : to fit 56.0
[61.0:66.0:71.0cm
(22[24:26:28]in) chest

35

Traditional tabard
tied at each side
seam.

Sizes : to fit 56.0
[61.0:66.0:71.0]cm (22
[24:26:28]in) chest

36

A collection of hats :
(top) cap, helmet
(left), beret
(centre) and jelly
bag hat (right)

Size : 10-14 years

111

37

Teenager's charming smock with long, full sleeves.

Sizes: to fit 71.0 [76.0:81.5]cm (28[30:32]in) chest/bust

38

Smart dress for a modern miss, worked in chevron stripes of three colours with a single colour yoke.

Size: to fit 61.0/63.5cm (24/25in) chest

39

Dainty dress for summer parties (far left) in a simple, sleeveless A-line shape.

Sizes: to fit 56.0 [61.0:66.0:71.0]cm (22[24:26:28]in) chest

40

Attractive, empire-line dress for a little girl (left) with neat, short sleeves and centre front opening.

Sizes: to fit 56.0 [61.0:66.0:71.0]cm (22[24:26:28]in) chest

41

Sensible raglan sleeved, v-neck jersey for a boy or girl with an interesting Aran look.

Sizes: to fit 66.0 [71.0:76.0]cm (26[28: 30]in) chest

42

Bright waistcoat with lace fastening and bands of contrast colour at lower edge.

Sizes: to fit 66.0 [71.0:76.0]cm (26 [28:30]in) chest

43

Useful v-neck cardigan or waistcoat with patch pockets. It can be adapted to suit a girl by reversing the buttonholes.

Sizes: to fit 66.0 [71.0:76.0:81.5: 86.5]cm (26[28:30: 32:34]in) chest

37 Teenager's smock

Sizes
To fit 71.0[76.0:81.5]cm (28[30:32]in) chest/bust
Length to shoulder, 63.5[65.0:66.0]cm (25[25½: 26]in)
Sleeve seam, 45.5[52.0:57.0]cm (18[20½:22½]in)
The figures in brackets [] refer to the 76.0 (30) and 81.5cm (32in) sizes respectively

Tension
24 sts and 12 rows to 10cm (3.9in) over tr worked on No.3.00 (ISR) crochet hook

Materials
11[12:12] x 50 grm balls Patons Cameo Crepe
One No.3.00 (ISR) crochet hook
One No.2.50 (ISR) crochet hook
9 buttons

Yoke
Using No.3.00 (ISR) hook make 216[240:264]ch. Join with a ss to first ch to form circle.
1st round (WS) 3ch to count as first tr, 1tr into each of next 26[29:32]ch, miss 2ch, 1tr into next ch placing coloured marker in this ch, miss 2ch, (1tr into each of next 49[55:61]ch, miss 2ch, 1tr into next ch, miss 2ch) 3 times, 1tr into each of last 22[25:28]ch. Join with a ss to 3rd of first 3ch. Turn.
Cont working in rows as foll:
1st row 3ch, 1tr into each of next 20[23:26]sts, *miss 2 sts, 1tr into next st, miss 2 sts, 1tr into each of next 21[24:27]sts, 2tr into next st, 1tr into next st, 2tr into next st, 1tr into each of next 21[24:27] sts, miss 2 sts, 1tr into next st, miss 2 sts, *, 1tr into each of next 45[51:57] sts, rep from * to * once more, 1tr into each of next 21[24:27] sts. Turn.
2nd row 3ch, miss first st, 1tr into each of next 18[21:24] sts, *miss 2 sts, 1tr into next st, miss 2 sts, 1tr into each of next 43[49:55] sts, miss 2 sts, 1tr into next st, miss 2 sts, *, 1tr into each of next 41[47:53] sts, rep from * to * once more, 1tr into each of next 19[22:25] sts. Turn.
3rd row 3ch, miss first st, 1tr into each of next 16[19:22] sts, *miss 2 sts, 1tr into next st, miss 2 sts, 1tr into each of next 18[21:24] sts, 2tr into next st, 1tr into next st, 2tr into next st, 1tr into each of next 18[21:24] sts, miss 2 sts, 1tr into next st, miss 2 sts, *, 1tr into each of next 37[43:49] sts, rep from * to * once more, 1tr into each of next 17[20:23] sts. Turn.
4th row 3ch, miss first st, 1tr into each of next 14[17:20] sts, *miss 2 sts, 1tr into next st, miss 2 sts, 1tr into each of next 37[43:49] sts, miss 2 sts, 1tr into next st, miss 2 sts, *, 1tr into each of next 33[39:45] sts, rep from * to * once more, 1tr into each of next 15[18:21] sts. Turn.
Change to No.2.50 (ISR) hook and work border.
5th row 1ch, 1dc into first st, 1dc into each of next 13[16:19] sts, *miss one st, 1dc into next st, miss one st, 1dc into each of next 35[41:47] sts, miss one st, 1dc into next st, miss one st, *, 1dc into each of next 31[37:43] sts, rep from * to * once more, 1dc into each of next 14[17:20] sts. Turn.
6th row 1ch, 1dc into first st, 1dc into each of next 12[15:18] sts, *miss one st, 1dc into next st, miss one st, 1dc into each of next 33[39:45] sts, miss one st, 1dc into next st, miss one st, *, 1dc into each of next 29[35:41] sts, rep from * to * once more, 1dc into each of next 13[16:19] sts. Turn.
7th row 1ch, 1dc into first st, 1dc into each of next 11[14:17] sts, *miss one st, 1dc into next st, miss one st, 1dc into each of next 31[37:43] sts, miss one st, 1dc into next st, miss one st, *, 1dc into each of next 27[33:39] sts, rep from * to * once more, 1dc into each of next 12[15:18] sts. Fasten off.

Skirt front
Using No.3.00 (ISR) hook and with WS of work facing, rejoin yarn into marked corner ch.
Base row (WS) 3ch, (yrh, insert hook into next st, draw through loop and draw up to height of 1.5cm (½in), (yrh, insert hook into same st, draw up to height of 1.5cm (½in) 3 times, yrh and draw loop through all loops on hook — called 1C1 —, 3ch, 1C1) into marked ch, *3ch, miss next ch, 1dc into next ch, 7ch, miss 1ch, 1dc into next ch, 3ch, miss 1ch, (1C1, 3ch, 1C1, 3ch, 1C1) into next ch, rep from * across front yoke, ending last rep with (1C1, 3ch, 1C1) into corner ch. 8[9:10] groups of 3C1 and 1 group of 2C1 at each end. Turn.
1st row 6ch, *(1dtr, 2ch, 1dtr) into next 3ch sp, 2ch, 1dtr into top of next C1, 2ch, (1dc, 9ch, 1dc) into next 7ch sp, 2ch, 1dtr into top of next C1, 2ch, (1dtr, 2ch, 1dtr) into next 3ch sp, 2ch, 1dtr into top of 3ch, rep from * ending last rep with (1dtr, 2ch, 1dtr) into last 3ch sp, 2ch, 1dtr into top of 3ch. Turn.
2nd row 7ch, miss first dtr, *1dc into next dtr, 3ch, (1C1, 3ch 1C1, 3ch, 1C1) into 5th of next 9ch, 3ch, miss 2dtr, 1dc into next dtr, 7ch, miss next dtr, rep from * ending last rep with 3ch, miss 2dtr, 1dc into next dtr, 3ch, 1tr into 3rd of first 6ch. Turn.
3rd row 9ch, 1dc into first st, *2ch, 1dtr into top of next C1, **2ch, (1dtr, 2ch, 1dtr) into next 3ch sp, 2ch, 1dtr into top of next C1, **, rep from ** to ** once more, 2ch, 1dc, 9ch, 1dc into next 7ch sp, rep from * ending last rep with (1dc, 4ch, 1dtr) into 4th of first 7ch. Turn.
4th row 3ch, (1C1, 3ch, 1C1) into first st, *3ch, miss next 2dtr, 1dc into next dtr, 7ch, miss next dtr, 1dc into next dtr, 3ch, (1C1, 3ch, 1C1, 3ch, 1C1) into 5th of next 9ch, rep from * ending last rep with (1C1, 3ch, 1C1) into 5th of next 9ch. Turn.
These 4 rows form patt and are rep throughout.
Cont in patt until front measures 49.5cm (19½in) from base of yoke, ending with a 2nd patt row.
Next row (5ch, 1dc, 5ch, 1dc) into first st, *2ch, 1dtr into top of next C1, **2ch, (1dtr, 2ch, 1dtr) into next 3ch sp, 2ch, 1dtr into top of next C1, **, rep from ** to ** once more, 2ch, (1dc, 5ch, 1dc, 5ch, 1dc) into next 7ch, rep from * ending last rep with (1dc, 5ch, 1dc, 5ch, 1dc) into 4th of 7ch. Fasten off.

Right sleeve
Using No.3.00 (ISR) hook and with WS of yoke facing, rejoin yarn to last corner ch worked into.
Base row (WS) 3ch, (1C1, 3ch, 1C1) into this corner ch, *3ch, miss 2ch, 1dc into next ch, 7ch, miss 2ch, 1dc into next ch, 3ch, miss 2ch, (1C1, 3ch, 1C1, 3ch, 1C1) into next ch, *, rep from * to * once more, **3ch, miss next 2dtr, 1dc into next ch, 7ch, miss 1ch, 1dc into next ch, 3ch, miss next ch, (1C1, 3ch, 1C1, 3ch, 1C1) into next ch, **, rep from ** to ** 2[3:4] times more, rep from * to * once more, 3ch, miss 2ch, 1dc into next ch, 7ch, miss 2ch, 1dc into next ch, 3ch, miss 2ch, (1C1, 3ch, 1C1) into corner ch. 6[7:8] groups of 3C1 and 1 group of 2C1 at each end. Turn.
Cont in patt as given for skirt front until sleeve measures 39.5[45.5:52.0]cm (15½[18:20½]in) from beg, ending with a 3rd patt row.
Divide for sleeve opening
Next row 3ch, (1C1, 3ch, 1C1) into first st, *3ch, miss next 2dtr, 1dc into next dtr, 7ch, miss next dtr, 1dc into next dtr, 3ch, (1C1, 3ch, 1C1, 3ch, 1C1) into 5th of next 9ch, *, rep from * to * 2[3:4] times more, 3ch, miss next 2dtr, 1dc into next dtr, 7ch, miss next dtr, 1dc into next dtr, 3ch, (1C1, 3ch, 1C1) into 5th of 9ch, turn.
Complete this side first. Work a further 4 rows for front of sleeve. Change to No.2.50 (ISR) hook and work front cuff.
****1st row** (RS) 3ch, miss first C1, 1tr into next C1, *2tr into next 7ch sp, 1tr into each of next

3C1, rep from * ending last rep with 1tr into each of last 2C1. **. 21[26:31] sts.
Next row 3ch, miss first st, 1tr into each rem st to end.
Rep last row 3 times more. Fasten off.
Using No.3.00 (ISR) hook, and with WS of work facing, rejoin yarn into 5th of 9ch where work was turned, 3ch, (1C1, 3ch, 1C1) into same st, patt to end.
Work a further 4 rows in patt for back of sleeve.
Change to No.2.50 (ISR) hook. Work as given for front cuff from ** to **. 16 sts. Work a further 4 rows in tr. Fasten off.

Skirt back
Using No.3.00 (ISR) hook and with WS of work facing, rejoin yarn into last corner ch worked and work as given for skirt front.

Left sleeve
Using No.3.00 (ISR) hook and with WS of work facing, rejoin yarn into last corner ch worked into and work as given for right sleeve to division for sleeve opening.
Divide for sleeve opening
Next row 3ch, (1C1, 3ch, 1C1) into first st, *3ch, miss next 2dtr, 1dc into next dtr, 7ch, miss next dtr, 1dc into next dtr, 3ch, (1C1, 3ch, 1C1, 3ch, 1C1) into 5th of 9ch, *, rep from * to * once more, 3ch, miss next 2dtr, 1dc into next dtr, 7ch, miss next dtr, 1dc into next dtr, 3ch, (1C1, 3ch, 1C1) into 5th of 9ch, turn.
Complete to match back cuff of right sleeve.
Using No.3.00 (ISR) hook and with WS of work facing, rejoin yarn into 5th of 9ch where work was turned, 3ch, (1C1, 3ch, 1C1) into same st, patt to end.
Complete to match front cuff of right sleeve. Fasten off.

To make up
Press under a damp cloth with a warm iron, omitting neck border. Join side and sleeve seams to within 6.5cm (2½in) of yoke, then join side edge to sleeve edge to form armholes.
Left front border Using No.2.50 (ISR) hook and with RS of work facing, work 3 rows dc along left front opening. Fasten off.
Right front border Mark position for 3 buttons on left front border. Work 3 rows dc along right front border, making buttonholes on 2nd row when markers are reached by working 2ch, miss 2dc. Sew down borders at base of opening.
Cuff borders Using No.2.50 (ISR) hook and with RS of work facing, work 3 rows dc all round cuff opening, working 3 buttonholes on front cuff on 2nd row as given for right front border. Fasten off. Press seams. Sew on buttons.

38 Chevron striped dress

Sizes
To fit 61.0/63.5cm (24/25in) chest
Length to shoulder, 48.5cm (19in)
Sleeve seam, 24.0cm (9½in)

Tension
21tr to 10cm (3.9in) worked on No.3.00 (ISR) crochet hook

Materials
Patons Limelight Crepe — knits as 4-ply
5 x 25 grm balls in main shade, A
3 balls each of contrast colours, B and C
One No.3.50 (ISR) crochet hook
One No.3.00 (ISR) crochet hook
4 buttons

Front
Using No.3.50 (ISR) hook and A, make 124ch.

Base row Into 5th ch from hook work 1tr, 1tr into each of next 7ch, *miss 1ch, 1tr into next ch, miss 1ch, 1tr into each of next 8ch, 1ch, 1tr into next ch, 1ch, 1tr into each of next 8ch, rep from * to last 12ch, miss 1ch, 1tr into next ch, miss 1ch, 1tr into each of next 8ch, 1ch, 1tr in last ch. Turn.
Commence patt. Join in B.
1st row (RS) Using B, 4ch, miss first st, *1tr into 1ch sp, 1tr into each of next 7 sts, miss one st, 1tr into next st, miss one st, 1tr into each of next 7 sts, 1tr into next ch sp, 1ch, 1tr into next st, 1ch, rep from * ending with 1tr into sp of turning ch, 1ch, 1tr into 3rd of first 4ch. Turn. Join in C.
2nd row Using C, as 1st.
3rd row Using A, as 1st.
Rep these 3 rows 3 times more.
Shape skirt
Next row Using B, 4ch, miss first st, *1tr into ch sp, 1tr into each of next 5 sts, (yrh, draw loop through next st, yrh and draw through 2 loops on hook) twice, yrh and draw through all loops on hook — called dec 1 —, miss one st 1tr into next st, miss one st, dec 1, 1tr into each of next 5 sts, 1tr into next ch sp, 1ch, 1tr into next st, 1ch, rep from * ending with 1tr into sp of turning ch, 1ch, 1tr into 3rd of first 4ch. Turn.
Next row Using C, 4ch, miss first st, *1tr into next sp, 1tr into each of next 6 sts, miss one st, 1tr into next st, miss one st, 1tr into each of next 6 sts, 1tr into next ch sp, 1ch, 1tr into next st, 1ch, rep from * ending with 1tr into sp of turning ch, 1ch, 1tr into 3rd of first 4ch. Turn.
Keeping striped patt correct, work 8 rows as now set.
Next row Using C, 4ch, miss first st, *1tr into ch sp, 1tr into each of next 4 sts, dec 1, miss one st, 1tr into next st, miss one st, dec 1, 1tr into each of next 4 sts, 1tr into next ch sp, 1ch, 1tr into next st, 1ch, rep from * ending with 1tr into sp of turning ch, 1ch, 1tr into 3rd of first 4ch. Turn.
Next row Using A, 4ch, miss first st, *1tr into ch sp, 1tr into each of next 5 sts, miss one st, 1tr into next st, miss one st, 1tr into each of next 5 sts, 1tr into next ch sp, 1ch, 1tr into next st, 1ch, rep from * ending with 1tr into sp of turning ch, 1ch, 1tr into 3rd of first 4ch. Turn.
Keeping striped patt correct, work 4 rows as now set.
Next row Using C, 4ch, miss first st, *1tr into ch sp, 1tr into each of next 3 sts, dec 1, miss one st, 1tr into next st, miss one st, dec 1, 1tr into each of next 3 sts, 1tr into next ch sp, 1ch, 1tr into next st, 1ch, rep from * ending with 1tr into sp of turning ch, 1ch, 1tr into 3rd of first 4ch. Turn.
Next row Using A, 4ch, miss first st, *1tr into ch sp, 1tr into each of next 4 sts, miss one st, 1tr into next st, miss one st, 1tr into each of next 4 sts, 1tr into next ch sp, 1ch, 1tr into next st, 1ch, rep from * ending with 1tr into sp of turning ch, 1ch, 1tr into 3rd of first 4ch. Turn.
Keeping striped patt correct, work 2 rows as now set ending with a row in C. Break off B and C.
**Next row Using A, 1dc in first st, *miss ch sp, 1dc in next st, 1htr in next st, 1tr into each of next 2 sts, ** (yrh) twice, draw loop through next st, (yrh and draw through 2 loops on hook) twice, rep from ** twice more, yrh and draw through all loops on hook — called dec 2 —, 1tr into each of next 2 sts, 1htr into next st, 1dc into next st, miss ch sp, 1dc into next st, rep from * ending with miss sp of turning ch, 1dc into 3rd of first 4ch. Turn. 61 sts.
Cont using A only. Change to No.3.00 (ISR) hook.
Shape armholes
1st row Ss over first 2 sts and into 3rd, 3ch, 1tr

into each st to last 2 sts, turn.
2nd row 3ch, miss first st, dec 1, 1tr into each st to last 3 sts, dec 1, 1tr into turning ch. Turn. ****.
Rep 2nd row twice more. 51 sts.
Next row 3ch, miss first st, 1tr into each st ending with 1tr into turning ch. Turn.
Last row forms yoke patt. Rep last row 7 times more.
Shape neck
1st row 3ch, miss first st, 1tr into each of next 15 sts, turn.
Complete this side first.
2nd row 3ch, miss first st, dec 1, patt to end. Turn.
3rd row Patt to last 3 sts, dec 1, 1tr in turning ch. Turn.
4th row As 2nd. 13 sts.
Work 1 row without shaping.
Shape shoulder
Next row 3ch, miss first st, 1tr into each of next 4 sts, 1htr into each of next 4 sts. Fasten off.
Return to where work was left, miss first 19 sts, rejoin yarn to next st, 3ch, patt to end. Complete to match first side, reversing shaping.

Back
Work as given for front until armhole shaping is completed. Work 13 rows without shaping.
Shape shoulders and back neck
Next row Ss over first 4 sts, 2ch, 1htr into each of next 3 sts, 1tr into each of next 5 sts. Fasten off.
Return to where work was left, miss first 25 sts, rejoin yarn to next st, 3ch, 1tr into each of next 4 sts, 1 htr into each of next 4 sts. Fasten off.

Sleeves
Using No.3.50 (ISR) hook and B, make 60ch.
Base row Into 5th ch from hook work 1tr, 1tr into each of next 4ch, *miss 1ch, 1tr into next ch, miss 1ch, 1tr into each of next 5ch, 1ch, 1tr into next ch, 1ch, 1tr into each of next 5ch, rep from * to last 9ch, miss 1ch, 1tr into next ch, miss 1ch, 1tr into each of next 5ch, 1ch, 1tr into last ch. Turn.
Keeping patt correct as now set, work in striped sequence as given for skirt. Work 19 rows patt, ending with a row in C. Break off B and C.
Work as given for front from ** to **. 41 sts rem after final chevron row. Rep 2nd row 7 times more. 21 sts. Fasten off.
Cuff
Using No.3.00 (ISR) hook, A and with RS of work facing, rejoin yarn to lower edge of sleeve.
Next row 4ch in first loop, 1tr into each of next 2 loops, 1htr into next loop, 1dc into each of next 2 loops, (miss next loop, 1dc into next loop) twice, *1htr into next loop, 1tr into each of next 2 loops, dec 2, 1tr into each of next 2 loops, 1htr into next loop, (1dc into next loop, miss next loop) twice, 1dc into next loop, rep from * ending with 1dc into next loop, 1htr into next loop, 1tr into each of next 2 loops, 1dtr into last loop. Turn. 43 sts.
Next row (1dc into each of next 2 sts, miss one st) twice, (1dc into each of next 3 sts, miss one st) 8 times, 1dc into each of next 2 sts, miss one st, 1dc into each of next 2 sts. Turn. 32 sts.
Work 1 row dc. Fasten off.

To make up
Press each piece under a dry cloth with a cool iron.
Front neck border Using No.3.00 (ISR) hook, B and with RS of work facing, work 1 row dc evenly round neck edge. Work 5 more rows dc, 1 row in B, 2 rows in C and 2 rows in A. Fasten off.
Back neck border Work as given for front.
Front shoulder border Using No.3.00 (ISR)

hook, A and with RS of work facing, work 2 rows dc along front shoulders, making 2 button loops on 2nd row, one at neck edge and 2nd in centre, by making 2ch and missing 2 sts.
Back shoulder border Work as given for front, omitting button loops.
Overlap front borders on to back and catch tog at armhole edge. Join side and sleeve seams. Set in sleeves. Press seams. Sew on buttons.

39 Sleeveless A-line dress

Sizes
To fit 56.0[61.0:66.0:71.0]cm (*22[24:26:28]in*) chest
Length to shoulder, 43.0[48.5:53.5:58.5]cm (*17[19:21:23]in*)
The figures in brackets [] refer to the 61.0 (*24*), 66.0 (*26*) and 71.0cm (*28in*) sizes respectively
Tension
2 rep of bodice patt to 6.5cm (*2½in*) worked on No.4.00 (ISR) crochet hook; 5 rep to 15.0cm (*6in*) worked on No.3.50 (ISR) crochet hook
Materials
8[9:10:11] x ¾ oz balls of Hayfield Courtier Bri-Nova Crepe Double Knitting
One No.3.50[4.00:3.50:4.00] (ISR) crochet hook
One No.3.50 (ISR) crochet hook for all sizes
4 buttons

Back
Using No.3.50[4.00:3.50:4.00] (ISR) hook make 40[40:49:49]ch and beg at right shoulder.
Base row (RS) Into 4th ch from hook work 1tr, *miss 3ch, (2tr, 2ch, 2tr) all into next ch, miss 3ch, 1tr into each of next 2ch, rep from * to end. Turn.
1st row 3ch, miss first tr, 1tr into next tr, *miss 2tr, (2tr, 2ch, 2tr) all into 2ch sp, miss 2tr, 1tr into each of next 2tr, rep from * to end. Turn.
Rep last row until work measures 7.5[8.0:9.0: 10.0]cm (*3[3¼:3½:4]in*) from beg, ending with a WS row. Fasten off.
Work left shoulder as given for right shoulder. Do not fasten off.
Shape armholes and join shoulders
1st row 3ch, 1tr into each of first 2tr, patt to last 2tr, place the first 2tr of right shoulder over these 2tr, work 1tr into each tr working through both tr on each shoulder, cont across right shoulder in patt, ending with 1tr into next tr, 2tr into 3rd of first 3ch. Turn.
2nd row 3ch, 1tr into first tr, 1tr into each of next 2tr, patt to end, ending with 2tr into 3rd of first 3ch. Turn.
3rd row 4ch, 2tr into first tr, miss next tr, 1tr into each of next 2tr, patt to end, ending with 2tr, 1ch, 1tr all into 3rd of first 3ch. Turn.
4th row 3ch, 1tr into 1ch sp, 2ch, 2tr into same sp, patt to end, ending with 2tr, 2ch, 2tr all into 4ch sp. Turn.
5th row 5ch, 1tr into 5th ch from hook, miss 2tr, *(2tr, 2ch, 2tr) all into next ch sp, miss 2tr, 1tr into each of next 2tr, rep from * ending with (2tr, 2ch, 2tr) all into last ch sp, join in a separate length of yarn to top of 3ch at end of previous row, make 2ch, break off yarn, work 1tr into each of these 2ch with main yarn. Turn.
Cont in patt without shaping until work measures 15.0[16.5:18.0:19.0]cm (*6[6½:7:7½]in*) from beg ending with a WS row.
Shape skirt
1st inc row 3ch, miss first tr, 1tr into next tr, *miss next 2tr, (2tr, 3ch, 2tr) all into next ch sp, miss next 2tr, 1tr into each of next 2tr, rep from * to end. Turn.
Rep this row 3 times more.

2nd inc row 3ch, miss first tr, 1tr into next tr, *miss next 2tr, (3tr, 3ch, 3tr) all into next ch sp, miss 2tr, 1tr into each of next 2tr, rep from * to end. Turn.
Rep this row 3 times more.
3rd inc row 3ch, miss first tr, 1tr into next tr, *miss 3tr, (3tr, 4ch, 3tr) all into next ch sp, miss 3tr, 1tr into each of next 2tr, rep from * to end. Turn.
Rep this row 3 times more.
4th inc row 3ch, miss first tr, 1tr into next tr, *miss 3tr, (4tr, 4ch, 4tr) all into next ch sp, miss 3tr, 1tr into each of next 2tr, rep from * to to end. Turn.
Rep this row 3 times more.
5th inc row 3ch, miss first tr, 1tr into next tr, *miss 4tr, (5tr, 4ch, 5tr) all into next ch sp, miss 4tr, 1tr into each of next 2tr, rep from * to end. Turn.
Rep this row 3 times more.
6th inc row 4ch, 1tr into sp between first 2tr, * miss 5tr, (5tr, 4ch, 5tr) all into next ch sp, miss 5tr, (1tr, 1ch, 1tr) all into sp between next 2tr, rep from * to end. Turn.
Next row 4ch, 1tr in 1ch sp, *(5tr, 4ch, 5tr) all into next 4ch sp, (1tr, 1ch, 1tr) all into next 1ch sp, rep from * to end. Turn.
Next row 5ch, 1tr into ch sp, *(5tr, 4ch, 5tr) all into next 4ch sp, (1tr, 2ch, 1tr) all into next 1ch sp, rep from * to end. Turn.
Next row 5ch, 2tr into ch sp, *(5tr, 4ch, 5tr) all into next 4ch sp, (2tr, 2ch, 2tr) all into next 2ch sp, rep from * ending with (2tr, 2ch, 1tr) all into last ch sp. Turn..
Rep last row until work measures 40.5[45.5: 51.0:56.0]cm (*16[18:20:22]in*) from beg.
Next row 4ch, 2tr into first sp, *(5tr, 4ch, 5tr) all into next 4ch sp, (2tr, 1ch, 2tr) all into next 2ch sp, rep from * ending with (2tr, 1ch, 1tr) all into last ch sp. Fasten off.

Front
Using No.3.50[4.00:3.50:4.00] (ISR) hook make 22[22:31:31]ch for left shoulder. Work base row as given for back.
1st row 3ch, work 1st row as given for back. Turn.
2nd row 3ch, 1tr into each of first 2tr, patt to end. Turn.
3rd row 3ch, patt to last 3tr, 1tr into each of next 2tr, 2tr into 3rd of first 3ch. Fasten off.
Using No.3.50[4.00:3.50:4.00] (ISR) hook make 22[22:31:31]ch for right shoulder. Work base row as given for back.
1st row 3ch, work in patt to end. Turn.
2nd row 3ch, patt to last 2tr, 1tr into next tr, 2tr into 3rd of first 3ch. Turn.
3rd row 3ch, 1tr into first tr, patt to end. Turn.
Join shoulders
Next row 3ch, patt to last 2tr, miss 1tr, 2tr into 3rd of first 3ch, make 28ch, 2tr into first tr of left shoulder, miss 1tr, patt to end. Turn.
Next row 3ch, patt to 28ch, (2tr, 2ch, 2tr) all into first ch, *miss 3ch, 1tr into each of next 2ch, miss 3ch, (2tr, 2ch, 2tr) all into next ch, rep from * to end of ch, cont in patt to end. Turn.
Cont without shaping on these 8[8:10:10] patt until armholes measure same as back to armhole shaping.
Shape armholes
Work as given for back. Complete as given for back.

Collar
Join shoulder seams. Using No.3.50 (ISR) hook and with RS of work facing, rejoin yarn at top of back opening and work 58[64:70:76]dc evenly round neck edge. Turn. Work 3 more rows dc.
Next row (buttonhole row) Work in dc to last 3dc, 2ch, miss 2dc, 1dc into last dc. Turn.
Work 1 row dc working 2dc into 2ch buttonhole. Work 10 more rows dc. Fasten off.

Armbands
Using No.3.50 (ISR) hook and with RS of work facing, work 64[70:76:82]dc evenly round armhole edge. Work 1 more row. Fasten off.

To make up
Do not press. Join side seams.
Border Using No.3.50[4.00:3.50:4.00] (ISR) hook and with RS of work facing, rejoin yarn at lower edge of side seam, work 1tr into first sp, 1tr into next tr, *miss next tr, 1tr into each of next 5tr, 4tr into ch sp, 1tr into each of next 5tr, miss next tr, 1tr into each of next 2tr, rep from * to end. Join with a ss to first tr. Fasten off.
Sew 3 buttons to back opening using holes in top edge for buttonholes, then sew 4th button to collar.

40 Short sleeved dress

Sizes
To fit 56.0[61.0:66.0:71.0]cm (*22[24:26:28]in*) chest
Length to shoulder, 43.0[48.5:53.5:58.5]cm (*17[19:21:23]in*)
Sleeve seam, 6.5[7.5:9.0:10.0]cm (*2½[3:3½:4]in*)
The figures in brackets [] refer to the 61.0 (*24*), 66.0 (*26*) and 71.0cm (*28in*) sizes respectively
Tension
6 patt to 10.0cm (*3.9in*) over skirt patt worked on No.3.50 (ISR) crochet hook
Materials
11[12:13:14] x ¾ oz balls of Hayfield Courtier Bri-Nova Crepe Double Knitting
One No.3.50 (ISR) crochet hook
4 buttons
One press stud

Back skirt
Using No.3.50 (ISR) hook make 109[121:133: 145]ch.
Base row *Miss 3ch, **yrh, insert hook into next ch, yrh and draw loop through, yrh and draw through 2 loops, working into same ch rep from ** twice more, yrh and draw through all 4 loops on hook — called 1C1 —, 4ch, 1dc into same ch as 1C1, rep from * to last ch, 1tr into last ch. Turn.
1st row 3ch, *1C1, 4ch, 1dc into ch sp, rep from * to end, 1tr into 3rd of first 3ch. Turn.
The last row forms patt. Cont in patt until work measures 28.0[30.5:33.0:35.5]cm (*11[12:13:14] in*) from beg. Fasten off.

Bodice
Using No.3.50 (ISR) hook and with WS of work facing, rejoin yarn to foundation row of skirt and work 57[65:73:81]dc evenly into ch. Turn. **
1st row 3ch, 1tr into first dc, *miss 1dc, 2tr into next dc, rep from * to end. Turn.
2nd row 1ch, 1dc into each tr to end. Turn.
These 2 rows form bodice patt. Cont in patt until work measures 33.0[37.0:40.5:44.5]cm (*13[14½: 16:17½]in*) from beg, ending with a 2nd row.
Shape armholes
1st row Ss across first 4dc, 3ch, *2tr into next dc, miss 1dc, rep from * to last 4dc, 1tr into next dc, turn.
2nd row 1ch, insert hook into first tr and draw loop through, insert hook into next tr and draw loop through, yrh and draw through all 3 loops on hook — called dec 1dc —, cont in dc to last 2tr, dec 1dc, turn.
3rd row 3ch, miss 1dc, yrh, insert hook into next dc and draw loop through, insert hook into next dc and draw loop through, yrh and draw through 3 loops on hook, yrh and draw through rem 2 loops on hook — called dec 1tr —, 1tr into same dc, cont in patt to last 4dc, miss 1dc, 1tr into next

dc then working into this and next dc, dec 1tr, 1tr into last dc, turn.
4th row 1ch, miss first tr, dec 1dc, work in dc to last 3tr, dec 1dc, 1dc in last tr, turn.
5th row As 3rd.
6th row As 2nd.
Rep 5th and 6th rows 0[0:1:1] times more.
Cont without shaping until work measures 43.0[48.5:53.5:58.5]cm (*17[19:21:23]in*) from beg. Fasten off.

Front
Work as given for back to **.
Divide for front opening
Next row Work 1st row of bodice patt on 26[30:34:38]dc, turn.
Complete this side first.
Next row 7ch, 1dc into 2nd ch from hook, 1dc into each rem ch, cont in dc to end. Turn.
Cont in bodice patt until work measures same as back to underarm, ending with a 2nd row.
Shape armhole
1st row Ss across first 4dc, 3ch, *miss 1dc, 2tr into next dc, rep from * to end. Turn.
2nd row 1ch, work in dc to last 2tr, dec 1dc, turn.
3rd row 3ch, miss 1dc, dec 1tr, 1tr into same dc, patt to end. Turn.
4th row 1ch, patt to last 3tr, dec 1dc, 1dc in last tr. Turn.
5th row As 3rd.
6th row As 2nd.
Rep 5th and 6th rows 0[0:1:1] times more.
Cont without shaping until work measures 40.5[44.5: 48.5:52.0]cm (*16[17½:19:20½]in*) from beg, ending with a 2nd row.
Shape neck
1st row Work in patt to last 10[12:14:16]dc, miss next dc, 1tr into next dc, turn.
2nd row 1ch, miss first tr, dec 1dc, cont in dc to end. Turn.
3rd row 3ch, patt to last 2dc, miss next dc, 1tr into last dc, turn.
4th row As 2nd. 6[7:8:9]gr.
Cont without shaping until armhole measures same as back to shoulder. Fasten off.
With RS of work facing, rejoin yarn at centre front to rem 31[35:39:43]dc. Work as given for first side to underarm, ending at front edge.
Shape armhole
1st row Work in patt to last 4dc, 1tr into next dc, turn.
2nd row 1ch, dec 1dc, patt to end. Turn.
3rd row 3ch, work in patt to last 4dc, miss 1dc, 1tr into next dc, then working into this and next dc, dec 1tr, 1tr into last dc, turn.
4th row 1ch, miss first tr, dec 1dc, patt to end. Turn.
5th row As 3rd.
6th row As 2nd.
Rep 5th and 6th rows 0[0:1:1] times more.
Cont without shaping until work measures same as first side to neck shaping. Fasten off.
Shape neck
1st row Rejoin yarn to 9th[11th:13th:15th]dc from front edge, 3ch, miss next dc, 2tr into next dc, cont in patt to end. Turn.
2nd row 1ch, patt to last 3tr, dec 1dc, turn.
3rd row 3ch, miss first dc, patt to end. Turn.
4th row As 2nd.
Complete to match first side.

Sleeves
Using No.3.50 (ISR) hook make 36[40:44:48]ch.
Base row Into 2nd ch from hook work 1dc, 1dc into each ch to end. Turn.
1st row (RS) 3ch, 1tr into first dc, *miss 1dc, 2tr into next dc, rep from * to end. Turn.
2nd row 1ch, work 1dc into each tr to end. Turn.
Cont in patt until sleeve measures 6.5[7.5:9.0: 10.0]cm (*2½[3:3½:4]in*) from beg, ending with a 2nd row.

Shape top
Work as given for back armhole shaping, then work last 2 rows once more. Fasten off.
Frills (make 2)
Using No.3.50 (ISR) hook make 29[33:37:41]ch.
1st row Miss 3ch, *1C1, 4ch, 1dc into same ch as 1C1, miss 1ch, rep from * to end of ch, 1ch, cont on other side of foundation ch, working 1C1, 4ch, 1dc into same ch as 1C1, miss 1ch, rep from * to end of ch. Fasten off.

Neck frill
Using No.3.50 (ISR) hook make 47[53:61:69]ch.
Work as given for sleeve frill on each side of ch.

Belt
Using No.3.50 (ISR) hook make a length of ch 112.0[122.0:132.0:142.0]cm *44([48:52:56]in)* long.
1st row Miss 1ch, *1dc into next ch, rep from * to end of ch, work 3dc into last ch then cont in dc along other side of ch. Fasten off.

To make up
Do not press. Join shoulder, side and sleeve seams. Set in sleeves. Sew frill to edge of sleeves, st through centre of ch. Sew neck frill to neck edge in same way. Sew 3 buttons evenly spaced on left front bodice and the 4th button in centre of frill on right front, then sew press stud to back of 4th button. Use tr row on right front to form buttonholes for 3 buttons. Thread belt through holes at top of skirt to tie at centre front.

41 Raglan sleeved jersey

Sizes
To fit 66.0[71.0:76.0]cm (*26[28:30]in*) chest
Length to shoulder, 40.5[44.5:48.5]cm (*16[17½: 19]in*)
Sleeve seam, 28.0[30.5:33.0]cm (*11[12:13]in*)
The figures in brackets [] refer to the 71.0 (*28*) and 76.0cm (*30in*) sizes respectively
Tension
16 sts and 10 rows to 10.0cm (*3.9in*) over tr worked on No.4.00 (ISR) crochet hook
Materials
11[12:13] x 1 oz balls of Lee Target Motoravia Double Knitting *or* Lee Target Super Crimp Bri-Nylon Double Knitting
One No.4.00 (ISR) crochet hook
One No.3.50 (ISR) crochet hook

Back
Using No.3.50 (ISR) hook make 61[65:69]ch.
1st row Into 2nd ch from hook work 1dc, 1dc into each ch to end. Turn. 60[64:68]dc.
2nd row 1ch to count as first dc. 1dc into each dc to end. Turn.
Rep 2nd row 4 times more. Commence patt. Change to No.4.00 (ISR) hook.
1st row 3ch to count as first tr, 1tr into each of next 21[23:25] sts. (miss next 2 sts, 1tr into each of next 2 sts then 1tr into each of 2 missed sts working with yarn and hook round back of 2tr just worked — called C4trB —, miss next 2 sts, 1tr into each of next 2 sts then 1tr into each of 2 missed sts working with yarn and hook across front of 2tr just worked — called C4trF —) twice, 1tr into each of next 22[24:26] sts. Turn.
2nd row 3ch to count as first tr, 1tr into each st to end. Turn.
3rd row 3ch to count as first tr, 1tr into each of next 21[23:25] sts, (C4trF, C4trB) twice, 1tr into each of next 22[24:26] sts. Turn.
4th row As 2nd.
These 4 rows form patt. Cont in patt until work measures 25.5[28.0:30.5]cm (*10[11:12]in*) from beg, ending with a 2nd row.

Shape raglans
1st row (RS) Ss across first 5 sts, patt to last 5 sts, turn.
2nd row 3ch to count as first tr, 1tr into next st, work 2tr tog, patt to last 4 sts, work 2tr tog, 1tr into each of last 2 sts. Turn.
Rep 2nd row until 20[22:24] sts rem. Fasten off.

Front
Work as given for back until front measures same as back to underarm.
Shape raglans
Work 1st and 2nd rows as given for back.
Divide for neck
1st row 3ch, 1tr into next tr, work 2tr tog, patt 12[14:16] sts, C4trB, 1tr into each of next 4 sts, turn.
Complete this side first.
2nd row 3ch, work 2tr tog, patt to last 4 sts, work 2 tr tog, 1tr into each of last 2 sts. Turn.
3rd row 3ch, 1tr into next tr, work 2tr tog, patt to last 3 sts, work 2tr tog, 1tr into last st. Turn.
Rep 2nd and 3rd rows 0[0:1] times.
Next row Patt to last 4 sts, work 2tr tog, 1tr into each of next 2 sts. Turn.
Next row As 3rd shaping row.
Rep last 2 rows until 6 sts rem.
Next row 3ch, (work 2tr tog) twice, 1tr into last st. Turn.
Next row 3ch, work 2tr tog, 1tr into last st. Fasten off.
Return to where work was left, rejoin yarn to next st.
1st row 3ch, 1tr into each of next 3 sts, C4trF, patt 12[14:16] sts, work 2tr tog, 1tr into each of last 2 sts. Turn.
Complete as given for first side, reversing shaping.

Sleeves
Using No.3.50 (ISR) hook make 27[27:27]ch.
Work first 2 rows as given for back. 26[26:26]dc. Rep 2nd row 10 times more. Change to No.4.00 (ISR) hook. Cont in tr throughout, inc one st at each end of next and every alt row until there are 44[46:48] sts. Cont without shaping until sleeve measures 28.0[30.5:33.0]cm (*11[12:13]in*) from beg, or required length to underarm.
Shape raglan
Work as given for back until 4 sts rem. Fasten off.
Neckband
Join raglan seams. Using No.3.50 (ISR) hook and with RS of work facing, rejoin yarn at left back raglan seam.
1st round 2ch to count as first dc, work 3dc across top of sleeve, 28[30:32]dc down left front neck, 28[30:32]dc up right front neck, 4dc across top of other sleeve and 18[20:22]dc across back neck. Join with a ss to 2nd of first 2ch. Turn.
2nd round 1ch to count as first dc, 1dc into each of next 47[51:55]dc, miss next 3dc, 1dc into each dc to end. Join with a ss to first ch. Turn.
3rd round 1ch, 1dc into each of next 28[30:32] dc, miss next 3dc, 1dc into each dc to end. Join with a ss to first ch. Fasten off.

To make up
Press each piece carefully, under a damp cloth with a warm iron for Motoravia or under a dry cloth with a cool iron for Br-Nylon. Join side and sleeve seams. Press seams.

42 Waistcoat with lace fastening

Sizes
To fit 66.0[71.0:76.0]cm (*26[28:30]in*) chest
Length to shoulder, 40.5[44.5:48.5]cm *16[17½: 19]in*

The figures in brackets [] refer to the 71.0 (*28*) and 76.0cm (*30in*) sizes respectively
Tension
20 sts to 10.0cm (*3.9in*) over patt worked on No.3.50 (ISR) crochet hook
Materials
3[4:4] x 40 grm balls of Wendy Marina Double Knitting in main shade, A
1[1:1] ball each of contrast colours, B, C and D
or
6[8:8] x 20 grm balls of Wendy Courtellon Double Knitting in main shade, A
1[1:1] ball each of contrast colours, B and D
2[2:2] balls of contrast colour, C
One No. 3.50 (ISR) crochet hook

Back
Using No.3.50 (ISR) hook and B, make 71[76:81] ch.
Base row Into 2nd ch from hook work 1dc, 1dc into each ch to end. Turn. 70[75:80]dc.
Commence patt.
1st row 3ch to count as first tr, *miss next dc, 1tr into next dc, 1tr into missed st working behind tr already worked, rep from * to last st, 1tr into last st. Turn.
2nd row 2ch, 1dc into each st to end, 1dc into 3rd of first 3ch. Turn.
3rd row 3ch to count as first tr, *miss next dc, 1tr into next dc, 1tr into missed st working in front of tr already worked, rep from * to last st, 1tr into last st. Turn.
4th row As 2nd.
These 4 rows form patt and are rep throughout. Break off B. Join in C. Rep 4 patt rows. Break off C. Join in D. Rep 4 patt rows. Break off D. Join in C. Rep 4 patt rows. Break off C. Join in A. Using A only cont in patt until work measures 25.5[28.0:30.5]cm (*10[11:12]in*) from beg, ending with a 2nd patt row.
Shape armholes
Next row Ss across first 9[11:11] sts, 3ch to count as first tr, work 2tr tog, rep from * of 3rd patt row to last 12[14:14] sts, work 2tr tog, 1tr into next st, turn.
Next row 2ch, 1dc into next st, work 2dc tog, 1dc into each st to last 3 sts, work 2dc tog, 1dc into turning ch. Turn.
Next row 3ch to count as first tr, 1tr into next st, work 2tr tog, rep from * of 1st patt row to last 4 sts, work 2tr tog, 1tr into next st, 1tr into turning ch. Turn.
Next row 2ch, 1dc into next st, work 2dc tog, 1dc into each st to last 3 sts, work 2dc tog, 1dc into turning ch. Turn.
Next row 3ch to count as first tr, work 2tr tog, rep from * of 3rd patt row to last 3 sts, work 2tr tog, 1tr into turning ch. Turn.
Next row 2ch, 1dc into next st, work 2dc tog, 1dc into each st to last 4 sts, work 2dc tog, 1dc into last st. 1dc into turning ch. Turn.
Keeping patt correct, cont without shaping until work measures 39.5[43.0:47.0] cm (*15½[17:18½] in*) from beg, ending with a WS row.
Shape shoulders
Next row Ss across first 5[5:5] sts, 3ch, patt to to last 6[6:6] sts, 1tr into next st, turn.
Next row Ss across first 5[5:5] sts, 2ch, 1dc into each st to last 5[5:5] sts, turn. Fasten off.

Left front
Using No.3.50 (ISR) hook and B, make 37[39:41] ch. Work base row as given for back. 36[38:40] dc. Cont in patt and striped sequence as given for back until work measures same as back to underarm, ending with a 2nd patt row.
Shape armhole
Next row Ss across first 9[11:11]sts, 3ch, work 2tr tog, rep from * of 3rd patt row to end. Turn.
Next row 2ch, 1dc into each st to last 3 sts,

120

work 2dc tog, 1dc into turning ch. Turn.

Next row 3ch, 1tr into next st, work 2tr tog, rep from * of 1st patt row to end. Turn.

Next row 2ch, 1dc into each st to last 3 sts, work 2dc tog, 1dc into turning ch. Turn.

Next row 3ch, work 2tr tog, rep from * of 3rd patt row to end, 1tr into turning ch. Turn.

Next row 2ch, 1dc into each st to last 4 sts, work 2dc tog, 1dc into next st, 1dc into turning ch. Turn.

Shape neck

1st row Patt to last 3 sts, work 2tr tog, miss last st, turn.

2nd row 2ch, work 2dc tog, 1dc into each st to end. Turn.

3rd row 3ch, patt to last 3 sts, work 2tr tog, 1tr into turning ch. Turn.

4th row As 2nd.

5th row As 3rd.

6th row As 2nd.

7th row 3ch, patt to end. Turn.

8th row 2ch, 1dc into each st to end. Turn.
Keeping patt correct cont without shaping until work measures same as back to shoulder, ending at armhole edge.

Shape shoulder

Next row Ss across first 5[5:5] sts, 3ch, patt to end, turn. Fasten off.

Right front

Work as given for left front, reversing all shaping.

To make up

Press each piece lightly under a dry cloth with a cool iron. Join shoulder and side seams.
Armbands Using No.3.50 (ISR) hook, A and with RS of work facing, work 1 round dc round armholes. Join with a ss to first dc, do not turn. Work 1 round crab st working in dc from left to right instead of from right to left. Fasten off.
Front bands Using No.3.50 (ISR) hook, A and with RS of work facing, work 1 row dc evenly up right front, round neck, down left front and along lower edge, working 3dc into each corner st. Complete as given for armbands. Fasten off. Using one strand each of B, C and D make a twisted cord long enough to lace down front opening, as required, and tie into a bow.

43 V-neck cardigan or waistcoat

Sizes

To fit 66.0[71.0:76.0:81.5:86.5]cm (26[28:30: 32:34]in) chest
Length to shoulder, 40.5[44.5:47.0:49.5:54.5]cm (16[17½:18½:19½:21½]in)
Sleeve seam, 30.5[34.5:38.0:40.5:43.0]cm (12[13½:15:16:17]in)
The figures in brackets[] refer to the 71.0 (28), 76.0 (30), 81.5 (32) and 86.5cm (34in) sizes respectively

Tension

8 sts and 6 rows to 7.5cm (3in) over htr worked on No.7.00 (ISR) crochet hook

Materials

Robin Vogue Double Double Chunky Knit
Cardigan 9[10:12:14:15] x 50 grm balls
Waistcoat 7[8:9:10:11] x 50 grm balls
One No.7.00 (ISR) crochet hook
One No.4.50 (ISR) crochet hook
4[4:5:5:5] buttons

Cardigan back

Using No.7.00 (ISR) hook make 37[40:43:46: 49]ch.
Base row Into 2nd ch from hook work 1htr, 1htr into each ch to end. Turn. 37[40:43:46:49]htr.

1st row 2ch to count as first htr, 1htr into each htr to end. Turn.
The last row forms patt. Cont in patt until work measures 25.5[28.0:30.5:33.0:33.0]cm (10[11:12 :13:13]in) from beg.

Shape armholes

Next row Ss across first 3htr, patt to last 3 sts, turn.
Dec one st at each end of next 3 rows. Cont without shaping until armholes measure 14.0[15.0: 15.0:15.0:20.5]cm (5½[6:6:6:8]in) from beg.

Shape shoulders

Next row Ss across first 3[4:4:4:5]htr, patt to last 3[4:4:4:5] sts, turn.

Next row Ss across first 3[3:4:5:5]htr, patt to last 3[3:4:5:5] sts, turn. Fasten off.

Cardigan left front

Using No.7.00 (ISR) hook make 19[20:22:23:25] ch. Work base row as given for back. 19[20:22: 23:25]htr. Cont in patt as given for back until work measures same as back to underarm. **.

Shape armhole

Next row Ss across first 3htr, patt to last 2htr, dec one. Turn.
***Dec one st at each end of next 3 rows. Keeping armhole edge straight, cont dec one st at neck edge on every RS row until 6[7:8:9:10]htr rem. Cont without shaping until armhole measures same as back to shoulder, ending at armhole edge. ***.

Shape shoulder

Next row Ss across first 3[4:4:4:5]htr, patt to end. Fasten off.

Cardigan right front

Work as given for left front to **.

Shape armhole

Next row Dec one st, patt to last 3 sts, turn.
Work as given for left front from *** to ***.

Shape shoulder

Next row Patt to last 3[4:4:4:5] sts. Fasten off.

Sleeves

Using No.7.00 (ISR) hook make 16[18:18:20: 22]ch. Work base row as given for back. 16 [18: 18:20:22]htr. Cont in patt as given for back, inc one st at each end of 2nd[4th:4th:6th:6th] and every foll 3rd row until there are 30[32:34:36: 38] sts. Cont without shaping until sleeve measures 29.0[33.0:37.0:39.5:42.0]cm (11½[13: 14½:15½:16½]in) from beg.

Shape top

Next row Ss across first 3htr, patt to last 3htr, turn.
Dec one st at each end of next 3 rows and foll 2 alt rows.

Next row Ss across first 2htr, patt to last 2htr, turn.
Rep last row once more. Fasten off.

Pockets (make 2)

Using No.7.00 (ISR) hook make 13[13:15:15: 15]ch. Work base row and patt as given for back until work measures 7.5[7.5:10.0:10.0:10.0]cm (3[3:4:4:4]in) from beg. Change to No.4.50 (ISR) hook. Work 2 rows dc, inc one st at each end of first row. Fasten off.

To make up

Press each piece lightly on WS under a damp cloth with a warm iron. Join shoulder seams. Set in sleeves. Join side and sleeve seams. Sew on pockets.
Front band Using No.4.50 (ISR) hook and with RS of work facing, rejoin yarn at side seam, work 1 round dc all round outer edges, working 2dc into each corner. Join with a ss to first dc. Mark positions for 4[4:5:5:5] buttons on right front edge, first to come 1.5cm (½in) above lower edge and last to come just below front neck shaping with 2[2:3:3:3] more evenly spaced between.
Next round (buttonhole round) Working in dc

to end, making buttonholes as markers are reached by working 2ch and missing 2dc. Join with a ss to first dc.
Work 1 more round dc, working 2dc into each 2ch buttonhole of previous round. Fasten off. Press seams. Sew on buttons.

Waistcoat back

Work as given for cardigan back.

Waistcoat left and right fronts

Work as given for cardigan fronts.

Pockets (make 2)

Work as given for cardigan pockets.

Armbands

Join shoulder seams. Using No.4.50 (ISR) hook and with RS of work facing, work 2 rows dc round armholes. Fasten off.

To make up

Complete as given for cardigan.

44 Bedroom set from squares

Sizes

Bedspread 178.0cm x 228.5cm (70in x 90in)
Rug 66.0cm x 122.0 cm (26in x 48in)
Cushion 47.0cm x 47.0cm (18½in x 18½in)

Tension

Each square measures 16.0cm (6¼in) worked on No.5.50 (ISR) crochet hook

Materials

Bedspread 36 x 50 grm balls Mahony's Bainin or Heatherspun in main shade, A
    8 balls of contrast colour, B
    13 balls of contrast colour, C
Rug 8 balls in main shade, A
    2 balls of contrast colour, B
    3 balls of contrast colour, C
Cushion 4 balls in main shade, A
    1 ball of contrast colour, B
    2 balls of contrast colour, C
Cushion pad
One No.5.50 (ISR) crochet hook

Square motifs

Using No.5.50 (ISR) hook and B, make 6ch. Join with a ss to first ch to form circle.
1st round 3ch, *(yrh, insert hook into circle and draw through a loop, yrh and draw through one loop, yrh and draw through 2 loops) twice, yrh and draw through all 3 loops on hook, *, (5ch, (yrh, insert hook under ch and draw through a loop, yrh and draw through 1 loop, yrh and draw through 2 loops) 3 times, yrh and draw through all 4 loops on hook — called 1 C1 —, 2ch, 1 C1 into circle) 3 times, 5ch, 1 C1 into circle, 2ch. Join with a ss to 3rd of first 3ch. Break off B. Join in A.
2nd round Using A, rejoin yarn into any 5ch sp, 3ch, rep from * to * of first round into same sp, 3ch, 1 C1 into same sp, **2ch, 3tr into 2ch sp, 2ch, (1 C1, 3ch, 1 C1) into 5ch sp, rep from ** twice more, 2ch, 3tr into 2ch sp, 2ch. Join with a ss into 3rd of first 3ch. Break off A. Join in C.
3rd round Using C, rejoin yarn into any 3ch sp, 3ch, rep from * to * of first round into same sp, 3ch, 1 C1 into same sp, **2ch, 2tr into 2ch sp, 1tr into next 3tr, 2tr into 2ch sp, 2ch, (1 C1, 3ch, 1 C1) into 3ch sp, rep from ** twice more, 2ch, 2tr into 2ch sp, 1tr into each of next 3tr, 2tr into 2ch sp, 2ch. Join with a ss to 3rd of first 3ch. Break off C. Join in A.
4th round Using A, rejoin yarn into any 3ch sp, 3ch, rep from * to * of first round into same sp, 3ch, 1 C1 into same sp, **2ch, 2tr into 2ch sp, 1tr into each of next 7tr, 2tr into 2ch, sp, 2ch, (1

121

C1, 3ch, 1 C1) into 3ch sp, rep from ** twice more, 2ch, 2tr into 2ch sp, 1tr into each of next 7tr, 2tr into 2ch sp, 2ch. Join with a ss to 3rd of first 3ch. Fasten off.

Bedspread
Make 154 square motifs in this way. Sew in ends. Press squares on WS under a damp cloth with a warm iron. Join each square by placing RS tog and stitching tog, taking only the back loop. Join into 11 strips of 14 squares. Join strips.
Edging Using No.5.50 (ISR) hook, A and with WS of work facing, rejoin yarn.
1st round 2ch, 1htr into each st, picking up back loop only, working 1ch at each join and 3htr into each corner. Join with a ss into 2nd of first 2ch.
Next round 2ch, 1htr into each st, picking up both loops, working 1htr into each ch sp and 3htr into each corner. Join with a ss to 2nd of first 2ch.
Next round 2ch, 1htr into each st, picking up back loops only and working 3htr into each corner. Join with a ss to 2nd of first 2ch. Fasten off. Press seams. Press edging.

Rug
Make 28 square motifs. Press as given for bedspread. Join in 4 strips of 7 squares, then join strips. Work edging as given for bedspread. Press seams. Make a fringe at each end of rug by cutting yarn into 28.0cm (*11in*) lengths and knotting 3 strands into every alt st along each short end. Trim fringe.

Cushion cover
Make 18 squares. Press as given for bedspread. Join 9 squares into 3 strips of 3. Join strips. Make other side of cushion in same way. Place 2 larger squares tog with RS of work facing and sew 3 side edges. Turn RS to outside, insert cushion pad and join last seam.

45 Practical carry-all

Sizes
30.5cm (*12in*) wide by 35.5cm (*14in*) deep
Tension
20 sp and 20 rows to 10cm (*3.9in*) over patt worked on No.1.25 (ISR) crochet hook
Materials
6 x 20 grm balls Coats Mercer-Crochet No.20
One No.1.25 (ISR) crochet hook
91.5cm (*1yd*) 91.5cm (*36in*) wide lining
45.5cm (*½yd*) 81.5cm (*32in*) wide interlining material

Main section (make 2)
Using No.1.25 (ISR) hook make 183ch.
1st row Into 4th ch from hook work 1tr, 1tr into each of next 2ch, (block made at beg of row), (2ch, miss 2ch, 1tr into next ch) twice, (2 sps made), 1tr into each of next 3ch, (block made), * (1 sp, 1 block) 4 times, 2 sps, 2 blocks, 2 sps, 1 block, rep from * 3 times more, omitting 1 block. 2 sps, and 1 block at end of last rep. Turn.
2nd row 3ch to count as first tr, 1tr into each of next 3tr, (block made over block at beg of row), 2tr into next sp, 1tr into next tr, (block made over sp), 2ch, 1tr into next tr, (sp made over sp), 1tr into each of next 3tr, (block made over block), (1 sp, 1 block) 4 times, *1 sp, 1 block, (1 sp, 1 block) 5 times, rep from * ending with 1 sp, 1 block, 1tr into each of next 3tr, (block made over block at end of row). Turn.
3rd row 5ch, miss first 3tr, 1tr into next tr, (sp made over block at beg of row), (1 block, 1 sp)

twice, 1 block, 1 sp, 2ch, miss 2tr, 1tr into next tr, (sp made over block), (1 sp, 1 block) 3 times, *2 sps, (1 block, 1 sp) twice, 1 block, 3 sps, (1 block, 1 sp) twice, 1 block, rep from * ending with 2ch, miss 2tr, 1tr into next tr, (sp made over block at end of row). Turn.
4th row 5ch, miss first tr, 1tr into next st, (sp made over sp at beg of row), *2 blocks, 1 sp, 1 block, 1 sp, 3 blocks, 1 sp, 1 block, 1 sp, 2 blocks, 2 sps, rep from * omitting 2 sps at end of last rep, 2ch, miss 2ch, 1tr into next st, (sp made over sp at end of row). Turn.
Beg next row with 3ch, cont to work from diagram from 5th row to top, turn diagram and work from row marked with * to end. Fasten off.

Gusset
Using No.1.25 (ISR) hook make 35ch.
1st row Into 8th ch from hook work 1tr, make 9 sps. Turn.
2nd row 5ch, work 10 sps. Turn.
Rep 2nd row 200 times more. Fasten off.

Join main sections to gussets
Using No.1.25 (ISR) hook and with WS facing, place gusset in position to main section and working over row ends, rejoin yarn to last row of both sections, 1dc into same place as join, 3ch, ss into last dc worked to form picot, 3dc over same row end, (1 picot, 3dc over next row end) 69 times, 1 picot, 2dc over next row end, 1dc into same place as base of next tr, 1 picot, cont in this way working into foundation ch at lower edge of front section and over row ends of next side. Fasten off. Join gusset to back section in same way.

Top edge
Using No.1.25 (ISR) hook and with RS of work facing, rejoin yarn to first free tr on front section

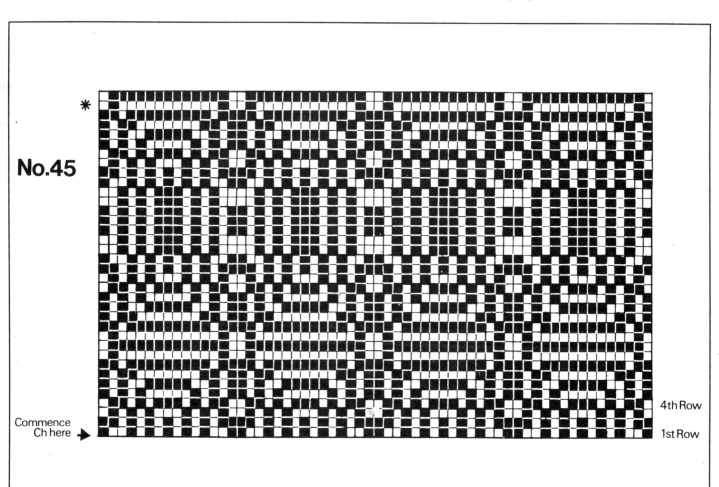

No.45

Commence Ch here ➤

4th Row

1st Row

1dc into same place as join, 1dc into each of next 2tr, 1 picot, *(2dc into next sp, 1dc into next tr, 1 picot) twice, (1dc into each of next 3tr, 1 picot, 2dc into next sp, 1dc into next tr, 1 picot) 5 times, 2dc into next sp, 1dc into next tr, 1 picot, (1dc into each of next 3tr, 1 picot) twice, rep from * 3 times more omitting (3dc, 1 picot) twice at end of last rep, 1dc into each of next 2tr, (2dc into next sp on gusset, 1dc into same place as base of next tr, 1 picot) 9 times, 2dc into next sp, 1dc into each of next 3 free tr on back section. 1 picot, rep from * once more working dc into top of tr on gusset and omitting 3dc and 1 picot at end of last rep. Join with a ss to first dc. Fasten off.

Handles (make 2)

Using No.1.25 (ISR) hook make 7ch.

1st row Into 2nd ch from hook work 1dc, 1dc into each ch to end. Turn.

2nd row 1ch, 1dc into each dc to end. Turn. Rep 2nd row 8 times more.

11th row 3ch, miss first dc, working into front loop only work 1tr into each of next 5dc, turn, working into back loop only of same tr, work 1tr into each of next 6dc, ss over turning ch.

12 row 3ch, miss first tr, 1tr over bar of each of next 11tr, ss over turning ch.
Rep last row until handle measures 38.0cm (*15in*) or required length, working last ss into 3rd of first 3ch.

Next row Working through both thicknesses work 1dc into same place as ss and into previous tr, (1dc through next 2tr) 5 times. Turn.

Next row 1ch, 1dc into each dc to end. Turn. Rep last row 8 times more. Fasten off.

To make up

Cut 4 pieces from lining 33.0cm (*13in*) by 38.0 cm (*15in*), for main sections. Cut 2 pieces from interlining 30.5cm (*12in*) by 35.5cm (*14in*). Cut 2 pieces from lining 7.0cm (*2¾in*) by 104.0cm (*41in*) for gussets, joining where necessary to obtain correct length. Cut one piece from interlining 4.5cm (*1¾in*) by 101.5cm (*40in*), joining where necessary to obtain correct length.
Baste one interlining main section centrally to WS of one lining for main section, noting that 1.5cm (*½in*) has been allowed throughout for seaming. Edge st interlining to lining. With RS tog, baste 2nd lining main section to interlining main section. Leaving one short edge open st round 3 sides. Trim seams and turn to RS. Turn seam allowance on raw edge to inside and sew tog, inserting each end of one handle 7.5cm (*3in*) from side edges. Make another main section in same way. Baste gusset interlining centrally to WS of one piece of gusset lining. Edge st to fabric. Having RS tog baste a gusset lining section to gusset interlining section. Leaving one long end open, st round 3 sides. Trim and turn to RS. Turn seam allowance on raw edges to inside and sew tog. Place gusset between main sections and oversew in place. Insert lining to crochet bag and sew round top edge.

46 Flower wall hanging

Size
Completed picture, 56.0cm x 40.0cm (*22in x 15¾in*)
Tension
Each flower measures 5.0cm (*2in*) diameter worked on No.2.00 (ISR) crochet hook
Materials
1 x 25 grm ball Twilleys Lyscordet
One No.2.00 (ISR) crochet hook
Material for backing

Embroidery cotton in green and white
Hardboard for mounting

Flower
Using No.2.00 (ISR) hook make 6ch. Join with a ss to form circle.

1st round 1ch, 9dc into circle. Join with a ss to first dc. 9 sts.

2nd round 4ch to count as first 1tr and 1ch, *1tr into next dc, 1ch, rep from * to end. Join with a ss to 3rd of first 4ch.

3rd round Ss into first 1ch sp, 3ch to count as first 1tr, 1tr into same sp, 2ch, *2tr into next sp, 2ch, rep from * to end. Join with a ss to 3rd of first 3ch.

4th round *1dc between 2tr, 3ch, 1dc into first of these 3ch — called picot —, 1dc into same place as first dc, 1dc into 2ch sp, 1 picot, 1dc into same place, rep from * to end. Join with a ss to first dc. Fasten off.
Make 14 more flowers in same way or required number.

To make up
Press flowers under a damp cloth with a warm iron. Stitch to backing material as shown in illustration, then embroider stems and leaves. Press work on WS. Stretch completed picture tightly over piece of hardboard and fix at the back with Copydex.

47 Four elegant cushions

Size
Each cushion measures 40.5cm (*16in*) by 40.5cm (*16in*) square
Tension
18 sts and 10 rows to 10.0cm (*3.9in*) over tr worked on No.3.50 (ISR) crochet hook
Materials
Cushion A 1 x 50 grm ball each of Madame Pingouin in 4 colours, A, B, C and D
Cushion B 2 x 50 grm balls of Madame Pingouin in main shade, A
1 ball of contrast colour, B
Cushion C As given for cushion A
Cushion D As given for cushion A
One No.3.50 (ISR) crochet hook
One cushion pad 40.5cm (*16in*) by 40.5cm (*16in*)

Cushion A
Using No.3.50 (ISR) hook and A, make 78ch.

1st row Into 4th ch from hook work 1tr, 1tr into each of next 3ch, *3tr into next ch, 1tr into each of next 5ch, miss 2ch, 1tr into each of next 5ch, rep from * 4 times more, 3tr into next ch, 1tr into each of last 5ch. Turn. 76 sts.

2nd row 3ch to count as first tr, work 2tr tog, 1tr into each of next 3tr, *3tr into next tr noting that this is centre tr of 3tr gr of previous row 1tr into each of next 5tr, miss 2tr, 1tr into each of next 5tr, rep from * 4 times more, 3tr into next tr, 1tr into each of next 3tr, work 2tr tog, 1tr into 3rd of first 3ch. Turn.
The 2nd row forms patt and is rep throughout. Cont in patt working (4 rows A, 2 rows B, 4 rows D, 2 rows B, 4 rows C and 2 rows B) throughout until work measures 81.5cm (*32in*) from beg. Fasten off.

To make up
Do not press. Fold in half with RS facing and join rem 3 sides, inserting cushion pad.

Cushion B
Using No.3.50 (ISR) hook and A, make 77ch.

1st row Into 4th ch from hook work 1tr, 1tr into each of next 22ch, miss 2ch, 1tr into each of

next 24ch, 3tr into next ch, 1tr into each of next 24ch. Turn. 75 sts.

2nd row 3ch to count as first tr, work 2tr tog, 1tr into each of next 22tr, 3tr into next tr noting that this is centre tr of 3tr gr of previous row, 1tr into each of next 21tr, 2tr into next tr, 1tr into each of next 21tr, miss 2tr, 1tr into each of next 21tr, 2tr into next tr, 1tr into 3rd of first 3ch. Turn.

3rd row 3ch to count as first tr, 2tr into next tr, 1tr into each of next 21tr, miss 2tr, 1tr into each of next 24tr, 3tr into next tr, 1tr into each of next 22tr, 2tr tog, 1tr into 3rd of first 3ch. Turn.
The 2nd and 3rd rows form patt and are rep throughout. Cont in patt until work measures 18.0cm (*7in*) from beg, then work 6 rows patt using B. Cont in patt using A until work measures 61.0cm (*24in*) from beg, then work 6 rows using B. Cont in patt using A until work measures 81.5cm (*32in*) from beg. Fasten off.

To make up
As given for cushion A.

Cushion C
Using No.3.50 (ISR) hook and A, make 69ch.

1st row Into 4th ch from hook work 1tr, 1tr into each of next 5ch, *miss 2ch, 1tr into each of next 7ch, 3tr into next ch, 1tr into each of next 7ch, rep from * twice more, miss 2ch, 1tr into each of next 7ch. Turn. 67 sts.

2nd row 3ch to count as first tr, 2tr into next tr, 1tr into each of next 4tr, *miss 2tr, 1tr into each of next 7tr, 3tr into next tr noting that this is centre tr of 3tr gr of previous row, 1tr into each of next 7tr, rep from * twice more, miss 2tr, 1tr into each of next 4tr, 2tr into next tr, 1tr into 3rd of first 3ch. Turn.
The 2nd rows forms patt and is rep throughout. Cont in patt until work measures 7.5cm (*3in*) from beg, then work 3 rows C, 5 rows B and 3 rows D. Cont using A only until work measures 61.0cm (*24in*) from beg, then work 3 rows D, 5 rows B and 3 rows C. Cont using A only until work measures 81.5cm (*32in*) from beg. Fasten off.

To make up
As given for cushion A.

Cushion D
Work as given for cushion C but working in striped sequence of (4 rows B, 2 rows C, 4 rows B, 2 rows D, 4 rows B and 2 rows A) throughout.

To make up
As given for cushion A.

48 Roller blind edging

Size
Each section is approx 30.0cm (*11¾in*) wide and 22.0cm (*8¾in*) deep
Tension
1 circle measures 5.0cm (*2in*) diameter
Materials
Pingouin Jericho
1 x 50 grm ball make approx 3 sections
One No.2.00 (ISR) crochet hook

Circle
Using No.2.00 (ISR) hook make 10ch. Join with a ss to first ch to form circle.

1st round 1ch, 15dc into circle. Join with a ss to first ch. 16 sts.

2nd round 1ch, 1dc into same place, 1dc into next dc, *2dc into next dc, 1dc into next dc, rep from * to end. Join with a ss to first ch. 24 sts.

3rd round 1ch, 1dc into same place, 1dc into each of next 2dc, *2dc into next dc, 1dc into each of next 2dc, rep from * to end. Join with a ss to first ch. 32 sts.

Cont inc 8 sts in every round twice more. 48 sts.

6th round 1ch, 1dc into each of next 3dc, 4ch, ss into first of these 4ch, then 1dc into same st as last dc — called picot —, *1dc into each of next 4dc, picot, rep from * to end. Join with a ss to first ch.

Arc

Next row Ss into next dc, 20ch, miss 2 picot, ss into next picot, 20ch, miss 2 picots, miss 1ch. ss into next ch, turn.

Next row 1ch, 1dc into each ch to end. Turn. 40 sts.

Next row 1ch, (1dc into each of next 3dc, picot) 5 times, 1dc into each of next 9dc, (picot, 1dc into each of next 3dc) 5 times. Fasten off.

Make 5 more circles and arcs, joining as illustrated. Make as many sections of 6 circles and arcs as required.

Top edging

Using No.2.00 (ISR) hook, rejoin yarn to 2nd picot of end arc, 5ch, 1dtr into same picot, **(2tr, 3ch, 2tr) into each of next 6 picots, *, (2dtr, 3ch, 2dtr) into next picot, (2dtr, 3ch, 2dtr) into 2nd picot of next arc, rep from ** for required length, ending last section rep from ** to *, then work 2dtr into next picot, turn.

Next row 5ch, 1dtr into next dtr, (2tr, 3ch, 2tr) into each 3ch loop to end, ending with 1dtr into dtr, 1dtr into turning ch. Turn.

Rep last row once more.

Next row *5ch, 1dc into 3ch loop, rep from * to end, ending with 5ch, 1dc into turning ch. Turn.

Next row Ss into 5ch loop, 3ch, (1tr, picot working dc into top of last tr, 2tr) into this loop, (2tr, picot, 2tr) into each 5ch loop to end. Fasten off.

To make up

Press lightly under a damp cloth with a warm iron.

Tassels Cut yarn into lengths of 20.0cm (7¾in). Using 40 strands tog, fold in half and tie about 2.0cm (¾in) from fold, work 24dc into this circle and fasten off. Sew one tassel to each point and one between each section as illustrated.

49 Traycloth edging

Size

Width of edging, 10cm (3.9in)

Tension

1 rep of patt (8 rows) to 5cm (2in) along inner edge worked on No. 1.50 (ISR) crochet hook

Materials

Coats Mercer-Crochet No.10

1 x 20 grm ball makes approx 51.0cm (20in) of edging

One No.1.50 (ISR) crochet hook

Edging

Using No.1.50 (ISR) hook make 36ch.

1st row Into 12th ch from hook work 1dc, 9ch, miss 9ch, 1dc into next ch, 4ch, miss 4ch, 1tr into next ch, 8ch, miss 8ch, 1dc into last ch. Turn.

2nd row 3ch to count as first tr, 11tr into 8ch sp, 1tr into next tr, 4ch, 1dc into next dc, 4ch, 1dc into 5th of 9ch sp, 4ch, 1dc into next dc, 4ch, miss 4ch, 1tr into next ch. Turn.

3rd row 11ch, miss 1dc, 1dc into next dc, 9ch, (1tr into next tr, 1ch, miss 1tr) 6 times, 1tr into 3rd of first 3ch. Turn.

4th row 12ch, 1dc into first 1ch sp, *turn, into loop just formed work 1dc, 7tr, turn, 6ch, 1dc into next 1ch sp along 3rd row, rep from * 4 times

more, turn, into loop just formed work 1dc, 7tr, turn, 2ch, 1dtr into next tr, 4ch, 1dc into 5th of 9ch, 4ch, 1dc into next dc, 4ch, miss 4ch, 1dc into next ch, 4ch, miss 4ch, 1tr into next ch. Turn.

5th row 6ch, 1dc into next dc, 9ch, miss 1dc, 1dc into next dc, 4ch, 1tr into dtr, 2ch, 1dc into 2ch sp, (5ch, 1dc into ch loop between tr groups) 5 times, 5ch, 1dc into ch loop at end. Turn.

6th row *6ch, 1dc into 3rd of these 6ch, (4ch, 1dc into first of these 4ch) twice, 1dc into same place as first dc, 2ch, 1dc into 5ch loop, rep from * 5 times more, 2ch, 1tr into next tr, 4ch, 1dc into next dc, 4ch, 1dc into 5th of 9ch loop, 4ch, 1dc into next dc, 4ch, miss 4ch, 1tr into next ch. Turn.

7th row 11ch, miss 1dc, 1dc into next dc, 9ch, 1tr into next tr, turn.

8th row 6ch, 1dc into 5th of 9ch, 4ch, 1dc into next dc, 4ch, miss 4ch, 1dc into next ch, 4ch, miss 4ch, 1tr into next ch. Turn.

9th row 6ch, 1dc into next dc, 9ch, miss 1dc, 1dc into next dc, 4ch, miss 4ch, 1tr into next ch, 8ch, 1dc into outer point of first picot group on 6th row, turn.

10th — 12th rows As 2nd — 4th rows.

13th row As 5th row but ending with 1dc into last loop, 1dc into outer point of 2nd picot group on 6th row, turn.

14th — 16th rows As 6th — 8th rows.

The 9th — 16th rows form patt. Rep patt for length required, ending with 15th row. Fasten off. Join into a circle, joining starting ch to last row to match patt.

Edging

Using No.1.50 (ISR) hook and with RS of work facing, rejoin yarn to inner edge, 4ch, *1tr into next row end, 1ch, rep from * to end. Join with a ss to 3rd of first 4ch. Fasten off.

To make up

Press under a damp cloth with a warm iron. Sew inner edge round material, as required.

50 Tough playroom rug

Size

101.5cm (40in) by 101.5cm (40in) square

Tension

18 sts and 10 rows to 10.0cm (3.9in) over tr worked on No.3.50 (ISR) crochet hook

Materials

5 x 50 grm balls of Madame Pingouin in main shade, A

5 balls of contrast colours, B and D

2 balls of contrast colour, C

One No.3.50 (ISR) crochet hook

Centre section

Using No.3.50 (ISR) hook and A, make 7ch.

1st row Into 4th ch from hook work 1tr, work 2tr into each of next 3ch. Turn. 8tr.

2nd row 3ch to count as first tr, 2tr into next tr, *1tr into next tr, 2tr into next tr, rep from * twice more. Turn. 12tr.

3rd row 3ch, 1tr into next tr, 2tr into next tr, *1tr into each of next 2tr, 2tr into next tr, rep from * twice more. Turn. 16tr.

4th row 3ch, 1tr into each of next 2tr, 2tr into next tr, *1tr into each of next 3tr, 2tr into next tr, rep from * twice more. Turn. 20tr.

5th row 3ch, 1tr into each of next 3tr, 2tr into next tr, *1tr into each of next 4tr, 2tr into next tr, rep from * twice more. Turn. 24tr.

6th row 3ch, 1tr into each tr to end. Turn.

7th row As 6th.

8th row 3ch, 1tr into each of next 4tr, 2tr into next tr, *1tr into each of next 5tr, 2tr into next

tr, rep from * twice more. Turn. 28tr.

9th row As 8th row but working 6tr between inc. Turn. 32tr.

10th row As 8th row but working 7tr between inc. Turn. 36tr.

11th row 3ch, 1tr into each tr to end. Turn.

12th row 3ch, 1tr into each of next 7tr, 2tr into next tr, *1tr into each of next 8tr, 2tr into next tr, rep from * twice more. Turn. 40tr.

13th, 14th, 15th and 16th rows As 12th row working one more tr between inc on every row. Turn. 56tr. Break off A. Join in C.

17th row Using C, 3ch, 1tr into each tr to end. Turn.

18th row 3ch, 1tr into each of next 12tr, 2tr into next tr, *1tr into each of next 13tr, 2tr into next tr, rep from * twice more. Turn. 60tr.

19th row As 18th row but working 14tr between inc. Turn. 64tr.

20th row 3ch, 1tr into each tr to end. Turn.

21st, 22nd, 23rd and 24th rows As 18th row working one more tr between inc on every row. Turn. 80tr.

25th row 3ch, 1tr into each tr to end. Turn.

26th, 27th 28th and 29th rows As 18th row working one more tr between inc on every row. Turn. 96tr.

30th row 3ch, 1tr into each tr to end. Turn.

31st, 32nd and 33rd rows As 18th row working one more tr between inc on every row. Turn. 108tr. Break off C. Join in D.

34th row Using D, 3ch, 1tr into each tr to end. Turn.

35th, 36th, 37th and 38th rows As 18th row working one more tr between inc on every row. Turn. 124tr.

39th row 3ch, 1tr into each tr to end. Turn.

40th, 41st, 42nd and 43rd rows As 18th row working one more tr between inc on every row. Turn. 140tr.

44th row 3ch, 1tr into each tr to end. Turn.

45th, 46th, 47th and 48th rows As 18th row working one more tr between inc on every row. Turn. 156tr.

49th row As 18th row working 38tr between inc. 160tr. Fasten off.

Make another section in same way. Make 2 more sections in same way, beg with D, changing to B on the 17th row and A on the 34th row.

Corner piece

Using No.3.50 (ISR) hook and B, make 114ch.

1st row Into 4th ch from hook work 1tr, 1tr into each ch to end. Turn. 112tr.

Shape edge

2nd row 3ch to count as first tr, 1tr into each tr to last 10tr, turn.

3rd row Ss across first 8tr, 3ch, 1tr into each tr to end. Turn.

4th row 3ch, 1tr into each tr to last 4tr, turn.

5th row Ss across first 4tr, 3ch, 1tr into each tr to end. Turn.

Rep 4th and 5th rows 3 times more.

12th row 3ch, 1tr into each tr to last 3tr, turn.

13th row Ss across first 3tr, 3ch, 1tr into each tr to end. Turn.

Rep 12th and 13th rows 6 times more.

26th row 3ch, 1tr into each tr to last 2tr, turn.

27th row Ss across first 2tr, 3ch, 1tr into each tr to end. Turn.

28th row As 26th.

Cont dec one st at same edge on next 6 rows, then on every foll 4th row until 3 sts rem. Fasten off. Make one more piece in same way. Make 2 more pieces in same way, reversing shaping.

To make up

Do not press. Join 4 centre sections tog, alternating colour sequence, to form a circle. With RS facing, join 4 corner pieces to edge of circle. Press seams very lightly under a dry cloth with a cool iron.

44

*Simple square motifs are used
to make up this bedroom set
of spread, rug and cushion.*

*Sizes : bedspread 178.0 by 228.5cm
(70in by 90in) ; rug 66.0 by 122.0cm
(26 by 48in) ; cushion 47.0cm (18½in)
square*

45

Practical carry-all worked in filet crochet.

Size: 30.5cm (12in) wide by 35.5cm (14in) deep

46

Intriguing wall-hanging using crochet motifs as flowers.

Size: 56.0cm by 40.0 cm (22in by 15¾in)

47

Four elegant cushions using variations of chevron stripes.

Size: each cushion measures 40.5cm (16in) square

48

Pretty edging for a roller blind, trimmed with tassels.

Size: each section 30.0cm (11¾in) wide by 22.0cm (8¾in) deep

49

Neat edging for your household linen.

Size: 10cm (3.9in) wide

CAMERA PRESS

50

Tough, colourful playroom rug
worked in separate sections.
(Toys not included.)

Size: 101.5cm (40in) square